Liverpool City RLI
Rugby league in a football

Mike Brocken

London League Publications Ltd

Liverpool City RLFC
Rugby league in a football city

A CIP catalogue record for this book is available from the British Library.

First published in Great Britain in October 2008 by:
London League Publications Ltd, P.O. Box 10441, London E14 8WR

ISBN: 978-1903659-40-3

Cover design by: Stephen McCarthy Graphic Design
                         46, Clarence Road, London N15 5BB

Layout: Peter Lush

Printed and bound by: CPI Antony Rowe,
                         Eastbourne, Great Britain

This book is dedicated to the memory of Bill Payne, a Liverpudlian by birth who excelled at the highest levels of rugby league.

Foreword

Ray Ashby was a legendary captain of Liverpool City, distinguished player for Wigan, with whom he received the Lance Todd Trophy in 1965, and later Blackpool Borough, Ray played almost 250 games in all for the Liverpool club and received Great Britain and Lancashire caps while at Knotty Ash Stadium.

I don't suppose any player is ever fully aware of the history behind a club when he signs. Players are only interested in one thing – playing – and when I arrived at Liverpool City from Blackbrook RLFC in 1956 I was only interested in playing rugby league. I'd played soccer and cricket at school (Lowe House R.C.) but I was rugby league born and bred. I had been on trial at St Helens but after a game against Wigan 'A' Saints' Harry Cook told me I was too slow (I was actually suffering from a dead leg at the time) and as a teenager I think I felt I had a point to prove.

My arrival at Knotty Ash was typical of the way Liverpool City went about recruitment: word of mouth! Apparently, there were so many injuries that their 'A' team was unable to fulfil its fixtures, so my dad was approached at work in Pilkington's (he'd played for St Helens Recs before the war) and he recommended that a few of us from the Blackbrook club, which had just won the Lancashire Junior Cup, help out the struggling Liverpool City. We made our excited way to Liverpool and played a few 'A' team games towards the end of the 1955–56 season. It was great fun and I learnt a lot. Most lads returned to Blackbrook, but along with my pal Harold Blythin, I'd been noticed by the board and was signed-on. The following season I was put straight into the first team at centre, and from that moment-on I spent the next eight seasons as a Liverpool City player (five years as captain), moving to full-back along the way. It was just brilliant: not only was the camaraderie exceptional, but when things 'clicked', Liverpool City could actually play to a very high standard.

Looking back, a few things spring to mind that contributed to our lack of success. Firstly the slenderness of our squad, which was usually strained to the utmost, and secondly the Knotty Ash pitch, which, wet or dry, I remember as a constant headache. Added to this was a third important factor of money (or lack of it): £4 match fees less tax were not exactly attractive to many professional players and only a few experienced pros such as Ike Fishwick came our way. But perhaps the biggest problem might have been the combination of a lack of a regular coach and the 'distance' of the Board. These two related problems actually bonded the players together, and when I became captain I tried to get the lads together after training for chats about tactics, but it wasn't always possible. So, we were inconsistent: we might beat (say) Salford one week, but lose to (say) Doncaster the next.

The City board appointed a new coach almost every season, but it was they – the directors – who insisted on picking the team! This was an unnecessary chain of command and at times led to players being treated poorly. For example I remember Harry Ody being dropped for no apparent reason after scoring two tries and, after playing well against the Australians in 1956, I was dropped for the very next game simply because the board 'wanted a change'. Even then, I thought it was an old-fashioned system that didn't help our cause.

Nevertheless, I have mostly great memories of my time at City both on and off the pitch. Even the possible near-death experience of a bus crash in the Lake District on our way home from a match in Cumberland now appears oddly exciting; our comradeship was so strong that even such potentially harrowing events can now bring about warm and happy memories.

I was ambitious, and after a short while I became aware that several bigger clubs were expressing an interest. From the late 1950s-onwards Barrow, Huddersfield, Hull, Rochdale Hornets, and Widnes had all, to my knowledge, made enquiries but Dr Roebuck and Mr Greenhill continued to insist I was 'not for sale'. Eventually in 1963 I became frustrated and put in a written transfer request – well, actually two written transfer requests, for the first one was torn-up by Dr Roebuck – they reluctantly agreed to place me on the list. It wasn't about the money – it was more to do with the possibility of testing myself, of playing at a higher standard on a more regular basis.

I thought I would soon be on my way out of Liverpool, but then spent the best part of 18 months on that transfer-list while Dr Roebuck knocked-back several serious enquiries. In the meantime, I represented both my country and my county as a 'listed' Liverpool City player – becoming the club's only post-war international cap. Eventually, after a run of games over Easter 1964 in which I was carrying a serious shoulder injury but played particularly well at Wigan's Central Park, I received a knock on the door on the evening of the Easter Monday 30 March. There stood my late father and City secretary Ken Grundy. My dad told me: "if you want to sign for Wigan now, you can". City had accepted Wigan's bid of £5,000.

So I became a Wigan player. There was never any possibility of a percentage coming my way, however! I was 'on the list' and as such forfeited the rights to a pay-out. However to this day I still feel a little hard done by: I had not actively sought a transfer at that moment in time, was unaware of the dealings going on behind the scenes, and was getting on with my job for Liverpool City. Ken Grundy in fact, informed me that I was going to receive 'something'. Needless to say, however, that 'something' never materialised.

The following season I went with my dad to Knotty Ash Stadium to watch City play Saints. I was now a Wigan player but these games were not to be missed: always won by St Helens, but the St Helens-born players in the City team felt they were playing for pride. Before the match I noted that a more durable concrete surround had replaced the old rickety pitch fencing. I bumped into Dr Roebuck's daughter: "that was paid-for with the money that should have gone to you", she said ruefully. Oh well – that was Liverpool City, I suppose. In any case, it was 'water under the bridge' for me by that time; after all, I was now playing for one of the crack teams of the 1960s and was to appear at Wembley twice.

To this day I still feel that the team spirit at Knotty Ash was not only wonderful but at times also a little eccentric. I would not wish to single-out any player in particular but on the pitch both Peter Twiss and George Walker were great thinkers, and could have easily played for a larger club. I also remember the mysterious second-row forward Greenhough who came up from the 'A' team, played a blinder against the Australians, and was never seen again.

So, back to that history: at first I was unaware of City's rugby league pedigree. I knew little of the club's past and did not realise until much later that it was something of a landmark club. For me, Liverpool City was somewhere to go for players who had been rejected or remained undiscovered by the larger clubs – an incredibly valuable asset to the sport of rugby league football in our area of south Lancashire. But I was aware of the general lack of interest in the sport in Liverpool and I thought this was a great pity. In fact, to us players 'Liverpool City' was just a name... we were Liverpool City. The sporting public of Liverpool didn't seem to care very much, and in the football-successful 1960s, who could really blame them? My playing career eventually spanned three decades: at Liverpool, Wigan, and latterly Blackpool, and when I look back now, it is quite clear that I became the player I was for Wigan because of my experiences at Liverpool. I will be forever grateful for those fantastic years spent at Knotty Ash. It also became clear to me that Liverpool City improved little-by-little every season throughout the 1960s. What a shame that the Knotty Ash ground was lost.

I suppose in some respects it was amazing that Liverpool City lasted as long as it did, but on the other hand it is a great pity that a professional rugby league club does not now exist in Liverpool. Just consider all those players from St Helens, Widnes, and Warrington who, each year, slip under the scouting radar. And what of the possibilities that there might be a 'Scouser' or two ready and willing to play the sport? James Graham certainly shows us that this is more than a pipedream. Without Liverpool City giving my professional career a start I too might have been lost to rugby league football. Maybe there is still a place for a 'Liverpool City' on Merseyside.

I hope you enjoy the book – it's been a long time coming!

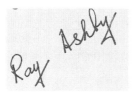

Thanks to:

Ray Ashby for writing the foreword and his help and support. Phil Babbs and Tom Fleet for use of Liverpool Stanley programmes, and everyone else who lent research material. Michael O'Hare for sub-editing, Steve McCarthy for designing the cover, Alex Service, Andrew Cudbertson, Mike Haddon, *Rugby League Journal* and many others for providing photographs. Everyone who was interviewed for the book, the staff at Antony Rowe Ltd for printing it, and Dave Farrar and Peter Lush for publishing it. Thanks to the Liverpool City Past Players Association for their support, without whom this book would not have been possible, especially Eric Seed, Harry Ody, Peter Twiss, and George Walker for their memories and friendship.

Mike Brocken

Publishers' note

Our first book, 13 years ago, was *Touch and Go, a history of professional rugby league in London*. Of course, for one season, 1933-34, the stories of rugby league in Liverpool and London become intertwined, as Wigan Highfield came to the capital for a year before moving back up north and transforming into Liverpool Stanley. I was fascinated by the story of the club, but particularly in their later incarnation as Huyton. How did such perennial strugglers keep going? Sports historian Chris Harte once told me that failure is much more interesting than success for a historian, and that concept certainly applied to Huyton. We even had a working title, *The wandering tribe of Lancashire*. But other projects intervened, and the book never got started. On reflection, that is probably good for the history of rugby league, as Mike Brocken, by focussing on Liverpool, has done a far better book than we ever could have done. We hope you enjoy this fascinating tale.

Peter Lush

Introduction

The June 2006 'capping' of 20 year-old Liverpool-born St Helens prop forward James Graham by Great Britain attracted only a smattering of attention from the media in Liverpool and, in turn, this absence served to highlight the intriguing non-relationship that has endured between the City of Liverpool and rugby league. Unlike its east coast partner, Hull – at the other end of the M62 rugby league 'corridor' – Liverpool has never really enjoyed a meaningful affiliation with the game. Perhaps this is cultural: the 'heavy woollen' areas of the North of England did not develop socially or culturally during industrialisation in the same way as the former Imperial power-base of Liverpool.

There are, however, several truisms concerning Liverpool and sport. For example there is the suggestion that Liverpool's migrant populations came to be involved in a sporting code, association football, that was considered more universal, less parochial and elitist – 'the peoples game' – than rugby. But the evidence for this assumption remains rather thin. The patterns of Liverpool's internal settlements and migrations do not necessarily coincide with such codal 'authenticities'. For example districts such as Walton, Tuebrook, and Stanley all played host to rugby sides prior to the rugby split of 1895. One might, therefore, argue that the growth and then decline of rugby in Liverpool has as much to do with the cultural geography of open spaces and the 1895 split, as it does with any politicised interpretation of association football as 'the people's game'. Indeed, this latter rather tedious stereotype leaves unanswered cultural inconsistencies such as the Roman Catholic Church's almost obsessive affinity with rugby union in their Liverpool schools, and the culturally elitist echelons surrounding certain association football leagues in the area such as the I Zingari League.

The Jewish King David Grammar School even enjoyed a somewhat egalitarian sporting history, incompatible with any such formalised narratives. For example, Steve Higginson remembers attending the King David School in Childwall, Liverpool, in the late-1960s. Due to the school having relocated, and its prime objective being its establishment as a 'quality' secondary school, team sports were played, but in the early days without any links to local schools competitions. This began to change from 1967–68 when football and cricket teams were entered into such competitions, but according to Steve: "attempts to initiate rugby league practice matches [were also made] on a regular basis. It was rugby league rather than union due to the teacher being from mid-Lancashire – another element in the outsider status of King David." Such partially hidden histories remain largely unexplored because the tyranny of local historical enquiry is that it often creates a unified narrative with the ultimate goal being to justify itself.

Once I had discovered spectator sport, the Liverpool that I knew as a child and then a teenager was made up of diverse club colours, harmonious relations between football codes, friendly rivalry, and steadfast support. But this Liverpool probably only existed in my head, and if it had existed, it had certainly ceased to do so well before my formative years in the 1960s. Oddly, 3d 'Lucky Bags' helped bring about these idealised 'Corinthian-Casuals' sporting images. Around 1964 some of these bags contained not only cheap sweets, but also football programmes and, while polishing off the former I began collecting the latter. These programmes illustrated to me how the presentation of club traditions were not simply acts of financial expedience, but at times also artistic endeavour. These football programmes were supplemented by *The Hornet*'s picture-stories of Bernard Briggs, that scrap metal-dealing goalkeeper who kept his club in the

Fourth Division by keeping clean sheets at a semi-derelict, empty-terraced football ground – this was surely the stuff of dreams and in my mind it wasn't really about winning anything, but about the 'fun' of survival. Furthermore, after devouring both football and rugby league results in the *News of the World* each Sunday morning, my own sporting rituals came to include watching rugby league ('A' team) matches on Granada Television: two mud-spattered teams playing-out a monochrome war of attrition against a backdrop of similarly empty terraces and dilapidated enclosures – it was all, I suppose, 'romantic' in a funny kind of way.

I came to follow both association football (South Liverpool) and rugby league (Liverpool City) teams who appeared evidently part of an ethos. This was an ethos also partially sustained for me by my membership of the Cubs, the Scouts, and the choir attached to St James' C of E Church in West Derby, and not one necessarily associated with playing for any particular football or rugby team. This kind of sporting history usually doesn't get recorded. It is more difficult to pin down, being based, for the most part, on ideas rather than in the supposed affirmations of an engagement with the real world. Indeed, I was often considered by schoolmates to be (in local parlance) a 'dickhead' for having such obscure interests – but it was real enough to me: even though I soon discovered that I lived in a city of fierce rivalries with a win-at-all-costs culture.

Historian John Tosh states that the writing of history is always partial in two senses of the word: firstly that it is never impartial, secondly that it is always incomplete. The history of sport in Liverpool of the past 40 years is an example of this, for it has been variously written as a history of affirmation, conformity, success, and legitimisation. This kind of narrative is of course woefully deficient. The latest in a long line of such texts is Ray Physick's *Liverpool at Play* (2007): a mostly worthy piece of work, dealing, as it does, with many forms of recreational and sporting activity in the city since team sports were 'formalised' – an attempt perhaps at 'levelling the proverbial playing field'.

However, sadly, Physick totally neglects to mention any of the four rugby league clubs bearing the name Liverpool during the 20th and 21st centuries (Liverpool City i, Liverpool Stanley, Liverpool City ii, Liverpool Buccaneers (not to mention the amateur sides Liverpool Rangers and Liverpool Hornets) – one of which actually played at the Stanley Greyhound Track, which **is** discussed. Furthermore he mentions Huyton RLFC only in passing: as having played at Alt Park prior to the arrival of the former-Kirkby-based non-league outfit Knowsley United FC and he does not discuss the code of rugby league at any stage in his narrative. The great irony of this limited discourse is of course obvious: the more detailed an examination of all team sports, the more complexities emerge concerning culture, socio-economics and political motivations.

Physick's partial discussion of sport and leisure in Liverpool, therefore, does not get at different ways of thinking about Liverpool's sporting heritages because it does not source its material in a thorough manner. This might have something to do with the primacy of association football narratives in the city. Physick does not necessarily place association football at the centre of his work (good), but its inclusion as a 'given' subsumes all other sports within its totalising discourse (bad). For example, he rather blithely states that at the beginning of the 20th century "football was now a mass spectator sport, with two clubs regularly attracting aggregate gates of over 80,000. By 1914 attendances for athletics, rugby, rounders, and even cricket, had tumbled in the great stampede of converts heading to watch the mighty Reds and Blues."

But he then fails to explain why this might have been the case, pays no attention to the fact that other football clubs in Liverpool such as South Liverpool (mark 1) experienced increased gates at this time, and totally ignores the 1895 rugby schism and its affects on rugby (indeed association football) in and around the city.

This kind of unfathomable 'up the reds' and 'up the blues' football-led narrative is common as far as sport in Liverpool is concerned and, to his credit, Physick attempts to referee this relative injustice by the inclusion of 'other' important sports such as baseball, bowls, golf and swimming (among others). But, like many such narratives of Liverpool's sporting past, *Liverpool at Play* ignores the inconsistencies, ambiguities and ambivalences surrounding Liverpool's perplexing relationship with rugby league. Surely, if questions are asked about this [non]-relationship, responses do not fit the usual episodic sporting narratives of the past.

For example, what motivates certain people to engage with specific football codes? Is it a class or race issue (as the stereotypes suggest)? Why did several Liverpool rugby clubs cease to exist after the rugby split of 1895? Did this effectively create a gap filled by football? How are we to understand the growth of greyhound and Speedway stadia in Liverpool? What were the motivations of those behind such hi-tech sports and what of the greyhound industry's relationship with rugby league? What are the 'parish boundaries' of sporting affiliation that appear to demarcate so clearly the failure quotient of rugby league? What kind of facilities might a rugby fan expect in the mid-20th century, and why?

But equally it would be a mistake to overemphasise the importance of rugby league in Liverpool. Liverpool was never a 'heartland', having different sporting values, beliefs and goals. As such, it is correct to state that the Liverpool and Everton football clubs have become the sporting and cultural symbols around which all others revolve and which all others obediently reflect. The over-arching hype surrounding the Liverpool and Everton football clubs knows no boundaries.

Yet, for some (such as this writer), the history of Liverpool City represents rugby league at its most sublime – for others, perhaps at its most ridiculous. The reader might already be aware that the club was undoubtedly an abject failure. But it is also worthy of note that it has a seminal place in the development of the Rugby Football League, despite its own visible dearth of success as a club. It is therefore worth recording that the city of Liverpool was actually host to a valiant professional rugby league club for approximately half of the 20th century.

A lot of courage is required to persist in presenting the values of one's own choice as sustainable; indeed, seen from this critical perspective it can resemble a voice crying in the (rugby league) wilderness. But the chequered and complicated history of Liverpool City serves to highlight the curious non-relationship twixt Liverpudlians and the code of rugby league in this seemingly unending era of 'prescription' spectator sport and the random cannibalisation of our sporting authenticities. It is a story of failure, in a city that in 2008 is intent on celebrating success. But history is not simply about success and success is surely relative. In fact, investigation of so-called 'failure' often reveals different kinds of success: essential if a true image of any city's sporting past is to be documented. Unless so recorded, the history of Liverpool City RLFC will be forgotten – erased by the propaganda of the Premiership and the simulacrum of 'Capital of Culture'.

Mike Brocken
Chester, September 2008

Contents

Photographs and illustrations

Some of the photographs in this book are quite old, and therefore have not reproduced perfectly. We thought that readers would prefer to have them like this than not at all. Unless otherwise credited, photographs and illustrations are from private collections. No copyright has been intentionally breached, please contact London League Publications Ltd if you believe there has been a breach of copyright.

Ray Ashby in his Great Britain shirt. Ray was Liverpool City's only international, and was their greatest player. (Courtesy Ray Ashby)

1. From the Bee Hotel to Mrs Walker's boys

In 1935–36, Liverpool Stanley finished runners-up in the Northern Rugby League, with 56 points from 38 matches. They won the Lancashire League, and cruelly lost in the Championship semi-final by a single point to Widnes, who had finished third in the league table. The following season, they finished fourth in the table, were runners-up in the Lancashire League, and again lost in the Championship semi-final, this time beaten 15–7 by Salford. In the Challenge Cup they lost to Keighley 7–2 in the quarter-finals after beating Leigh and Hull KR. What difference would a Wembley Cup Final appearance have made?

Those two seasons were the high point in the history of one of rugby league's most remarkable stories – the sport's attempts to establish itself in Liverpool. Seasons of struggle followed, with a new name, Liverpool City, and a new stadium. In 1968, the club abandoned Liverpool and moved to Huyton. The story finished ignominiously with the club, by then known as Prescot Panthers, withdrawing from the Rugby Football League in 1997.

It is interesting to speculate how different that history might have been if Liverpool Stanley had won the Championship in 1936, and whether the club could have become a major force in the game. Nevertheless, the story of rugby league's attempts to build the game in Liverpool – which is usually seen as a football city – is a fascinating one.

******

By the dawn of the 20th century there were only a few clubs playing rugby in and around Liverpool and its districts, but interest in the game did exist, and had done so for some time. Rugby was played with some enthusiasm at the local grammar and fee-paying schools and former pupils formed one or two clubs such as Liverpool College Old Boys and Parkfield Old Boys. A September 1906 edition of the *Liverpool Mercury* also records a Liverpool Old Boys rugby side playing in the parish of Stanley.

However in both a cultural and a sporting sense, senior rugby clubs such as Liverpool, founded in 1857, and Birkenhead Park, founded in 1871, were somewhat remote, and local junior clubs such as Waterloo – formed in 1882 by a group of former Merchant Taylor's School pupils as Serpentine RFC – Liverpool Gymnasium, and Tuebrook a little thin on the ground. Rugby football certainly had its supporters among middle class young men and Liverpool probably had more than its fair share of such individuals. The Liverpool club did play an important role in establishing county structures for rugby in Lancashire. The Reverend Frank Marshall, in his 1892 history of the game, recognises this, and the "invaluable services" which it gave to the sport's development in its early days.

While manufacturing played a relatively minor role in Liverpool's economy, enterprise created myriad clerks – 19,000 in 1872 – and upwardly mobile white-collar workers; but some who wished to join but could not find an approachable rugby club will no doubt have turned their attentions instead to association football.

These days it is rather odd to consider association football a late arrival in Liverpool – but it most certainly was. While 30 clubs had formed the Lancashire Football Association in 1878, the Liverpool and District Football Association did not appear until 1882. Yet it was in the absence of a substantial number of either community or works-related rugby clubs during this period that association football made great strides in Liverpool. This was not only from the top down with the Liverpool and Everton clubs being among the foremost professional clubs in the country, but also via the amateur game. Football leagues such as the I Zingari League, formed in 1897, and the Liverpool County Combination, which was launched in 1908, came to play a prominent role in the sporting currencies of the city. The 'County Comb', as it came to be known, was itself a late arrival for it was formed ostensibly to prevent local amateur clubs from joining the popular West Cheshire League which originally existed for teams on the other side of the River Mersey.

The I Zingari League, however, was socially and culturally dissimilar from the County Combination in that it catered for the more Corinthian middle-classes and grammar schools old boys teams, some of whom, such as Beresford Old Boys, also played rugby football; the County Combination, on the other hand consisted in the main of aspiring working-class sides, many drawn from dock and factory workers such as Prescot Wire Works FC and Garston Gas Works FC. Sides from these two leagues met only occasionally in Liverpool County FA competitions and it was not until 2006, after over 20 years of declining memberships that the two amalgamated as the Liverpool County FA Premier League.

Some historians look upon this works-related sporting culture as a form of social control, however, within a relatively short space of time, many of these works teams had outstripped their factory beginnings and were being run as sports clubs in their own right. One example of this process is African Royal FC, which began as a docks-based team and played most of their football in the West Cheshire League, but merged with the pre-First World War semi-professional South Liverpool FC who in the 1930s moved across the Mersey and became New Brighton.

From the onset, then, it is clear that association football plugged a gap in the participatory sporting landscape of Liverpool. One glance at any pre-First World War map of the city reveals innumerable recreation grounds and open spaces and it was on these unenclosed fields, rather than simply one more famous enclosed pitch on Anfield Road – home of first the Everton and then the Liverpool football clubs – that association football truly developed. The game was easy to learn and play and playing areas easy to locate. On purely practical terms, football goal posts were far easier and cheaper to construct and erect than those for the rugby code.

However, one might also cite the rugby schism of 1895 as a precursor to rugby's loss in profile in Liverpool. The division between the public school based southern rugby establishment, and clubs in the north with a working class following, had been growing for some years. The development of cups and league competitions had lead to allegations of professionalism and the consequent suspension of players and clubs in Yorkshire and Lancashire from the so-called amateur game. The defeat at the RFU Annual General Meeting of proposals to allow 'broken time' payments – compensation for working class players who missed work to play matches or travel to games was the final straw. So, on 29 August 1895 representatives of 22 northern clubs met in the George Hotel, Huddersfield to form the Northern Rugby Football Union.

Prior to this historic moment the game of rugby undoubtedly had its followers in Liverpool and by the late-19th century local junior sides such as Walton and Bootle Wasps were developing fixture lists. However, following this schism several junior rugby clubs in and around the city, such as the two above, rather than having to decide whether to align to one form of rugby or the other folded altogether. Others changed to the association code but none, it seems, chose to align with Northern Union rugby. Rugby historian Tom Fleet notes "the Northern Union game itself was not a variant at that time, it was only about the broken time payments issue. Maybe some of the folded clubs lost their fixtures. The RFU banned games against the breakaway clubs." [1] Mike Latham in *League Express* describes the years following the schism as "carnage". [2]

2

The dearth of local junior rugby activity was so visible by 1907 that The Aliens RFC, formed around non-native Liverpool teachers, could not find a pitch and every game was played on their opponents' ground. Indeed, the club was unable to find a suitable home ground until 1908–09, at Clubmoor Cricket Club. Furthermore, club membership at first restricted to the teaching profession was, after only a couple of seasons, opened to all because of a general shortage of players. The club was then forced to move a second time to a larger recreation ground on Townsend Lane, Clubmoor where it remained until the outbreak of the First World War.

The Aliens later became Sefton RUFC and continue to be an active junior club to this day, while also playing host to Rugby League Conference side Liverpool Buccaneers at their Leyfield Road ground in West Derby. These early difficulties highlight not only the relative scarcity of junior rugby in the city but also, as the city of Liverpool and association football grew abreast of each other, the premium that came to be placed on open spaces. These were mostly given over to association football, rather than rugby of either code. There was also an almost total lack of interest in semi-professional Northern Union (NU) rugby within Liverpool.

Liverpool City RFC

At a Northern Rugby Union committee meeting on Tuesday 28 November 1905 a letter was read aloud from Mr H. Wallace Langshaw and his associates regarding the proposed formation of a new professional rugby football club in Liverpool. The letter was greeted enthusiastically because the Northern Rugby Union had over the previous few seasons lost clubs, including Manningham, the first NU Champions, to association football as Bradford City FC. Perhaps it was thought that a team from such a large conurbation as Liverpool, with a population in 1901 of 684,958, would bring strength and prestige to the Northern Union at an evidently uncomfortable stage in its evolution.

It was decided that Messrs Smith and Houghton, the chairman and secretary respectively of the NU, would attend the first meeting of this prospective new club to consider the appropriateness and seriousness of the bid.

Liverpool City RFC was launched at a meeting held on Wednesday 21 December 1905 at the Bee Hotel on St Johns Lane in Liverpool city centre. The two aforementioned committee members together with representatives from all the NU clubs attended the meeting. Mr Albert Abel was appointed honorary secretary and it was proposed that a £5,000 share capital, with shares at £1 each, be issued in order to fund the club. Whether this capital was ever realised however is another matter, for Liverpool City appears to have lurched from crisis to financial crisis throughout its short existence and in all probability the NU covered a great deal of the club's expenditure during their season of humiliation. Nevertheless, the Wednesday 31 January 1906 edition of the *Liverpool Mercury* announced that the 'Stanley Athletics Grounds', ostensibly on Edge Lane, had been secured as Liverpool's home venue and that an exhibition match between rivals Salford and Swinton scheduled for 17 February would provide the people of Liverpool and their new club with an opening event.

This fixture duly took place, with Swinton beating Salford 8–6 in front of 4,000 spectators – seemingly a promising start, although such an away day 'derby' would have been an attractive proposition for fans from these two clubs even in 1906. A second exhibition match also took place between Runcorn and Warrington on 17 March 1906 before, it was reported, "a crowd of interested spectators".

There has been some debate among rugby league historians about the location of these 'Stanley Athletics Grounds', with the Police sports ground where Stanley later trained as one possibility. Ray Physick (2006) places the Stanley Athletics Grounds on the site later occupied by the Stanley Track: "The Stanley Greyhound Stadium, the first of its type in Liverpool, was opened on 17 August 1927 by the Electric Hare Greyhound Company. Prior to this the site had been occupied by the Stanley Athletics Ground, one of several privately owned sports ground to have been laid out in the city during the late 1880s and 1890s." [3]

According to correspondence between Tom Webb of Oldham and Norman Lloyd of Liverpool City dated 19 June 1956, the Swinton versus Salford game was played "on a ground adjoining Edge Lane **railway station** [my emphasis] on Saturday 17 February 1906. The attendance was 3,000." The correspondence continued: "in season 1906–7 Liverpool City played at the Stanley Ground (the Liverpool Athletic Ground)... the ground was on the present Stanley Abattoir." [4]

Furthermore, the Liverpool City programme editorial for Monday 20 August 1956, states: "Our first club went under the title of Liverpool City (Rugby) Football Club (Northern Union) and they played at The Athletic Grounds, Fairfield, **a site now covered by the abattoir** [my emphasis]. Mr J.T. Blenkinsopp, 12 Ardmore Road, Liverpool, 18, has kindly presented the club with an original fixture card for the old club (of which he was a member), dated 1906-7, and this is to be framed and honourably placed in the new directors' room." [5]

In my opinion the original Liverpool City club did not play at the site later designated for the Stanley Track, but at the privately owned Liverpool Athletics Grounds on the edge of Newsham Park, to the rear of the Cattle Market, in Stanley, also known as the Stanley Athletics Grounds. This ground was not only well appointed but also well served by the local railways with stations at West Derby Road, Stanley, and Edge Lane. Other high profile events took place at this ground. For example, it was reported in the *Liverpool Echo* of 17 August 1907 that a spectacle to celebrate the 700th anniversary of the foundation of Liverpool was to take place at this venue between 3 and 6 August. The *Echo* also said in the same edition that the Sefton Harriers Athletics Club was based at the Stanley Athletics Grounds. Nonetheless, whichever ground was used, it was certainly not used for long.

On Tuesday 10 April 1906 the Northern Union committee accepted Liverpool City as a member for the 1906–07 season. This was followed by Lancashire County membership on 18 July 1906 and all was set for the club's first (and last) season in the ranks of the professionals. 'Bee's Notebook' from the Saturday 28 July 1906 edition of the *Liverpool Football Echo* records: "The new organisation, Liverpool City Rugby Football Club, promoted by a small body of Northern Union enthusiasts gathered together by Mr H. Wallace Langshaw, has met with so much encouragement and support that the coming season promises to prove a most successful one for the new venture. The attractiveness of the fixture list will be understood by all followers of the Northern Union League, when it is stated the following clubs will be played during the season – namely, Runcorn, St Helens, Warrington, Broughton Rangers, Wigan, Salford, Swinton, Widnes, Rochdale Hornets, Leigh, Morecambe, Dewsbury, Huddersfield, Keighley, Pontefract, and Wakefield Trinity. The club has entered for the Northern Union and Lancashire Senior Cup, and have had the good fortune to be drawn against Broughton Rangers at Liverpool for the first round of the latter competition. A good team is being formed and the committee have also a desire to encourage local talent. All players desirous of being played in the trial games should send their names to the secretary. The ground, which is one of the most important factors in the success of a club of this character, has received the careful consideration of the club

4

committee and the club will make the Stanley Athletic Grounds their headquarters, having a lease upon the same for seven years." [6]

This report not only highlights the significance of an enclosed ground – rather than, say, an open field – but its tone also expresses a level of hopeful perhaps cock-eyed optimism, rather than confidence, about the future of the club. This style of writing was to recur over the next 60 years concerning rugby league in Liverpool. It is also worthy of note that in the wake of this news a stony silence fell over the Liverpool Rugby Union Club - at least as far as press reports were concerned.

Graham Williams (1989) records that by the end of August 1906 Liverpool City had registered some 35 footballers but a trial match on Saturday 1 September attracted only 30 spectators, suggesting little local enthusiasm. This was further exacerbated by several of the leading Northern Union clubs backing down from their agreement to bring a team to play Liverpool City. At this time, due to the size of the league, not every team played every other one, and teams arranged fixtures between themselves. The league table was decided on a percentage basis, because not only did the teams not all play each other, but they did not play the same number of matches. Some played 34, others as few as 20.

That same day in his 'Northern Union' column for the *Liverpool Football Echo* 'Veteran' was to complain bitterly about this apparent backsliding: "At the meeting to inaugurate the coming of the Liverpool club, promises of fixtures were made by representatives of all the big clubs and yet we find that in reality they have not been kept. Then why make the promises and gull the promoters into optimistic security? They naturally built their highest hopes on these promises to find them half-blighted." [7]

This decision not to send sides to Stanley would certainly have created severe problems for the new club who, having guaranteed the owners of the Athletics Grounds some kind of rental for the use of the facilities would have naturally wished to recuperate outgoings by substantial gate receipts. If high profile fixtures were not to take place against the leading Northern Union clubs during Liverpool City's gestation period, how was the club to survive?

This concern was confirmed by City's first competitive games. At 5.45pm on Monday 3 September 1906 at the Edge Lane enclosure and sporting colours of green and white [8] Liverpool City lost 41–8 to Wigan in front of 1,000 onlookers. The following Saturday a crowd of only 500 witnessed another heavy defeat, 28–3 to Salford. It is highly likely that the vast majority of these two crowds consisted of visiting supporters. By 15 September *The Echo's* 'Veteran' was to pen these far less optimistic words: "I am glad to see that at the last meeting of the Northern Union committee more fixtures are ratified in which the new Liverpool club is included. No one, I think, will grumble if one gives a few words to the latter, for they are making a hard and brave struggle to rehabilitate the game in this quarter. Their difficulties are stupendous and if only the public will help – and I think we might appeal to those who once were red-hot followers of the handling code, but now go to see the sister code – we might hope for success... I am told that the management have this week secured the services of three good backs (and they were badly needed)." [9]

However by October 1906 the Liverpool City rugby team was pointless, perhaps in more ways than one, and the Northern Union authorities attempted to come to its assistance by allowing six loan players to join from Oldham, Warrington, and Wigan. A reserve team was also mooted in the hope that locals might progress through the ranks, but it was all to no avail. Apart from a 3–3 draw with Bramley in front of a poor attendance on 4 November 1906, the club continued to lose heavily and in early December the home games against Runcorn and Warrington were viewed by only a handful of spectators. By 15 December Liverpool could field only eight men against Leigh – the club was in freefall.

The situation reached a critical stage in the new year of 1907. Heavy snow falls in January made the City pitch unplayable and games were, somewhat randomly, cancelled. As punishment the Northern Rugby Union forced Liverpool City to play all remaining fixtures away from home. Perhaps, too, the club was unable to pay rent to the Athletics Grounds. After all, the wretched attendances were probably insufficient to pay even match fees. City began their travels on Wednesday 30 January at Fartown, Huddersfield. The match was lost 63–0. This trip instigated a run of six defeats in which the team was unable to score even a point but, in the process, conceded 337. A trip to Salford on 2 February resulted in a 78–0 defeat; this was followed by a 46-0 loss at Swinton the following week. Rochdale Hornets then inflicted a 42–0 trouncing on City on 12 February and this was followed four days later by a 56–0 crushing at Broughton Rangers. Returning closer to home on 18 February Warrington defeated the 'green-and-whites' or 'all-blacks' 52–0. Williams further illustrates Liverpool's ineptitude: "So bad were their performances that a *Yorkshire Post* reporter was moved to write that they were 'hopelessly outclassed – their feebleness at times being painful to witness'" [10] On 23 February 1907 Liverpool City finally scored two points in a 53–2 'thumping' at Hull Kingston Rovers. In all only 20 tries were scored and only 15 goals kicked by Liverpool throughout this wretched season – "hopeless" hardly seems the word.

When problems arose concerning the re-arrangement of a previously postponed away fixture at Bramley, a Northern Rugby Union committee meeting on 19 February 1906 decided to cancel this outstanding fixture. As a consequence, they also took the decision to wipe the November 3-3 home draw from the records, stripping Liverpool City of its one non-defeat. By the end of the season City's record read: played 30, lost 30, points for 76, points against 1,398, percentage 0%. Liverpool also lost to Pontefract 20–8 actually making the total losing figure 31, but this result was expunged from the championship records because Pontefract withdrew from the league over the Christmas period. The season's fixtures were disrupted by the atrocious January weather and cancelled games were not always rescheduled.

Northern Rugby League 1906-07 (bottom six)

	P	W	D	L	F	A	Pts	Percentage
21 Batley	24	8	1	15	228	326	17	35.41%
22 St Helens	26	9	0	17	374	353	18	34.61%
23 Hull	32	11	0	21	337	515	22	34.37%
24 York	24	5	0	19	217	514	10	20.83%
25 Bramley	20	1	0	19	85	466	2	5.00%
26 Liverpool City	**30**	**0**	**0**	**30**	**76**	**1398**	**0**	**0.00%**

Such appalling results, mediocre attendances, and not least partial responsibility for that season's disorder ensured that Liverpool City RFC was not re-elected at the June 1907 Northern Union AGM – and a good thing too, one might suggest. It had been an unsuccessful and costly experiment for both Wallace Langshaw and the Northern Union, and the Liverpool City club was not deemed worthy of professional status. Perhaps the city of Liverpool was also viewed as a rather hard nut to crack, as far as the NU code was concerned.

For the following season, 1907–08, two Welsh clubs, Merthyr Tydfil and Ebbw Vale replaced them. Liverpool did at first attempt to soldier on by joining the second-tier regional NU rugby competition: the Lancashire Combination. Here they were scheduled to play against the 'A' teams of the professional Lancashire and Cheshire-based Northern Union clubs: Broughton Rangers, Oldham, Rochdale Hornets, Runcorn, Salford, St Helens,

Warrington, Wigan, and Widnes plus three amateur sides: Highfield (about which, more later), Leigh Shamrocks, and Pemberton Rovers.

This season started well when on 7 September 1907 Liverpool defeated St Helens 'A' by 11–5, presumably back at "Edge Lane". A half-time report in the *Football Echo* from 28 September notes Liverpool City playing at Highfield. Predictably the score was 12–0 at half-time to the Wigan side with a certain Jimmy Green on the score sheet. But this was ostensibly a Highfield match report and City had effectively fallen from the *Football Echo's* sphere of interest. As rugby league historian Harry Edgar [11] affirms, within a few weeks of the start of the new season, Liverpool's miserable excuse for a Northern Union club was failing to fulfil its fixtures. Matters came to a head on Tuesday 19 November 1907 when at a committee meeting of the Lancashire Combination, the Salford club accused Liverpool of failing to turn up to play Salford 'A' on 19 October – a heinous crime. The committee endorsed Salford's compensation claim of £1/2/6d and the Liverpool City club was ejected from the Lancashire Combination with immediate effect, leaving the city of Liverpool without a Northern Union (rugby league) representative for nearly 30 years.

At the same time, however, one of the aforementioned Lancashire Combination clubs actually scheduled to play against Liverpool City during the 1907–08 season – Highfield – was developing from nascent beginnings in Wigan. It was the Highfield club that later evolved into Liverpool Stanley.

Wigan Highfield

Highfield Rugby Football Club was formed around 1880 in the coal-mining district of Pemberton, Wigan. The club then went out of existence for a while following the great rugby schism of 1895. There were various reformation attempts – both 1902 and 1919 being cited in later years – but the Highfield that came to be elected to the professional ranks played rugby football at a pitch originally behind and to the west of Tunstall Lane in Pemberton, using the changing facilities at the nearby Hare & Hounds pub, which is still there to this day, as their headquarters – here they were referred to locally as 'Mrs Walker's Boys' presumably in tribute to the landlady of the hostelry. 'Airedale' of the *Rugby Leaguer* was later to write: "They were immediately a success – almost a counterpart of Featherstone Rovers in Yorkshire and, like them, carried all before them in the amateur field. They won four Lancashire Junior Cups in succession, before being barred from further participation, and in season 1921-22 played off with Wigan 'A' for Lancashire Senior Competition honours." [12]

So, after competing successfully as an amateur club in the Lancashire Combination the Highfield committee decided to upgrade and turn professional. In spite of meagre resources they applied for membership of the Northern Rugby Union for the 1921–22 season. This application was refused because the NRU Council decided that the Tunstall Lane enclosure was neither large enough nor indeed well enough equipped for first-class rugby league. So, during the club's extended stay in the Lancashire Combination, a field between Billinge Road and Queen Street was added to the ground, thus increasing its capacity and facility to cater for the kind of attendances common to professional rugby league in the post-First World War era, turning the pitch at right angles in the process. The club erected dressing rooms and installed baths at the ground, rather than continue to use the pub facilities. With these structural changes put into place, Highfield RFC reapplied and was duly admitted to the re-titled Northern Rugby Football League for the 1922–23 season after a successful ground-grading visit from League officials during the summer of 1922.

A remarkable draw at Widnes in the 1921–22 Challenge Cup also contributed to this successful application by raising their already formidable profile. The now professional Highfield players were to receive £2 for a home victory, 10 shillings extra for an away win and £1 for a defeat, although there were no contract payments. Despite limited finances, Highfield continued to develop the ground in their first season in the professional ranks, adding covered accommodation for around 2,000 fans at the Queen Street West end of the ground in 1922–23, and a seated stand for 500 along the north side of the ground in 1924.

The popularity of rugby league in the Wigan area during the early 1920s was paramount and the rugby league authorities were confident – perhaps over-confident – that the town could support two professional league clubs. The other well-supported Wigan-based amateur side, Pemberton Rovers, also competed in the Lancashire Combination until 1928. Highfield duly played their first league game against local rivals Wigan, who won 25–10, on 2 September 1922 in front of an estimated crowd of 15,000 (Latham, 1997, states 18,000).

The official programme editorial, 'Witticisms', for that fixture celebrated the value of this additional derby to the Championship: "Now then, Central Park-ites, a mighty send-off for the Highfield lads, to show them that you welcome them in their new sphere." [13] The aforementioned Jimmy Green played one last time for Highfield that day, scoring two goals in the process.[14] One wonders whether the groundsman remembered to cut the grass, however, for the *Wigan Examiner*'s 9 September 1922 'Artist's Impressions' stated wittily that "the phenomenal rise of the Highfield club was nothing compared with the phenomenal rise of the grass on the field... there were quite a good number of exciting moments when the players came up to breathe." [15]

Wigan Highfield finished their first season 25th out of 27 clubs – a somewhat inauspicious start – but improved considerably over the next few years. The record ground attendance at Tunstall Lane was achieved via another Wigan 'derby' in September 1924 when an estimated 16,000 paid £502. Highfield even reached the semi-finals of the Challenge Cup in 1925–26 before losing 15–6 to Oldham in front of 18,200 spectators at Salford. A crowd of 13,350 had paid more than £700 to watch Highfield beat Leeds at Tunstall Lane in the previous round. The club climbed as high as seventh in the 1927–28 championship table, with Wigan one place behind them.

In 1928 Nat Bentham became the club's first Australasian tourist and its first test player. He played at hooker for Great Britain seven times, six as a Wigan Highfield player. Reportedly, his signing-on fee for Highfield was a modest 4 pence, which, according to 'Airedale' in the aforementioned edition of the *Rugby Leaguer* was: "promptly spent on a packet of Woodbines!" [16]

Throughout this period of improved results, however, the club continually struggled for respectable gates and their resources remained meagre – with only a small paid-up membership of 250 during this period of senior status. They evolved as something of a nursery club – spotting and nurturing players and then moving them on at a profit in order to keep the club alive. Mike Latham records one unnamed columnist waxing lyrically in 1925 "Highfield is the football factory where they hew the rough material from the coal face and mill it into gems." Several players subsequently became noted professionals elsewhere, some receiving international and county honours along the way. The list includes Billy Belshaw, Great Britain's full-back by 1937 who began with Highfield and was capped while with Liverpool Stanley and Warrington; Tom Blinkhorn, another to attain test status with Warrington; Tommy Bradshaw with Wigan; Billy Cunliffe with Warrington; Bill Derbyshire with Liverpool Stanley and Warrington; Ken Gee with Wigan; Stan Langshaw with Rochdale

Hornets; Jack Maloney, who was perhaps Liverpool Stanley's greatest player; Tommy Maloney with Halifax, and Bob Smith with Leeds.

The availability of all these talented players in one side would have been sufficient for Highfield to attain at least a play-off place. But the problem for the club was that they seldom played together at one time. A somewhat ritualised exodus, initiated by the club to sustain its resources, ensured that talent was moved on at a remarkable pace. Great credit must be awarded to the Highfield scouting and coaching set-up which, led by Jimmy Green, was second to none. But scouting alone could never fully compensate for the club's diminutive size and when the local economy of Wigan also experienced a severe downturn brought on by the mining slump of the early to mid-1930s, Highfield's gates, income, and ability to nurture players reduced exponentially and their chances of survival looked bleak indeed. Their lowest recorded gate receipts came for a home game with Bramley in 1931 when the takings were a mere £2/19/0.

Northern Rugby League 1922–23 (bottom six places)

22 Widnes	34	11	1	22	195	350	23	33.82%
23 Keighley	38	12	1	25	236	449	25	32.89%
24 Broughton Rangers	32	10	1	21	230	319	21	32.81%
25 Wigan Highfield	**32**	**7**	**1**	**24**	**208**	**432**	**15**	**23.43%**
26 Bradford Northern	34	6	1	27	180	676	13	19.11%
27 Bramley	36	5	2	29	184	572	12	16.66%

Northern Rugby League 1927–28 (top eight)

1 Swinton	36	27	3	6	439	189	57	79.10%
2 Leeds	42	32	0	10	619	307	64	76.19%
3 Featherstone Rovers	36	25	1	10	387	234	51	70.83%
4 Hunslet	40	28	0	12	546	308	56	70.00%
---------------								
5 St Helens Recreation	36	24	0	12	499	251	48	66.66%
6 Oldham	36	23	1	12	422	261	47	65.27%
7 Wigan Highfield	**32**	**19**	**1**	**12**	**272**	**240**	**39**	**60.93%**
8 Wigan	40	24	0	16	601	345	48	60.00%

To further extend the frail finances of this struggling rugby club, a decision had been made in 1926 to purchase the Tunstall Lane enclosure via a locally arranged mortgage. The land had previously belonged to a neighbourhood colliery owner, Colonel Blundell, but he wished to dispose of it and with the future security of tenure in some doubt the club decided to acquire the ground. Club director Harry Swift provided Highfield with a £450 mortgage and a loan for working capital but it soon became clear that both mortgage and loan were going to be difficult to repay. By the end of the decade Swift had served a winding-up notice on Highfield and by May 1930 this financial instability precipitated a tender from a Liverpool-based consortium to relocate the club, probably to either the Stanley or Breck Park greyhound tracks, but the members unanimously rejected the bid.

Jimmy Green and White City

Jimmy Green was the guiding light of Wigan Highfield. He was in turn, player, player-coach, manager/secretary-cum-scout, and chairman. Green's playing career began in rugby union with Leigh RFC but he transferred his allegiance to the Northern Union code and moved to Highfield. In 1907-08 Green proved to be a more than useful centre and scored 20 tries; he was subsequently transferred to the professional Wigan club. After returning to Highfield following the end of the First World War he ended his playing career with them and helped guide them into the Rugby Football League in 1922.

Green was regarded as one of the most judicious talent spotters in rugby league. Harry Edgar wrote of him: "Described in some quarters as 'their guide, philosopher and friend', Jimmy Green was the father figure for the team through their various guises as Wigan, then London and onwards into Liverpool Stanley. It is easy to draw a comparison between Jimmy and the man who performed a similar role in keeping the club alive through its various reincarnations in later years, one Geoff Fletcher... in manager Jimmy Green they had the Harold Genders [the founder and first managing director of Fulham RLFC] of their day." [17]

As Edgar affirms, it was Green who would remain with the club throughout their next two incarnations. Indeed, upon the imminent arrival of Green's club in Liverpool in 1934, the *Liverpool Echo* was to observe: "Mr Green has spent a life's service in the cause of the game and his fame for picking up young players is unequalled. He has helped to keep the flag flying in Wigan through periods of poor gates, by selling off their best wares. In Liverpool he hopes there is a public here content to watch the best of football, even if they are locals. He has already got a team of rare strength." [18]

However, back in 1933, the Wigan Highfield club was in dire financial straits. On 24 January members of the RFL's finance committee visited Wigan Highfield to consider the future of the club after it had once more defaulted on repayment of the aforementioned Swift loans. But the RFL officials found that Swift was prepared to withdraw the winding-up order on Highfield. It was agreed, therefore, that if the club could renegotiate an equitable repayment figure with Swift, the RFL would assume responsibility for the repayments. So, the existing mortgage and loan between Swift and Highfield resumed but with the RFL footing the bill – a financial arrangement that would, with some variation, become habitual for the rugby league authorities and the club over the next 60 years.

Highfield finished their 1932–33 league campaign second from bottom, their gates had fallen to well below break-even levels and expenditure far exceeded income but, thanks to the RFL, they were still in business – just. Jimmy Green, however, was reported in the local press admitting "he could not see the club carrying on... A few people had been carrying the club on their shoulders, and money was owing to tradesmen." [19] The intervention of the Greyhound Racing Association's Canadian-born managing director Brigadier-General A.C. Critchley CMG, DSO, as head of the controlling body of the White City Stadium in Shepherd's Bush, London effectively saved the club from extinction – but came at a cost.

Northern Rugby League 1932–33 (Bottom five) - Wigan Highfield's final season

24 Dewsbury	38	14	0	24	361	503	28
25 Batley	38	12	1	25	293	450	25
26 Featherstone Rovers	38	8	2	28	302	594	18
27 Wigan Highfield	**38**	**8**	**2**	**28**	**240**	**734**	**18**
28 Bramley	38	6	1	31	219	768	13

The White City Stadium was built for the London Olympics in 1908 and boasted (an unlikely) capacity of 150,000 – 68,000 of which was seated and 17,000 more covered. It has also been reported that the grandstands held 93,000 but this figure probably came about when at a later stage the terracing was partially roofed. White City was the very first purpose-built Olympic stadium and was at that time the largest sports enclosure in the world. Constructed in only 10 months at a somewhat modest cost of £60,000, facilities were

Left: The teams from Wigan versus Wigan Highfield, September 1922.

Middle: Wigan Highfield RLFC 1927-28.
Back: Silcock, Newburn, Gore, Osbaldeston, Connelly, Bentham, Green, Calderbank; front: Cowley, Jerram, Parkinson, Lyon (c), Winstanley, Grimes, Blinkhorn.
Bottom: Wigan Highfield 1932-33 at Birch Lane.
Back: Cayzer, Gray, Wade, Halsall, Woods, Davies, Stock; front Hanson, Winnard, Barnes, Lowe, James Walker, John Walker. James and John Walker were the uncle and father, respectively, of Liverpool City's captain George Walker. (Courtesy Alex Service)

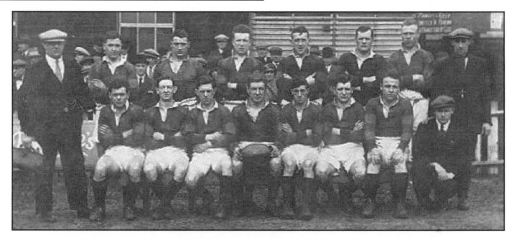

11

decidedly varied with a restaurant in the grandstand but rather basic amenities on the mostly open terraces. The great advantage of White City was its oval shape and steep banking, allowing almost the entire stadium to be viewed from any part of the ground, but it was an expensive ground to manage and following the Olympics lay underused and in a state of semi-dereliction until it was purchased by Brigadier-General A.C. Critchley of the Greyhound Racing Association (GRA) in 1927 to stage the new 'hi-tech' sports of dog racing and later on speedway.

On 24 July 1926, in front of 1,700 spectators, seven greyhounds had leapt out of the traps at Belle Vue Greyhound Stadium, Manchester and raced to catch an electric hare. This was the first modern greyhound race in England. The sport had been imported from the USA and within a year 30 more greyhound tracks opened across the UK, attracting over six million spectators.

Critchley was a business opportunist, to be sure. He had prospected for oil in Mexico, joined the Canadian Mounted Police, and had been the editor of the strike-breaking *British Gazette* newspaper during the 1926 General Strike. He even tried without success to stage cheetah racing at the White City grounds and later became a Tory MP for Twickenham. One might, therefore consider his political allegiances to be rather incompatible with rugby league, a predominantly working-class sport. However, anything resembling sporting philanthropy as a motive should be disregarded; Critchley was a mogul. Indeed, upon learning of White City's 1933 rugby league initiative, leading sportswriter of the day Tom Stenner awarded Critchley "full marks for enterprise". When the new sports of greyhound and speedway racing were introduced by the GRA from 1927 and 1928 respectively – with betting allowed at the trackside for the former – these two pursuits turned the White City Stadium and its parent GRA into a seriously profitable enterprise and the GRA was able to purchase the freehold. In fact, in those days of betting restricted to the racecourse, at least officially, other White City tracks were opened across the country to capitalise on this extra opportunity to place a non-equine trackside bet. New stadiums sprung up at Liverpool, Manchester, Newcastle, Hull, Nottingham, Cardiff, and Glasgow.

As for its associations with rugby league, Farrar & Lush (1995) and Collins (2006) highlight the problems associated with greyhound tracks in the inter-war rugby league development programme, in various venues outside the game's heartlands, including Newcastle.

By 1928 a night at the dogs was second only to association football in popularity. But unlike football, stadium-based limited companies controlled all activities at the grounds and track owners, who were businessmen first and sportsmen second, were constantly in search of additional income streams. Speedway (or 'dirt track' racing as it was also known) proved to be one such stream of income. Speedway was developed in Australia in 1923 and first appeared in Britain in Essex in 1928. This sport initially bolstered the finances of many newly built greyhound stadia across the country. However, speedway was also a promotion-based enterprise and team-owners franchised their teams to tracks, rather than the traditional football or rugby set up of a team owning their own stadium. Furthermore it was a seasonal sport, costly to stage and did not allow trackside betting. Profit margins for the track owners could be thin and as a consequence, speedway promotions tended to come and go, somewhat, while the greyhound track proprietors searched for more profitable revenue sources.

As with other such stadium-founded organisations, the GRA wished to exploit the floodlit use of the grassed area within the White City track, but the Football Association and the Rugby Football Union discouraged and forbade its members respectively from talking to the

Greyhound Racing Association. In fact the FA had already a passed a resolution on 25 August 1930 stating the "playing of matches [under for example, dog track floodlights was] undesirable and prohibits members from taking part in such a game". Unlike football, rugby union was, although well embedded in London and the Home Counties, principally a participation rather than a spectator-led sport and clearly unable to command gate receipts capable of sustaining such a venue as White City. Rugby league therefore became a third-choice target for these profit-seeking promoters, especially when the successful arrival of the Challenge Cup Final to Wembley in 1929 probably left them slavering. Tony Collins outlines that: "In 1929 the GRA approached the RFL about the possibility of forming clubs at various greyhound stadia around England. On the morning of the first [rugby league] Wembley cup final a delegation from the RFL had met with Brigadier General A.C. Critchley to discuss the formation of a rugby league club in London." [20]

Farrar & Lush also reveal another likely stimulus for Critchley: the opportunity of a White City-based side entering a competition at its highest level. This was, of course, impossible in the Football League. However with rugby league's one professional division any side playing at the White City would automatically be in the top flight.

However, it was another four years before any plans between the GRA and the RFL would come to fruition; in the meantime, hungry for greater cash flow, the GRA continued to scrutinise association football as their biggest potential cash cow. For example, despite rumblings of discontent from the FA, Queens Park Rangers FC vacated their petite Loftus Road ground in 1931 and played their Football League fixtures at White City for the 1931-32-season. But QPR and the GRA and White City failed in their attempts to persuade the FA to stage league matches under floodlights. At this time QPR were one of the poorest Football League sides in London and their meagre Saturday afternoon attendances looked lost inside White City. The appeal of playing football under lights may well have increased attendances but the FA's refusal proved costly and despite a record crowd of over 40,000 for an FA Cup tie versus Leeds United, QPR returned to Loftus Road during the following season £7,000 the poorer. It has been variously reported that during the 1932-33-season mid-week floodlit football was played at the White City. Certainly on 4 January two London representative sides played in front of 12,000 spectators. However, Wembley Stadium aside, the Football Association was still a long distance from sanctioning deals with greyhound promoters or permitting competitive floodlit football, which was only approved in 1950. Without the competitive edge of Football League games, White City floodlit football involved only one or two matches within one season and was ultimately unsuccessful.

That same 1932–33 season, the first rugby league football match under floodlights at White City also took place – on the evening of Wednesday 14 December 1932 – when the GRA management staged an exhibition match between Leeds and Wigan[21]. Unlike the football experiment, the rugby league match was deemed a success, attracting "a curious crowd of over 10,000" (Latham) to the White City arena, a figure confirmed by Trevor Delaney. John M. Jones in his short history of London rugby league[22] disputes the figure (he places the attendance at a massive 40,000), but it is almost certain that around 10,000 curious sports fans and expatriate northerners attended proceedings that evening.

From the beginning rugby league at White City was advocated with the sole purpose of being another revenue stream for the GRA. Farrar & Lush maintain "Obviously Critchley was encouraged by this gate, but his plans were that rugby league would always play second fiddle to greyhound racing." [23] Nevertheless, the Rugby League Council duly reversed a ruling that did not allow competitive fixtures to be played under lights and cleared the way for a side to play at White City. Yet Critchley felt that building a team from scratch would be time consuming. With the Empire Games due to be staged at White City during the summer of 1934 finding a pre-existing club willing to move to London would be a far more astute quick fix. Negotiations therefore re-opened between the White City management and the Rugby League Council concerning the promotion of rugby league football in the capital and it was during these discussions that the financially unstable Highfield club came under the spotlight. Jimmy Green was approached and, aware that his club was on the verge of folding, agreed with the plan. The approval of the Rugby Football League membership was then sought.

Brigadier Critchley, his co-director Captain Walsh, and Jimmy Green all attended the Grosvenor Hotel in Manchester on Wednesday 8 June 1933 to place their proposals before the RFL's AGM. They asked that Highfield's home league fixtures for the following season should be played under floodlights at the White City Stadium, London on Wednesday evenings to avoid weekend fixture clashes with neighbouring Queens Park Rangers FC and the other London football and rugby union teams who all played on Saturday afternoons. They would reimburse opposing clubs for the inconvenience of travelling to London, and the White City Company would create a fund to be administered by the RFL to cover players' lost wages caused by the midweek fixtures. Finally, the White City Company proposed to purchase the Tunstall Lane enclosure outright, but would permit Highfield to continue their training, reserve, senior competition and junior matches at the enclosure. The three men also boasted that within five years Highfield would be the strongest team in the Rugby League.

The RFL minutes for that day record the general mood of the meeting as not initially in favour of the proposals and it can clearly be seen why this might have been the case: the plans were financially very ambitious but also somewhat denigrating towards the district of Pemberton and the few remaining faithful Highfield supporters. This attitude might not have been quite so important had the club emerged from a development area such as South Wales, however Highfield was a Wigan club – right in the middle of the rugby league heartlands – and an act of such blatant disloyalty to their supporters was rather alarming. The *Wigan Examiner* on 27 May 1933 reported: "A gentleman who had followed the fortunes of the Highfield club for over 40 years told our representative that about 20 or 30 members attended the historic meeting on Monday [concerning the London bid]... One informant expressed himself in favour of the scheme, however, but not without regret. 'I've watched the matches of the Tunstall Lane club since I was a lad... before the break with the Rugby Union, and I shall be sorry to see them go. Interest has been waning' he declared 'but what can you expect when we have to sell our best players in order to keep going. I've been getting fed up lately'." [24]

At first Highfield insisted that the Tunstall Lane ground should remain the property of the club. Item 3 of the conditions as printed in the local *Wigan Examiner* newspaper stated that the "ground and appurtenances" would remain the property of Highfield. However, the GRA did not agree to this condition and effectively asset-stripped the club by purchasing outright the Tunstall Lane ground. The GRA even announced that improvements were to be made to the diminutive stadium, which would not have been the case had Highfield remained as owners. The land was practically worthless in these severe financial years; however one might perhaps speculate that the GRA had eyed up Tunstall Lane as a potential greyhound track development. Monetary issues aside, the purchase did not bode well for the club should any problems arise concerning tenancy, expansion or indeed, a rise in land values.

In spite of these dangers, it appears that the mood of the AGM was excited by the prospect of a move to London and realistic enough to appreciate that it averted Highfield's imminent demise. Jones records: "The White City Company representatives obviously made a great impact on the delegates at the initial meeting. Although the matter was adjourned, permission was granted a few weeks later and it was announced that Wigan Highfield would be renamed London Highfield and would play all their home games at the White City Stadium, London. London had obtained its first professional Rugby League club." [25]

The vote was 20–3 in favour of the proposal, with four abstentions. With the Rugby Football League effectively standing as guarantor, should the experiment prove to be a failure, the club's short-term future was assured and Highfield's debts were paid-off.

Wigan Highfield came under the auspices of the White City Company Ltd (and ultimately the Greyhound Racing Association) and Jimmy Green – still based at Tunstall Lane – remained as chairman/secretary/scout-cum-manager. Notwithstanding several previous development initiatives in Wales, this move was notable as the first big-money attempt to expand the Rugby Football League membership beyond its borders and into the association football stronghold of the capital city. It was, admittedly, to a great extent artificial – as all transplants inevitably are – but undoubtedly daring and perhaps, like the formations of rugby union clubs such as London Irish and London Scottish, an unwitting recognition of the growing transience of British society. Furthermore, by allowing London Highfield to play all their league home fixtures on Wednesday evenings, with a 7pm kick off and a whitewashed ball under floodlights, the Rugby League Council introduced the concept of floodlit evening matches almost 20 years before the Football Association approved the use of floodlights as a viable alternative to afternoon fixtures.

There had been other floodlit experiments prior to this, but both the profile and the technology of this adventurous move far exceeded earlier 19th century attempts to establish all codes of football as evening events. However, given the previously wretched record of the RFL Council's business dealings with greyhound proprietors in South Wales at Cardiff and Cumberland at Carlisle, it is amazing that they were still willing to consider such a transaction worthy of the sport they represented. One might even argue that to concede to the soliciting of a consortium of greyhound racing entrepreneurs wishing to establish rootless clubs in non-heartland areas for the benefit of the latter's revenue streams surely smacked of commercial inexperience.

In some respects the London Highfield concept was indisputably groundbreaking – a precursor, in fact, to the Fulham project, which did much to promote rugby league football in London in the early 1980s – and it has been argued (Fleet, 1991) that had Highfield continued in London beyond that solitary season they might have become the vehicle on which rugby league became an established sport in the capital.

Furthermore the RFL did countenance what became one of the very first professional sports club 'franchises' in Great Britain, establishing a precedent that still applies today – that is a proprietor, with the long-term interests of the club in mind, and the approval of the Rugby League Council, can move a team away from its apparently indigenous area and relocate it to a perhaps more profitable site. But any such rugby league relocation remains a key concern linked as it is with issues surrounding the class basis of rugby union, the stereotyping of rugby league by the rest of England, and the ambiguously parochial nature of rugby league. From this historical distance the whole affair seems an unlikely alliance fraught with both cultural and financial headaches: indeed both of these two central points were not far from the surface during London Highfield's brief existence.

Mr H.J. Carver of the GRA (right) and staff foreman Mr Bull inspecting
the White City pitch prior to the trial match on 12 September 1933.
Below: the programme teamsheet at Rochdale, and the programme from the Australians match.

TEAMS & SCORING SHEET.—Saturday, September 30th, 1933.

HORNETS			London Highfield		
Selected from	SCORE. Goals	Tries	Selected from	SCORE. Goals	Tries
Full Back			*Full Back*		
1 W. Gowers			1 Fraser or A. N. Other		
Threequarter Backs			*Threequarter Backs*		
2 A. C. Falwasser			2 Walker		
3 A. L. Davies			3 Haigh		
4 R. Gaunt			4 Hunter		
5 T. Tolan			5 Maloney		
Half Backs			*Half Backs*		
7 J. Helme			7 Gordon		
6 C. J. Aynsley			6 Salmon		
Forwards			*Forwards*		
8 E. D. Milne			8 Ilsley		
9 R. Lister			9 Fairhurst or A. N. Other		
10 R. Thompson			10 Oakley		
11 B. Walker			11 Griffen		
12 G. E. Mills			12 Woods		
13 L. V. Armbruster			13 Welsh or Gray		
14 M Campbell					
Referee: Mr. A. S. Dobson, Featherstone.			Kick-off at 3.30		

THE RUGBY FOOTBALL LEAGUE

LONDON HIGHFIELD

Wednesday,
22nd November,
1933

AUSTRALIANS

versus

(Black No 8)

WHITE CITY STADIUM

2D. OFFICIAL PROGRAMME 2D.

RIGHT OF ADMISSION RESERVED

London Highfield

First match in London for Highfield. The team at Euston before going on to White City and their match against Wakefield Trinity on 20 September 1933. (Courtesy Alex Service)

Success Of Floodlight Rugby In London

HIGHFIELD JUST LOSE GREAT GAME

Fine Scrummaging :: Intense Marking :: Faulty Finishing

One newspaper's headlines about the first game.

In the first case, the promotion of the club was very tricky owing to most of the London or national newspapers handing this newsworthy item over to their disapproving rugby union correspondents. Sadly for London Highfield the majority of these writers were decidedly anti-rugby league and declared that the brand of professionalism espoused by the new club should be actively discouraged in the capital. The only notable exception was Trevor Wignall of the *Daily Express* who campaigned for the code and condemned the 'union-ites' as pessimists.

Jones records the positive impressions of visiting Australian journalist Claude Corbett who described his first visit to a floodlit rugby match as follows: "I had looked for something beyond the ordinary when I visited the White City. I am glad nobody told me what to expect, otherwise that element of complete surprise which came when I saw the home team in the spotlight behind the goalposts, would have been destroyed. Standing there in their immaculate uniforms, the players with their greyhound mascot presented as pretty a picture as anyone could hope to see. The whole staging of the match was perfect; the ball boys in their white uniforms, the shadowless light, the perfect turf; the alacrity with which the balls were thrown to the players, and above all the absence of partisanship among the spectators, made it a night of memories never to be forgotten. White City floodlit rugby as I saw it, will always be among my cherished recollections." [26]

But while Corbett displays a somewhat poetic enthusiasm, the "absence of partisanship" comment draws attention towards the fundamental value of the project. Surely, the very success of rugby league is determined by partisanship. So the question has to be asked: from where and how was London Highfield to acquire this partisanship in adequate numbers especially when the Rugby Football Union campaigned to dissuade all union followers, players and fans alike, from participating in any such professional activities? On the other hand, the support for rugby league from union followers in areas outside league's heartlands has never been great. Even with the slower, more scrum-dominated game of the 1930s, a rugby union follower would only see the differences from the fare they were used to watching, and vice versa for a league supporter watching union. Also, at that time the antipathy to league among union followers would have been far greater. In reality, association football fans were a greater potential pool of support.

The first floodlit Highfield game took place on Wednesday 13 September 1933, one year after the experimental Leeds versus Wigan match. It was an exhibition match that also invited any rugby union amateurs to have a trial in the game itself. However, when the RFU heard of this they were furious and instructed all of their clubs to forewarn players, at the risk of being disqualified *sine die* from playing rugby union football, not to endorse the White City project. Upon hearing of this, most local amateurs pulled out – with the notable exception of Plymouth Albion and England half-back L.H. 'Eddie' Richards who was subsequently signed by the London club and went on to play successfully for Liverpool Stanley, and W.B. Welsh a back or loose-forward from Hawick in Scotland who also signed for Highfield, but then left for York before the start of the club's first season in Liverpool.

Even worse, some weeks following this inaugural match, the RFU again circulated clubs instructing them to inform all their members - playing or non-playing - that merely attending London Highfield games would result in suspension. As Tony Collins affirms: "Whether in Britain or France, rugby league symbolised much more than a set of alternative rules for rugby – a fact that was sometime more obvious to the indifferent and the hostile than it was to supporters of the game." [27]

Meanwhile, White City's floodlighting technology was also not without its problems. Tom Mather (2007) states: "White City's floodlights had 40 million candle-power (although various sources say 25 or 35 million), and the teams came out solely lit by spotlight, with the stadium lights gradually coming on." [28] But the White City lights failed completely during one trial match and when a practice match had taken place one evening following a dog meeting, onlookers were unable to distinguish between those in yellow and black and those in black and white jerseys. However, there were no reports of viewing problems for supporters during the league matches.

None the less, reports of opposing sides blaming results on the lighting do exist. Latham writes "One highlight [of London Highfield's season] was a 30-12 win over Wigan. 'They blamed it on the lights, but that was nonsense' Harry [Woods, the Highfield forward] recalled. 'We were simply the better team.'" [29] John M. Jones further records that one sportswriter referred to the stadium as resembling "a sunlit meadow on a June day" – whether this comment was poetic or ironic remains open to debate. It is probable that the lights were certainly not up to brightness ratings of even the post-1950 association football levels, especially in such cavernous surroundings as the White City arena.

With the exception of Eddie Richards, the London Highfield players were based in the north. They trained locally at the White City-owned Highfield enclosure at Tunstall Lane, Pemberton and travelled to London on the train for matches. Mike Latham explains: "Many years later Highfield forward Harry Woods recalled how he would work in the foundry until 2pm, then catch the afternoon train down to Euston with his team mates, returning overnight to start work again early the following morning." [30]

The photograph of the London Highfield players at Euston prior to their first match against Wakefield on 20 September 1933 shows them looking happy and fit. It beggars belief that, having played 80 minutes tough rugby league, these men were expected to return home in the early hours and then clock-on at work the following morning.

London played 38 games and finished 14th in the table. Twenty games were won and 18 lost – not a bad record for such a season of upheaval. The first home league match was on the evening of 20 September 1933 when they lost narrowly to Wakefield Trinity 9-8 in front of 6,000 spectators. The rugby correspondent for *The Times* remarked "if play in the second half can be taken as a standard of football played by the Rugby League in London, there seems no reason why this game should not attract its regular devotees." However, in general terms there was very little newspaper interest in London Highfield. This was due in part to the Wednesday evening kick-off time, which proved to be troublesome for copywriters and editors at the London papers.

Notwithstanding the previously mentioned rugby union 'bias', the papers frequently missed the matches. The highest recorded Highfield attendance at White City that season was for the fixture between London Highfield and the Australian tourists. The Australians won 20-5 in front of 14,500 spectators, with a gate of £1,007. The lowest recorded was, predictably for one of two Saturday afternoon cup fixtures – a first round Challenge Cup tie against amateurs Hull St Mary when only 1,000 attended to see Highfield, two points down inside four minutes, cruise to a 32–2 victory. There was also a disappointing attendance for the visit of the first French tourists: Tom Mather notes that only 1,922 spectators paid to see the visitors lose to Highfield 19–17 on 21 March 1934.

However, despite all of the promises to the RFL before the season, and respectable crowds of between 5,000 and 7,000 – a good rugby league crowd indeed, if somewhat lost in the echoing spaces of White City - and despite some level of media attention, prejudiced or otherwise, the White City management deemed the venture unprofitable and decided, in May 1934, to call it a day after only one season of promoting rugby league in London, despite the relatively successful season the pitch.

Northern Rugby League 1933–34 (Top 14)

1 Salford	38	31	1	6	715	281	63
2 Wigan	38	26	0	12	739	334	52
3 Leeds	38	26	0	12	597	376	52
4 Halifax	38	26	0	12	457	340	52
5 York	38	24	1	13	481	370	49
6 Hunslet	38	23	1	14	608	441	47
7 Widnes	38	21	4	13	393	324	46
8 Warrington	38	22	1	15	508	370	45
9 Swinton	38	22	1	15	418	322	45
10 Hull	38	21	3	14	553	438	45
11 Keighley	38	22	1	15	429	367	45
12 Huddersfield	38	20	1	17	500	330	41
13 St Helens	38	20	0	18	550	500	40
14 London Highfield	**38**	**20**	**0**	**18**	**509**	**489**	**40**

Their losses for the season, it has been reported amounted to £8,000. Critchley had expected deficits during the first season at White City but this figure was far greater than envisioned. On 8 June 1934 Critchley and Captain Lorne Bartram met the Rugby League's emergency committee to inform them of this financial loss. A press statement issued after the meeting reported that London Highfield would continue as members of the Northern Rugby League the next season, but probably the side would return to the north of England. It was initially presumed that another White City venue would accommodate them.

This deficit of £8,000 seems credible, for quite how the Highfield committee, the board of White City Ltd and the Rugby League Council expected to create the required cash flow to meet players' match fees and expenses and to make a profit after compensating the opposition for travel costs is anybody's guess – especially in the mid-1930s. Even in the 1980s with better sponsorship, travel networks, and publicity, the Fulham RLFC experiment proved how fraught it was trying to establish league in the Metropolis.

There exist reports of considerable away support travelling to London – 600 Wakefield fans for the opening match, for example – but the novelty value of this fixture should be taken into account. The prospects of midweek winter visits to London, with some fans perhaps losing at least a half-day's wages for the trip, were not attractive to away supporters. And surely no Pemberton-based fans would have travelled to these 'home' fixtures, if there were any fans left after the move to London. It would have been far less difficult and considerably less costly for these fans to attend most away games.

In these depression days of the mid-1930s one is also left wondering how many expatriate Northerners attended the fixtures. The White City Company probably expected some to turn up, as did the later short-lived Acton & Willesden and Streatham & Mitcham clubs. Collins notes one London supporter, J. Steel, writing to the *Daily Mirror* in 1935: "With the transference of workers to the South during the last few years, many of whom are rugby league enthusiasts, I think that there has never been so good a chance of establishing a rugby league club as now. At Dagenham alone there are now working hundreds of former supporters of the Salford club." [31] These were optimistic words, and the support was perhaps due to the relocation of Ford Motors from Manchester to Essex.

In the short term, the decision to end the agreement was also affected by the forthcoming Empire Games. The GRA and White City Ltd saw rugby league as a potential cash source – a stopgap prior to this money-spinning event due in the summer of 1934.

Perhaps they were surprised at the cost of running a professional rugby league team – the cost of travel, alone, was high – maybe even their lighting bills had been underestimated. It was probably a combination of these factors and others that prevented the London experiment continuing. When the club moved back to Lancashire it was the Liverpool-based Electric Hare Greyhound Company that offered them a new home.

The fact that the Rugby League Council also sanctioned the creation of two new London clubs, to commence playing in the 1935–36 season, in the way of compensation for the loss of London Highfield seems an act of financial irresponsibility and over optimism. Acton & Willesden and Streatham & Mitcham were also created around new metropolitan stadiums, with the potential to become greyhound track venues, this time those belonging to Sydney Parkes, managing director of Modern Homes and Estates Ltd and proprietor of the Wandsworth Greyhound Stadium. And sure enough, problems soon emerged when it became clear that Parkes was only using rugby league to establish new greyhound racing stadia, which because of trackside gaming, required the appropriate licences. Acton & Willesden Rugby League club was created to give the stadium a local profile and soon after a licence to race dogs at the Acton Park Royal ground had been granted in November 1935, the Acton side, having apparently done its job for Parkes, was moved to the Mitcham ground in December 1935. This stadium had previously been refused a racing licence and Parkes moved the Acton team to increase gate revenue while Surrey County Council further considered greyhound racing.

Jones writes: "Because of declining attendances at Park Royal [the home of Acton], S.E. Parkes announced that all home games would, in future, be played at Mitcham Stadium. He claimed the reason for this was to provide weekly football at Mitcham so as to boost attendances, which were already higher [for the Streatham & Mitcham team] than Park Royal, and provide increased finance to cover the high costs of running the stadium. In November, when the London County Council granted a racing licence for Park Royal, Surrey County Council had rejected a similar application for Mitcham, so the South London club were unable to augment their income from racing."[32]

Parkes disbanded Acton & Willesden at the end of the 1935–36 season. Following a third licence refusal in July 1936 he also put Mitcham Stadium up for sale and then disbanded the Streatham & Mitcham side in February 1937. The team had been successful on the pitch in the first half of the season but, as the better players were sold, attendances declined. Both teams had the problem of clashing with well-established football clubs in London by playing on Saturday afternoons. The continuation of White City style Wednesday evening matches, combined with more foresight and a development strategy for the game could have established rugby league in London and changed the sport's whole history.

Endnotes

[1] Tom Fleet, email correspondence with author 25 August 2007
[2] Latham, Mike (1997), 'Panthers Extinct on Merseyside', *League Express,* 8 December 1997, p.11
[3] Physick, Ray (2007), *Played in Liverpool: Charting the Heritage of a City at Play*, Manchester: English Heritage, p.96
[4] Correspondence housed at the University of Huddersfield; sourced 2 November 2007
[5] Unaccredited 'Editorial', *Liverpool City Official Programme* [versus St Helens], Monday, 20 August 1956, p.2

[6] 'Bee's Notebook', *Liverpool Football Echo*, Saturday 28 July 1906, p.1

[7] 'Veteran', 'Northern Union', *Liverpool Football Echo*, Saturday 15 September 1906, p.1

[8] This might be disputed, for the Liverpool City [mk2] programme for the 20 August 1956 fixture versus St Helens states: "The club colours were all black" (p.2).

[9] 'Veteran', 'Northern Union', *Liverpool Football Echo*, Saturday 15 September 1906, p.1

[10] Williams, Graham (1989), 'Initiating The Liverpudlians: A History of the First Liverpool City 1906-07', *Code 13*, issue 13

[11] Edgar, Harry (2003), 'League and Liverpool', *Rugby League Journal*, 1/5 winter 2003, Egremont: Edgar Publishing, pp. 20-22

[12] 'Airedale' (Austin Birch?), ' 'Begun and Continued' a New Series of RL Club Histories No. 18: Liverpool C', *Rugby Leaguer*, 16 January 1959

[13] 'Witticisms', *The Rugby League Football Programme*, official programme for Wigan Highfield versus Wigan, Saturday 2 September 1922

[14] The Highfield team that day was: Winstanley, Sammons, Crossman [T], Bate, Langshaw [T], Chapman, Johnson, Green [2G], Gaskell, Jackson, West, Thomas, Shield

[15] Unaccredited 'Artist's Impressions', *Wigan Examiner*, 9 September, 1922

[16] 'Airedale' (Austin Birch?), ' 'Begun and Continued' a New Series of RL Club Histories No. 18: Liverpool C', *Rugby Leaguer*, 16 January 1959

[17] Edgar, Harry (2003), 'League and Liverpool', *Rugby League Journal* 1/5 winter 2003, Egremont: Edgar Publishing, p.21

[18] 'Bee's Notes On Sport', *Liverpool Echo*, 8 August 1934, p.9

[19] Farrar, Dave & Peter Lush with Michael O'Hare (1995), *Touch And Go, A History of Professional Rugby League in London*, London: London League Publications, p.76

[20] Collins, Tony (2006), *Rugby League In Twentieth Century Britain*, London: Routledge, p.68

[21] For earlier experiments with floodlights see: Mather, Tom (2007), *Snuff Out The Moon: The Development of Floodlit Rugby League*, London: London League Publications

[22] Jones, John M. (no date), *The History of London Highfield, Acton & Willesden, Streatham & Mitcham Rugby League Football Clubs 1933-1937*, no publishing details: privately published monograph, p.2

[23] Farrar, Dave & Peter Lush with Michael O'Hare (1995), *Touch And Go, A History of Professional Rugby League in London*, London: London League Publications, p.77

[24] Unaccredited 'Highfield RFC Offer From London Syndicate Accepted By Members', *Wigan Examiner*, 27 May 1933

[25] Jones, John M. (no date), *The History of London Highfield, Acton & Willesden, Streatham & Mitcham Rugby League Football Clubs 1933-1937*, no publishing details: privately published monograph, p.2

[26] *ibid*

[27] Collins, Tony (2006), *Rugby League In Twentieth Century Britain*, London: Routledge, p.73

[28] Mather, Tom (2007), *Snuff Out The Moon: The Development of Floodlit Rugby League*, London: London League Publications, p.96

[29] Latham, Mike (2004), 'The Leaving Of Liverpool', *Rugby League World*, February 2004, p.41

[30] *ibid*

[31] Collins, Tony (2006), *Rugby League In Twentieth Century Britain*, London: Routledge, p.69

[32] Jones, John M. (no date), *The History of London Highfield, Acton & Willesden, Streatham & Mitcham Rugby League Football Clubs 1933-1937*, no publishing details: privately published monograph, p.17

2. 'On Stanley, On!'

Such was the popularity of greyhound racing in the inter-war period that three dog tracks existed within close proximity of each other in 1930s Liverpool. The first to open in 1927 was the Stanley Greyhound Stadium in Stanley, Liverpool 13. The Breck Park Stadium on Townsend Lane, Clubmoor, Liverpool, 6 followed in 1928 and a third was opened by White City Ltd on a former baseball diamond on Lower Breck Road, Anfield, Liverpool 4, in August 1931. A fourth greyhound stadium also existed in Seaforth in Bootle. Despite costing a lavish £70,000 to build, the GRA showed no signs that they wished to house the nomadic rugby league team in their well-appointed dog track in Anfield. Instead they were keen to offload the Highfield outfit onto a perhaps less suspecting victim from within the greyhound stadium network. This turned out to be John Bilsland of the Electric Hare Greyhound Company at the Stanley Greyhound Track.

According to most narratives concerning this period in Liverpool Stanley's history Bilsland stepped in and, with assistance from the Rugby Football League General Purposes Committee, acquired the players' registrations and equipment that once belonged to London Highfield – including Jimmy Green – lock, stock and barrel. John Bilsland is certainly credited by those in the know; for example, the Liverpool Stanley programme editor of 1950 rather graciously states that "Mr John Bilsland **started** [my emphasis] the club in season 1934–35", although this comment was made just as the club were about to leave the ground. It was not, however, quite as simple as that.

The Electric Hare company did indeed assume control of the assets of the Highfield club – at least as far as coaching and playing staff was concerned – but they provided little more than a pitch and the use of the Stanley Track facilities for every first team home fixture. In return they took the gate money and any transfer revenue that might accrue from Jimmy Green's dealings hoping in the process to make a profit. Liverpool Stanley RLFC, as the team was renamed, existed simply as a trading arm of the Electric Hare Greyhound Company – no more, no less. In any case, the Rugby Football League effectively sponsored the move to Liverpool as a way of saving face. They needed to show the sporting public that they were not mistaken in bolstering this second-tier Wigan club, despite the failure of the overly ambitious GRA and White City deal in London. But by getting into bed with yet another greyhound promoter their raw optimism was exposed to the monetary priorities of the greyhound track network.

In fairness, this financial sting wounded both ways. Greyhound promoters must have initially viewed the rugby league tie-in as a potential money tree. But this overt optimism was closely followed by the realisation that development area rugby league required much more than a rather patronising 'build-it-and-they-will-come' approach – it was probably bad business all round.

By all accounts the Stanley Track owner knew little about rugby league football; so while Bilsland incorporated Liverpool Stanley into the administrative structure of the Electric Hare Greyhound Company, the day-to-day rugby business of the new Liverpool club remained firmly at the Tunstall Lane headquarters in Pemberton – as it had throughout Highfield's exile in London, but now with GRA and White City Ltd as owners of the land. Perhaps as a result, the news of the impending arrival of Liverpool Stanley in the late summer of 1934 was saluted neither with great publicity nor rapture by the Liverpool sports pages. Indeed the tone of the *Liverpool Echo* summer sports writer 'Blackstaff' was only cautiously optimistic. He revealed immediately, in fact, that the rugby heart of the club was to remain firmly rooted in Pemberton, and that the old Highfield ground at Tunstall Lane was to stay in use for training, 'A' team and youth team fixtures. It was odd that a team named Liverpool Stanley 'A' should play their home games in Wigan – but this did change. His 'Notes on Sport of the Day' from the Wednesday 25 July 1934 edition of the *Liverpool Echo,* headlined "Liverpool Stanley" make for interesting reading: "Lovers of the rugby league code in Liverpool will have an opportunity this coming season of watching the game in their own city. Liverpool Stanley, the former London Highfield club, who played at the White City Stadium last season, will have a strong side, and efforts are being made to strengthen the team before the opening match. The Stanley ground is situated in a thickly populated district, and there is covered accommodation for 4,000 people [an exaggeration]. Apart from Welsh, the Scottish international forward, and Haigh, a threequarter, who have been transferred to York, all last season's players who did so well are available, including Maloney, international wing-three quarter; Oster, international stand-off half; Richards, the former Plymouth Albion scrum-half; and Oakley, who kicked 99 goals in the League for London Highfield, and nearly 130 in all matches during the season. The principal players on the list are: Maddock and Fraser, full backs; Maloney, Hunter, Belshaw, and Walker, threequarters; Salmon, Gordon, Oster, Unwin, Davies, Woods, Ray, Griffin, Stock, Sherrington, Atherton, and Hitchin, forwards. The players will train at Tunstall Lane, Highfield, Wigan, where the team played before going to London. The 'A' team fixtures in the Lancashire Combination will be decided at Tunstall Lane, while three junior teams will be run. 'I think we shall field an exceptionally fine team', said one of their officials." [1]

There is some disparity between Blackstaff's information and contemporary source material. Match programmes from the time suggest that 'A' team matches did take place at the Stanley Track, nevertheless the last paragraph of the *Liverpool Echo* article is especially revealing in other ways. Any rugby league-curious Liverpool sports fan may have been more than a little discouraged to find that, notwithstanding the Liverpool Stanley moniker, the everyday comings-and-goings of the club remained firmly rooted on its authentic home turf in Wigan. A scan of the above-mentioned squad of rugby league footballers by an educated 1930s sports fan would also have revealed a list of Lancashire-based semi-professional journeymen. These were, by and large, the same specialists who performed so admirably for London Highfield the previous season – without upping sticks - northern, yes, but 'Scouse'? Decidedly **not**. Most were probably Lancashire miners and mill workers who would not have relished travelling to Liverpool for training after a hard day's work. While the Tunstall Lane enclosure continued to be operational, this they did not have to do.

Notwithstanding, it was also apparent that Electric Hare were certainly not going to allow any training nights to interfere with the primary business of the Stanley greyhound track, and Bilsland's arrangement between his company and the Rugby League Council would have been apparent to any *Liverpool Echo* reader familiar with that paper's back pages. Here one could clearly find the details of almost nightly dog racing at the Stanley Track – even in the depths of winter. Other than Sunday, when the track was forced to close by law, there were simply no nights (or lights) available for training. Furthermore, any evening dog meeting that proved unprofitable in the summer months would, at the first opportunity, be given over to Speedway. The Stanley Track chairman might have been committed to the rugby league project sufficiently to permit Liverpool Stanley the use of the stadium every other Saturday, but not so dedicated as to allow players to train at the ground at the expense of a lucrative dog race meeting.

The Stanley Track development programme

In fact one might suggest that the real motives of Bilsland and his board, the expansion of Electric Hare's sporting *modus operandi,* clarified as the rugby league project took shape. In a replication of both the White City and Sydney Parkes's Modern Homes & Estates strategies in London, rugby league football was but one experiment among many for the Stanley Track management team as it developed into previously unfamiliar sporting territories during the mid-1930s. For example, one cursory glance at the Liverpool Stanley match programme for their Championship semi-final fixture against Widnes in May 1936 reveals clear expansionism. As the rugby league season closed for business that day, Saturday 2 May, so the baseball season commenced the following week. A baseball side named Liverpool Giants was due to begin its North of England Professional League season with a reserve fixture against Rochdale Greys on 9 May; this was to be followed by a first team fixture against the same opponents the following Saturday – both games to be played at the Stanley Track. Bilsland had poached The Giants from their previous home at Wavertree Playground.

Of course baseball has a fascinating history in Liverpool. It is rumoured that the game actually left the city and travelled across the Atlantic to the USA. It was there, with some variation, that it became the leading summer sport in the United States. In 1933 Pools magnate John Moores re-established baseball in Liverpool with American rules in order to keep a pools coupon going during the summer months. He offered competing clubs £100 each to join his National Baseball Association and seven clubs took the bait. Baseball was further exposed to the Liverpool public when a few Liverpool and Everton soccer players such as Everton's Bill 'Dixie' Dean and Liverpool's Lance Carr, Alf Hanson, and Berry Niewenhuys – all subject, of course, to the maximum wage – played professional baseball in the summer months as a way of paying the bills and keeping fit. There were many summers when the National Baseball League held deciding games at the Stanley Track, and this continued in the post-Second World War era with the occasional American side from Burtonwood US Air Base also being involved. A *Liverpool Echo* photograph exists in Liverpool Central Library of local sportsman N. Edgar playing baseball at the Stanley Track in August 1951. So, perhaps unlike the code of rugby league football, there was some kind of authentic sporting foundation, indeed a centre of operations, for this pursuit in Liverpool – but the Stanley Track was never regarded as the sport's home ground, as such - this was the Wavertree Playground - and attendances did vary dramatically from a few hundred to a man and his dog.

Furthermore, page 6 of the Liverpool Stanley versus Widnes programme reveals that on the following Monday, 4 May, the first speedway fixture of the new season was to take place at Stanley. This "Grand Opening Event" was to begin at 8.00pm and take the form of a *Daily Mail* Trophy challenge between Liverpool Stanley and Nottingham with a "special star match race" between Max Gosskreutz and Bill Kitchen. This was not the first time speedway had been tried in Liverpool. Les Graham the winner of the inaugural 500cc Grand Prix Senior World Championship [now MotoGP] in 1949 started his motorbike career by racing on the dirt at Stanley in 1929, but it was the first time that a franchise proper had been arranged between a promoter and the Electric Hare management. Since its inception in 1928 speedway had also grown as a spectator sport throughout the United Kingdom in both the pre and post-war era but rather like rugby league football, proved only sporadically popular in Liverpool. The Liverpool side competed in Division Two of the second-tier National League as opposed to the premier standard British League. However, the sport did have its fans and ran for a few interrupted years at the Stanley Track. It would be fascinating to discover whether the Liverpool Stanley and Liverpool Chads speedway sides ever balanced their books.

The team was not unsuccessful and gave a start to the Liverpool–born speedway world champion Peter Craven in 1949. He made eight league appearances for the Liverpool Chads in Division II during 1951, and rode with both the Chads and Belle Vue Aces the following summer. Speedway, however, was primarily a commercial activity built around franchises, deals, and perhaps even backhanders, and abounding in area monopolies, closures and reorganisations – not altogether conducive to the average 'Scouse' indicators of authenticity.

As with most sports the peak spectator period for Speedway in the UK was in the late 1940s and early 1950s but despite this popularity it never appeared to generate long term sustainable economic stability – even at Wembley Stadium. By 1955 and the advent of Independent Television, the writing was on the wall for speedway, although the sport did survive and had a new period of growth from 1960. In my experience, boyhood visits to the by then rather decrepit Stanley dirt track were in the early 1960s to watch the Liverpool speedway team. The phrase 'financial stability' did not immediately spring to mind – but the smell of *Redex* and / or methanol was amazing. As any follower of football at Cowdenbeath's Central Park, Halifax Town's Shay, New Brighton's Tower Grounds, or indeed rugby league at Odsal, would probably confirm, motor sport played absolute havoc with sporting enclosures, indelibly scarring and weakening facilities. Paddocks were invariably taken over for maintenance, pitch surrounds were often loosened or broken and oil and dirt literally reached all parts. In the north west, supporters watching non-league soccer at both Ellesmere Port (Speedway and greyhounds) and New Brighton (stock cars) demanded endurance and vision above and beyond the call of duty. As with greyhound racing, motor sport also enforced an intolerable distance between the spectator and the football action in the middle of the race track.

Bilsland also embraced athletics and there were several high-profile athletics meetings held at Stanley even beyond the year that the rugby league club left for Knotty Ash. For example, a triangular athletics tournament took place during Liverpool's Festival of Britain celebrations of August 1951 where world champions from the USA competed against the Amateur Athletics Association and Northern Counties selects. Electric Hare was evidently empire building (and good luck to them, one might argue), however to expect sports fans to blithely consume everything on offer at the Stanley Track rather than via a gradual processes of adoption, was somewhat dictatorial, and attendances varied significantly from sport to sport. In the long run, and as ideas began to run dry, the track became available for hire to any organisation wishing to hold an event.

Over the years Stanley Track was put to a variety of different sporting and pageant uses. For example when the Stanley rugby team vacated the stadium in 1950, a local civil service football team immediately moved in. The Stanley Track also housed several pageants during the Festival of Britain. On 31 August 1963 it hosted arguably one of the UK's first pop festivals when a battalion of Liverpool groups – excluding the Beatles – played at an all-day beat show entitled 'The Daily Herald Big Beat Festival'. Former local resident Bill Hinds recalls: "I remember the 'Beat Day' really well. My cousin and I spent the whole day hanging out of my gran's upstairs sash-windows listening to it. Obviously at nine years old it was the first 'live' pop music I'd ever heard, and mighty impressed I was, too. Couldn't see a thing but the sound was loud and clear. My cousin was six years older than me and a Cavern [club] regular so could keep up a running commentary of who was who – which I remember was just about everybody apart from the Beatles. This must have been the absolute peak of Mersey beat fame." [2]

But when the final incarnation of a Liverpool Speedway team ceased to exist in the mid-1960s the Track management was left with a crumbling venue without a purpose. Bill Hinds further remembers: "My mates and I used to spend a lot of time in there around then – this would be 1964 or '65... The place certainly looked semi-derelict then, although all of the paraphernalia of dog racing was still in place. I can remember us mucking about in the traps, and the lights were still on, but the bar or café on the Prescot Road side by the turnstiles was clearly not used. We spent an entertaining afternoon breaking the windows once. The grandstand was on the railway side, which we never approached as underneath it lived two cocky watchmen, who legged us more than once."

At the same time the popularity of greyhound racing had declined to a hard core of devotees and eventually in the late-1960s the Track was compulsory purchased for a wholesale fruit and vegetable market, which still stands and trades to this day. By this time the Stanley Track had long outlived its usefulness, and most Liverpudlians did not overly mourn the loss of a rather ugly landmark although Bill Hinds was to later remark: "We certainly did mourn its passing when the fruit market deprived us of our adventure playground – but that would be 1968 by which time such delights were history anyway. Last time I walked down Edge Lane, I paused for a Proustian moment by scrambling up the railway wall by the sub-station on the bridge where we used to climb on to the railway. Lovely."

Back to the 1930s

So, while a knowledgeable sports aficionado might have welcomed the arrival of professional rugby league to Liverpool, a fleeting glance at the local press would have revealed this entire set-up for what it evidently was: a marriage of convenience, propped-up, one might suspect, by the ever-resourceful and optimistic Rugby League Council. Perhaps the death warrant of rugby league in Liverpool was already sealed at this preliminary stage by its visible lack of authenticity. These days the many sporting franchises across North America have discovered that embryonic fan acceptance is an enormous challenge. Fan adoption is a long-term process with a framework that guides clubs through a programme of very specific strategies: from creating fan awareness through to the actual procedure of adoption – but even then there are no guarantees of success and many franchises fold. However, even today, the majority of the British public, less used to sports franchising and suspicious of sporting imports, have deep reservations about sporting activities that do not appear to be authentically embedded.

Certainly, in the case of Liverpool, where cultural identities were so strong, so distinctive, importing a pre-existing rugby league side, bearing the name of the city as a flag of convenience, would not have conveyed the required imagery, and may have been viewed by some sports folk as a rather cynical act. The challenge of proceeding from awareness to adoption, therefore would have been burdened with immense cultural difficulties from the word go, as they probably were during that season in London.

Code disparities

There were also the disparities to be ironed-out between the association, rugby union, and rugby league codes of football. The *Liverpool Echo* of 8 August 1934 reported: "The first view of the new Liverpool Stanley Rugby League Club will take place on the 15th when the hon. sec. Mr J.H. Green, will formulate two sides to play at 6pm., the proceeds to go to the Red Triangle [boxing] Club. This will give those who do not know the manly game a chance of seeing what is done with the handling code." [3]

By 23 August, the *Liverpool Echo's* Bee's Notes On Sport of the Day even felt compelled to give the readers "an outline of the differences between rugby league and rugby union football".[4] Perhaps the practice match of the previous week left a few spectators somewhat baffled.

Nevertheless, in the following day's edition of the *Echo*, the rugby league correspondent, Hooker reported enthusiastically: under the headline "Liverpool Take Up Rugby League": "... We are breaking new ground in Liverpool, not for the first time, but I think the project has now been launched under more favourable circumstances. Followers of the rugby league game in Liverpool can take it for granted that Liverpool Stanley, if they reproduce some of the form they showed at White City last season, will beat more clubs than will beat them. They are a much better side than the old Wigan Highfield, and Liverpool folk need have no fears as to the ability of the players who will wear the Liverpool Stanley jersey." [5]

Retaining their London colours of yellow with a blue band, they began well on 25 August with a late victory: 17–9 at Rochdale Hornets. But the following Monday evening the *Liverpool Echo* reported that "the Liverpool team have been recruited from local clubs, the names are very familiar to the supporters of most clubs, and no doubt old-timers from all round the district will roll up at Stanley to see the 'Highfielders' in their new home". The tone of this piece suggests, perhaps, that the local rugby league correspondents were fully aware that the team was an assemblage of journeymen, including some veterans, conspicuously the article still referred to them as 'Highfielders' at the Stanley Track rather than the Stanley rugby league team.

Bee's Notes on Sport of the Day from the following Wednesday evening edition of the *Liverpool Echo* provided more detail: "Liverpool Stanley make their first actual appearance in the city on Saturday when they entertain St Helens Recs at the Stanley Greyhound Track (6 o'clock) and some idea will be gained of how the club is going to fare. The prospects are rosy enough, for there is no doubt that Liverpool's new club will play Rugby League football in its most attractive style. This was amply demonstrated when they opened the season at Rochdale and came away with full points."

'Bee' continued: "'Leeds Loiner' writes this – 'Allow me space in your valuable notes to sing the praises of Liverpool Stanley's glorious win. According to the varied reports their second half display at Spotland was really brilliant. A continuance of such form will ensure them support. My suggestion to the management is that on the morning of your first home Rugby League game they engage at least three sandwich men advertising the game, and also distributing fixture cards in the club's colours, and enclosing a small leaflet explaining the main and vital points of the Rugby League game.'" [6]

The first home fixture on the following Saturday, 1 September versus St Helens Recreation was also won – with some style, 21–5 – but whether Liverpool Stanley's advent was glorious or somewhat inglorious remains a moot point. 'Leeds Loiner', mentioned above evidently detected a sizeable PR job to be done in the city of Liverpool.

There does appear to have been some initial success, with secretary/coach Jimmy Green largely responsible. Gates and publicity were satisfactory for the 1934–35 season. Stanley finished halfway up the Championship with attendances at their new home on Prescot Road usually hovering around the 3,000 mark – pretty good for a club playing an unfamiliar sport in somewhat unconventional surroundings. As predicted, the teams fielded by Jimmy Green were very competitive – a credit to Green's ceaseless talent for spotting footballers of merit. In fact, the aforementioned threequarter Jack Maloney scored 25 tries that season for Stanley, which remained a Liverpool record throughout the entire existence of the club. Oakley kicked 45 goals, with Belshaw scoring 40 and six tries. The Stanley Track was also awarded an international match towards the end of that first season as a way of promoting the sport. England beat Wales 24–11 in front of more than 7,000 spectators, paying £462, with Stanley's Belshaw and Woods starring for the victors. Exactly how many Liverpudlians attended that day will never be known. Liverpool Stanley finished 15th, with 38 points from 38 matches, 18 wins and two draws.

In the following season, 1935–36, the team performed even more successfully, losing only nine games overall. Stanley won the Lancashire League section of the competition outright, a complicated - and some might say incongruous – 'league within a league' that existed in rugby league football until 1970, and finished second in the Northern Rugby League Championship behind leaders Hull. The record for the Lancashire League fixtures was impressive with Stanley playing 28 games, winning 19, drawing one and losing only eight. Their Championship record was even more striking: Stanley played 38 games, winning 27 and losing only nine, with two draws – there was also an unusual 0–0 draw at Acton & Willesden in the Challenge Cup.

Northern Rugby League 1935–36 (top four)

1 Hull	38	30	1	7	607	306	61
2 Liverpool Stanley	**38**	**27**	**2**	**9**	**426**	**248**	**56**
3 Widnes	38	25	4	9	433	190	54
4 Wigan	38	25	1	12	543	328	51

According to Harry Edgar[7]: "Stanley were reported to be very unlucky to lose their Championship semi-final to Widnes (10–9) after the Chemics had kicked a last minute goal, on a day when a record crowd of 14,000 attended at the Stanley Greyhound Stadium."

Edgar's reportage is accurate, although the loss that day might be attributed to the absence of the injured Billy Belshaw and Harry Woods. Belshaw was replaced by Baxter and Woods by Shaw. Until the last minute of the game, Liverpool led by one point – Woodcock had scored Stanley's only try, Howarth with two and Shaw kicked the goals.

When one of the Stanley forwards infringed at a scrum, Jacks of Widnes took the resulting penalty from what was a very awkward field position. With the wind at his back, however, he kicked the penalty, and won the game for the Chemics. Oddly, when the goal was scored, the ground erupted, for far more Widnes fans were there that day than those rooting for Stanley, despite, it was reported, many old Wigan Highfielders being present. In an odd and somewhat disappointing anticlimax to that afternoon's fixture, the Stanley team were presented with the Lancashire League Championship Cup after the defeat to a half-empty ground: the jubilant Widnes fans were on their way home. Try-scorers were evenly spread that season: Robinson 12, Howarth 11 (plus 29 goals) Maloney 11 and Belshaw 9 (plus 21 goals) topped the list, suggesting a very effective squad.

By the 1936–37 season Stanley were once again a top-four club in the Rugby League Championship, but were beaten in the semi-final play-offs, 15–7 at The Willows by the eventual winners, Salford. It was reported that poor goalkicking was largely responsible for Liverpool's defeat that day. Glover scored the only try with Belshaw and Howarth kicking a goal apiece.

But, as a further honour, Liverpool Stanley had two players selected for the 1936 Lions tour of Australia: full-back (or centre) Billy Belshaw and front-row forward Harry Woods. Belshaw won six caps while with Stanley, and Woods five. Both players gained additional international and county honours once they had been transferred to Warrington and Leeds, respectively. Maloney top scored that season with 22 tries and Belshaw kicked 68 goals.

Northern Rugby League 1936–37 (top four)

1 Salford	38	29	3	6	529	196	61
2 Warrington	38	28	3	7	468	189	59
3 Leeds	38	28	1	9	627	262	57
4 Liverpool Stanley	**38**	**26**	**3**	**9**	**425**	**226**	**55**

All of this boded well, but the 'catch 22' of this successful spell was that Liverpool Stanley had to continue to provide a winning team in such a football-mad city just to attract book-balancing support. Literally thousands of spectators had to cross the threshold of the ground to pay for these talented journeymen turning out in the yellow and blue of Liverpool Stanley. When part-professionalism was adopted by the Northern Union in 1898–99 it was agreed that players were paid per match rather than weekly. Wage agreements stipulated that payments were dependent upon the outcome of the game. For the Electric Hare Company, therefore, their Liverpool Stanley side was a successful but consequently costly brand.

Furthermore, while at this stage they were mostly victorious, there was another snag: there were no locals, no budding apprentices, nor kids from the back streets of Liverpool to champion. No Scouse Cinderella story could ever emerge from this franchise arrangement because the players were not, effectively, local heroes. Their accents were not even locally bred. It was quite clear to all interested parties that it would take years before any Liverpool-born player could compete at this level of rugby league – if ever. Indeed, any remaining members of the older brigade who had watched the pre-First World War Liverpool City club would have recalled that particular tam failing to survive because it was essentially faceless and rootless. Liverpool Stanley RLFC was an import, a transplant – and an expensive one, at that.

There was the other aforementioned drawback: Stanley played their rugby in the middle of a dog track. This stadium was not erected for the purpose of watching rugby league and every spectator who paid admittance to the Stanley Track found themselves several yards away from the pitch. Even crowds of 3,000 were unable to generate the required atmosphere. A similar situation existed at the rather gaping Rochdale Hornets' Athletic Grounds and when this latter enclosure was used for high profile matches such as the 1924 Challenge Cup Final, overcrowded spectators would rush across the cinder track to the pitch touchline in order to get an improved feel and view of the game.

Liverpool Stanley RLFC 1935-36: Back: H. Woods, D. McDonnell, G. Davies, F. Openshaw, R. Smith, J. Lowe, A. Gutteridge, W. Shaw; front: J. Green, R. Stock, W. Belshaw, J. Robinson, J. Maloney (c), C. Glover, J. Woodcock, J. Welsby; on ground: W. Howarth, R. Burkhill.

Liverpool Stanley around 1938 (Courtesy Alex Service)

Liverpool Stanley versus St Helens Recs 1 September 1934:
Salmon and Kelly (Courtesy Denis Whittle)

Liverpool Stanley versus St Helens Recs 1 September 1934:
Salmon and Horace Randolph. The Recs player on the right is Jumbo Highcock
(Courtesy Denis Whittle)

Programmes from the 1930s

PRICE ONE PENNY

THE
Nᵒ 1077
OFFICIAL
PROGRAMME

ST. HELENS RECS
v
LIVERPOOL S.

Saturday, November 10, 1934
Kick off 3-0 p.m.

It Cured your Grandmother!

It will Cure YOU.

**WEBSTER'S OLD ST. HELENS
COUGH BOTTLE**

1/3, 2/9, 4/6. Sold by Chemists. Wholesale :

GLOVER'S PHARMACY
14 ORMSKIRK STREET, ST. HELENS

LIVERPOOL STANLEY
GROUND : STANLEY GREYHOUND TRACK, PRESCOT ROAD.
TELEPHONE: OLD SWAN 122.

NORTHERN RUGBY LEAGUE
CHAMPIONSHIP—SEMI-FINAL

LIVERPOOL STANLEY
VERSUS
WIDNES

SATURDAY, 2nd MAY, 1936
KICK-OFF 3-30 P.M.

1d. OFFICIAL PROGRAMME **1d.**
RIGHT OF ADMISSION RESERVED

ADMISSION :
GRAND STAND 2'-. GROUND 1/-. LADIES HALF-PRICE. BOYS 2d.

Next Saturday, 5th September

LIVERPOOL STANLEY
v.
BARROW

KICK-OFF 3-30 p.m.
ADMISION 1/- and 2/- (Ladies Half Price . BOYS 2d.

Saturday, August 29th. 1936 .   Kick-off 3-30 p.m.
Liverpool Stanley 'A' v. York 'A'

1 GUTTRIDGE	8 PHILLIPS
2 WOOD	9 DERBYSHIRE
3 ASHCROFT	10 BRERETON
4 KILGANNON	11 NOLAN
5 BAXTER	12 PRESCOTT
6 SALMON	13 RILEY
7 KIRK	

SEASON TICKETS ARE NOW READY
Grand Stand 35/-.   Ladies 17/6.
Popular Enclosure 17/6.   Ladies 8/9.
All including Tax.

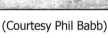
(Courtesy Phil Babb)

**LIVERPOOL
STANLEY**
(Yellow and Blue).

Players will appear in their respective numbers.

(1)
Guttridge
(2)   (3)   (4)   (5)
Robinson   Halsall   Glover   Howarth
(7)   (6)
Burkhill   Salmon
(8)   (9)   (10)   (11)   (12)
Davies   Lowe   Nolan   Smith (Capt.) Shaw
(13)
Stock

Referee : Mr. T. Marley   Touch Judges :
         (Yorkshire).   Mr. W. Connelly (Wigan).
                             Mr. G. E. Rhodes (Warrington).

Forwards—   *Backs*—
(3) Curran   (7) Gilbert
(5) Fairall   (16) Norman
(8) Heidke   (24) Robinson
(18) Narvo   (21) Reardon
(6) Gibbs   (27) Williams
(11) Lewis   (4) Dawson
(17) Norval   (25) Ward
(20) Prigg   (1) Beaton
                              (23) Thompson

AUSTRALIANS

The Scores will be shown in Electric Lights at the foot of the
Main Indicator.

Liverpool versus Australians 1937 (Courtesy Alex Service)

33

Furthermore, the rugby league fan would have been additionally infuriated by the fact that, grandstand and paddock aside, most of the covered accommodation at this greyhound stadium had been erected at the Prescot Road end of the ground specifically to give shelter to those who wished to view the dogs turning. To gain shelter from the elements, rugby spectators were forced to huddle under eight timber and curved corrugated iron 'Belfast' lean-tos erected against the perimeter fencing on the unterraced banking: the furthest possible distance from the pitch. Fans were condemned to gaze at a distant rugby field across yards of track and through the shadows and gloom of an unlit winter's afternoon.

It has been suggested that the grandstand held 2,500 and that there was cover for 10,000 souls on the opposite side, but both estimates are generous. The stand held barely 500 spectators and no cover existed at all at the Edge Lane end of the ground. There were two small shelters on the side opposite the main stand close to the halfway line but they were also far from the pitch side. Indeed several of the eight small shelters located on the Prescot Road and Fairfield sides of the ground fell down during the war and by the 1960s only a little patched up covered accommodation existed to the left hand side of the grandstand. Denis Whittle, the St Helens rugby league journalist and historian recalls: "despite its grandiose name, the ground was a tip". 'Merman', writing in the *Rugby League Review* (24 February 1950), just prior to Stanley's removal to Knotty Ash stated: "The Stanley Track... never really leant itself to Rugby. Spectators were too far away, atmosphere was lacking, and seating accommodation inadequate." [8]

So while Liverpool Stanley had built an enviable reputation on the pitch, the Stanley Greyhound Stadium quickly gained a label as an unwelcoming, impractical and altogether unsuitable venue. It was neither beloved by visiting supporters, nor able to provide the practical weatherproofing necessary to tempt curious Liverpudlians. Indeed one might argue that as a venue it failed almost immediately in its primary purpose: that of raising the profile of rugby league in Liverpool. One might speculate both the Acton and Streatham enclosures suffered from similar deficiencies in ambience. In these pre-legalised bookmaking days a poorly appointed ground did not necessarily detract the enthusiastic punter from a legal flutter on the dogs. Enduring 80 minutes of a somewhat unfamiliar team sport from a distance – whether in London or Liverpool – was an altogether different proposition.

It is not surprising to discover, in fact, that the crowds for many of these Stanley home games consisted of a mixture of away supporters and rugby league aficionados from the fringes of Liverpool. Crosville and Wigan Corporation bus services regularly carried a few fans from Stanley's roots in Pemberton, Wigan. In any case, these routes were advertised on the front covers of the Stanley programmes. But what's more, rugby league football supporters from St Helens, Whiston, Cronton, Penketh, Widnes and even Warrington, joined them. This was the era of the genuine rugby league fan and the Liverpool Stanley club became for them a kind of second club when their own club was playing away from home. The convenience of that L&NW railway station and depot almost adjacent to the Stanley Stadium further aided this effect.

A reader of the *Liverpool Echo's* 'Bee's Notes on Sport of the Day' going under the pen name 'Oval', was moved to join a debate within that column concerning the apparent unwillingness of Liverpudlians to support their rugby league side. Oval stated: "What a team Stanley are, with a reserve team almost the equal of the first team. Lancashire Cup winners last year and, perhaps, this year – Wembley finalists. You know what a word from you can do. You've kept New Brighton [FC] going by continued appeals... And I'm just one of Stanley's keen supporters who is earnestly asking you for support. Stanley have the enthusiasm and there's room in the city for another 20,000 gate. Did you hear about the Leigh trip? Eight chara loads, over a hundred people left behind, who went by train and taxi, and 1,000 on the train excursion. Stanley are not a Lancashire team to be bracketed in the 'Rugby Notes' with others. It's our city's team – Liverpool Stanley – and the only club in the town that can bring honours to it this year."

However, 'Bee' also quoted another reader, writing under the pen name 'An Old Red', who argued: "I think that 'Yellow and Blue' [a previous correspondent] is letting himself get a little upset over nothing. What you wrote, and have consistently written, about Stanley and the lack of support is, and has been, perfectly in accord with facts. I would have gauged Stanley's crowd a little more than 4,000, say 5-6,000, but I bow to your very much superior knowledge in this direction. You strike the nail dead centre when you state that you are aware of the fact that some of the matches have attracted big crowds, but that these were mainly from outside.

True, indeed, and anyone with half an ear could easily pick out the varying dialects decidedly not Liverpudlian. In the recent match lost to St Helens Recs there were at least as many Recs supporters as Stanley supporters, and in the Widnes semi-final last season, Stanley supporters were well outnumbered, even with the assistance of the Wigan section which came to shout for 't' Ifield'.

Stanley, I am pleased to say, have a very loyal and enthusiastic band of supporters which has grown immensely in three seasons, and there can be little doubt that we will see a big increase in that band in the next year or two, for the lads have fairly caught hold of the game.

I think Stanley supporters should be grateful to you for having appealed time and again to Merseyside sportsmen to support so fine a team as is Stanley. The appeal is slow in bearing fruit, but that is not your fault, nor can you do anything with those many foolish folk who say that they would go only they don't understand the game. Understanding is not absolutely essential to enjoyment of the game, although enjoyment increases with understanding, and it is surely hopeless to expect to understand a game without watching it. Now then Merseyside sportsmen! Come along and try the best 'bob's' worth in the city." [9]

But severe problems loomed for Liverpool Stanley. Although, as has been seen, the side continued to perform solidly in the league – a strong Wigan side was defeated 8–7 and condemned to fifth place during March 1937 to ensure Stanley's place in the play-offs – on 13 March the Challenge Cup quarter-final against Keighley was unexpectedly lost. It was a closely fought encounter that, by all accounts, should have belonged to the Liverpool team.

On page 3 of Monday 15 March's *Liverpool Echo* Stanley even received the 'honour' of a George Green cartoon depicting 'Stanley's Cup K.O. by Keighley'. But it was no laughing matter: the defeat was very disappointing coming as it did at a time when an appearance at Wembley would have done the Liverpool club no end of good, both locally and nationally.

An even bigger bombshell hit the club on Thursday 1 April 1937 when following a short illness, Jimmy Green passed away. No one man could be given full credit for developing the profile of rugby league in Liverpool but history says that Jimmy Green was indeed one such key individual and a great loss to Stanley and indeed to the game of rugby league. The *Liverpool Echo* reported:

Liverpool Stanley Manager – Death of Mr James Green

"Mr James H. Green, of 18 Grove Road, Upholland, manager of Liverpool Stanley Rugby League Club, died at the Wigan Infirmary this morning after an illness lasting a few weeks.

Mr Green, who was 50 years of age, was a prominent figure in the Rugby League world. In his younger days he was a player of great ability. He started his playing career with the Leigh District Rugby Union club, and scored 15 tries in 16 matches. Subsequently he joined the old Highfield club, and after scoring nearly 20 tries in the 1907–08 season he was transferred to Wigan, and figured many times in the first team in the centre position. He had a good turn of speed and passed with great judgement.

Mr Green's association with the Rugby League game extended up to the time of his death. At the close of his playing career, he continued in an administrative capacity with the Highfield club, then members of the Lancashire senior competition. Later they became members of the Rugby League and Mr Green built up a very successful team, several members of which became internationals. When the Highfield club went to London he was appointed manager, and held a similar position when the club came to Liverpool later. He was also a noted horticulturist, and won many prizes at Lancashire shows.

One of the best judges

Mr R.F. Anderton, the Warrington secretary and joint manager of the English touring team in Australia said: "Mr Green's death is a big blow to the development of the Rugby League game in Liverpool. Few men have done more for the game. He was one of the best judges of a player the code ever had, and many of the present Rugby League stars owe their introduction to professional football to Mr Green's foresight. The old Wigan Highfield club had always been regarded as a nursery for Rugby League players." [10]

In that same edition of the *Echo*, via the 'Bee's Notes on Sport of the Day' column, the tribute read:

The late 'Jimmy' Green

The Rugby League has lost one of its best and most respected friends in Mr 'Jimmy' Green the man who was responsible for Liverpool Stanley's appearance and success on Merseyside.

The game and the club are much poorer by his death. He will be mourned everywhere, for it is safe to say that every team today playing the Rugby League Code has in its ranks one man who was 'discovered' by Mr Green.

Rugby League football was his work and his hobby, and there never was, and never will be, a man who could better assess the merits of a player, be he a tried player or just a youngster seeking advancement. You needed to be in his company no longer than a few minutes to realise that here was the true and honoured sportsman who was never afraid to express his opinion and demanded equal frankness by return.

I am convinced no one except he could have built up Liverpool Stanley to its present eminence in the code, or could have proved to Merseyside that the Rugby League code was an attractive game.

That was the only reward he asked for his untiring enthusiasm and labours – that Merseyside would come to pay due homage to a game it was rather inclined to ignore. Something of a martinet in his control and training of the players under his control, he nevertheless was loved and respected by them. They knew that he had their welfare as well as that of the team and the code at heart – that this was the reason for his strictness, and that he did not merely seek to bask in the reflection of his team's glory.

I journeyed with him (writes 'Winger') to Hull for the cup-tie game. That was the last time he was 'abroad'. One chat will be a pleasant memory. He had much valuable comment on Rugby League matters in general to make.

I shall not forget his last remark. He said "our lads have done well today. They were a credit to the game, and I would like them to get to Wembley. It would do the game and the team such a deal of good on Merseyside. But I think Liverpool is realising that there is something in this code of ours."

Such was the man, and sportsman, 'Jimmy' Green.

It has been a great shock to everyone at Liverpool Stanley. Mr J. Bilsland and Mr Perkins paid their tributes to him "We could not have suffered a greater loss" they said. "He will be sorely missed – no one more so. His enthusiasm was amazing, and he earned the wide-spread respect that he commanded".[11]

The *Echo* later reported that John Bilsland had called for a two minutes silence prior to the 3 April 1937 fixture versus Warrington. A crowd of 6,000 stood in silence to honour Jimmy Green. Despite Stanley beating Warrington 11-5, it was a sad day for all those who attended the Track. Ultimately Green's demise was to be not only an untimely but also a very costly event.

It was reported that John Tinsley would be Stanley's new manager. Tinsley had not played rugby league to the standard experienced by Green, but had been his disciple. Not only had Tinsley been Green's lieutenant for many years but he and Green had also been schoolboy friends. He stated to the *Echo* "whatever I can do, I shall do, if only as a tribute to my pal and mentor Jimmy Green", a somewhat disconsolate comment, to be sure. Indeed as the season drew to a close the atmosphere around the Stanley Track was grim and it appears that John Bilsland took this as an opportunity to reassess his own involvement with Liverpool Stanley.

Jimmy Green had done much to bring players to Liverpool Stanley at a cut price and maintain a high profile for Stanley with the somewhat reluctant local press. But more than this he attempted to encourage schools rugby league football in the city of Liverpool.

John Belcham (2007) provides an inventory of all sports played in Liverpool in 1931 prior to the arrival of Liverpool Stanley and neither rugby code is included. Although the precise nature and impact of Liverpool Education Committee's adoption of rugby league remains unclear (see chapter 6), an initiative to raise the game's profile among the young people of Liverpool most certainly took place. Sadly, as with other such programmes in the future, the scheme's waning was in direct relationship with the departure of individuals from the city.

So, as this outwardly successful but secretly calamitous season came to a close in May 1937 the *Liverpool Echo's* rugby league columnist 'Winger' reviewed the Stanley achievements for that season. The words reproduced here serve as a measure: firstly that despite a top four finish for Stanley, Liverpool as a city was not enamoured by the XIII-man code, and secondly that John Bilsland was perhaps making plans:

Stanley's achievements
"Naturally, it is a disappointment that Liverpool Stanley did not achieve any specific honours. Yet, there is no gain-saying the fact that Stanley have had a most successful

season that augers well for next year and a season that offers its reproof to Merseyside's rather strange coldness in accepting both the team and the code.

When Stanley... came first to the Stanley track there were those who said 'we give them a season. Perhaps not a season'. Even now, the idea of Stanley being mere 'birds of passage' has not entirely disappeared, and an odd query of whether they will be at the Stanley track next year has been asked... Stanley as a Wembley side would have been just one more reproof to Merseyside's aloofness... the only trouble (if it can be described as that) for next season would seem to be whether the crowds will grow in the same ratio as they have during the past months." [12]

The "odd query" discussed by 'Winger' was more than conjecture. Despite (or perhaps as a consequence of) the playing successes of the previous three seasons, by the end of their trading year 1937 The Electric Hare Greyhound Company announced that the Liverpool Stanley sector of their operations was in severe financial difficulties. They disclosed a trading deficit of £15,000 for 1936-37, although this figure probably included all sporting acquisitions. Nevertheless this was a vast amount of money for a provincial greyhound track to lose - almost twice the level of the London White City losses – and placed Liverpool Stanley in an invidious position. In fact, according to a *News Chronicle* report on 15 July 1937, such was the impact of Green's death, together with what appeared to be appalling financial mismanagement, the Stanley Track administration wanted Liverpool Stanley to resign from the Rugby Football League and cease trading with immediate effect. According to a later *Rugby League Review:* "In went the letter of resignation to the League".[13]

Following on the heels of Green's death this announcement came as a mighty blow to the Stanley supporters, who also discovered that John Bilsland was holding clandestine discussions about a possible wholesale relocation of the entire team to Sheffield, Morecambe or Doncaster (further greyhound and/or speedway tracks, no doubt). Bilsland and his small board of directors felt that Electric Hare could no longer continue to financially sustain the rugby league team – at least as part of their own sporting stable. According to Tom Fleet, Bilsland's resignation from the RFL (on Stanley's behalf) was only averted at the last minute by the Stanley Supporters' Club guarantee that "1,000 season tickets would be sold. In the event 800 was a dramatic increase from the previous 79 and sufficient to ensure the survival struggle continued." [14]

Dramatic is hardly the word; indeed one wonders not necessarily how this figure was achieved in such a short space of time, but rather, if there were 800 potential season ticket holders around the Stanley Track, how had the Liverpool Stanley venture reached such an appalling financial nadir? It clearly didn't add-up. The supporters' club were evidently suspicious of Bilsland and were not easily persuaded to part with their hard-earned cash. In fact, Tony Collins states that the Liverpool Stanley supporters were keen to accept "Direct... responsib[ility] for the survival of their side. When the club's owners, the Electric [Hare] Greyhound Racing Company, tried to shut it down in 1937 they took it over and formed a limited liability company to ensure it carried on playing," [15] which suggests that relations between the supporters and Electric Hare were not as they should have been. It would actually be another 12 months before the Liverpool Stanley Supporters Club was able to float their limited company, but Collins's point is well made. Although Bilsland was claiming a large loss on the club, the numerical strength of the Stanley Supporters' Club suggests a solid backbone of support. Perhaps Electric Hare did not enjoy what they might have considered interference in the running of their business.

This underestimation of supporters' cultural investment in the side was probably typical of the greyhound industry as a whole which, as a rule, dealt with punters rather than supporters. It seems likely that the monetary announcement was deliberately portentous: Bilsland could begin selling-off the Liverpool Stanley assets (i.e. the players).

John Bilsland viewed Jimmy Green, and his ability to turn "rough material into gems", as Liverpool Stanley's prime asset and Green's demise meant the disappearance of potential long-term transfer profits. Stanley's few remaining assets lay in the players brought to the club by Green at almost no expense, so, for the 1937–38 season Bilsland set about transferring these players to help square Electric Hare's accounts.

The Stanley Supporters' Club had no say in this policy for, quite simply, the players' registrations were the property of Electric Hare. They could only stand and watch as Bilsland whittled away at their team. Nevertheless, prior to the advent of their limited company, the Liverpool Stanley Supporters' Club duly took over the administration of the rugby team, soldiering on, and providing as much financial support as they could muster – and to all intents and purposes they made a pretty good fist of it.

The 1937–38 season kicked-off with a 17–2 defeat at Swinton but, by the beginning of October, Stanley had climbed the table. Home victories against Leigh, Wigan, and Barrow, together with a win at Wakefield meant a top four place. But all was not well: 'Winger' from the *Liverpool Echo* reported candidly on 11 September 1937: "It has to be admitted that the opening match with Leigh attracted no attendances [sic] that confirmed expectations of a wider interest being manifest in the code on Merseyside.

"I was told officially that the attendances were less than 2,000. That is no good if Stanley are to continue in a smooth and unburdened course in Liverpool." [16]

The first player to leave Stanley was Harry Woods, sold at the start of the 1937–38 season to Leeds for a fee of around £1,000. 'Winger' then received rumours of the next player to depart and reported on 25 September 1937: "I see that someone has written that he is willing to make a substantial bet that when Belshaw plays for England against the Australian tourists he will not be a Stanley player... If Belshaw were transferred, it would be one of the most vital pointers as to the consequent fading success of Stanley. The officials, I know, are fully aware of how such a transfer would be interpreted by supporters. It would be more or less the beginning of the end... This is certainly going to be a testing season for Stanley – and the code itself – on Merseyside. I hate to think what would have happened had Stanley proved to be merely a mediocre side, which never approached top-four honours. It is certain that it would have been just another blank page in the history of introducing the rugby league code in 'foreign country'." [17]

But Billy Belshaw did indeed leave Stanley soon after – for Warrington - and cost the Wire £1,400 – a mighty transfer fee for the 1930s and clearly intended to maximise income. Ironically, while Liverpool Stanley struggled, the sale of Belshaw resulted in high profile charity matches being staged between Stanley and the Wire at both the Prescot Road and Wilderspool enclosures, with local charities benefiting. Tom Blinkhorn later accompanied Belshaw to Warrington for an undisclosed fee, whereas forward George 'Porky' Davies (who had scored London Highfield's first-ever try) was transferred to St Helens after their supporters' club raised £250 of the required £275 transfer fee. And more were to follow; Bilsland viewed the squad as 'fees on legs' and moved them on as soon as was convenient.

That season's visit of the Australian Rugby League touring side was a major sporting event, but illustrates Stanley's rapid decline well. After losing to England in front of almost 32,000 spectators at Swinton's Station Road ground that November, the

Australians travelled down the East Lancashire Road to play Liverpool Stanley, one of the form teams of the previous season. The Kangaroos won 28-9 – a Glover try and three Nolan goals for Stanley – in front of a paltry crowd of only 1,500 spectators. The successful Stanley side from the previous season had already largely been dismantled. The Australians' next fixture against Huddersfield attracted a throng of more than 9,000 to Fartown.

By 2 October 1937 Bilsland's plans had evidently filtered through to the Stanley fans. The *Liverpool Echo*'s 'Winger' remarked on his postbag:

Stanley and apathy

"Will Liverpool Stanley survive? I dislike pessimism in any matter but this question of Liverpool Stanley ending its connection with Merseyside, is revived by the tone of several letters I have received this week... The fact must be faced that the attendances are still unsatisfactory. The Supporters' Club are striving to arouse enthusiasm whenever it is possible, and they realise that this is going to be a ticklish season. They 'saved' the club for this season. Have they 'saved' it for other seasons? I hope so." [18]

Despite the exodus, almost unbelievably Liverpool actually finished the 1937–38 league season in a very respectable league position, 17th, with 35 points from 36 matches, just below halfway in the table. However, they were playing their home games in front of depleted gates. Stanley had performed well, winning almost half of their fixtures, but they could not attract the population of Liverpool along to the Track in the required numbers. Stanley's campaign during a packed April was characteristic of an erratic season. Nine games were played that month, four were won and five lost. The best result was on the 16th: a 17–4 win at St Helens. In all, Maloney top-scored with only 12 tries, Nolan kicked only 36 goals – a tough season, all round.

One additional, but seldom discussed factor in Stanley's unending search for respectable attendances was the arrival in 1935 of Liverpool's third professional football club, South Liverpool FC, in its second incarnation. The history of the 'South' is an equally complex tale and both clubs suffered many analogous twists and turns in their existences, including members' club problems and dreadful vandalism to their enclosures during the 1970s and 1980s.

But in the mid to late 1930s South Liverpool FC was a booming club and attracted regular attendances of 6,000 to its Lancashire Combination fixtures. Many South Liverpool members resided not only in Allerton and Garston – ostensibly South's home districts – but also in the Wavertree, Edge Hill, and Lodge Lane areas of Liverpool – just to the south of the city. South's successes: several league titles and cup victories almost lifted them into the Football League.

They certainly gave Stanley yet another unwelcome rival spectator attraction with which to deal. Indeed South Liverpool's practice and reserve games drew on average more than Stanley's first team rugby league fixtures. This must have been a matter of consternation to Bilsland, who also witnessed the South Liverpool Caledonians baseball team turn out on a regular basis at the well-resourced and atmospheric Holly Park ground during the summer months.

Once the family silver of players had been sold to cut the company's losses, Liverpool Stanley was just a name: a team without its best players and a club without any tangible possessions – effectively valueless to Electric Hare. Rugby league had been brought to the Stanley Track to promote the venue and greyhound racing; it was not, in and of itself, of great value to Bilsland. Once it could no longer help promote or sustain the

40

commercial side of the business, it was of little further use. As Collins correctly suggests "doggedness was not a quality that was valued by greyhound entrepreneurs... The entrepreneurs mistakenly believed that rugby league's professionalism was the same as that of the new commercialised spectator sports that blossomed in the early 1930s." [19] It must be borne in mind as well that Liverpool Stanley was completely asset-less. The GRA and White City Limited now owned the Tunstall Lane training ground.

Liverpool Stanley was duly floated as a limited company in April 1938 and the directors relinquished daily use of the Pemberton ground by the end of the 1937–38 season. Bilsland was forced to reconsider allowing Liverpool Stanley increased use of the Stanley Track for training and 'A' team fixtures. He agreed, at a price, to the 'A' team fixtures, but not to supplying training facilities, which would have eaten into his profitable race meetings.

However, it must be said that Electric Hare did not stand in the way of this group of people determined to see the continuation of their club. There were now genuine supporters of Liverpool Stanley who, having fought to keep the club in existence, were beginning to develop roots for this previously rootless outfit. Adversity often sheds light on loyalties and convictions that undoubtedly represent a kind of kinship, however just how much of this kinship represented the broader sporting and cultural communities within Liverpool remains open to debate. Without a rugby team, towns such as Wigan, Widnes, St Helens and Leigh would be bereft of valuable cultural signifiers. But for Liverpool, Stanley's presence meant little to the local communities in and around the Stanley Track.

In April 1938 an agreement had been drawn up between the new limited company and Electric Hare for the purchase of the team and for rent payable on match days: £5 for first team games and £2/10/- for 'A' team fixtures. The new company carried with it the full support of the Rugby League Council and this support included intermittent financial assistance. The new Liverpool Stanley Rugby League Football Company Limited opened its shares subscription list on 19 April 1938. Capital was set at a modest £5,000 and divided into 40,000 shares of 2/6d each. There were nine directors, four of whom were Wigan-based. The name of supposed founder John Bilsland is notable by its absence from the list of directors: John Charnock of Pemberton, Wigan; Sydney Craven of Liverpool 14; Hubert Groghan M.B. of Garston, Liverpool; Alfred Drennan of Liverpool 13; Peter Green of

Pemberton, Wigan; Humphrey Thorne of Birkenhead; John Tinsley of Upholland, near Wigan; Edward Finch of Liverpool 19 and Thomas Chadwick of Upholland, near Wigan. It was hoped that the share capital would provide working capital. However, as one share certificate suggests, this was perhaps more challenging than originally envisaged. A Liverpool Stanley Limited share certificate, held and displayed by www.world-rugby-museum.com, shows that by July 1938 only 895 shares had been sold out of a total of 40,000. Mr Joseph Porter of Portelet Road, Liverpool 13 had purchased 10 of these (worth £2/10/-). It is possible that the new Stanley directors were in a position to purchase the remainder, however, no evidence exists of that and it is likely that the balance of the shareholding remained unsold while the Rugby League Council were financially available to back the club and provide a modicum of stability.

The supporters, however, were constantly fund-raising throughout this period and dinner-dances abounded to help with administration costs and to contribute to players' fees. Ten years later in 1950, the board were to publicly admit at the final Stanley

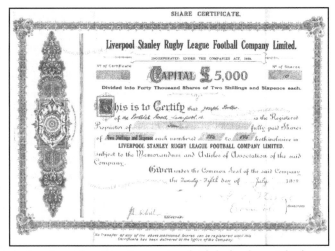

fixture at the Track: "the great help given by the Supporters' Club had mainly been responsible for the club's continued existence".[20]

Stanley's new management was also able to subscribe to the Northern Rugby League Pool – the system of gate sharing whereby five percent of gate income from all league matches was paid into the pool and then divided between all clubs. With Liverpool barely surviving on such low gates, this brought in important revenue. Liverpool's income from such a system would have been far greater than its contributions and would have substantially aided the club's survival.

However, it could be argued that the limited company strategy was not very sound. While on the one hand it kept debtors away and did not make any director personally liable for the debts that might be incurred, major investors would not be attracted because the club did not have any assets, as such. Its two greatest resources (Belshaw and Woods) had already been sold off by the old organisation and the new company had little in the way of share stock. Certainly Mr Porter of Portelet Road might have been able to attend an AGM and shareholders meeting, but he would not have had any discernible power with only 10 shares. In any case, Stanley paid rent on a thoroughly unsuitable ground, could no longer afford transfer fees, and had nowhere to train. Sales of shares, under these 1938 circumstances, were little more than charitable donations.

Two Liverpool Stanley sides were able to fulfil their fixtures for 1938–39 and despite dwindling finances the club prevailed. The first XIII fell to a final place of 19th in the Rugby League Championship table prior to the outbreak of war, which actually wasn't a bad effort. Despite a weakened squad Stanley managed 18 victories, with both local rivals St Helens and the soon-to-be-disbanded St Helens Recs finishing beneath them in the table. There were one or two notable victories: Stanley won at St Helens on 12 September in the Lancashire Cup 10–5 and, on 8 October, 9-7 in the League. Stanley also achieved the double over St Helens Recs: 7–3 at home and 13–3 away. Maloney top-scored again, but this time with a rather paltry 12 tries whereas Nolan achieved more success with the boot and registered 55 goals. The side was certainly far closer to the middle of the table than to the bottom and it says something about their first three seasons that the team was viewed as 'struggling' – after all, a few middling seasons on the pitch are not really cause for concern.

But there was more to it than this; the city of Liverpool had lost what little interest it had in Liverpool Stanley and the attendances at matches throughout this final pre-war season reflected a general indifference. John Belcham records that by the 1930s the two Liverpool professional football teams were attracting average gates of 30,000 – some of the best attendances in the country – those at Stanley hovered around the 2,000 mark. The local press did not help Stanley's cause, of course. They either largely ignored the club or else fed their readers a stream of conjecture about the club's financial instability.

As far as finances were concerned it is highly likely that the Rugby Football League stepped-in periodically throughout this season to help maintain the club. But if this was indeed the case, they were at least doing so for what they perceived to be correct motives: keeping an, albeit tenuous, toehold for rugby league football in the city of Liverpool. Of course, by 1939 all attendances were reducing, reflecting the impending war, for the conflict with Germany did not come as a surprise. The 1938–39 season was played out against a backdrop of diplomatic tensions and, while life went on as usual, and, like the rest of professional sport, rugby league players tried to carry on regardless, the forthcoming 1939–40 rugby league season was about to be interrupted. In some ways it was a surprise that it even got under way at all.

It was clear that the latest version of Liverpool Stanley could only exist on a shoestring and rumblings of discontent were not restricted to the local press. Restlessness also began to emerge among the rugby league fellowship about the viability of the club. Around 10 years later in November 1950 rugby league's most high profile personality, Eddie Waring declared Liverpool Stanley to be the Rugby League Council's "costliest toy". This dissatisfaction had its roots in the immediate pre-war era when Stanley evidently existed by virtue of a Rugby Football League crutch.

Seven years on from Waring's acerbic remark, the Warrington RLFC secretary Les Hockenhull wrote about the fading reputation of the pre-war Liverpool Stanley: "The game on Merseyside would have been much stronger today had it not been for a certain Mr Hitler. There were several times during the pre-war years when Stanley reached the later rounds of the Challenge Cup. In season 1936 they were Lancashire champions and if Percy Jacks of Widnes hadn't kicked a last-minute goal, Widnes would not have fought out the League Championship against Hull in the same season. Yes, men like Billy Belshaw, Jack Maloney, Billy Howarth, 'Porky' Davies, Jock McDonnell, Harry Woods, etc., put Stanley on the map. And if you care to look up the records Stanley beat Warrington twice in one season. Billy Belshaw and Harry Woods were tourists in 1936 and Billy eventually came to Warrington playing some grand games before the war. He was also at Wilderspool for a short while after the ending of hostilities." [21]

However, one might state as a postscript that, as a whole, the Liverpool Stanley rugby league club performed brilliantly even to survive until the outbreak of the war. Not only did the new limited company prevail under the chairmanships of Humphrey Thorne and then Tom Ashcroft, but the *ad hoc* playing staff under the management of John Tinsley worked wonders in winning 36 league matches over the two seasons of their so-called degeneration.

There must have been those at the club very satisfied with the way Stanley had survived Jimmy Green's death and the subsequent financial trauma. The Warrington secretary's notes above are indicative of many sporting histories that begin or end with the expression "but for the war..." or (in this case) "had it not been for Mr Hitler". It continues to be one of the foremost clichés in British sporting history. However in Stanley's case this truism does appear to have some context. But for the war there might have been a resurgent Liverpool Stanley – less ambitious perhaps, but leaner, used to hardships, and working well within their means.

The days of struggling to pay incessant winning bonuses to the likes of Harry Woods and Billy Belshaw were well behind them, but this was no bad thing for a club barely able to record attendances of 2,000. On the other hand, the problem of being unable to control its own destiny was a constant torment, and was never far from the agenda. As long as Stanley remained at the 'dirt track' the destiny of the club lay in the hands of John Bilsland, not the directors of Liverpool Stanley Ltd – something clearly had to be done about finding a new headquarters for the club.

The Stanley Greyhound Track was requisitioned by the RAF in September 1939 for a balloon barrage and after only one home league game versus Warrington on 2 September, a 15–8 win for Stanley, Liverpool Stanley moved to a temporary home at Prescot Cables Football Club's Hope Street ground, which is still there today: now renamed 'Valerie Park'. Bilsland pocketed the War Department payments for the use of the Stanley Track throughout the war. This move away from Liverpool has historical significance for it appears to have held the potential of a more permanent relocation.

NORTHERN RUGBY LEAGUE
Season 1939-40.

Liverpool Stanley v. Warrington

Saturday, September 2nd, 1939
Kick-off 3-30 p.m.

1d. OFFICIAL PROGRAMME 1d.
RIGHT OF ADMISSION RESERVED.

Admission :

Grand Stand 2/-   Ground 1/- Ladies Half-price   Boys 2d.

Ground: Stanley Track, Prescot Rd., Liverpool, 13
Telephone   ·   Old Swan 3641.
Railway Station: Stanley (L.M.S.)   Cars 9, 10 and 10b.
Crosville and Wigan Corporation Buses.

Indeed, the *Rugby League Review* of 24 February 1950 records "despite the times, they looked like taking on a new lease of life. Gates were showing improvement". Tom Fleet also provides testimony that "gates... showed some initial improvement". The club officials had decided to move proceedings physically closer to the spiritual home of rugby league football in Lancashire, and the public appeared to have responded positively – suggesting perhaps that the bulk of their support came from this area, in any case.

The Liverpool Stanley board had already decided that their club needed a new home – away from Bilsland – and Hope Street, Prescot was seen as a way out of Liverpool. Here at Hope Street, Stanley continued playing rugby league for a further two seasons in the hastily arranged Lancashire division of the War Emergency League. But it became clear in the second of these seasons that on Merseyside rugby league was somewhat surplus to requirements. With the exception of one match staged at Hunslet on 19 April 1941, Stanley's 1940–41 season ran only until Christmas 1940 and the 9 November 13–5 victory at home to Leigh was played with only 12-a-side. Stanley suspended operations for the duration in 1941 after finishing seventh in a nine team league.

Sadly it was not possible to continue at Prescot after the War. 'Merman' of the *Rugby League Review* wrote in 1950 that the Stanley board explored many avenues in their efforts not to return to the Track – but to no avail: "After the war, it was not possible to return to Prescot, as the ground was required for soccer, but determined efforts were made to take over the City Road ground, formerly occupied by St Helens Recs. The directors of Pilkington, the owners of the site, ruled that the ground in future should be used solely for amateur games. There next came the bid to find a home at the old St Helens Town ground in Park Road, which had been converted into a greyhound track, but after progress had been made, negotiations broke down. The Orrell district was explored, but avenues were closed and back Stanley came to Liverpool." [22]

Fleet concurs: "Six years on, resumption at the Prescot Cables ground was not possible and efforts to move to either St Helens or Orrell came to nought. The only option proved to be a return to the vast emptiness of the unsuitable Stanley Track."[23]

The irony of Stanley's inability to resume rugby at Hope Street was probably not lost on the Prescot Panthers officials and supporters who, in 1997, saw the end of this club at the ground Stanley's board wanted. 'What ifs' count for little in history, but what if, in 1945, Stanley had been able to resume rugby league at Prescot Cables FC?

1939–-40: War Emergency League Lancashire section

1 Swinton	22	17	0	5	378	158	34
2 Salford	22	16	2	4	328	171	34
3 Wigan	22	16	1	5	301	157	33
4 Widnes	22	15	2	5	305	176	32
5 Warrington	22	11	1	10	281	258	23
6 St Helens	22	11	1	10	288	224	23
7 Barrow	22	10	1	11	303	286	21
8 Oldham	21	8	2	11	241	242	18
9 Rochdale Hornets	21	8	0	13	197	306	16
10 Leigh	22	6	1	15	188	346	13
11 Liverpool Stanley	**22**	**4**	**3**	**15**	**152**	**350**	**11**
12 Broughton Rangers	22	2	0	20	153	441	4

1940–41: War Emergency League Lancashire section

1 Wigan	16	15	1	0	297	71	31
2 Warrington	16	13	0	3	236	42	26
3 St Helens	14	10	1	3	280	83	21
4 Salford	14	9	0	5	216	95	18
5 Oldham	16	6	1	9	161	205	13
6 Swinton	13	6	0	7	121	132	12
7 Liverpool Stanley	**14**	**2**	**1**	**11**	**147**	**270**	**5**
8 Broughton Rangers	10	0	0	10	71	247	0
9 Leigh	13	0	0	13	62	446	0

As for Tunstall Lane, on 23 April 1938 the *Wigan Observer* confirmed that local slipper manufacturers Messrs Lord & Sharman of Pemberton purchased the old Wigan Highfield ground, presumably from the GRA, and no greyhound track was developed there. As a further postscript, Trevor Delaney's 1991 *The Grounds of Rugby League* is of some interest here. In the section on 'Highfield' he states that in March 1939 Lord & Sharman built a wooden pavilion for the use of their employees on the site of the "old embankment at Tunstall Lane" (or Billinge Road according to the RFL guide of the time). It further reads that Liverpool Stanley later used this area for training. This remains in some doubt.

The club's programme editorials say that Stanley trained at the Clock Face Colliery ground in St Helens in the late 1940s and at the Liverpool Police Sports and Social Club bordering their home ground in their final season at the Stanley Track. So it is possible to say that they had severed all connections with their ancestry by at least, 26 August 1948 (the date of the pertinent programme editorial). The Tunstall Lane site was developed for housing in the 1980s.

As a rather poignant postscript, Pemberton man Jimmy Caddick recalls in a way that turns Wigan Highfield's accomplishments into fading and half-remembered legends: "I was born in Tunstall Lane in 1946 and I remember this rugby ground. It was between the slipper works and Valley Rd. When I was going to Highfield School in the early 1950s it was still there; whether it was still used, I don't really know. I can't remember a clubhouse, but the goalposts were still there".[24]

The principal tales of rugby league history are usually concerned with glorification of its heroes. But the history of any great sport should also take account of the barely visible and scarcely remembered: those characters such as Jimmy Green who once existed in a shifting and blurring light, flickering between success and failure, between the hopefulness of kinship and the gloom of rejection.

Endnotes

[1] 'Blackstaff's Notes On Sport of the Day', *Liverpool Echo*, Wednesday 25 July 1934, p. 10
[2] Bill Hinds – email correspondence with author 24 December 2007
[3] 'Bees Notes On Sport', *Liverpool Echo*, 8 August 1934, p.9
[4] *ibid*, 23 August 1934
[5] 'Hooker', 'Liverpool Take Up Rugby League', *Liverpool Echo*, 24 August 1934, p.11
[6] 'Bee's Notes On Sport Of The Day', *Liverpool Echo*, Wednesday, 29 August 1934, p.10
[7] Edgar, Harry (2003), 'League and Liverpool', *Rugby League Journal* 5 winter 2003, Egremont: Edgar Publishing, pp.20-22
[8] 'Merman', 'On, Stanley, On! New Haven and Rising Hopes at Liverpool', *Rugby League Review*, 24 February 1950, p.5
[9] 'Bee's Notes On Sport Of The Day', 'Liverpool Stanley', *Liverpool Echo*, Wednesday 3 March, 1937, p.14
[10] 'Liverpool Stanley's Manager, Death of Mr James Green', *Liverpool Echo*, Thursday, 1 April, 1937, p.8
[11] 'The Late "Jimmy" Green', 'Bees Notes On Sport Of The Day', *Liverpool Echo*, Thursday, 1 April 1937, p.10
[12] 'Winger', 'Stanley's Achievements', *Liverpool Echo* 1 May 1937, p.7
[13] *ibid*
[14] Fleet, Tom (1991), 'A History Of Highfield, Part 6: 'The Struggle For Survival'. Series written for the *Highfield RLFC Official Programme* 1991-92-season
[15] Collins, Tony (2006), *Rugby League In Twentieth Century Britain - A Social and Cultural History*, p.32
[16] 'Winger', *Liverpool Echo*, 11 September 1937, p.7
[17] *ibid*
[18] *ibid*, 'Stanley And Apathy', *Liverpool Echo*, 2 October 1937, p.7
[19] Collins, Tony (2006), *Rugby League In Twentieth Century Britain - A Social and Cultural History*, p.70
[20] J.C. Gregson [probably], 'A New Era', *Liverpool Stanley Official Programme* [versus Dewsbury], Thursday 20 April 1950, p.7
[21] [Probably club secretary] Hockenhull, L., 'Liverpool's Second Visit', *Rugby League Football Programme* [the official programme of Warrington RLFC: versus Liverpool City] 11/3, 31[t] August, 1957, pp.1-2
[22] 'Merman', 'On, Stanley, On! New Haven and Rising Hopes at Liverpool', *Rugby League Review*, 24 February 1950, p.5
[23] Fleet, Tom (1991), 'A History Of Highfield, Part 6: The Struggle For Survival'.
[24] Jimmy Caddick - email correspondence May 2007

3. Hard times at Stanley

"Improved public spending power and the boom in spectator sports generally saw most sporting organisations flourish but Stanley did not share in this euphoria, either financially or on the field." [1] Tom Fleet's comment was correct. Liverpool Stanley duly resumed their rugby league fixtures for the 1945–46 season and reluctantly returned to the Stanley Track; quite simply there was nowhere else to go. But both boardroom and the supporters' committees established immediately that the number-one priority for the club's survival was a new home ground; it was to be an almost soul-destroying task.

On the pitch the situation was no less anxious. However, there was a strong Furness feel to that inaugural post-war season side and new player-coach Norman Fenton had recruited several players from his home district of Barrow-in-Furness. Full-back Cliff Carswell, utility player Newson and prop Newsham, together with Val Cumberbatch (brother of Jimmy, one of the first black players to represent England) had all been recruited from the Barrow side. But despite the inclusion of winger Aspinall – who had gained wartime international honours and also played for Lancashire in 1945–46, and the equally reliable Bill Riley, also a county and international player that season, the rest of the side consisted of pre-war veterans such as the redoubtable Jack Maloney, Stock and Norman, and St Helens cast-offs Dixon and Preston: a piecemeal squad, indeed.

Limited finances precluded anyone other than travelling journeymen from turning out in the new Stanley colours of white. The coffers were clearly empty in the immediate post-war era and, with gates even lower than the 1930s average of between 2,000 and 3,000, rental outgoings to Bilsland, and a playing staff consisting of largely ageing professionals, Liverpool Stanley's existence – win, lose or draw – was tenuous indeed.

The 1945–46 Stanley squad was certainly ill-equipped to cope with the rest of the resurgent Rugby League. The team began well enough, recording an 18–13 home victory over York and a 9–8 win at Broughton Rangers. Two drawn games followed – one in the league against Swinton, 10–10, and the other a Lancashire Cup home leg against Broughton. But following this promising start, fortunes plummeted. Ominously on 20 October 1945, Bradford Northern inflicted a humiliating 67–0 defeat on Stanley. This score remained a Bradford club record for some years, as did Ernest Ward's points tally of 34 from four tries and 11 goals. Despite that early promise of better things to come, Stanley finished the season second from bottom. Including the defeat at Bradford Northern, a run of 25 straight league defeats ensued. A narrow 7–5 victory in the Challenge Cup on 16 February at Keighley (not enough for passage through to the second round after a 5–0 loss in the first leg the previous week) broke the overall run, but four further league defeats followed in February and March. The *St Helens Reporter* on 26 February 1946 praised Stanley's display at Hull Kingston Rovers, describing it as "commendable" with "Stanley's defensive work [standing] them in good stead". But it was all to no avail as Hull KR easily ran out 16–5 winners. The Stanley squad's efforts were no doubt "commendable" but, in truth, the team was woefully inadequate.

Rumblings of discontent again began to emerge from the RFL's membership about Stanley's viability. However, they were possibly saved from expulsion by a curious end to the season. Stanley played eight league matches in quick succession between 6 April and the final match on 13 May – and won three of them. There were narrow victories against Widnes 7–5, Hunslet 16–15, and Rochdale Hornets 9–3. Liverpool also forced a 10-10 draw at Hunslet in the penultimate game of the season. Overall Stanley won only six games during this first post-war season and had that mini-recovery not taken place in the closing weeks their continued membership of the RFL might have been placed under pressure. As it stood, the final table revealed Stanley's meagre playing record to have exceeded that of York and they were effectively saved for another year.

The ever-loyal pre-war favourite Jack Maloney threw in the towel in December 1945 after making a record 413 appearances since his debut for Wigan Highfield in 1926. He just missed out on joining Belshaw and Woods in the Great Britain tour of Australia in 1936 and was very unlucky not to receive an international award throughout his illustrious career – perhaps had he moved to another club, as did most of his team mates during the mass exodus in 1937–38, he might have received greater recognition. As it stands, he was probably Liverpool Stanley's greatest player but he was never given a testimonial by the club.

1945–46 Northern Rugby League (bottom six teams)

22 Keighley	36	9	2	25	307	640	20
23 Leeds	36	9	1	26	351	581	19
24 Rochdale Hornets	36	9	1	26	221	513	19
25 Bramley	36	9	0	27	271	620	18
26 Liverpool Stanley	**36**	**5**	**2**	**29**	**263**	**700**	**12**
27 York	36	4	1	31	328	769	9

Off the pitch it is likely that the Rugby Football League was still to some extent interceding financially in order to keep the club in the city of Liverpool. They certainly contributed towards the match fees of the small staff of professionals – there was no 'A' team. The arrival of on-loan Val Cumberbatch during January 1946 was almost certainly via the expediency of the Rugby League Council. Most important, perhaps, was the 5 per cent gate levy system, which clearly kept Stanley afloat. Their average attendances hovered around the 1,500 mark so a regular financial subsidy from the RFL gate levy and Challenge Cup pool was welcome. But the supporters' club was also ever active. Indeed, its membership by April 1946 was over 500 strong according to the Liverpool Stanley programme of 6 April 1946, and to the good financially.

The following season, 1946–47, Stanley performed well on the rugby field. Fenton was released as coach and in his place came a veteran of the old Wigan Highfield side, Jack Bradbury. He was entering his twilight years as a player with St Helens and as a way of returning to his roots became player-coach at Stanley. With his vast experience and local knowledge, Bradbury was able to coax locally based players to turn out for Liverpool and he gradually dismantled the 1945–46 side and reassembled a capable team around forwards Bill Derbyshire and Bill Riley. Predictably those two were stars throughout the season as Stanley won 14 matches – a vast improvement on the previous campaign.

Liverpool even reached the third round of the Challenge Cup after overpowering reformed amateurs Pemberton Rovers over two legs in round one and then narrowly defeating Hull in the second round. It was only their inability to register any points at Wakefield that prevented further progress. Forward Bill Riley was out of the side that day and his absence contributed to the defeat. In the league Stanley recorded their highest post-war winning margin on 9 November 1946 by walloping Halifax 44–0 at home, and to crown it all achieved the double over St Helens. Stanley narrowly and spectacularly won 17–16 at Knowsley Road on Christmas Day with Winstanley landing four decisive goals, and then followed up with an 8–7 home victory on New Year's Day

1947 when former Saints stalwart, player-coach Bradbury, apparently played out of his skin, scoring a try and a goal to win the game. Other notable victories over Swinton and Leigh capped off a far more rewarding season for the Liverpool minnows on the pitch and helped to sustain interest from the stalwarts in the supporters' club, who had donated £550 to the cause the previous August.

Predictably, however, the big guns circulated, sniffing around the Stanley squad for tasty morsels. Warrington moved first and by the following season Derbyshire and Riley were both Wilderspool-based. This was sad in some respects, but even if Stanley could turn out a competitive side on the pitch they were in a no-win situation off it. Attendances were weakening, debts once more mounting, and it was only the sale of these two international-standard players that balanced the books. 'Merman' of the *Rugby League Review* recalled "The wolf was at the door again and to keep him out the two Bills — Riley and Derbyshire — were transferred to Warrington. The fees, and generous assistance from the Supporters' Club, kept Stanley alive." [2]

The Stanley supporters really were quite amazing. They were able to contribute to the rugby club in the most practical of ways: by providing a regular throughput of cash. But even this proved to be insufficient when the big freeze winter of 1946-47 hit. Many games were postponed and what little income Stanley usually received through the turnstiles dropped to almost zero. In February 1947 Stanley did not play any championship matches and in March only one home match, the Challenge Cup win over Hull, took place. When rearranged home matches were eventually played, they came thick and fast and attendances suffered as a consequence.

Rugby league attendances in this period were often rounded up or down and precise figures remain to this day difficult to locate. However the *Rugby League Review* did collate these somewhat inexact totals each month. The late running of the 1946–47 season — it ran until 21 June — owing to the freezing weather certainly illuminates the losing battle for decent attendances fought by Stanley on a week-by-week basis. For example while on Saturday 12 April 1947 the highest rugby league gate was at Swansea where Wales beat France in front of 20,000 fans; of the 14 league matches that day, the largest attendances were at Barrow with 13,700, Huddersfield with 13,000 and Swinton who attracted 12,000. Liverpool Stanley drew a meagre 2,500 for the visit of relatively unattractive York.

The following Saturday, 19 April, fell on the weekend of the Challenge Cup semi-finals at Swinton and Huddersfield. These two fixtures attracted an aggregate figure of almost 70,000 spectators. Liverpool Stanley were at home to Batley that afternoon in front of a gate of 1,000 — a long way from the attendance record of 14,000 set in 1936. The same day Wigan attracted 30,000 to Central Park for the derby match against Leigh. A midweek Stanley derby fixture against Warrington on Wednesday 21 May attracted a healthy 5,000 to the Stanley Track on the same evening that Leeds attracted more than 40,000 for their derby fixture against Bradford Northern. Probably a majority of the crowd that evening at Stanley were Warrington supporters. The final home fixture against local opposition Leigh on 31 May 1947 attracted a good crowd of 4,000; however, in context, five-figure gates were recorded at Hunslet, St Helens, Wigan and Workington on the same day. It must also be stated that Liverpool Stanley was not the only minnow in terms of attendances. Bramley, Featherstone Rovers, Keighley, and York in Yorkshire and Rochdale Hornets, St Helens, and Swinton in Lancashire, all registered low gates during these congested closing months of the season. It largely depended on how many fixtures were played over a period of a week and whether the opposition brought many travelling fans with them. However Liverpool Stanley's gates appear to have been the most consistently low of all the clubs.

On New Year's Day 1947, the Stanley directors had publicly expressed hope that the "ground trouble would be settled in the year to follow" but financial matters came to a head at the end of this weather affected season. The team had finished an adequate 23rd out of 28 clubs but, owing to the shortage of cash partially brought about by the lack of home games during the winter months, the directors were unable to meet their financial responsibilities and the limited company established in 1938 was wound up in March 1947, owing Electric Hare unpaid rent in the process. However, it could be argued that Bilsland had already done well from the rugby league club.

1946–47 Northern Rugby League (bottom six teams)

23 Liverpool Stanley	**36 11 1**	**24 322**	**497**	**23**
24 Swinton	36 11 1	24 262	466	23
25 Keighley	36 10 1	25 299	509	21
26 Featherstone Rovers	36 9 1	26 217	477	19
27 Rochdale Hornets	36 9 0	27 223	430	18
28 Bramley	36 5 0	31 232	706	10

The supporters' club immediately stepped in and took control: by March 1947 they had handed over £1,000 to a committee of volunteers headed by George Facey and J.C. Gregson, the supporters' club secretary and chairman respectively. The Stanley programme for 12 April versus York contains a picture of the famous rugby league official Mr Harry Sunderland handing over on 18 March 1947 a supporters' club cheque for £1,000 to Mr Lunt of the Stanley committee. Under the title of "A Milestone Passed and A Promise Kept" this substantial aid to the Stanley club was probably, pound-for-pound, without equal among the members of the RFL.

This new committee was aided once more by generous subsidies from the RFL and an official rent-free period was agreed with track owner John Bilsland for the remainder of that season, with the caveat that Stanley should attempt to vacate the ground as soon as possible. The bottom of the barrel had once more been scraped, but the financial acumen shown by the erudite supporters' club meant that money was made available for an escape plan. The club yet again lived on to fight another day and the first priority was to get out of the Stanley stadium as soon as possible.

Moving on

By 1947 the stadium was a dreary enclosure in an equally dreary location; the war years had not been kind to the ground and the greyhound and speedway activities surrounding the pitch rendered it dilapidated even by rugby league standards – which were not always high. The one diminutive grandstand did not properly cover a partially exposed paddock, and the changing rooms and bathing facilities were cramped and neglected. While, as previously stated, to the left of the stand some cover did exist, it was yards away from the playing area. Several of the eight Belfast shelters had collapsed and the rest of the ground was lacking the most basic requirements of hard terracing, cover, female toilets, and refreshments. It was a classic example of an experiment that had all but failed: team sports and speedway tracks did not mix well, at least at this rather modest level and especially in a city where every sporting venue was sized-up in perhaps unfair comparison with the mighty Anfield and Goodison Park football grounds. Rugby league correspondent Tom Reynolds, using the pen-name 'Lancastrian' was to write in February 1948 "if football stands had been available, Liverpool Stanley would have been paying its way in Fairfield by now."

Furthermore, in these immediate post-war years of building permits, licences and the scarcity of construction materials, track proprietor John Bilsland showed little interest in upgrading the meagre facilities – and who could blame him? It took an age to get permission to alter a building and even longer to obtain expensive supplies. In those days of chancellor of the exchequer Sir Stafford Cripps instructing the general public on a regular basis to tighten their collective belts, supplies for even the most undemanding improvement jobs – for example a little concreting or roofing replacement – required permits. Buildings of all varieties in Liverpool were allowed to fester. There was, of course, the residue of a long-standing slum problem, but even by the mid-1960s bomb-damaged buildings and spaces left by buildings demolished after being hit by a bomb were still commonplace in inner city Liverpool – the now famous Albert Dock tourist trap was a good example.

Entire streets were left unaided with only the ubiquitous prefabricated temporary homes being erected to ease the housing crisis. Three thousand pre-fabs were dotted around the city, including over 1,000 on a single estate on the outskirts of Liverpool at Belle Vale.

The city of Liverpool was in deep crisis in 1947; financially broke yet with a socialist building agenda aiming for the city to turn itself into a 'new Jerusalem'. True to form, the city fathers did it on the cheap and took their building programmes to the east of Queen's Drive (such as Belle Vale) leaving the ageing and crumbling inner city pretty much to itself. British movies of the post-war era set on Merseyside such as *The Magnet* (1950) and *Violent Playground* (1957) clearly show this inner-city neglect. One should not, of course, overly blame the Liverpool Corporation for this malaise. Developing the city's periphery had already begun in the 1930s. There was a planning initiative as early as 1933 and building began prior to the outbreak of the war at Speke and Huyton: overspill was the key word, rehousing people away from the city centre.

The passing of the Town and Country Planning Act of 1947 also meant that central government pulled the strings as far as development was concerned. But development or not, the responsibility of Liverpool City Corporation to revitalise the inner city was spurned time after time for the sake of new housing on the perimeter; something that contributed to the city losing almost half its population between 1951 and 2001. There were plenty of jobs, of course, and upwardly mobile families thus began expeditions into the new council house estates and privately built suburbs. It took another 30 years for Liverpool's inner city crisis to come to a head in the Toxteth riots of 1981.

So, with little to no say about the degrading amenities at the Stanley track, yet with a manifest passion to either promote rugby league football in Liverpool or simply keep the club alive, all rugby parties concerned – the Stanley board, supporters, and the council members of the Rugby Football League – felt that Liverpool Stanley needed to be in control of its own destiny. It had been agreed that a search for a new headquarters and ground was essential and perhaps this could also result in a return to the successes of the 1930s. This search for a new enclosure had already begun in earnest – the temporary removal of the club to Hope Street in 1939 sealed Stanley's future in the minds of the directors: it lay away from John Bilsland and his deteriorating dog track.

During the early months of 1947 the new Stanley committee identified a potential enclosure. This was a plot in Mill Yard, originally one of the many small hamlets leading out of Liverpool towards Prescot, in close proximity to Knotty Ash, Little Bongs and West Derby. This Prescot-bound road was the original packhorse and turnpike conduit between Liverpool and south Lancashire and still runs intermittently alongside the A57 dual carriageway.

But there were several problems concerning the provenance of the land. The plot, part of which was used for allotments, existed a little to the south of the Broughton Hall Catholic School playing fields – a portion of a vast area of land owned by the Roman Catholic Church. This swathe also accounted for the Cardinal Allen School, St Vincent's Blind School and a Carmelite Convent. On first enquiry all of the land appeared to belong to Liverpool City Council, but there was a snag – the boundaries between this site and that owned by the Church were blurred; it took three years of searches, negotiations and permits to sort out this quandary and, in the meantime, the Stanley club was forced to slowly decline at the Track. Looking back now it appears almost inconceivable that Liverpool Corporation, the Roman Catholic authorities and the Rugby Football League should allow matters to drag on at such a slow and chaotic rate; but this was late-1940s Britain and the reinvigoration of a tired and dishevelled Liverpool did not necessarily include a rugby league team which did not have a long history in the city.

At the commencement of the 1947–48 season, *Liverpool Echo* rugby league correspondent S.H. Yates penned a special article for the Stanley official programme for the match against Warrington on 13 September 1947. He outlined Liverpool's dual plight in their search for both an enclosure and playing staff of the required standard: "If a fact-finding commission were appointed to inquire into the position of the Stanley Club, I can well imagine, in bold type at the head of the findings, would be: 'Progress will never be made unless and until the club acquires its own ground.'

There is nothing very profound in that. It is self-evident. Efforts have been made right, left and centre. Some promises held out temporary hope before petering out as just other disappointments, and here we are, back at the starting point, with supporters more and more confused and club officials struggling against a feeling of frustration.

No useful purpose will be served simply by reviling the directorate. Whatever the explanation of their inability to find a new home, it is certainly not for want of trying. If you, the Supporters who are the life-blood of the club, have influence which you could use to advantage it is your duty to co-operate.

Most of you are aware that there is a site, which holds out every promise of being the answer to the club prayers. Wrangling proceeds apace, but progress is very much an also ran. If the City Council was impressed by the strength and righteousness of your clamour, doors which are now heavy and unyielding might swing back far more easily on their hinges. Speed is essential. The club cannot afford to drift on throughout the season in a spirit of uncertainty of the future.

Stanley's tradition is bound up with the discovery and development of juniors, but how can they proceed to enrol the promising young players, who are as numerous as ever for the persistent and observant, if they cannot offer them a game in the 'A' team and adequate training facilities.

Bramley and Featherstone have weathered storm after storm throughout the years and now all Rugby League enthusiasts are heartened that the tide appears to be on the turn for them. They have their grounds. Stanley too, must have a home or.....

You have your part to play. Disappointments there will be, but if everyone will stand and pull together, not as observers only, Stanley can still establish a rugby cornerstone in Liverpool." [3]

Yates was never a great supporter of Liverpool Stanley and was forever sceptical about the club's existence. For him the authentic history of rugby league excluded the city of Liverpool and in many respects he was not incorrect in this conviction – but there was no point in blaming the club for this cultural aberration, as the tone of the first two paragraphs appear to do.

Yates was fully aware that the committee had already spotted a piece of land in Knotty Ash and his advice, while appearing pragmatic, was actually dogmatic and somewhat patronising. It must have been quite evident to all Stanley supporters, devoid of the pointed language of a rugby league fundamentalist, just what needed to be done. By January 1948 the Stanley committee was able to announce: "Last New Year's Day we expressed the hope that Stanley's ground trouble would be settled in the year to follow, and such has been the case. On Tuesday, 22 December [1947] arrangements were made to sign the lease of the new ground, and this should be an accomplished fact by the time these notes appear in print. A great deal has now to be done to get the ground ready for August next, and 1948 will be a year of high hopes and hard work! Supporters will be kept posted up to date with information as to future arrangements, and we ask for the full support of all in this great opportunity to give Stanley a ground worthy of Merseyside." [4]

A supporters' club meeting was held at the Bents Cattle Market Inn on Tuesday 6 January 1948 to discuss the signing of the lease for the new ground. A flyer, written by Tom Reynolds, 'Lancastrian', was put into the Stanley programme for the 7 February 1948 fixture to induce supporters to assist the club. Reynolds remarked that "deeds not words will be needed" and while asking Stanley fans to purchase shares in the future holding company – a long way in the future – for the new ground, stated that he had "sounded supporters of surrounding clubs" to provide "flying squads of skilled workers" to work on the prospective new ground – rather hard to believe, but certainly enthusiastic.

He also gave an indication that the Rugby League Council was behind the new project by continuing: "It is, without a doubt, a tremendous thing to attempt to establish a new sports stadium at Knotty Ash at a time like this. A private company can only get over the knotty problem of being unable to advertise by using its supporters to canvass for backing.

The 775 members of the Supporters Club are pledged to throw in their resources for several years' rent. The Rugby League is pledged for a loan of £2,000. Can Liverpool back this with a company for £5,000 in ten shilling shares? ...What a film it would make. The local club, on the village green, fighting for life; its transition to London to play floodlit rugby at White City; its next journey to Liverpool, in greyhound track surroundings; its last stage at Knotty Ash, in a brand new ground. Wandering finished. Home at last." [5]

Reynolds was not completely familiar with the structural and financial arrangements at Stanley which, to be fair were changed on a regular basis. A new committee had been formed out of the supporters' club but a limited company was not constituted while the team remained at Stanley.

Instead, a directorate of leading supporters' club officials was to coordinate matters relating to the acquisition of the new lease and the supporters' club would effectively continue to run the rugby team via its appointed committee representatives. This meant that all monies raised would go directly and speedily to the areas of greatest need.

Warrington versus Liverpool Stanley 21 January 1946

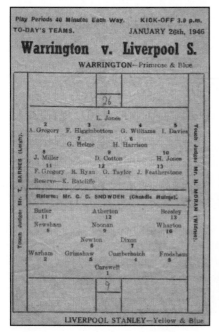

Left: The teams in the programme.

Middle: Fred Higginbottom (Warrington) passing the ball.

Below: Higginbottom tackles a Liverpool Stanley player.

(Courtesy Fred Higginbottom & Neil Dowson)

Liverpool Stanley 1946-47 (Courtesy Alex Service)

Programmes from the 1946-47 season: versus Belle Vue Rangers
(Courtesy Alex Service) and versus York.

Top left: The announcement of meetings to form the members club in 1950.
Top right: Harry Sunderland presenting a cheque to Liverpool Stanley in 1947.
Bottom: The Stanley players being presented to the Earl of Derby.

A new holding committee, formed with J.E. Jones as 'chairman of directors' agreed at a meeting on Tuesday 6 April 1948 to hand over the "domestic affairs" of the team to the 'directors' for the following season (a rather misleading title because despite being described as 'directors' there was no board, as such). The supporters' club placed four representatives on the ground committee – Messrs Jump, Facey, Draper, and Gregson.

Good news concerning the Knotty Ash venture was, however, sporadic at best. There was a hitch concerning the lease whereby the owners of the land, ostensibly the City Council and the Catholic Church, wished the new holding committee to provide a substantial four-figure financial guarantee. This came as a great blow - there was simply not enough money around for such a large pledge. Furthermore, Ministry of Works permits were not immediately forthcoming for what was considered 'non-essential work' and the deal at this stage looked scuppered. However, the Stanley programme editorial for Good Friday, 26 March 1948, gave supporters a more optimistic update:

The new ground – progress reported
"The last month has been one of great activity by the Directors and Supporters' Club officials. As promised, we are keeping you in the picture and now give you a brief account of what has been done. The gloomy outlook of a month ago has gone to make way for one with real hope of success. The Chairman of Directors made a start the day after his appointment! And with three others offered to sign the lease.

Then came check number one. A personal guarantee of £5,000 was wanted from the signatories, and the necessary permits to commence enclosing the ground must be obtained by mid-April. Messrs Jones and Parry saw the owners who altered the terms, making them more favourable – a guarantee by the club of £1,500, but permits still to be obtained by mid-April. Mr Jones has been successful in finding that materials can be obtained for the fencing and enquiries are out re dressing rooms, turnstiles, etc.

A joint committee of Directors and Supporters' Club Officials has been formed and met on Thursday 18th, together with Mr James Hilton (Chairman of Leigh) who is giving us most valuable help. The permits went to the Ministry of Works on the 19th with all the necessary details of material, costs, etc. The Supporters' Club and Directors have seen to the matter of £1,500.

Summing up – we want the permit by mid-April. Then the lease will be signed and the Holding Company formed immediately." [6]

In May 1948, right in the middle of this deepening crisis concerning the financial bond, Liverpool Stanley took the unusual but wise step of appointing another club's director – Tom Brown of Wigan – as their representative on the Rugby League Council. This appeared to achieve two objectives. Firstly it enabled the ambitious Brown to become RLC chairman – a rapid rise indeed - but secondly, alongside James Hilton of Leigh, it also gave Stanley a strong voice on the Council, creating a higher profile for the club among members than had previously been the case. Via the badgering of Brown and Hilton, RFL secretary Bill Fallowfield reviewed Stanley's plight and drew up a dossier on the future of the club. In the considered opinion of both Brown and Fallowfield, the Council was advised to financially support Stanley as a development area club, thus retaining the all-important city moniker. The Liverpool name was considered crucial to the development profile of the Rugby Football League. As shall become clear, the Stanley holding committee, with the assistance of Brown and Fallowfield eventually secured a new ground, while creating plans for a new fee-paying members' club.

However it took three years of time and energy to create a new rugby league ground out of nothing in this era of post-war austerity. 'Merman' of the *Rugby League Review* later stated in February 1950: "For a tantalisingly long period the lease remained unsigned, and while interest waned people were asking if the lease would ever be signed or would Stanley go out like the snuff of a candle?" [7]

Furthermore, within weeks of the ground's opening, it became obvious to all that the seemingly generous financial package provided by Fallowfield was actually woefully inadequate. Tom Brown continued his active support for Stanley right up until the time when the Members' Club was formed in May 1950. But, by 1950, Brown reverted to his original love – Wigan RLFC with some degree of frustration at the goings-on at Knotty Ash, but he was certainly one of the unsung heroes of the Liverpool Stanley rescue plan.

Results and receipts for 1947–48 season were predictably dismal: Stanley's pockets were usually all but empty and the team was very fortunate to finish away from the bottom of the final table. There were eight league victories but avoiding the wooden spoon was largely thanks to truly dreadful seasons from Yorkshire sides Featherstone Rovers and York. Liverpool found scoring very difficult; Stanley failed to register any points at all in eight matches and scored six points or less on 28 occasions. Ronnie Preston was leading try scorer with only eight tries to his name. Pat Murtagh and Peter Forsyth top-scored with only 10 goals each. The season did end on an optimistic note but this had nothing to do with Stanley's playing strength; finally an opportunity had arisen to escape Bilsland's grasp.

1947–48 Northern Rugby League (bottom six teams)

23 Bramley	36	12	0	24	330	482	24
24 Batley	36	11	1	24	281	482	23
25 Hull Kingston Rovers	36	10	1	25	303	470	21
26 Liverpool Stanley	**36**	**8**	**1**	**27**	**192**	**550**	**17**
27 Featherstone Rovers	36	6	0	30	270	724	12
28 York	36	4	1	31	216	849	9

Austerity

Like many sports clubs in the immediate post-war era, shortages and rationing in addition to almost daily money difficulties directly affected Stanley. The aforementioned hoped-for construction permits did not appear by April 1948 and supporters experienced a frustrating summer, waiting for clearance from the Ministry of Works to commence building work at Knotty Ash. Only then, of course, could any lease be signed. But it still remained unsigned as Stanley kicked-off the following 1948–49 season. In the Stanley official programme for opening fixture versus Warrington, 26 August 1948, J.C. Gregson admitted: "It has been a great disappointment to everybody that for the time being we have been unable to secure the necessary permits to enclose the proposed new ground at Knotty Ash. Thanks to Mr Bilsland we have been able to carry on again at the Track and the least we can do to show our gratitude is to see that no damage is done to his property. We feel sure all supporters will help in this direction. We shall make every effort to secure the new ground and shall continue to try and obtain the necessary permits. Both Directors and Supporters' Club officials are bitterly disappointed that their continued efforts in the close season have not borne fruit." [8]

Two further examples contextualise the austerity and frustrations of this post-war era well. Not only were sports people stymied by government officialdom, but they were also limited by acute money shortages. Firstly, unable to play in their more colourful pre-war strip of yellow and blue owing to the additional expense brought about by a scarcity of dyes, Stanley resorted to wearing whatever shirts they could lay their hands on. Up until their final season at the Track they were forced to wear various permutations, mostly based on white, and were reliant on clothing coupons donated by supporters. Indeed, the 1946 Stanley side was only able to wear a new strip thanks to the generosity of a Mrs Rosalie Kyle, a Liverpool convert to the game who made and then presented an entire white and black outfit to the club for free. Sadly Mrs Kyle left Liverpool in 1950 – another significant loss to the club infrastructure. A black and white picture of the Stanley team in 1947–48 in *Rugby League Journal* shows the side is decked-out in what appears to be white shirts with a dark 'V', perhaps blue or black, stitched over the white. Another photograph at the Liverpool City Record Office shows Stanley in all white with a large but rather primitive 'S' stitched to the shirt pocket area. A third, printed on the front cover of the March 1950 *Rugby League Gazette*, shows the Stanley team being introduced to Lord Derby in December 1949 at Oldham wearing rather worn plain white shirts with dark, perhaps black, shorts, and black-and-white hooped stockings. This strip was possibly the one presented to the team in September 1948, as reported by J.C. Gregson: "We should like to take this opportunity to thank the Supporters' Club for the gift of two complete outfits, one each for the first team and juniors – white jerseys with black collars and cuffs, white shorts with black line, and black and white ringed stockings. Both committee and players appreciate this splendid gift." [9]

The penultimate home fixture for the 1948–49 season versus Widnes records Stanley playing in blue – a change strip owing to Widnes's black and white hoops. It was not uncommon in rugby league for home sides to change strips thus allowing supporters to see perhaps more illustrious visitors in their more famous colours. It was not until the final season at the Stanley Track, in 1949–50, that the latterly more recognisable – and probably more expensive - white with a green band appeared. It was this distinctive strip that went with the club to Knotty Ash. In Liverpool this livery was also known as 'Corporation Green', adorning, as it did, everything from buses to council house drainpipes.

Secondly, as discussed by S.H. Yates, severe financial restrictions prevented the Stanley committee from fielding an 'A' team in the Lancashire Combination. The gap between the Lancashire Combination and the Northern Rugby League was always difficult to surmount, but the county league certainly had its uses and intermittently a young player of talent might emerge. For Stanley to play a team in one competition and not another was tantamount to rugby league suicide: a throughput of match-fit players did not exist and the club could not hang on to squad members desperate for a game of rugby. In September 1948, programme editor J.C. Gregson stated that several unsettled and unwanted irregulars were to be transfer-listed for the benefit of the club. The editor affirmed optimistically: "The recent report of transfers of players has given rise to the usual rumours! These transfers have no financial significance whatever. With no 'A' team we had a surplus of players who could not get even a reasonable number of games, and the players concerned are being placed on the transfer list at their own request. We cannot of course, allow all our experienced players to leave and we must build up our playing strength with young junior players... there is no reason why the team should not settle down and win matches." [10]

But if Stanley's squad players were not good enough to hold down a place in this ineffective side, how could they be transfer market material? One suspects a little gentle dishonesty here, brought about by the ramblings of an eternal optimist. In truth the situation of the playing staff was in a sorry state; the club was fielding only one other side: a junior team in a local Merseyside Amateur League – Merseyside not Liverpool, reflecting the weakness of the amateur game in the city itself. This team found the going very tough against what were little more than district-based sides and youth club teams from the fringes of Prescot, Whiston, and St Helens and, as usual, Bilsland would not accommodate them at the Stanley Track.

Perhaps it just wasn't practical, for player recruitment for this team was mainly from east of Queens Drive, but the non-availability of the pitch for more than 80 minutes every other week was ludicrous. It must have been dismal having to play for Liverpool Stanley Juniors on an open field, rather than running out at one's own enclosure.

For example, by the commencement of the following 1949–50 season, the Stanley official programme for 27 August reports their juniors sharing a pitch with Huyton Juniors on Liverpool Road opposite the Oak Tree Hotel in Longview. At the same time another local junior side, Liverpool Rangers, were also playing their fixtures in Longview. While all of this was portrayed somewhat optimistically, it actually tells a different story – if Liverpool Stanley had any kind of future, it most certainly lay to the east of Liverpool and away from the punitive restrictions at the Stanley Greyhound Track. Liverpool Stanley was a very weak and impoverished club that had been unable to develop a sufficient degree of social integration within its chosen area. In fact, by this time the district to which Stanley appeared committed was in a state of disintegration and was already a shadow of its former self.

Naturally, as a consequence of their continued impoverishment, matters worsened on the playing field during the 1948–49 season. Stanley failed to win any of their 28 championship or cup matches between September and April and only three games were won all season: at home to Batley in September 19–3, at Halifax in April 6–5, and at home in the final game of the season to Rochdale Hornets 11–4. A further game in March at home to Rochdale was abandoned with the score at 3-0 to Stanley, but the result did not stand. Only 35 tries and 31 goals were scored all season and the selectors were unable to field the same team in successive fixtures. Leading try-scorers for this calamitous season were Clare and Jackson with only six tries a-piece. Peter Forsyth kicked 12 and Pat Murtagh 11 goals. The club was well adrift of the rest of the league by April 1949 and finished the season at the bottom of the table – and the popular Murtagh left the club.

1948–49 Northern Rugby League (bottom six teams)

24 Bramley	36	12	2	22	362	546	26
25 Halifax	36	11	3	22	258	372	25
26 Featherstone Rovers	36	9	3	24	305	519	21
27 Whitehaven	36	6	2	28	216	597	14
28 York	36	5	2	29	194	597	12
29 Liverpool Stanley	**36**	**3**	**2**	**31**	**145**	**758**	**8**

The club had become something of an embarrassment and the next season, 1949–50, once again finished bottom of the Rugby League Championship with only eight points to their name. Stanley won four games as opposed to the previous season's three and improved their try and goals tally to 40 and 52 respectively. But they still registered fewer than 200 points (198), 76 behind close rivals York. By the end of that equally bleak season 'Merman' of the *Rugby League Gazette* was describing Stanley as the "League's gift to point seeking teams... a chopping block for the virile and healthy".[11]

Liverpool suffered the humiliation of having 40 or more points scored against them on five occasions, and in two games Wigan helped themselves to an aggregate of 93. Without the kicking skills of Peter Forsyth (recruited from the St Helens-based Vine Tavern junior side) who kicked 47 goals, Stanley would have been even further adrift. Rugby matters further deteriorated as a consequence of the enforced transfer of Stanley's other Vine Tavern recruit Ted Cahill in December 1949. Rochdale Hornets paid a cool £1,000 transfer fee for the St Helens-based player, and the money probably saved the club's bacon.

In any case, RFL secretary Bill Fallowfield had by this time committed the RLC to the Stanley cause, and there was no turning back. Ted Cahill of course, was worth every penny – how had he slipped under St Helens' radar? – and he later went on the 1954 Lions tour to Australia, sadly suffering an injury in a match at Rockhampton and making an enforced early return home.

1949–50 Northern Rugby League (bottom six teams)

24 Batley	36	10	0	26	346	555	20
25 Featherstone Rovers	36	9	2	25	299	550	20
26 Bramley	36	6	1	29	258	676	13
27 Rochdale Hornets	36	5	2	29	200	547	12
28 York	36	6	0	30	274	807	12
29 Liverpool Stanley	**36**	**4**	**0**	**32**	**198**	**820**	**8**

Prior to the 1950–51 season 'Premier' of the *Rugby League Gazette* highlighted, if not actually offering any kind of solution to, Liverpool Stanley's unenviable circumstances. He suggested that the Stanley policy of using experienced players, possibly past their prime, had not been successful, despite the declared optimism of incoming player-coach Bill Riley. He also drew attention to the continual dearth of young rugby league players in the city of Liverpool: "Because Liverpool Stanley have a list of signings as long as the secretary's arm some of the supporters took it for granted that there would be a quick change in their fortunes... There is a substantial leaven of experienced players round which to build a new team and... Liverpool should do more. Young players at St Helens, Widnes, Wigan and Warrington are responding really well to Stanley's overtures. Any idea that Stanley could turn soccer followers to rugby were foreign to those members of the board with practical experience. Only a Wigan or Warrington organisation could do that, if it could be done. What Stanley have to do is train their own juniors, and bring them up as players or supporters using the club as the focus point of interest. A good deal has already been done that way, but more is required. St Helens, a few miles away, used to give free admission to parties from different schools every week." [12]

Rational sentiments, indeed – at least concerning grassroots development; but from this historical distance it is plain to see that despite being close geographic neighbours, Liverpool and St Helens were separated by something far more substantial than a few geographic miles. Whereas the Saints were at the very heart of the St Helens community, Liverpool Stanley was an anomaly: a club out of synch with the sporting rituals of its adopted city, and residing in an area of Liverpool that was uneven and deteriorating. Perhaps all it could ever do was rely upon experienced old-timers or inexperienced cast-offs. The Barrow RLFC secretary was to comment much later in his programme notes for the visit of (by that time) Liverpool City on 8 November 1958, that

Liverpool's playing policy was a paradox: both fundamental to its very existence as a short-term fix, but in the long term fatally flawed: "The policy forced financially on them [Stanley] in the years immediately following the last war was to try and build a team around several older and experienced players who had been discarded by their own clubs; although these players had both the experience and skill to do just that, they came up against the old snag of players living in different towns and training individually – a system which all clubs try to avoid, and which can be avoided to a certain degree if you have the money to go out and buy players, house them and find them employment. Liverpool City were never in this happy position." [13]

What might have facilitated success in this seemingly eternal search for decent players was more access to the actual ground, itself: the one place that would have encouraged younger players – perhaps those rejected by St Helens or Widnes – to give Liverpool Stanley a go. It was a stadium after all – albeit dilapidated – and the distances between, say, Widnes, St Helens and Stanley could be easily negotiated by road and rail. But once a player was signed by Liverpool Stanley he was forced, at least up until the hire of the Fairfield Police Ground for the 1949–50 season, to either train alone, or with the club that had rejected him, or on a field at Clock Face Colliery in St Helens: hardly inspiring stuff. How Stanley's coach Albert Harris and trainer Jim Gerrard coped with this ineffectual set of circumstances is anybody's guess.

Joe Bourke, a former Widnes-based full-back or centre who played 113 post-war games for the Chemics received a free transfer and played a handful of times for Liverpool in the club's remaining few games at the Stanley track. Owing to being forced to train alone Joe didn't move when the club finally decamped to Knotty Ash and instead retired from his long professional career. He recalled in 2007 a protégé by the name of Tom Spark. Spark, a fellow-Widnesian, was a very talented player - a powerful teenage forward who could also kick from anywhere on the field. But during the 1949–50 season Spark fell out with the Liverpool club, and was then transfer-listed during the first season at Knotty Ash. Joe Bourke stated that like himself, Spark "got fed up training on his own". Young Spark's talents seem to have been lost to the game of rugby league football partially as a consequence of Liverpool Stanley's lack of direction.

The new ground

The redoubtable J.C. Gregson's programme editorials throughout 1949 are very instructive concerning relocation and development. For example, from the programme notes for the match against Barrow on 1 January 1949 – a heavy 44–2 defeat – Gregson announced: "The start of another year still finds us without a ground of our own, and many major problems still to be solved. This time last year we thought we were sure of the ground at Knotty Ash and the disappointment caused by the failure of that scheme has no doubt been one of the chief causes of the present poor support being given to the club. The present committee are still doing all they can to get the ground question settled, but are encountering many set-backs and difficulties. Everything that can be done will be done and all is not lost yet." [14]

From the 26 February 1949 Featherstone Rovers match programme his editorial draws attention towards the problems brought about by the disputed ownership of the land: "Although we have no definite news of the new ground and are not yet in a position to re-organise the club, we shall carry on team building on the assumption that all will be well! And that this is the darkest hour before the dawn of better times." [15]

Gregson's programme notes for the opening fixture of the 1949-50 season versus Barrow on 20 August 1949, a 31-19 defeat, highlighted the seemingly interminable inconvenience of post-war building permits:

The new ground
"It has been a great disappointment to the Ground Sub-Committee that they have not been able to get the lease signed by the owners and the Rugby League before the start of the season. The necessary permission has been given to develop the land as a football ground and now all that is wanted is the permits to enclose the land and equip the ground. Plans have been drawn up and there should be no difficulty in obtaining dressing rooms and other accommodation. We are now at the point we got to twelve months ago as far as the final permit is concerned, but this time we feel there is a much better chance of success.

Stanley news
The permission to use the Police Ground for training has been a great boon. We tender our very sincere thanks to the Police Athletic Society and also to Mr. John Bilsland for the use of the Track." [16]

But the Boxing Day 1949 programme editorial announced triumphantly: "The lease is signed and this is the news we have all been patiently waiting for. The Committee, together with the Supporters' Club Committee, now have the satisfaction of knowing that the first major obstacle is overcome. The League have placed the contract for the erection of the fence with Messrs J. Yearsley & Son, St Helens, and the work will begin immediately. There is now no need to evacuate Liverpool Stanley to some place else as some people thought! Immediately the holiday is over we shall proceed to carry out our plans to form a Members' Club and this is where every Stanley supporter comes into the picture!" [17]

During February 1950, a tender to take the club to Blackpool had been received by the Liverpool Stanley directors. The offer was taken seriously enough to warrant a mention in *Rugby League Review* on 24 February 1950. However, as 'Merman' recorded, the bid was received with a protective stance and "only ma[de] the die-hards keener still to hold on to the club that commands the whole of their spare-time efforts" and was rejected. It was at this stage that the RFL secretary Bill Fallowfield finally went public on the aforementioned assistance portfolio for Liverpool Stanley - enough was evidently enough. Fallowfield was most certainly in favour of a rugby league club in Blackpool, but did not wish to lose Liverpool, as a consequence.

In any case, the Blackpool cartel was well-grounded enough to start a professional rugby organisation from scratch and well-connected enough at the Blackpool Council to create a serviceable rugby stadium over the next two or three years, or use the existing greyhound track – they didn't really need a team of no-hopers from Liverpool. So to avoid further speculation about the future of this rugby league outpost, Fallowfield announced publicly that a development programme had been formulated in an attempt to revitalise the fortunes and finances of the Liverpool club.

On behalf of the Rugby Football League he announced that a sum of £5,000 had already been committed to the Liverpool Stanley cause, presumably in addition to the £2,000 loan mentioned by 'Lancastrian' in February 1948. In a note of clarification to all

63

rugby league supporters about this project to revitalise Stanley he penned the following in the *Rugby League Gazette,* the RFL's official journal, in March 1950:

The Future of Liverpool Stanley

"Support during this [post-war] period has been insufficient to meet the expenses of the club and local officials have long felt that a ground of their own with facilities for running first and second teams was essential for further progress."

He confirmed that the club's future resided elsewhere in Liverpool and that the RLC was standing as guarantor. He said that the ground was "rented" but it was, of course, a lease: "During the last two seasons the Rugby Football League has subsidised the club in order to keep it in being and furthermore have rented a new ground at Knotty Ash. In addition a new fence is now being erected and the cost of materials and erection is being met by the Rugby Football League.

The Council of the Rugby Football League feel that every effort should be made to establish the game in an important city such as Liverpool, but no amount of help will be of any use if local officials are not prepared to get the work done and arouse interest in the game... An appeal for funds has been launched and these funds will meet the charges for levelling the ground, erection of dressing rooms and possibly, in the future, a stand." [18]

And so it was disclosed to all member clubs that the RFL General Purposes Committee was once more on hand to assist Liverpool Stanley. In fact it was the RFL and not the club who finally acquired the lease at the aforementioned Mill Yard site near the corner of East Prescot Road and Kings Heath Avenue in Knotty Ash, Liverpool 14. Only the RFL could have provided the sufficient financial guarantee. Had this monetary caveat remained Liverpool Stanley's burden, the lease would probably never have been signed, for the holding committee could not afford the requested bond. Without the intercession of Bill Fallowfield the club would in all likelihood have folded at the end of the 1949-50 season.

Off to Knotty Ash

With some relief Stanley duly ended its now free occupancy of the Stanley stadium at the conclusion of the 1949-50 season. Local rugby league columnist S.H. Yates, however, did not share Fallowfield's optimism, and he penned this somewhat pessimistic note in the *Liverpool Echo* on 15 April: "Still requiring to raise £1,700 to meet liabilities in connection with their new ground at Knotty Ash, Stanley's kitty is embarrassingly bare when it comes to producing cash to make youngsters' eyes light up. Getting a home is one thing, but making it ship-shape and ready for action is quite another. If any clubs are looking for a good home for part of their next season curtain-raising gates they would find a wide open purse and ready welcome at Stanley." [19]

By Wednesday 19 April, Yates's comments were a little more accommodating:

End of Chapter - Last Rugby Game At Stanley Track

"Another chapter in the storm-tossed career of the club which began as Wigan Highfield, continued as London Highfield, and is now Liverpool Stanley draws to a close at the Stanley Track tomorrow evening, when the club play their last Rugby League game on the ground, with Dewsbury as visitors.

Next season will find them still pioneering at their new home at Knotty Ash, where work is proceeding unceasingly to have it ready for play with the raising of the curtain on season 1950–51.

When Stanley first came to Liverpool in 1934, they enjoyed average gates of about 6,000 [incorrect]. Can they conclude as they began?" [20]

And by Saturday 22 April, in reference to the newly published rugby league fixtures for the 1950–51 season which allotted St Helens, Wigan and Warrington visits to Knotty Ash over the first month of the new season, as requested by Stanley, Yates was to state: "Stanley can top two season's receipts in two games... there is no turning back now".

While Yates's pragmatism about the general plight of Liverpool Stanley's bank account should be commended, his cynicism towards the club seems more than a little jaundiced. His readers, and Yates himself, had long since lost interest in the future of Liverpool Stanley and regarded the club as something of a joke. Like others within the rugby league fold, he resented the RFL Council forever throwing money at the club for the sake of the Liverpool name. While Bill Fallowfield, on the one hand, for whatever reasons, wished to see Stanley survive, Yates seemed determined to belittle the club's efforts. Perhaps Yates realised that £5,000, plus the matter of the £2,000 loan from 1948, would not even touch the sides as far as ground expenditure was concerned. He was right - the 1 June Liverpool Stanley minutes include a secretary's report stating that £290/7/2 was due to Stanley from the Challenge Cup pool but that the RFL were retaining the money as "part payment of the loan". [21]

This debate of heartlands versus expansion represented by Yates is still as prominent today as it was in 1950. There still exist two camps: one that sees the future of the game resting firmly in the hands of its founder clubs – strength through unity; the other that considers expansion and development as the future of the game. Yates certainly subscribed to the former opinion. Both arguments have their merits but perhaps the history of Liverpool Stanley shows that, however apparently attractive, a 'top down' approach of franchising and RFL Council financial support only creates an anomaly that is forced, as Yates suggests, to reinvent itself over and over again and in the process resort to adventurous schemes to sustain itself.

The concluding Liverpool Stanley programme editorial of the 1949–50 season was to at long last proclaim: "Tonight's game is our last in season 1949–50 and our last game at the Stanley Track. The end of the season sees us in a much better position than last, for work on the new ground is well advanced and next month the club will be reformed as a Members' Club. Details of the first general meeting is on page 8 and we hope as many supporters as possible will join before the meeting... A winning team is essential if we are to attract enough support to pay our way, and the new ground with facilities for a reserve team and training will be a great help to the future management." [22]

The Members' Club model will be outlined in due course, but the key statement here is the admission that the chronic lack of both decent training facilities and reserve team football had certainly contributed to the club's near-extinction. These problems had not only exacerbated Stanley's financial difficulties but also disabled the club during its most exposed period by illustrating its powerlessness regarding professional-standard facilities. It was clear that these issues were of little interest to the stadium management for whom it was simply a case of economics: the income from the dog and Speedway meetings were of considerably greater importance than the provision of training facilities for what was clearly perceived to be a tenth-rate rugby league team.

By the time of the above editorial the Stanley squad was using for training the Liverpool Police Sports Club pitches at Fairfield for free. Upon leaving the area for that final time the Stanley committee donated the old Stanley Track baths and fittings to the Police Club as a way of thanks, [23] in the process leaving John Bilsland without adequate facilities for any prospective tenants.

Despite the influx of the £2,000 and £5,000 sums, together with the constant supplies of cash raised by the supporters' club, Stanley remained financially unstable and it took a great amount of ad hoc fund-raising to bring the move to fruition. The Wigan programme editor's notes for the visit of Liverpool Stanley in February 1950 illuminate this well: "Our visitors today are Liverpool Stanley, who are having a most difficult time. They are, however, looking forward to a brighter future. Next season they hope to occupy their own ground at Knotty Ash, a thickly populated area on the outskirts of Liverpool. In addition to financial assistance, which is and has been given by the Rugby League they have issued a general appeal for help. No club has done more in the latter regard than Wigan. The Wigan Board sent them a cheque for £387/15/0 as a result of the seven a side competition held before the present season commenced, and in addition gave them a donation of £50. They also gave the Stanley Supporters' Club permission to hold collections at Central Park and one such collection raised nearly £100. The Liverpool people are extremely grateful to the Wigan club, and to the Wigan public generally, for what has been done to assist them." [24]

This fundraising at Central Park was but one activity among many during Stanley's final season at the Stanley Track. Although a dedicated cherry-and-white, RLC chairman Tom Brown had been spreading the gospel on Stanley's behalf and much petty cash was raised during the late season of 1950. Workington Town supporters were generous with their cash, as were the ever-reliable St Helens Board and fans. A collection was taken at the 1 April fixture at Saints' Knowsley Road and over £45 was raised. This should be compared with the meagre £4/15/- collected at the previous Stanley home game versus Salford. Ground fund donations were collected on weekly and the final Stanley programme of the Track era reported: "Mr John Moores, £100; Collection at Widnes, £18; Collection at Warrington, £65; Home v. Leigh, £5; Games v. Widnes, £13/10/0; Messrs Guinness Ltd., £10."[25]

Previously, on Tuesday 27 December 1949, a friendly at Naughton Park between Stanley and Widnes had raised funds for Stanley's move. The Widnes programme editor for that game stated: "To have a home of their own has always been their ambition and their tenacity of purpose in surmounting what appeared to many, impossible obstacles, reflects great credit on this happy band of enthusiasts, and is generally admired throughout the rugby league. We hope that the fixture today will assist them to attain their objective and that the happy relationship which has always existed between us will ever continue." [26]

It looked as if almost everybody involved in rugby league supported the continuance of Liverpool Stanley, but this was not quite the case.

As their complimentary tenure at Stanley was drawing to a close, two timely league fixtures against Widnes meant more funds could be extracted from ever-willing rugby league fans. However, following Widnes's successful Challenge Cup semi-final victory one week previously, the local press expressed some concern that the Widnes coach might, understandably, rest his best players when Stanley were attempting to raise as much money as possible. Prior to the first game against Widnes, in Liverpool, S.H. Yates reported: "Nobody likes to see clubs fielding weakened sides towards the end of a

66

season, especially away from home, for the temptation to put other than full strength into the field is almost invariably associated with sides which have reached the final stages of the major competitions. The home club [Liverpool Stanley] looks forward to a full strength visit, knowing full well that gate receipts are almost certain to show an appreciable jump. It is often the case that to battle through cup rounds to the final involves many cases of injury, some possibly small, but if played on, might become more serious affairs. Consequently cup-conscious teams are not at all inclined to take the slightest chance in anything other than the real thing.

Can you blame them? If Warrington and Widnes field weakened sides from now to April 20, when the tourists leave this country, who will, with jurisdiction, be able to point a finger of accusation against them?" [27]

To their great credit, and despite their forthcoming Wembley appearance, Widnes dutifully fulfilled their commitments to Stanley by fielding sides near to full strength in both Easter fixtures. Scorers for the Chemics in the two games included Bradley, Davies, Hutton, Malone, Parkes, and Sale: all first-team regulars. While only 1,200 saw the match at Liverpool, more than 5,000 paid to get in at Widnes and the combination of Stanley's home gate receipts and the Widnes collection receipts helped the club survive the barren months of the close season. The Stanley editorial duly acknowledged: "These sporting actions by clubs in the Rugby League are not going unnoticed, particularly on Merseyside, and are not only a help to Stanley but to our game generally." [28]

Moving on in Liverpool

"Perraps, one day we'll 'ave a splash,
When Littlewoods provide the cash,
We'll gerra 'ouse in Knotty Ash
And buy yer da' a brewery":
(*Liverpool Lullaby* sung by Cilla Black, written by Stan Kelly)

The aforementioned hamlet of Mill Yard was only three miles from the centre of Liverpool but it was also significantly closer to Lancashire than it was to the Liverpool docks. More than this, the designated new enclosure was to be on the eastern side of the outer (now inner) ring road of Queens Drive. The symbolic importance of this road in the history of Liverpool in the post-war era must never be underestimated and the pragmatics of crossing this arterial route should not be neglected when discussing the progress of Liverpool Stanley. While remaining geographically in Liverpool, the movement east meant that a different Liverpool to the one in Stanley – one of inter-war fringe development and upwardly mobile population expansion – was being embraced. In a city such as Liverpool this had great symbolic resonance, of both positive and negative varieties - positively in that it was a move intended to coincide with a new area of middle-class affluence, but negative in that it was perhaps yet another symbol to the more inner-city dwelling Liverpudlian that the club had effectively migrated away from the epicentre of the city.

One memory-based example illustrates this latter opinion well. As a young boy with more than a passing interest in rugby league football, and living just on the city-side of Queens Drive in Stoneycroft, Liverpool 13, a short walk away from the dog track, I had made a conversational acquaintance with our local newsagent, Mr Thompson, a rugby league supporter originally from St Helens.

He was typically opinionated concerning the significance of Liverpool City – often deriding them as 'no-hopers'. But he did tell me that City had "already lost any chance of support in Liverpool" by uprooting "years ago" from Stanley to Knotty Ash. I also recall him telling me in no uncertain terms that he, as a St Helens man, considered the districts to the east of Queens Drive as belonging to "Lancashire, really". He didn't like Liverpool's suburban and council house expansion along the Prescot Road – "bringing trouble closer to St Helens" – and viewed the club's migration as a retreat towards rugby league's sporting roots in Lancashire.

I vividly remember him describing City as a "second-rate attraction for St Helens fans". He further stated that he considered the Hope Street ground at Prescot "a better home; they should call themselves Prescot Town", a name with which for several years the football team toyed before reverting back to their original title of Cables, and where ironically the rugby league team ended up.

Rugby league historian Tom Fleet later acknowledged the accuracy of this position: "Mr Thompson's was, I think, typical of the views held by many about invading Scousers into Hale via Speke, Widnes at Halebank and Hough Green, and Winsford in mid-Cheshire." [29]

Through Mr Thompson's eyes, the resettlement of Liverpool Stanley appeared to be a kind of admission of defeat. Perhaps Bill Fallowfield encouraged the club to move east because of the upward mobility of this developing area – Fallowfield was a renowned snob - but also perhaps because it was closer to the cultural spirit of rugby league. Close enough, then, to retain the 'Liverpool' moniker – so useful for the Rugby Football League to cite as an example of their expansion into what is still described as a development area, but near enough to entice the Lancastrian rugby league football fan. It is difficult these days to contemplate housing estates as offering anything other than problems, but these new expansion areas in Liverpool incorporated several former villages and were considered by some to be semi-rural idylls, such as Knotty Ash itself, while the council estates to the east of Knotty Ash were regarded by the authorities as 'garden suburbs'.

Knotty Ash was also adjacent to other prominent suburban developments such as West Derby and Childwall (both in fact are mentioned in the Domesday Book – the former as the 'Derbei hundred'). Therefore the move across the 'Styx' of Queens Drive needs to be seen within this post-war suburban landscape of semi-detached and council properties on the fringes of a city; yet, despite the continuation of the 'Liverpool' moniker, this resettlement was most decidedly from one distinctly inner district to another outer suburb.

Tom Fleet further recalled how he and his friends would travel from Halebank in Stanley's first season at Knotty Ash Stadium precisely because: "They had moved to Knotty Ash. We didn't go to the Stanley Track. We thought of Knotty Ash as being only on the verges of Liverpool, as such. It was hardly the Pier Head - it was a nice area, not in the least bit threatening. Two buses took us from Halebank and the second bus eventually stopped in Honey's Green Lane. There were no noticeable Liverpool accents at the ground. You could look back now and question how many Liverpudlians actually were there – the answer would be 'hardly any'." [30]

Several former players such as George Walker and Harry Ody have disputed the issue of local accents. Nevertheless we can see a planned, specific flight from inner city Liverpool. Another small article in the aforementioned March 1950 edition of the official mouthpiece of the Rugby League Council the *Rugby League Gazette* stated:

Liverpool Stanley's Year

"After years of struggle Stanley have a real chance to build up and establish themselves and the game on Merseyside. With the help of the Rugby League a ground has been secured and for the first time since the club started their spectators will have that close contact and touch with the players so necessary to create enthusiasm in team and supporters alike. The ground is in a central position, served by 15 tram and bus routes and can be made to hold 50,000.

The club is being organised as a members' club and everything should be in order for next season. Lots of cash is wanted, £5,000 at least, and all Rugby sportsmen are invited to help keep our game on Merseyside." [31]

But the centrality of which the Rugby Football League spoke was in point of fact quite irrelevant. Knotty Ash Stadium was not, in Liverpool terms, central for anything, other than a row of shops on East Prescot Road and the Greyhound pub. In the rugby league world, however, it all appeared to make perfect sense.

Endnotes

1 Fleet, Tom (1991), 'A History Of Highfield Part 6: The Struggle For Survival'. Series written for the *Highfield RLFC Official Programme* 1991-92-season

2 'Merman', 'On, Stanley, On!' New Haven and Rising Hopes at Liverpool', *Rugby League Review,* 24 February 1950, p.5

[3] Yates, S.H., 'As I See It', *Liverpool Stanley Official Programme* [versus Warrington] 13 September 1947, pp.6-7

[4] Gregson, J.C., 'Editorial', *Liverpool Stanley Official Programme* [versus Widnes] 1 January 1948, p.3

[5] Reynolds, Tom a.k.a. 'Lancastrian', insert from *Liverpool Stanley Official Programme* 7 February 1948

[6] J.C.G.[probably], 'The New Ground – Progress Reported', *Liverpool Stanley Official Programme* [versus Belle Vue Rangers] Good Friday, 26 March 1948, pp.6-7

[7] 'Merman', 'On Stanley, On!' New Haven and Rising Hopes at Liverpool', *Rugby League Review,* 24 February 1950, p.5

[8] J.C.G.[probably], 'Editorial', *Liverpool Stanley Official Programme* [versus Warrington], 26 August 1948, p.3

[9] *ibid*, versus Batley, 25 September 1948, p.3

[10] *ibid*

[11] 'Merman', 'On Stanley, On!' New Haven and Rising Hopes at Liverpool', *Rugby League Review,* 24 February 1950, p.5

[12] 'Premier', 'Tough Job At Liverpool', *The Rugby League Gazette* 2/4, 30 September 1950, p.4

[13] [probably] Hurst, A., 'Our Visitors', *Barrow Rugby Football Club Official Programme* [versus Liverpool City], 8 November, 1958, p.4

[14] Gregson, J.C., 'Editorial', *Liverpool City Official Programme* [versus Barrow] 1 January 1949, p.3

[15] *ibid*, versus Featherstone Rovers 26 February 1949

[16] *ibid*, versus Barrow 20 August 1949

[17] *ibid* versus Swinton 26 December 1949

[18] Fallowfield, W, 'The Future of Liverpool Stanley', *Rugby League Gazette*, March 1950 edition [no number], p.11

[19] Yates, S.H. *Liverpool Football Echo*, Saturday 15 April 1950

[20] *ibid*, 'End Of Chapter', *Liverpool Echo*, Wednesday 19 April 1950, p.7

[21] Source: minutes of the Liverpool Stanley RLFC Committee 1 June 1950 – housed at the University of Huddersfield

[22] J.C. Gregson, 'Editorial', *Liverpool Stanley Official Programme* [versus Dewsbury], 20 April 1950, p.3

[23] Source: minutes of the Liverpool Stanley RLFC Committee 5 June 1950 – housed at the University of Huddersfield

[24] Unaccredited programme editor's notes, *Wigan Official Programme* [versus Liverpool Stanley], 18 February 1950, p.4

[25] Unaccredited 'Stanley News', *Liverpool Stanley Official Programme* [versus Dewsbury], 20 April 1950, p.6

[26] Unaccredited editor, *Widnes RFC Official Programme* [versus Liverpool Stanley], 27 December 1949, p.3

[27] Yates, S.H., *Liverpool Echo* [possibly 7 April 1950], reprinted in 'What The Critics Say', *Rugby Leaguer* 36 w/e 15 April 1950, p.3

[28] J.C. Gregson, 'Editorial', *Liverpool Stanley Official Programme* [versus Widnes] 8 April 1950, p.3

[29] Fleet, Tom, personal correspondence with author 10 June 2007

[30] Interview with Tom Fleet, August 2007

[31] Unaccredited correspondent, 'Liverpool Stanley's Year', *Rugby League Gazette*, March 1950 edition [no number], p.30

4. A New Era?

A little confusion exists concerning the ownership of the freehold of what became Knotty Ash Stadium. According to Mike Latham, the original lease was drawn up between the Rugby Football League and St Francis Xavier Catholic Church. Although this church was not part of the buildings to the north of the hamlet of Mill Yard, it was the leading Catholic organisation in Liverpool prior to the erection of the Metropolitan Catholic Cathedral. Latham also correctly states that the Knotty Ash ground lease was later pulled because of the imminent arrival of a Catholic Blind Institute. According to Liverpool City player George Walker the squad assumed that, "at least as far as we could tell, the ground belonged to the nuns".[1] However the new Blind Institute was mostly erected on land already belonging to the Broughton Hall Convent School and infringed only partially upon what became Knotty Ash Stadium. In fact, the remainder of the site where the rugby ground once stood now houses a day-centre named Mayfield Court – under the auspice of the local authority and nothing to do with the church.

Land-ownership and boundary complications do have a habit of going hand-in-hand in Liverpool. What further obscures the history is that there is no evidence of Liverpool Stanley/City making any payments to either Liverpool Corporation or the Roman Catholic authorities; this was because, as Mike Latham confirms, the rugby club was effectively a sub-tenant of the Rugby Football League. The original lease between the RFL and the owners lasted until 31 December 1960. The lease was then redrawn to run until the last day of 1970. A Liverpool City balance sheet from May 1962 reads: "The stand at Knotty Ash Stadium remains the property of the Rugby Football League until the loan is repaid. The ground improvements at Knotty Ash Stadium are subject to a lease for 10 years from 31 December 1960 in favour of the Rugby Football League of which the club are sub-tenants." [2]

Primary source material certainly suggests that the Catholic Church was not only at least a part-owner of the land, but also wished to expand upon its holdings. For example, when in the summer of 1964 Liverpool City were informed about the lease retraction, J.C. Gregson reported that "We have recently been informed by the [unnamed] owners of the ground that they will not be able to renew the lease, as owing to town planning their property in town is to be demolished and will be rebuilt here." [3] This property was the Catholic Blind Institute, a landmark that had had stood on Brunswick Road for 130 years. Liverpool Corporation wished to widen Brunswick Road and purchased the Institute for £75,000 in order to demolish it, but was only able to do this on the proviso that help should be offered to find a replacement. This they did by allowing the boundary between that land owned by the Catholic Blind Institute to be extended into the area belonging to the Corporation, where prior to the arrival of Knotty Ash Stadium there had been allotments. Any remaining land that was left from the demolition of the rugby ground went into the hands of the Corporation – where it effectively remains to this day.

Apathy?

Despite the general apathy surrounding rugby league football in Liverpool, the *Liverpool Echo* did show some interest in Stanley's move to Knotty Ash that summer of 1950, but most of the news items concerning Liverpool Stanley were small. The main source of information regarding the club's progress came from 'Ranger' who primarily dealt with Liverpool and Everton football clubs, but also wrote a few gleanings every day concerning other local sporting activities. 'Ranger' probably did not exist in person, being an amalgam of the sports staff at the *Echo*. During August 1950 Liverpool Stanley were occasionally awarded a little paragraph or two, usually in a less significant typeface. For example 'Ranger's Notes' on Thursday 3 August carried the following rather sardonic item: "Enthusiasm has reached a new high level in the affairs of Liverpool Stanley and with so few newcomers so far added to their strength it is surprising how so much optimism could be generated. There is the incentive of starting off with a programme more attractive than that boasted by any other club [this comment refers to the opening home fixtures versus St Helens, Wigan, and Warrington].

They have their own ground, with regular training facilities, an experienced coach in Bill Riley, whose humour is infectious and whose playing knowledge is admitted on all sides, and probably the most enthusiastic committee the club has ever had." [4]

The "infectious enthusias[m]" shown by the committee was evidently not altogether shared by the correspondent, probably S.H. Yates, and one suspects his usual ambivalence about the future prospects for rugby league in Liverpool. However, by the day of the first public trial, Saturday 5 August, 'Ranger's' colleague, 'Winger' was a little more constructive: "Liverpool Stanley had a number of prominent youngsters from Warrington and Widnes showing their paces in their first public trial at Yew Tree playing fields. Another impressive youth who was at full-back for the Blue and Whites is a Cheshire Rugby Union man whose name, for obvious reasons, is not being revealed. Stanley's new committee was encouraged by the enterprise of some of the youngsters who were interspersed with Stanley stalwarts like Clare and Cockram – who, incidentally, showed excellent promise in a new position for him at loose-forward." [5]

These trials were held under the supervision of Bill Riley, Stanley's new player-coach, who himself turned out in the second practice match. Apart from the rugby union trialists mentioned above, the club had a list of 36 players retained from the previous season. Following the report by 'Winger' of the 5 August trial, the Thursday 10 August edition of 'Ranger's Notes' provided news of a more practical nature: "Liverpool Stanley hold their final practice on Saturday at the Yew Tree playing fields, adjacent to their new ground at Knotty Ash. The two strongest sides have been picked. The new ground was visited yesterday by [RFL] Secretary W. Fallowfield. Part of the opening game against St Helens is to be broadcast. Work on the new stand is to start on Friday and part will be ready for the opening game." [6]

Notwithstanding the – maybe over – optimistic news about the potential part-completion of the grandstand in little over a week, the report provides information that the pitch was not yet available for training. The late summer of 1950 was wet - very wet - and the turf was too precious, and the ground too soft, to be used until the last possible minute. 'Ranger' was again reporting on Stanley in the Tuesday 15 August edition of the *Liverpool Echo*. Here he confirmed:

Stanley's Final Trial
"Liverpool Stanley's final trial is to be played tonight at Yew Tree playing field, West Derby after which the side will be chosen for the opening game at Featherstone on Saturday. The players will have their first run out on their new ground at Knotty Ash next week. Big crowds are assured for their opening home games: August 26th v St Helens, August 30th v Wigan and September 2nd v Warrington." [7]

'Ranger' then proceeded to highlight one important problem that had previously dogged Liverpool Stanley when he assured "The new ground is in excellent condition and will provide what was always missing at the track – a touch line atmosphere." [8] By Friday 25 August, 'Ranger' was affirming with some degree of doom that Stanley had "no great hope" in their inaugural Knotty Ash fixture against St Helens, which was probably true; however the general tone of 'Ranger's' comments were once more sceptical about the quality of footballers at Knotty Ash. Riley and the Stanley committee were attempting to make changes and introduced six new names for the opening match against Featherstone on 19 August 1950. Todd, Waring, Clinton, Beesley, O'Mara, and the returning Pat Murtagh were the additions to the selection that lost the opening game 27–13 at Post Office Road.

At this stage, the *Rugby League Review* was more supportive and it ran a two page article on the dilemmas and desires of Liverpool Stanley in its close-season edition of 9 June 1950. Here, 'Merman' discussed the club's unsteadiness as the first season at Knotty Ash approached. He welcomed the return towards the end of the previous season of Bill Riley as player-coach – initially on loan from Warrington: "The return home of 'Big Bill' Riley transformed the Stanley pack. I am glad to think that the Stanley Committee had sufficient good sense to see there was still plenty of useful football life to Riley when Warrington made their magnanimous offer to loan him. Stanley are now fearful lest Warrington should decide to recall him to Wilderspool. I should not be surprised if Warrington did not hand Riley to Stanley as an expression of goodwill when the gong sounds for the start of the trials of 1950–51." [9]

Riley did commence the new season in the Liverpool pack but his player-coach tenancy at Knotty Ash Stadium was to last a mere six calamitous matches. Moreover, while there appeared to be "sufficient good sense" in the committee room, all was not well behind the scenes. Everything had looked so promising in May: the valiant Members' Club idea was officially implemented at a meeting held at Radiant House on the appropriately named Bold Street, Liverpool (the local Gas Board headquarters) on Wednesday 3 May 1950. Ninety new members attended this meeting where rules were approved and officials appointed to oversee the new membership.

Members were invited to pay £2 or £5 per season and were known as founder members for the first season. For this privilege they were allowed into the ground free-of-charge. The members' committee included E. Kinsella, E.S. Carey, T. Mann, Mr Quine, Dr Gore, H. Andrews, G. Plank, and G. Lawrenson. Rugby League Council representative W. Brown of Wigan gave the club £45 from a dance held at Wigan for the Stanley ground fund. At a meeting held six days later on 9 May Tommy Mann was appointed chairman of the football club and George Facey stepped up from the supporters' club to be appointed honourable secretary. Sadly, Facey's position did not last long owing to ill health, exacerbated by intense friction within the committee room.

However, despite raising some much-needed cash, the membership fund could not provide enough substantive capital. Following the Radiant House meeting, the members' subscriptions, amounting to about £1,800 at this stage, lasted barely a few weeks. It soon became clear that fundraising among the faithful few hundred, at £2 per head, would not go far in ground development and by October 1950 the club had once again run out of money. The Liverpool Stanley minutes of 30 October record "Finance: Overdraft at bank and £1,400 owed in invoices. Overdraft had been guaranteed by the bank manager rather unwillingly, and would require guarantees before loaning any further cash, RFL to be informed of the position." [10] The £5,000 assistance (plus it must be remembered that further £2,000 loan) from the RLC had turned out to be a drop in the ocean.

The 9 June *Rugby League Review* article by 'Merman' attempted to focus upon Stanley's playing staff in a positive manner, but inadvertently drew the reader's attention towards committee room instability by highlighting the previous season's dispute between the talented young forward Tom Spark and the club: "It was disconcerting to see him dropping out of the team... as a result of a difference of opinion with the club". 'Merman' then drew attention to the club's inability to attract players of the right standard or age by contrasting the youth of Spark with "veteran loose forward" Ronnie Preston: "Not only does he wear well, but like good wine he goes better with keeping." There were also two cast-offs close to retirement - Bourke (formerly with Widnes) and Heitzman (from Rochdale). A young former Port Sunlight rugby union full-back, Cox, trying his hand at league was also mentioned, but it was scarcely rousing stuff.

Furthermore, 'Merman' highlighted the continued lack of a Stanley 'A' team and the increasingly pitiful gates upon which the club was forced to rely. Gates had certainly slipped over the past season or so; 'Merman' recorded Stanley's best takings of the 1949–50 season had been £370 against St Helens, producing "wealth almost beyond Stanley's dreams". However he also stated the average attendance at the Track for 1949–50 had been in the region of only 600 with receipts of around £40 and added: "on occasions it had sunk as low as 325 spectators and £19".

His call went out to the club to make a pitch to the RFL fixtures secretary: "If Liverpool Stanley fail to cash in on a 'derby' start at Knotty Ash with St Helens as visitors, they will pay dearly for a lack of clear vision." [11] At least the Stanley committee showed the vision to do exactly that. When the fixtures were published not only was the St Helens side the first to visit the new ground, but also Wigan, Warrington (twice), and Leigh followed in rapid succession.

So, with the new lease signed, sealed and delivered by the RFL, with Liverpool Stanley as sub-tenants - to run until 1960 - the ground was ready for the first home match of the 1950–51 season. In truth it wasn't ready at all, as J.C. Gregson admitted in his 'Editorial' column of the official souvenir programme to mark that first home game on 26 August 1950: "Our new ground will not be as advanced as we had hoped, but a tremendous lot has been done in six all-too-short months. Shortage of materials and labour and the obtaining of permits for so many things have retarded our progress, but we shall carry on as quickly as possible and the new dressing rooms, baths, etc., with a stand on top should be ready in about five weeks." [12]

The 56th season of the Rugby Football League kicked-off with the Rugby League Council's pet project – Liverpool Stanley – playing their home games on little more than an enclosed field in Liverpool 14, inauspicious to say the least. Nevertheless, A.N. (Norman) Gaulton of the *Rugby League Review* considered he was speaking for all of the rugby league community when in his preview for the forthcoming season he declared: "It is to be hoped Liverpool Stanley have at last found a permanent home. They have also signed several new men, including Ernie Large, the former Oldham, Workington Town and St Helens wingman. News of continued progress on Merseyside will be a source of delight to all Rugby League adherents and everyone will wish them well on the opening of their new ground." [13]

That opening home fixture on 26 August 1950 against St Helens received only moderate advance publicity from the *Liverpool Echo.* Yet there was the aforementioned match report by S.H. Yates together with two photographs on page 6 of the *Football*

Echo - one showing Lord Derby shaking hands with the Liverpool Stanley players be-decked in their white with green band jerseys and the other a view of the empty new ground, where, apart from a railed-off pitch there existed very little to show in the way of facilities. What appears to be the first phase of a building comes into view in the right of the picture, presumably the site of the changing rooms and grandstand. Rather perversely, the official *Rugby League Gazette* of September 1950 published a picture on page 10 of Lord Derby being introduced to the St Helens, rather than the Liverpool Stanley, team that day.

To make it in time for the Saturday football special edition of the *Liverpool Echo* – known locally as the *Football Echo* or *Pink Echo* and devoured by the sporting public of Liverpool – Yates, like his fellow correspondents, phoned in his report to the Echo offices at Old Hall Street at half-time. The details of the first half proceedings therefore were usually full of atmosphere whereas those of the second half were usually little more than scribbled notes and scoring additions. The reader could become engrossed in the game via beautifully economic yet descriptive journalism, only to turn to the (usually front) page of the *Echo* to find little more than potted notes. Nevertheless Yates' combined news item and match report on page six of the paper makes for interesting reading:

Lord Derby opens new stadium - Saints in Scoring Burst after Stanley Penalty By S.H. Yates

"The results of six months high-speed endeavour were seen at the new Stanley Stadium today, which was opened for Rugby League football for the visit of St. Helens.

Considering their limited resources the ground reflects great credit on the struggling Liverpool Stanley organisation. The pitch, despite the week's torrential rain, was in remarkably good condition, the playing surface comparing favourably with any in the game. Although the rain before the game undoubtedly kept away quite a number of the St Helens supporters, the bankings quickly filled, and it became apparent that Stanley would start the new phase of their career with a bigger crowd than any enjoyed last season at the Stanley track. The ground, estimated to have accommodation available at present for 20,000, seemed at least half full when the teams took the field.

Lord Derby, president of the Rugby League, accompanied by Councillor Tommy Mann, chairman of the Stanley club, the Mayor of Eccles (Mr W. Blackburn), the mayor of Wallasey (Alderman J. H. Wensley), and the chairman of St Helens RFC. (Mr Harry Cook) were present. Telegrams of good wishes were received from almost every club in the League. Lord Derby kicked off in brilliant sunshine, a happy augury for the latest venture by the club to find a permanent home. In addition to the Stanley track, the club have played at Wigan Highfield and at London.

Liverpool Stanley: Robinson, Jackson, Todd, Clinton, Large, Molyneux, Lea, Martin, O'Mara, Riley, Spark, Murtagh, Preston.
St Helens: Lowe, Lawrence, Greenall, Harrison, McCormick, Honey, Holland; Norris, Blakemore, Whittaker, Ashton, Parsons, Parr.
Referee: Mr S. Abrams, Wigan

Mighty Cheer

It soon became apparent that Stanley, in their new surroundings, had gathered in a large number of newcomers to the code, for there was a mighty cheer as Jackson raced for the line in the opening minute. He tried to round Lowe, but the St Helens full-back brought off a grand tackle. Greenall brought relief with an interception. The chance to open the scoring on the new ground fell to Murtagh, who kicked a goal when Blakemore was penalised four minutes after the start. Stanley were on their toes and slow passing by St Helens' backs did not look like breaking through the green and white barrier. Ashton slung out a wide pass to Greenall, who sent on to Lawrence whose effort was brave but unavailing.

Harrison made the best move of the match with a tricky, side-stepping run in which he beat three players in rapid succession, but when he passed he found McCormick had cut inside and the good work was wasted.

Harrison was again the hero a moment later. A rapid side-step and he was straight through down the middle. Lowe took the pass to beat the full-back. Finding he had not sufficient pace to outpace Molyneux, he sent on to Honey who crossed under the posts, Harrison improving.

St Helens were in the ascendant and an apparently aimless-looking kick by Ashton stopped just short of the dead ball line. Lawrence gave chase and cut down for a try. Harrison failed at goal.

This represented a scoring burst of eight points in nine minutes."

The notes for the second half of the game were then transferred to the front page of the *Echo* and announced that the "Crowd now numbered more than 10,000", suggesting all manner of transport hold-ups, late arrivals, and perhaps a large degree of 'bunking-in'!

It was a pity that the *Echo* deadline did not allow for a more elaborate reading of the second half, for Yates's first half observations are superb. His discussion of the opening gambits of the match are also historically interesting for he appears to suggest that there were a lot of newcomers to the sport on the embankments (no terracing) despite the fact that the rain had come down in torrents before the game began. One can only imagine what chaos heavy late-summer rain caused to the cinder embankments – probably reducing their height as the game progressed. St Helens historian Denis Whittle confirms that "the ground was primitive; there were large cinder bankings, but they provided no cover for the spectators and the pitch was enclosed by a rickety wooden fence." [14] These basic amenities had cost the club £3,402 from their RFL loan of £5,000.

As predicted by 'Ranger', the St Helens side were by far the more accomplished and before the end of the first half had already established a comfortable lead. Stanley's also-rans were eventually well beaten 36–2. The goal from Pat Murtagh was the solitary Stanley score. It was immediately clear to all interested parties that the side was in need of all-round improvement. Nevertheless the financial signs were promising at this stage. A truly wonderful attendance of around 10,000 uncovered spectators had given the club a good start and there were two more local derby matches against Wigan and Warrington to follow. That opening attendance was probably the largest ever seen at Knotty Ash Stadium, but it was not documented as such. It was later recorded by the Liverpool Stanley official programme of 2 September 1950 that 6,600 spectators paid a gate of £407 that day: "Not too bad considering the weather just prior to the match." Financial expediency might have massaged these figures, maybe giving rise to a little creative accounting, or more likely, as Harold Pimblett, a renowned Liverpool sportsman, said some years later "at least half as many again never paid to get in that day; it was easy to get into for nowt at Knotty Ash".

Significantly, that programme of 2 September 1950 also announced the sudden death of John Bilsland. He died shortly before the first match at Knotty Ash Stadium and at least from the evidence of the programme, his passing was not greatly mourned by the club. Indeed the programme notes are hardly of obituary length at all. The editor merely pays credit to Bilsland for his agreement to Stanley's use of the Track, and offers sympathy to his widow.

One suspects amid the proprieties of language, little more than lip service being paid to the Electric Hare man. The programme item suggests that the editor had no forewarning of Bilsland's demise and perhaps contact was non-existent by this stage. Certainly by the latter stages of the Stanley Track arrangement track manager Baker acted as the go-between. The Stanley committee had previously voted in May 1950 to present both Bilsland and Baker with tankards as a way of thanking them both. When it was noted, however, that the tankards were to cost a considerable amount of money, the offer was reduced to life memberships of the rugby and members' clubs. It is not known whether this offer was ever accepted.

The first months of the 1950–51 season did not bode well for the Liverpool side. Stanley lost the well-attended home encounter with Wigan on 30 August 22–0. The two-legged Lancashire Cup-tie against Warrington played on 2 and 13 September 1950 further illustrated Stanley's ineptitude on the pitch as they conceded an aggregate 91 points while scoring only five. The first leg – played in front of 3,000 spectators on the cinders at Knotty Ash – was far from a disgrace with Stanley going down to the mighty Wire by 18–5. The second leg, however, was a humiliation. With more than 10,000 spectators at Wilderspool, the Stanley side was routed 73–0. Not only did this margin sustain as Liverpool's heaviest first class defeat throughout the next 28 years but the 14 conversions kicked by Warrington captain Harold Palin that day created a Wire club record that stands to this day.

It would, of course, be unfair to cite one Lancashire Cup result against a rampant Warrington – who also defeated York at this stage of the season 75–3 – as a measure of Liverpool's lack of success. The borough of Warrington was, and remains, a rugby league stronghold and the club has been able to nurture some of the finest players in the sport's history. Of the 51 post-Second World War encounters between the two clubs, from 1945 to 1968, Liverpool Stanley/City were to win only four and they did not defeat Warrington in any post-war competition until a hard-fought 5–2 victory in March 1954. Indeed Warrington's Brian Bevan scored 69 tries against Liverpool Stanley/City in his illustrious career. But it was evident that, at least on the pitch, this new season was to be like all of Stanley's previous post-war efforts, one of attrition. Indeed the following week a home league clash against the Wire resulted in another sizeable, 23–0, defeat in front of a vastly reduced crowd of fewer than 700. Coach Bill Riley was having mixed feelings about his new appointment. He had already been noticeable by his absence from the club before these two Lancashire Cup fixtures, but certainly seems to have made up his mind about his future following the 13 September match – and it was not at Knotty Ash Stadium.

Bill Riley

The Warrington programme said in April 1950 that "No doubt a special cheer will be reserved for our old pal Bill Riley when he steps on to the field today... one of the most popular players to have donned the 'primrose and blue' in recent years. Indeed there have been many expressions of regret that Bill has been precluded from making the trip to Wembley, which would have been a grand wind-up to his career." [15]

Riley was initially interviewed for the position of Liverpool's full-time coach on 5 June 1950 and he was offered a 12-month contract subject to Warrington's agreement - Warrington had loaned Riley to Stanley the previous season. His wages were to be £8 per week plus playing fees and his hours were from 10am until 4pm except for training days and Saturdays. However, following this appointment, Bill Riley was seldom seen at the ground and constantly missed training. The committee began to express misgivings about his employment in August when discontent began to break out among the playing squad and factions developed.

There were apparently 'pro-Riley' and 'anti-Riley' blocs and this evidently left the team in disarray. Some players, such as Fay, Holmes, Prescot, Rankin, and Robinson were removed from the retained list as a consequence. On 11 September 1950 former Welsh international Stan Powell of Castleford was sent a telegram inviting him to meet the Stanley committee. Powell duly signed on loan with Stanley and played his first game for the club on 13 September at Warrington in the 73–0 defeat. Importantly, Bill Riley also featured in this game, but Powell and Riley did not see eye-to-eye and there was discontent between the two men on the pitch that day. When Powell pulled on the number 4 shirt the following week against the same opposition, Riley was missing from the squad – indeed he was missing from the club. In fairness, Riley's playing days were almost at an end; despite beginning his professional career with Liverpool Stanley, he was a Warringtonian at heart and, one suspects, the ignominy of such a defeat at the hands of his former colleagues and in front of his former supporters was probably too much to bear. Nevertheless he left his Liverpool employers almost totally in the lurch – yet another unfortunate and unnecessary embarrassment for the Liverpool minnows.

It was reported by the club secretary at the Stanley committee meeting on 2 October that match posters remained undelivered "due to W. Riley's absence." It was also at this meeting that more factionalism among the players came to light with Lea being identified as a "troublemaker" (inevitable perhaps for a bunch of disparate, coach-less players). By 10 October 1950, Riley was still promising to formally take up his duties and attend committee meetings, but neither event transpired and by the meeting on 23 October the Stanley club minutes had noted: "W. Riley: discussion on position as coach, problem over paying his wages, also felt he had not fulfilled his contract. Agreed to give him two weeks' pay in lieu of notice and that he be returned to Warrington. Felt he had been absent from ground at times he should have been there, also failed to do many jobs asked to do." [16]

Significantly, the Stanley committee still picked the team. Committee member Kinsella was effectively the team manager and reported directly to his colleagues, whereas Riley – actually the man with his head on the block – was regarded merely as a servant of the club. The committee minutes exemplify this by recording that Riley failed to execute some of his duties, such as cleaning the ladies' toilets.

In an attempt to help matters on the pitch the on-loan Stan Powell was officially signed by Liverpool Stanley – at the cost of £400 – and in November 1950 he assumed the role of player-coach. But the minutes of the 6 November Stanley committee meeting point out that some players opposed this move and Powell did not prove a popular figure with the Stanley players. He played only intermittently until December before bailing-out and returning to Yorkshire, having cost the Liverpool club £400. As a way of attempting to bolster their meagre and faction-riven playing resources, other ageing players were brought in, but this time at little or no expense. Bob Ayers arrived from Barrow, Fred Hughes from Workington Town (the father of Liverpool FC's Emlyn Hughes), Hunt from

Wigan, and Myers from Swinton in October 1950, but between 19 August and 11 November 1950 Liverpool Stanley played 13 games and lost every one. In five matches the side failed to score at all and an aggregate of only 54 points was registered in the rest, indeed they scored only eight tries.

They then, perhaps bizarrely, won two matches on the trot in November: at home versus Rochdale Hornets on the 18th, 7–0, and at Batley, 12–2 on the 25th. After the first win, A.N. Gaulton of the *Rugby League Review* noted: "Those elusive first points have at last, after 19 consecutive defeats, been captured by Liverpool Stanley and although their 7–0 victory over Rochdale Hornets does not lift them from the foot of the table they can, at least, now claim as many League points as their companions in distress, Salford." [17]

But Gaulton's anticipation was misplaced, for following these two freak results Stanley proceeded to lose every single game until the final match of the season when a 9-9 draw at home to Bramley ensued. On the pitch the entire season was an unmitigated disaster.

'A ploughed field'

The pitch, too, was in a desperate condition and within a short space of time it was practically unplayable. After an extremely wet autumn it had, by winter, become a mud heap and it was only by virtue of the supporters and directors working on it that games were staged at all. Subsequent programme editorials talk of "The condition of the ground is still a headache" (28 October 1950), "the torrential rain this week has more than tested the draining capabilities of the pitch" (18 November 1950) and "The elements once again have dealt us a cruel blow" (9 December 1950). Tom Fleet records: "The drainage system for the pitch proved inadequate through the first few winters and the pitch was often waterlogged. The state of the ground [later] received wide exposure with a photograph of Tom Smith, a Widnes forward of the 1950s, and more recently Widnes chairman, leaving the field at Knotty Ash in February 1957 – the picture carried the caption 'Man-size in mud!'" [18]

By 23 October 1950 chairman Tommy Mann was in discussions with Prescot Cables FC about the possibility of Stanley playing at Hope Street for the 1951–52 season. Other committee members were talking to the Stanley Track management (now minus Bilsland) about the prospect of training there – a civil service football team, who were now based there, stood in the way of this initiative. No former Stanley players have been found to comment about this first season at Knotty Ash, but Bill Adair, who joined City from St Helens in the 1952–53 season, describes the pitch as "a ploughed field; it was always a mess and had no proper drainage as far as I can recall. In fact when it was originally marked out, I don't think it had any drains - it was just a field – and it wouldn't drain at all. Terrible, really." [19]

Finances and publicity

As winter approached, finances were described in committee minutes as "grave". Some players were unpaid and officials were digging into their own pockets. It was noted in the 30 October minutes that the supporters' club should receive this news as soon as possible, presumably in case their pockets were a little deeper than those of the club committee. This beleaguered working group then decided on 2 November 1950 that a private limited company was the "best way" to guarantee the club's survival. But, attending a committee meeting on 6 November, Rugby League Council representative Brown became very agitated; he was bitterly disappointed by both this decision and the way that Stanley had gone about its business thus far. He claimed to have sold the members club idea to the RFL on Stanley's behalf and complained that he felt Stanley had "no chance with the foundation of a limited company", suggesting that they would "not raise £500, never mind £5,000".[20]

Brown had been a true friend of the club but was evidently worried about the prospect of financial irregularities brought about by limited liability. Perhaps he saw future repayments to the RFL disappearing before his eyes. The RFL was paying the ground lease, which it naturally wished to pass back to the club at the club's earliest convenience. This was not simply an act of financial expedience on their behalf; the RFL desperately needed Liverpool Stanley to stand on its own two feet to counter the claims of Liverpool's non-viability. The RFL could be left with debts and a lease for a useless plot of land should the proposed Stanley limited company cease to trade.

The rugby league press was also getting wind of Stanley's problems and, in contrast to both 'Merman's' and Norman Gaulton's genuine expressions of optimism in June and August 1950 concerning the future of rugby league on Merseyside, by 24 November 1950 the tone had changed and fellow *Rugby League Review* columnist Vincent Firth was beginning to doubt gravely the wisdom of Liverpool Stanley's continued inclusion in the Rugby League Championship:

Action Wanted
"With three wins in a row – two of them away from home – York seem all set for becoming a club able to take care of itself and no longer the object of our compassion. That will be a good day for all of us as there can be no future for clubs who are compelled to take up a permanent position at the foot of the League Table. Something far more bold and imaginative than anything that has been attempted so far must now be done about Liverpool Stanley. In the light of Eddie Waring's searching on-the-spot survey, published in this journal a fortnight ago, it is imperative the RL Council should make their intentions on Merseyside very clear to all followers of the game. Unless the club can be brought up to a reasonable professional standard during the present season there is no point in Liverpool Stanley being included in the Northern League in season 1951–52." [21]

There is no doubt that Liverpool's hopeless displays on the pitch were a cause for concern, but Firth's final remarks appear somewhat ill-conceived. While the Rugby League Council was investing heavily in the club off the field any suggestion that Stanley should be ejected from the Championship was out of the question. However, as Firth reveals, his own concerns regarding the future of Liverpool Stanley had been written in concordance with a much larger on-the-spot survey penned by the journalist known as 'Mr Rugby League', Eddie Waring.

It was becoming evident that not everybody saw Liverpool Stanley's preservation as advantageous to the profile of rugby league football. Indeed both Firth and Waring were effectively charging Stanley with bringing the game into disrepute and these charges were supported by a small groundswell that considered Stanley a dead duck. This might have had something to do with the Lancashire-Yorkshire split inherent in the Rugby League. The rivalry between the two camps was intense and Waring, Firth and the *Rugby League Review* were all Yorkshire-based. They had been watching a post-war

RUGBY LEAGUE REVIEW

The Journal of Rugby League Football

FIFTH YEAR CONTINUOUS PUBLICATION   EDITOR—STANLEY CHADWICK

Vol. 5 No. 107   FRIDAY, NOVEMBER 10th, 1950   Price 7d.

Over to Eddie Waring . . .

Back to Nature !

DISTRESSING STATE OF AFFAIRS AT LIVERPOOL

IS the Rugby Football League concerned over the future of Liverpool Stanley? Is this the best we can offer the sporting public on Merseyside? While this article reveals the full plight of Liverpool Stanley, it also suggests a way by which the club could be saved.

RUGBY LEAGUE'S costliest project—I nearly said toy—is no nearer success to-day than it was on its inception. To what do I refer? Liverpool Stanley, of

take you near the ground in about twenty minutes.

ROUGHING IT

Rugby League Championship that was being dominated by Wigan, Warrington and St Helens. Perhaps any dig at south west Lancashire was considered fair game – and Liverpool Stanley was the easiest of all targets. The contentious Eddie Waring piece had been published as a front page *Rugby League Review* news item earlier that month (November 1950: volume 5, number 107) and concerned Liverpool Stanley's status in their first few months at Knotty Ash Stadium. Waring's individual but informed impressions of a home fixture versus Whitehaven at the new ground, together with his strongly worded concerns for the Rugby League Council's position regarding Liverpool Stanley were considered burning issues.

Waring's article was somewhat premature – the season had only barely kicked-off and Stanley were building facilities at Knotty Ash as and when finances and permits allowed. Furthermore, the article probably says as much about his own ego as the '*j'accuse* everyman' of the rugby league supporter, as it does about the plight of Liverpool Stanley. It appears on first reading to be a blistering attack on Liverpool Stanley, the Knotty Ash enclosure, and the prospects of rugby league ever gaining a toehold in the city of Liverpool, but on closer inspection the real target reveals itself as the Rugby League Council:

Over to Eddie Waring...
Back to Nature!
Distressing State of Affairs at Liverpool
"Is the Rugby Football League concerned over the future of Liverpool Stanley? Is this the best we can offer the sporting public on Merseyside? While this article reveals the full plight of Liverpool Stanley, It also suggests a way by which the club could be saved.

Rugby League's costliest project – I nearly said toy – is no nearer success today than it was on its inception. To what do I refer? Liverpool Stanley, of course. Strong words, but it is my studied opinion after a recent visit to Liverpool and Knotty Ash."

Waring's article delivered a scorching indictment on the club, directors and ground, leaving no doubt as to his impressions and feelings. He had opted to see a Stanley home game versus Whitehaven and initially experienced some trouble on the morning of the game ascertaining whether it was actually on. Attempting to phone the ground had proved difficult and when he eventually got through he found that secretary Facey was unavailable. Nevertheless, he decided to risk the trip. Arriving in the city and hailing a taxi, Waring found that the driver had no idea about the location of a 'Liverpool Stanley rugby league ground' (handily for his readership the correspondent pointed out that the ground was accessible by the local number 10 bus).

Waring was less than impressed on arrival. Colleagues were searching for boxes on which to sit and tin cans on which to rest their typewriters. Thanks to Ned Hodgson, the Whitehaven manager, Waring secured a place on the trainer's bench. He records about a thousand or so spectators standing around and reports: "They couldn't have sat down had they wished", but praises their enthusiasm in view of so little to cheer about. The Whitehaven side stripped in a hut, but then went back to their coach to keep warm. Waring was further intrigued to see a Liverpool official selling raffle tickets and one of the directors generously helping out. He continued: "Thanks to a Press colleague I was given the loan of a telephone, and with the help of another was able to get into the city after a welcome cup of tea from a friendly lady in a converted bus. Get away from what? From the most depressing professional RL football I have experienced for a very long time."

Waring expressed his sorrow for the faithful spectators, for the players who have to play on what he described as the worst ground he has seen, for the directors, too – but went on to add that the club is no longer a joke but a tragedy "which either wants stopping or altering". He further cast considerable doubt on the viability of the club in the future: "My present opinion of Liverpool Stanley is that their future is as vague, as doubtful, and as disappointing as ever in their long unfortunate career. I would not be doing justice to the game or to Liverpool Stanley supporters if I glossed over their failings as obviously everyone else has been doing to date. But I am not going to criticise without offering some constructive advice."

Among all this negativity, Waring offered guidance on all points, feeling that the RFL should urgently appoint a full-time manager. Bill Riley had, of course, already flown the coop by this time. Waring stated that the club directors should be out looking for players rather than selling raffle tickets. Further, he felt improvements to the playing surface were a priority because no player was able to play decent rugby on it. He gave all connected with the club the benefit of the doubt where their own efforts were concerned but felt that their best was far from good enough for a professional club. Waring also questioned the profile of Liverpool Stanley, for having spent a day in the city of Liverpool reckons he might as well have been talking to the locals about American Football for all the knowledge shown to him about the club.

He proposed that the RFL to either spend enough money to ensure Stanley's viability or let them play as amateurs in the Lancashire Combination. Although he thought there was room for rugby league in the city, it would have to be a lot better than the standard he had just witnessed. In conclusion he stated:

New outlook required
"Liverpool Stanley appear to have the Cinderella complex throughout. That will get them nowhere except the bottom. There is room for Rugby League football in the Liverpool

area, but not the sort I saw the side put up against Whitehaven. Ernest Pollard has shown what enterprise can do over at York. Stanley have a motto, "On Stanley, On!" I suggest they change it to "Up Stanley, Up!" Cut out this small-time Rugby League and get down to running the club as a real professional club should be run, and away with part-time methods with part-time results.

No one wants to see any club go out of the League but that is where Stanley are heading for if they don't brighten their ideas. And please do not come back and say Stanley shouldn't be criticised, and should be helped and sympathised with. They have been helped; they have been sympathised with; and now I suggest they try the other side a bit.

There are some loyal Leagueites at Knotty Ash, some hard working folk around the place, but the results are not up to the required standard.
THEY MUST HURRY AND MAKE IT GOOD ENOUGH, FOR THIS TIME THEY WILL NOT BE GIVEN ANOTHER CHANCE." [22]

For the record, Whitehaven inflicted a predictably heavy 22–5 defeat on the Stanley side that afternoon, despite the Stanley team containing three former internationals in Powell, Ayres, and Hughes. However, both in its roles as diatribe and manifesto, Eddie Waring's article inflicted far greater long-term damage on the club.

Eddie Waring

Waring was a man of many parts. He began his professional life as a journalist and then became manager of his hometown rugby league club, Dewsbury. He was, in fact, the youngest and also one of the canniest managers in the wartime rugby league, winning trophies for Dewsbury by signing any international player who happened to be stationed nearby. The Rugby League Council declared the 1943 championship null and void and fined Dewsbury £100 for such irregularities and this punitive action forever placed Waring in opposition to those in rugby league authority.

After the war, Waring was one of the first to spot the potential of the media as a way of drawing the public's attention towards rugby league football. He was successful in this campaign and it was largely via his machinations that the BBC came to televise the Rugby League Challenge Cup Final – with himself as commentator. By 1950 this former Dewsbury manager was gaining a reputation for being the supporters' champion and it is within this self-appointed trailblazing visage that his polemic must be understood.

Moreover the position of the *Rugby League Review* journal and its relationship with the Rugby League Council needs some explanation, for by the 1950–51 season, this relationship was practically non-existent. Editor Stanley Chadwick was a renowned dissenter, a staunch left-winger and a member of the Independent Labour Party, and after a major disagreement concerning the right of the *Review* to criticise RL Council decisions, the Rugby Football League had imposed a ban on *Rugby League Review* correspondents reporting on games.

Press facilities at grounds were refused to all who represented the journal. For example in the 24 November 1950 edition, the editor reported on page 157: "It was our intention to give readers a report of last Saturday's Huddersfield v. Leeds match at Fartown, but once again the secretary was forbidden to send a Press ticket." [23] The *Rugby League Review* was also in *de facto* direct competition with the official journal of the Rugby Football League, the *Rugby League Gazette* – a rather staid publication that propounded whole-hearted support for any initiative stemming from the council. The *Review* on the other hand attempted to serve its readership with a jaunty non-aligned approach, redolent of its editor. The conservatives at the Rugby Football League, therefore, regarded Chadwick, self-publicist Waring and their outspoken colleague Vincent Firth as 'mavericks' and somewhat leftfield.

Evidently rugby league football in 1950 was rife with divisions concerning the future enlargement of the sport. There were the traditionalists who, in appearing to speak for the fans, saw development, as such, as a rather pointless exercise; they wished to see the game consolidate in its heartlands and urged the council to spend money on assisting clubs with ground improvements and youth and schools rugby – from the bottom up, as it were. There were the officials of the Rugby League Council, however, who jumped at any available opportunity to develop the game in new areas. The council saw its job as partly developmental and was constantly looking for new opportunities to expand the game – from the top down. So it is clear that holding onto a professional side bearing the name 'Liverpool' in 1950, was as imperative to those controlling rugby league as the development of the game in, say, Neath or Cardiff. In contradistinction was Vincent Firth's declared joy in 1952 at the folding of the Cardiff club.

It is not known whether the Liverpool Stanley committee that day received Eddie Waring with any salutation; however, given their wholehearted allegiance to the decision makers of the RFL it is likely that they did not. Indeed, one might presume the curious unavailability of secretary George Facey on the day of the match could indicate a distinct lack of co-operation. In truth Facey had all but resigned as secretary by this time. Nevertheless, the Stanley officials certainly expressed open disapproval of two further press articles concerning their plight. One written in November 1950 by Waring's pal S.H. Yates brought about a strongly-worded rebuff from the committee in December; the other, penned in December 1950 by the *Prescot Reporter*'s 'Searchlight' (pen name for a Mr Eaves) induced an invitation from the committee for Eaves to explain himself in front of them – which he promptly did. Despite its obvious bias, Waring's study of Liverpool Stanley remains of value, confirming several key issues.

First, that Eddie Waring saw this 'new' Liverpool Stanley and their Knotty Ash enclosure as the "toy" or plaything of the Rugby League Council – representing a further episode in a long-running saga of pouring rugby league's cash into the seemingly bottomless pit entitled 'Liverpool'. Waring's comments, therefore, all but confirm (in so many words) that the very survival of Liverpool Stanley as a professional rugby league club in the immediate post- (and possibly pre-) war era was a bone of contention; the charge was that it was almost solely due to the interventions of the Rugby League Council. Furthermore, this conviction (indeed possible verification) that the club only existed by virtue of the Rugby League Council's direct involvement, also brings into doubt the validity of its role, especially when on Waring's visit to the city of Liverpool he "might have well been talking about American grid-iron football as talk of Rugby League" - further exemplified when his taxi driver knew nothing about the location of the ground.

Waring's recommendation, therefore, that Liverpool should have a new player-manager is directed less at the Stanley Board but at the Rugby League Council. In a sideswipe at the council, his suggestion effectively de-bars the Liverpool committee from any constructive decisions about their own future. What's more, this advice actually proved to be productive, for the following season the Rugby League Council agreed to take responsibility for the appointment of a new coach. The problem was that it took a long time and in the meantime Liverpool Stanley had to appoint the recently retired Pat

Murtagh in a caretaker role. Waring's aversion towards the - admittedly primitive - conditions at Knotty Ash Stadium is also directed towards what he viewed as the misguided RL Council rather than the Stanley officials - whom he seems to regard as willing, but naïve, enthusiasts. This additionally implies that ground improvement at Knotty Ash was the RFL's responsibility, rather than Liverpool Stanley's.

Limited company

At a special members' meeting on 15 December 1950, moves were announced to commence preparations for the limited company after statistics showed how financially ineffective the members' club contributions had been. The debt stood at £1,840 with an additional debt of £707 owed to the Rugby League Council. The bank account was £100 overdrawn (and only available via Councillor Mann's personal guarantee); cash in hand was nil. Income for the season had fallen after the first three home games to only £40 per senior game and £5 per 'A' team match. Bad weather was partially blamed together with the poor state of the ground and fittings. The non-erection of the stand was described as a "bitter blow", especially given the parlous financial state currently endured by the club. Dr Gore mentioned that a company in Blackpool was showing interest in taking over the Stanley team (effectively asset-stripping the club) and to avoid such eventualities a limited company should be formed as soon as possible.

Whether this was a smokescreen or not remains questionable. After all, who would be interested in Stanley's struggling side? It was more likely that an investor was waiting in the wings. It was agreed unanimously that a limited company should be formed as soon as possible. In January 1951, a major investor duly joined the fold – effectively securing Stanley's future. Wealthy builder William Rainford, a resident of Huyton, was co-opted onto the committee on 21 January 1951 and offered to put several hundreds pounds into the limited company kitty if other future board members promised to match his offer. In all, a five-figure investment was agreed by all that evening and the limited company concept was able to move forward with some degree of confidence.

Meanwhile, the Knotty Ash playing surface was so badly damaged it required at least a week between games to recover – and Stanley were now also running an 'A' team. Supporters' Club secretary A.V. Turland asked in February 1951 for "volunteers to help with the spreading of ashes on the car park. The team manager is anxious to have this ready to use as a training ground for the players." [24] This embarrassing failure to cater for their professional squad directly reduced the club's capacity to attract players - or attendances - of the required standard.

For example, the players were forced to use the local Harold Davies Swimming Baths' showers, on the opposite side of Prescot Road, after training. Apart from losing the aforementioned Spark, old pros such as Bob Ayres and Harry Todd decided not to stay with the club a moment longer than was necessary. As the season drew to a close in March 1951, the Leigh programme editor provided confirmation of Stanley's problems: "The weather and bad drainage of their playing pitch have had the effect of keeping their gates down to a low level this season but they plan on re-draining the pitch in the close season and also to provide covered accommodation for next season."

The editor added optimistically: "They do feel however that they are stimulating local interest and enjoying increased local support which, after all, is essential if they are to succeed." [25] But that season's paltry two victories at the Knotty Ash enclosure meant that Stanley's 1950–51 record was far worse than the final season at the Stanley Track.

Stanley fielded a variety of highly vulnerable sides, scoring few points and conceding many, and the two wins gained in the weeks following Eddie Waring's visit in November 1950 were hardly awe inspiring. Between 25 November 1950, the date of the win at Batley, and 2 May 1951, that final 9–9 draw against Bramley, Liverpool Stanley had lost 24 league and cup matches consecutively. Furthermore, only 37 tries and 50 goals were scored during the entire season – a soul-destroying record for a club celebrating its first season at a new home; as one might expect these diminishing returns had been witnessed by equally diminishing crowds. The same Leigh programme editor was predictably generous in welcoming Stanley for their 17 March fixture, a 24–2 victory for Leigh, but also realistic enough to provide rational grounds for Stanley's on field failures:

Our visitors
"Liverpool Stanley have only two wins to their credit so far this season and occupy the bottom position in the league table. Reports indicate however that their playing standard at times belies their league position and with a little more steadiness would have enjoyed the fruits of victory on far more occasions.

One of the main difficulties facing both management and players in the sad lack of training facilities and very often the players don't handle a ball from Saturday to Saturday. Efforts are proceeding to try and remedy this by floodlighting their ground and when this is done there should be a marked improvement in their standard of play... two of their forwards Wright and Spark are attracting considerable attention at the moment and both are on the transfer list at £1,000 and £1,500 respectively." [26]

Training problems once again and mention of the mercurial Spark suggesting he was to go down in Stanley's modest history as both a 'find' and a 'loss'. He had, like Peter Forsyth before him, been picked-up from the Vine Tavern side of St Helens, but did not settle at Liverpool. His earlier disagreements with the committee while still at the Track caused his demotion from the 1949–50 side at a time when a reserve team did not exist and his eventual agreement to play for the club was only part of a deal that saw him placed on the transfer list. A transfer did not ensue – partially one suspects because City had suspended him again in December 1950 in a row over failing to turn up for training.

He eventually left, apparently disillusioned at the general lack of infrastructure. The Liverpool Stanley minutes of 11 December 1950 state that the discussion that evening was very heated. Councillor Mann had accepted Cook's resignation without deferring to his colleagues. Training, he claimed, was a mess and, alongside Spark, Leyland had also been suspended. Feelings were so strong that the committee (perhaps understandably) walked out. Mann's tenure as chairman only lasted until the end of the season.

Similarly disillusioned – albeit temporarily – was supporters' club stalwart and programme editor, J.C. Gregson. He had fallen out with the Stanley committee after he had voiced his disapproval rather too publicly: firstly by a scathing item penned for the local press in October 1950 and secondly by a strident argument on a match day in December 1950. He resigned as liaison officer between committee and supporters and refused to compose any more editorials for the programme. It was left to committee-man F. Woolley to pen the following awkward programme notes for the final evening home game versus Bramley: "the last match of a most unfortunate season and in many senses we shall be glad to see the end of it" and this sentiment was not simply referring to the team's woeful performances.

Woolley's editorial also went on to criticise the "carpers and obstructionists" and while it seems that his remarks were directed at members of the crowd, one cannot help but feel that some journalists, together with an editorial predecessor were the real targets.

Silcock's Fun Fair had a 10-day residence on the Stanley car park in the last week of April 1951. "It will mean a little something in the kitty for our cause" stated Woolley on 19 April. In truth, it was probably the only fun witnessed at the stadium all season.

1950–51 Northern Rugby League (bottom six teams)

24 Bramley	36	11	3	22	380	530	25
25 Castleford	36	12	1	23	376	548	25
26 Featherstone Rovers	36	12	1	23	375	562	25
27 Widnes	36	10	1	25	265	382	21
28 York	36	8	1	27	266	706	17
29 Liverpool Stanley	**36**	**2**	**1**	**33**	**193**	**712**	**5**

To conclude, how important was the Eddie Waring article in damaging the future prospects of Liverpool Stanley? Did the *Rugby League Review* wreck the expectations of this rugby league outpost? It remains difficult to ascertain. The *Review* began its run in 1946 and it would certainly have been neither widely sold, nor read in Liverpool – unless Stanley had given permission for its sale at the ground - which under the circumstances is unlikely. In representing the voice of rugby league's elite the attitude of the *Rugby League Gazette,* on the other hand, which was available for sale at the ground, ensured that its values were generally upheld and reinforced for the rest of the decade. So although numbering in thousands, the readership of the *Review* was by no means vast and such contentious articles perhaps admired mostly with a passive indolence. Yet it is also quite obvious from his views on rugby league football in Liverpool that *Liverpool Echo* rugby league correspondent S.H. Yates concurred with Eddie Waring's opinions and Yates' writings did hurt the Liverpool club in the years to come. To his credit, Yates's position concerning the Liverpool club was ambivalent (he saw it all as a waste of time, money and effort) and he seldom deviated from this opinion; but this degree of malice blighted Liverpool Stanley and later City by stereotyping the club as perennial losers.

So, while Waring inflicted some degree of harm on Liverpool Stanley, Yates perhaps meted out the greater long term damage. It is certainly worth speculating that both this *Review* piece and Yates scepticism contributed to the following season's name change from 'Stanley' to 'City'. By the time a degree of comfort actually existed at the ground (the grandstand and changing rooms were partially erected during the following season) the name change came to represent yet another new beginning. The message was simple for those all-important visiting supporters to the Knotty Ash ground: the 'Eddie Waring' Stanley of old was dead and buried. But the 'Liverpool' stigma was more difficult to remove – especially when recruitment remained a constant problem, the team lurched from crisis-to-crisis, and the local press treated City somewhat shoddily. It seems odd to think that taking the title of 'Liverpool' from the club's name could be conceived as progressive. But there must have been those at the club who felt blighted by this label.

It would be another 17 years before this part of the club's moniker was finally abandoned as a lost cause. As for Eddie Waring, while Yates remained at the *Echo*, he went on via the *Sunday Pictorial* and then *Daily Mirror* to become the BBC's voice of rugby league, thus somewhat complicit in his own institutionalisation. Yet, despite this 'Mr Rugby League' national persona, some rugby league players in southwest Lancashire found him somewhat undependable. Former Widnes and Liverpool City player Tom

Galligan says: "He wasn't popular in Widnes. He was the type of bloke who would come into the dressing room after the match and say to a player 'did you have a good night last night at such and such a place?' and the player would say 'oh aye', and the next day in the paper it would read 'who was the well known rugby player who was seen last night at'... and you can work out the rest."

Liverpool City's John McGrath – another Widnesian - agreed: "People reckon he did a lot for rugby league with the people in the south but a lot of the time we hated what he was saying – things like 'up and under' just pigeonholed us; for me he became a personality on the back of rugby league football." [27]

It is worthy noting that many Liverpudlians saw Eddie Waring – once he had reached a position of national fame – as the quintessential 'woolly-back'. While his northern-ness was authentic to many, and helped to advance the sport beyond its parochial perimeters via the new media (Waring, in the process becoming for many the embodiment of rugby league), he also existed in the Liverpool of the 1960s and 1970s as a figure of ridicule. Authenticity to one is anathema to another and his profile being higher than the game itself only confirmed to Scousers such as Huyton resident Mick O'Toole that Eddie Waring was not only "a bit of an idiot, appearing on *Morecambe and Wise* and all that", but that the game that had brought him this celebrity status was "rubbish as well".

Endnotes

[1] Discussion with George Walker, 2 November 2007
[2] Liverpool City Balance Sheet May 1962 – housed at the University of Huddersfield
[3] J.C. Gregson, 'Editorial', *Liverpool City Official Programme* [versus Workington Town], 22 August 1964, p.2
[4] 'Ranger's Notes', *Liverpool Echo*, Thursday 3 August 1950, p.3
[5] 'Winger', *Liverpool Echo*, Saturday 5 August 1950, p.1
[6] 'Ranger's Notes', *Liverpool Echo*, Thursday 10 August 1950, p.3
[7] *ibid*, Thursday 15 August 1950, p.3
[8] *ibid*
[9] 'Merman', 'Third Time Lucky?', *Rugby League Review*, 9 June 1950, p.10
[10] From Liverpool Stanley RLFC minutes housed at University of Huddersfield
[11] *ibid*
[12] Gregson, J.C., 'Editorial', *Liverpool Stanley Official Souvenir Programme* [versus St Helens], Saturday 26 August 1950
[13] Gaulton, A.N. 'They're Off!', *Rugby League Review* 4 / 95, 18 August 1950, pp.1-2
[14] Denis Whittle to Mike Latham (2004), 'The Leaving Of Liverpool' *Rugby League World*, February 2004, p.42
[15] Unaccredited editor, *Warrington RLFC Official Programme* no. 3 vol. 27 [versus Liverpool Stanley], 15 April 1950, p.3
[16] Minutes of the Liverpool Stanley RFC committee – source University of Huddersfield
[17] A.N. Gaulton, *Rugby League Review*, 24 November 1950, p.159
[18] Fleet, Tom (1991), 'A History Of Highfield Part 7: 'Knotty Ash'. Series written for the *Highfield RLFC Official Programme* 1991-92-season
[19] Discussion with Bill Adair 2 November 2007
[20] Paraphrased from the Liverpool Stanley committee minutes 6 November 1950 – at University of Huddersfield
[21] Firth, Vincent, 'Today In Rugby League', *Rugby League Review* 5 / 109, November 24 1950, p.152
[22] Waring, Eddie (1950), 'Over To Eddie Waring: Back To Nature! Distressing State Of Affairs At Liverpool', *Rugby League Review* 5/107, 10 November 1950 p.125, p.131 not inclusive
[23] Chadwick, Stanley, *Rugby League Review*, 24 November 1950, p.157
[24] A.V. Turland, 'Supporters' Club Announcement', *Liverpool Stanley Official Programme* [versus Barrow], 24 February 1951, p.7
[25] [probably] G.E. Sims, 'Club Commentary', *Leigh Official Programme* [versus Liverpool Stanley], 17 March 1951, p.5
[26] *ibid*, p.11
[27] Interview with Tom Galligan and John McGrath, 21 September 2007

5. Liverpool City - revisited

Although the Liverpool Stanley Supporters' Club, numbering an impressive 800, pledged to take over payments for the ground prior to the formation of a new limited company, this did not fully materialise and the RFL continued to pay the owners of the land at least until the end of that first season. Indeed when the Liverpool City Limited Company finally surfaced in May 1951 it was this group and not the supporters club who were the legal sub-tenants.

The direct involvement of all supporters in the repayments proved more difficult than originally imagined because of the Knotty Ash ground's propensity to swallow up all available funds. On several occasions during the first season – 1950–51 – at Knotty Ash the football committee was compelled to go cap-in-hand to the Supporters' Club for extra funding. This proved to be challenging for all those involved but especially the supporters, for their scepticism had a logic: there had been little history of success for any controlling group at Liverpool Stanley – indeed the supporters had time and again bailed out this unprofitable (and some might say unmanageable) rugby league club. So, not only was a strong sense of guarded ownership prevailing among many supporters, but also a general feeling of unwillingness to back anything that appeared overly ambitious. The idea, therefore, that the club could be totally reconstructed, was greeted by some with a level of hard-nosed cynicism.

The members' club concept was at the outset thought to be a wise move and had been considered by both the Stanley supporters and the Rugby League Council as a viable alternative to the club's unending financial difficulties. Supporters were invited to buy not shares (a clearly unsuccessful scheme prior to the war) but memberships, paying a subscription fee for an entire year, and having a vote apiece – far more democratic, one might argue, than larger shareholders calling all the shots.

As has been seen, the proposal – promoted by Rugby League Council representative W. Brown – had taken shape during the final season at the Stanley Track and was officially implemented at Radiant House in Bold Street, Liverpool on Wednesday 3 May 1950. However, despite raising some much-needed cash, the membership could not provide enough capital and by the autumn of 1950 the rugby club had once again run out of working capital. Committee member F. Woolley was to admit to all supporters on 23 December 1950: "It has been proved that to run the business of a first class rugby club needs capital and the small amounts subscribed by members in their nomination fees – which incidentally allowed free access to the ground on match days and thereby reduced prospective gate monies – even allowing for the generous assistance given by the Rugby League authorities, was completely inadequate. Big business – and that is what this class of football is today – needs big capital and your committee had had a nightmare of a time in having this fact brought home to them." [1]

Woolley refers to securing substantial business capital, but does not go on to explain how this might be introduced. Obviously a share subscription for a limited company could provide the club with working capital but from whence might this come? Woolley also fails to discuss how many shares might be made available and who might purchase them.

It has also been seen that William Rainford, the successful building and road materials supplier, was able to provide an injection of cash from his well-established company. He was not an existing member of the Liverpool Stanley committee but had donated and built a scoreboard for the club. Rainford officially joined in January 1951 what eventually became the new Liverpool City board of directors. So, the committee, members and supporters were tireless in their attempts to keep the club on an even keel, but there were several factions at play as Stanley moved to Knotty Ash. For example, despite most supporters contributing their £2 to join the new members' club, the scheme was viewed with considerable suspicion and the supporters' club was not altogether hand-in-glove with either the members' or football club committees.

All parties wisely viewed the members' club model as a possible way of creating regular sources of income not dependent upon turnstile revenue, but nobody had realised just how expensive Knotty Ash Stadium was to prove; and this caused further frustrations and subsequent friction by emptying several pots of money at a stroke. As early as June 1950 Woolley had reported to his fellow football club committee members that at: "... the S.C. AGM bouquets had been handed out to some of our committee, but this had been turned to abuse against the committee in general. Our decision to refuse the general issue of tickets had been questioned and our liaison-officer had upheld their decision to re-open this question with us. Election of committee had caused trouble." [2]

Members of the Liverpool Stanley Supporters' Club over the age of 21 usually met at the Bents Cattle Market Inn, opposite the Stanley Track on Prescot Road (which is still there today) and provided that establishment with a regular source of income. With this in mind, it was correctly considered that beer profits should flow through the club via a members' bar. But, while this proposal was seen as pragmatic and members duly set about locating suitable premises for a drinking establishment for social activities and all-important cash flow, the supporters' club continued to raise much of the money that was going into the ground development fund.

These strands of income, if managed correctly, could have provided the parent club with constant and frequent sources of cash, with the limited company free to search for capital investment. However, the 'supporters' and 'members' dichotomy had already developed – something that would eventually lead to the dissolution of the supporters' club in the 1960s. Following this termination, the members' social club that had eventually come into being, moved further and further away from the rugby club until a stage was reached when it no longer felt obliged to fund any rugby-related activities.

Indeed, by the time Huyton RLFC emerged, relationships between the two bodies was so acrimonious that the new social club built on the Alt Park site was seen as a way of funding the rugby club without going cap-in-hand to a reluctant and by this time almost totally autonomous members' club in Stoneycroft.

One might also initially consider the formation of the limited liability set-up as a means of giving control of the club into the hands of the wealthy, such as William Rainford, but this could hardly be the case with Liverpool Stanley. Tony Collins correctly states: "The minutes of Liverpool Stanley committee's discussion about the conversion of the club in 1950 suggest that it was their eagerness to avoid personal liability for the clubs debts that animated their desire for limited liability status." [3] Indeed the Stanley minutes for 2 November 1950 clearly state: "Heavy expense bill for players. Payment to players for loss of time was also a big item. Proposed that in future no loss of time be compensated, except by special arrangement. Thought best to form a limited liability company, should endeavour to contact people of substance to take shares. Agreed to propose to a special general meeting." [4]

So, rather than being the domain of a wealthy hierarchy, Stanley's limited company status was established with the - perhaps half-hearted - view that there would be no threat of individual legal responsibility should the club go under: a cautious move, and not an ideal message to send to any potential investors (or indeed the RLC). Luckily a willing person "of substance" had already been identified.

Under the guidance of chairman, Councillor Tom Mann and vice-chairman, Bill Demmings, together with new investor William Rainford, procedures were put into place so that by the 1951-52-season a new limited company would assume the running of the rugby football club and begin to pay the sub-lease on the new ground. A preliminary meeting of investors took place at Pilch Lane on 3 May 1951 where it was declared that £1,400 had been invested so far.

The next meeting scheduled for 24 May was to appoint 12 directors including a secretary and treasurer. 'Stork's Notes' in the *Liverpool Echo* of 15 May 1951 revealed: "Liverpool Stanley's limited liability company will come into being on May 24th when it is expected directors will be appointed. A meeting will be held next Thursday in the billiard room of the Knotty Ash Hotel, East Prescot Road, Liverpool, when efforts will be made to accommodate small investors in the new company." [5]

By all accounts the limited company was not completely finalised that day – and only a smattering of small investors turned up for the meeting. But it appears that Thursday 24 May 1951 was the day when Liverpool Stanley effectively became Liverpool City Ltd. The new board felt this process should involve a re-naming of the club. The team no longer played in Stanley, Eddie Waring had effectively discredited the 'Stanley' designation, and the new board of directors had raised enough capital to see them through the next phase of operations at Knotty Ash. So the title of Liverpool City ('Liverpool City Rugby League Football Club Ltd') was re-born after 44 years.

'Ranger's Notes' in the *Liverpool Echo* on Monday 9 July 1951 reported: "Liverpool City believe that their drainage problem at Knotty Ash will have been completely cured by the start of the season, and even if there are patches with only the barest covering of grass, it will be infinitely better than the mud of earlier games.

Mr Joe Carson has again been appointed trainer, and will welcome the players to Knotty Ash tomorrow night when they begin training. For the time being, Pat Murtagh and Eli Dixon are sharing coaching responsibilities, but there are prospects of an appointment being made before the programme opens with a home game against Leigh. A stand may also be in position for the first game and improvements have been made to the clubhouse by the installation of a bath in both the home and visitors' dressing rooms. Although the club has changed its name, there will be no change of club colours. ... Legal considerations have so far prevented the completion of the company formation, but these should be resolved in the next few days." [6]

On 25 July 1951, construction engineers J. Jones of Woolton and Widnes received a cheque for £500 for work to commence on the Knotty Ash stand. The footings for the building had already been filled and sporadic construction work had taken place over the previous season, but there was now enough money in the kitty for the structure to be roofed. If that 1962 balance sheet, quoted in chapter 4, is anything to go by it is likely that this cheque for £500, like many before it, began its life at the Rugby Football League.

By the beginning of the 1951–52 season, this new limited company had finally been put in place, but by its very constitution was forced to distance itself from the honorary committees serving members and supporters. This further exacerbated the divide between the various bodies who already felt a responsibility to distribute funds where they (and not the board) felt was necessary. Furthermore, the day-to-day running of the limited company was naturally demarcated and players' fees and expenses became the sole responsibility of the limited company. So, although the club was undoubtedly privileged in having such an enthusiastic, hard-working group of officials and supporters – especially given that diabolical first season on the pitch at Knotty Ash – it does appear that the system was over-complicated by sub-committees slowing down decision-making, often in the process leaving the limited company desperately and unnecessarily short of cash. This was, of course, the age of the sub-committee and even the most humble of associations appeared to thrive on such petty symbols of control; in truth many such groups were manned by people whose self interests came first.

For example, during the pre-season of 1951–52, the supporters and members combined spent more than £700 to pay for a full-time groundsman, the re-draining and reseeding of the pitch, and the installation of a public address system and training lights. While all this does appear to be imperative, one is left wondering how much cash was allocated by the limited company to spend on improving the inadequate playing staff.

On the pitch, the new season opened with a visit to Knotty Ash by Leigh on 18 August 1951. City lost heavily, 27–12, but the side registered a couple of tries through Leyland and Radcliffe and, by and large, the defeat was considered far from disastrous. The following Monday, 21 August, 'Ranger' (on this occasion S.H. Yates) recognised: "Although the gate was still only about 2,000 strong a pleasing feature was that the vast majority of them were Liverpool supporters, which shows a big advance on last season."

He also commented on the pitch and ground that "For the first time City have no need to fear the rains and spectators may soon be similarly placed, for negotiations are proceeding for the covering of the stand." [7] However, although Yates recognised an improvement of the playing surface, there was no real improvement on the pitch: the team won only twice before Christmas 1951 and, to add insult to injury, the playing surface once more cut-up – inevitably attendances dropped.

It could be argued that the £700 spent by supporters actually restricted potential income for the limited company. By spending their cash on both a groundsman and a tannoy system, rather than donating it to the company to help fund, say, a half-decent pack, the supporters shot the club in the foot. The team was losing, the pitch had not settled, and as a consequence the City board was deprived of vital gate money and match day sales that a winning team would generate – it didn't make economic sense.

Ironically this lack of foresight inspired several young, curious rugby league fans to travel from Halebank in Widnes to West Derby to inspect "the squalor of the place and the set-up compared to Widnes". One of the teenagers in question, Tom Fleet, subsequently a director at Widnes RLFC, prefers these days to call his interest 'romantic': "It was a very welcoming place when they were still playing as Stanley and the following 1951–52 year as City. There was one turnstile next to the grandstand; we didn't bother about getting wet because there was nowhere to keep dry in any case. The players came out of a hut type place at this stage. I don't remember Waring's 'old bus' [of the offending *Rugby League Review* article]. Latterly, it must have been 1956 when the Australian tourists played there and I stood on what was known as the 'popular side' but there was still no cover."

So, what was the attraction?

"Hard to define, really, there is something almost masochistic although romance is the better word: a fight against the odds. To go to the upmarket grounds wouldn't have seemed so attractive. I think people were more receptive to our being there because so few people went in the first place. It was a sad place but there was tangible enthusiasm." [8]

These romantic ideals can be compared to the feelings expressed by Steve Higginson, one of Liverpool City's few Liverpool-born and bred supporters. As a youngster he was taken to Knotty Ash Stadium by his father and became a City fan after the fashion of his dad. The Higginsons lived in suburban Childwall and Higginson Senior was a sportsman of the old brigade. Steve recalled it was: "Anfield every other week with Liverpool City filling in the gaps; wrestling on a Friday night at the Liverpool Stadium and a healthy interest in athletics. Only horse racing was banned and dad and I used to walk from Childwall to Knotty Ash, crossing three different postal zones – Liverpool 16, 15 and 14 to get there. The pleasure of visiting Liverpool City together with my dad was, of course irreplaceable. But he was different from those in our close. This particular cul-de-sac in Childwall was very quiet, very empty – it hardly stirred of a weekend, but dad was a sportsman and would come and go to various sporting and political events. I suppose as an active member of the Labour Party, he found some kind of authenticity, maybe romantic ownership, in rugby league that many others in Liverpool did not find or did not consider. There was usually a good, encouraging atmosphere at the ground that appealed to both of us." [9]

Steve's sense of genuine belonging is evident in the above quote and both his father's and his own beliefs in sporting authenticity are never far from the surface. This 'romance' is a central concept in attempting to understand the dialogues surrounding both rugby league and non-league football in Liverpool. Here, authenticity is imbued with considerable symbolic value. In its common-sense usage, authenticity assumes that the instigators of such clubs have undertaken the work not only for themselves but also for their communities; that there is an element of pioneering communality present, along with connotations of sincerity and uniqueness. For Tom Fleet and Steve Higginson, such authenticity was also a statement concerning emblematic opposites: integrity versus commerce. The very existence of Liverpool City as a rather messy and misguided collective was for some a physical representation of ideology, and not dissimilar in many respects to the equally waning support for non-league football in Liverpool.

The 1951–52 season replicated the previous season in almost every conceivable way. City doubled their victories to four from the previous campaign's two: Salford 8–4; Featherstone 13–11; Doncaster 18–16 and Belle Vue Rangers 8–2. They increased their try-scoring from 37 to 45, but 1951–52 would have to go down as another inept campaign. Key goalkicker Peter Forsyth was largely unavailable after August and he was undoubtedly missed, but there were shortcomings in every position on the pitch and Liverpool City failed to field the same team twice.

In fact, apart from approximations posted in the Friday evening edition of the *Echo*, most supporters were probably unaware of the team they were paying to see in City's colours until the announcement was made on the new tannoy system at the ground. Additionally, popular forward Pat Murtagh suffered an injury in a collision that finished his playing career. In all fixtures only 41 goals were kicked and five of these were in the two-legged Challenge Cup tie against Warrington. City failed to cross the try line at all on 14 separate occasions and in eight fixtures conceded more than 40 points. During the first half of the season they lost 52–5 at Barrow in the Lancashire Cup, 46–6 at Wigan, 44–8 at home to Workington Town, 50–5 at Halifax and 57–10 at Warrington. In the New Year of 1952 Barrow inflicted another pasting on City 47–5, Widnes won 42–0 at Naughton Park and Leigh ran out 45–17 winners in the last match of the season. It was desperate stuff and even the most hardened fan could be forgiven for expressing tangible gloom.

One look at that 1951–52 final table would suggest that to all intents and purposes Eddie Waring's candid statements of the previous year were accurate (and the aforementioned Yorkshire-Lancashire equilibrium was restored that season). Tom Fleet was to later admit "We felt a bond with City; not as supporters, as such but more as rugby league fans in general. I don't think we considered the football as second class [but] to all intents and purposes Waring's comments were probably accurate... They had cobbled together a team and at times you were left wondering how it could continue." [10]

1951–52 Northern Rugby League (bottom six teams)

26 Rochdale Hornets	36	10	1	25	328	585	21
27 Bramley	36	10	1	25	300	577	21
28 Castleford	36	8	1	27	370	579	17
29 Keighley	36	8	1	27	351	617	17
30 Cardiff	36	5	0	31	342	1024	10
31 Liverpool City	**36**	**4**	**0**	**32**	**199**	**915**	**8**

So supporters were understandably wavering, but backing from within the ranks of the Rugby League Council remained steadfast. It could not be otherwise, for following the package of financial aid to the club, further expansion by the inclusion of Doncaster and Cardiff for the 1951–52 season, followed swiftly by the calamitous demise of the Cardiff club immediately prior to the start of the 1952–53 season, the Council could not lose face and eject Liverpool City. Too much time, money and effort had been put into this club to see it disappear alongside the short-lived Cardiff. Should the Rugby League Council have demoted Liverpool, the League would be seen from both inside and outside the sport as a rather farcical operation.

By October 1952 rumours once again linked Liverpool City to Blackpool. Gossip abounded that a couple of Lancashire clubs had been canvassed about relocating to Blackpool for the following season. It was quite obvious to all interested parties just who one of these two clubs actually was – Liverpool City. Blackpool Council had already allocated a former tip as a possible new rugby league ground but they were not averse to the old, cheap, 'greyhound stadium' idea of transporting a pre-existing club lock, stock, and barrel to the seaside – and the Council owned such a ground on St Anne's Road. But the RFL would not countenance such a move and in due course a new Blackpool Borough side was assembled from scratch for the 1954–55 season.

While the Rugby League Council was being canvassed by the Blackpool consortium, the following official *Rugby League Gazette* item from October 1952 had been written to celebrate the organisational structure of Liverpool City, disregarding their obvious limitations on the pitch. The article was also a point of order to the rest of the rugby league community: the announcement was clear that "this club would continue – if necessary with the help of the RFL" – and, in the absence of enthusiasm for the game in Liverpool, the rest of the League was duty-bound to support City. The article also stated that "They also have a mixed social committee who look after the refreshments. In the near future they aim to build a small stand on the popular side, and continue with the banking, which has already been started... After the [pre-season] get-together, which was a very successful event, the Liverpool papers reported on the enthusiasm of the club, and forecast a successful playing season. "All City require now," said the *Rugby*

League Gazette, "is larger gates. 'We were greatly surprised', said [board member] Mr Rhodes, 'when we received a quotation from a local builder as follows: To supplying and fitting larger gates at the Knotty Ash ground, and gave a price. I wish it was as easy as that,' concluded Mr Rhodes." [11]

Notwithstanding the humorous intent, there is a tinge of sadness about this priceless piece of reportage. Certainly the item deals with apparently renowned Scouse wit, but it also consciously focuses upon the general ignorance of the local populace concerning what exactly was taking place at Knotty Ash Stadium. The message was clear – as far as the RFL was concerned, it was 'hands off Liverpool City'. They would remain in this development area and, although welcome, any side from Blackpool would have to start from the beginning.

The members find a home

Evidently, the zeal displayed by the *Rugby League Gazette* reporter was most certainly not widely held in Liverpool and the aforementioned plans for a Liverpool City Members' Social Club were increasingly viewed as a necessity. After much searching, suitable premises for a members' club were at long last located in 1955 at the old May White's drinking establishment at Derby Lane, Old Swan. The location of these premises was by no means ideal, being a bus ride away from Knotty Ash Stadium and although this geographical remoteness between social club and ground was not initially considered an issue, it probably contributed greatly to the distancing that developed between the organisations. A social club still exists at Derby Lane today.

As with all things Liverpool Stanley/City, the progress towards opening the club took considerable time and energy. It was in fact another two and a half seasons before the club became operative. The programme notes penned by supporters' club correspondent and publicity officer E.G.W. Terry for the match against Widnes on 12 February 1955 state excitedly: "The decision of the Main Club to acquire the premises of May White's at 19, Derby Lane, Old Swan, has been warmly received by your Supporters' Club committee. It has long been our wish that there should be some social focal point for all Rugby League interests in the Merseyside area and we feel that this latest move will be of considerable benefit to the Club. The final plans for the proposed use of the premises have yet to be drawn up but, as soon as this information becomes available, it will be communicated to you."

From the match programme against Workington Town on 20 April 1955, notes by E.G.W. Terry informed the fans that: "Supporters were no doubt very pleased to learn the news that premises for our new Social Club in Derby Lane, Old Swan, had definitely been acquired. Much work will have to be done there during the coming weeks to create a club and centre for Rugby League interests in Liverpool of which we are all proud. So remember to watch for the opening date and when you come along to join, bring your friends with you."

The new 1955–56 season began in an equally optimistic mood concerning the new social club, as the 20 August 1955 notes for the match against Bradford Northern (probably written by the now reinstated J. C. Gregson) indicate: "Undoubtedly the most encouraging sign our organisation [the supporters' club] has experienced since its foundation in Liverpool, is the creation of a real home for our many social activities, at Derby Lane. We know that the premises, its appointments, and facilities, have been more than a surprise to many people, and we can all feel very proud of the establishment, which was opened by Mr Jim Hilton, [chairman] of Leigh [RLFC], in July last. Mr Hilton expressed the view that it would be a good thing for the Rugby League in general if other clubs followed suit. We feel that they will. Once again we are indebted to stalwarts, Messrs Greenhill and Rainford, and Doctors Gore and Roebuck, who, as trustees, have given guarantees to the bank for the advance of the necessary capital. We can best thank them by giving the club and its activities – which will be many – our wholehearted and unstinted [sic] support. This club will be a substantial means of spreading the rugby game in the city, to say nothing of the financial support to the Main Club."

The news updates continued; this is from the match programme editorial against Widnes on 8 October 1955, probably written by J.C. Gregson: "Further progress is being made on the [social club] premises, and the upper rooms have been vacated by the former owner, allowing for them to be decorated and adapted for our many needs. Additional toilet facilities have been arranged for ladies, and arrangements are now in hand for the accommodation of a newly appointed steward and his wife... please note that your rugby match programmes, which may be now regarded as something of a club bulletin, are on sale at the club on the Friday evening, prior to the match."

And from the 5 November 1955 edition of the programme for the fixture against Hunslet (also most likely from the pen of J.C. Gregson): "New furniture has recently been acquired to answer ever-growing needs, and the club has acquired a really homely atmosphere. The socials on Saturday and Sunday evenings have proved so successful that admission is restricted to members only who now total near to 600!"

The development of the social club was summarised in the programme notes for the 19 November 1955 derby fixture versus St Helens (again, almost certainly written by J.C. Gregson) as follows: "If all our ventures were as successful as our [social] club there would be little to worry about. Under careful control and good management – and our thanks go to the many willing helpers – we will soon be a substantial bulwark to the main club. The standard of entertainment and the social amenities make the club a real attraction and more patrons are talking rugby." [12]

As something of a failsafe, the supporters' club applied for and was furnished with a licence to open a bar every Saturday afternoon between 2pm and 6pm at the Knotty Ash ground. This bar, run by the supporters' club officials, was located under the newly-roofed grandstand and as decreed by the licensing laws of the day was also 'For Members Only' although a home or visiting supporters' club membership card was sufficient to be allowed over the threshold. The bar proved to be at its most profitable when posses of visiting supporters arrived at the ground, and it became a valuable source of cash for the supporters' club.

By the mid-1950s some kind of working capital was flowing around the three bodies, the club, supporters club and social club, but it can be seen even at this early stage that each group had distinct agendas: a Supporters Club AGM notice, held on 29 May 1956, stated that their income and expenditure account showed rental payments for the year of £22 for Derby Lane and £10 for the Knotty Ash Hotel.

So the Liverpool City Members' Social Club in Derby Lane was charging the Liverpool City Supporters' Club rent for meeting room space. This seems punitive and hints at the aforementioned rift in the club, although it at least suggests that the social club was being managed professionally. The main problem was that the parent limited company was forced to go cap-in-hand to each respective committee when it needed cash. This was an all-too frequent occurrence, for gates were barely able to meet players' expenses. Nevertheless it can be seen that despite these challenges, together with the indifference of Liverpool's sporting population, subsequent secretaries Messrs Burns, Turland, Skinner, (briefly) Strutt, and then Grundy - together with successive chairmen Bert Greenhill and Harry Roebuck, proceeded to run the club in a relatively effective manner, giving the supporters a rugby league side to watch every other week, and the drinkers a watering hole or two.

One might argue, in fact, that the Liverpool City club was among the earliest of all rugby league football clubs to realise the need for fostering the social side of the game. It was certainly one of the first senior clubs to possess a flourishing, professionally-organised social club. It came as a blow when the sudden death of Tom Bailey, the honorary treasurer of the Liverpool City Social Club was announced on 9 March 1957. Bailey was much more than an honorary officer and devoted a great deal of time and energy into the establishment of the Derby Lane-based club. His loss, like that of Jimmy Green two decades before, was greatly mourned and in retrospect it can be seen that a key link between the rugby club and the members' club had been broken.

Bailey ensured that the rugby club received its fair share of the profits from the social club and also helped to establish the crucial pools income stream with the supporters' club. After his death the relationship between rugby and social clubs was never the same and the gradual drift away of the Derby Lane-based social club commenced. In any case, the mood of the social club had already begun to change. Being physically dislocated from the stadium meant that a clique had developed and following Bailey's untimely death the board of the limited company began to get nervous about their relationship with the social club.

Indebted

By 1958 this highly valued members' club income, together with weekly pools takings, illustrated to the Liverpool City board the unpalatable truth that – win, lose or draw – gate receipts alone could never sustain the club. The programme notes from 20 December 1958 are revealing: "The Directors are getting very anxious regarding the financial position of the Club. Whilst the income from the lottery is helping in a very big way, the receipts from the turnstiles are very disappointing; take, for instance, the last three first team games at home, the actual cash taken was less than £140, this meagre total is most discouraging, especially when these games were won, i.e. Whitehaven, Doncaster and Dewsbury. This meant paying out winning money, which was around £400, plus 'A' team money, Coaches, Groundsman, Turnstile men, playing kit, travelling expenses, catering, advertising and a hundred and one other incidentals which crop up in running a rugby club.

These few facts are given, just to give you an idea of what a struggle it is to keep the flag flying at Knotty Ash Stadium. I think everyone will agree the team have improved greatly, although again everyone knows, we have lost games, which should have been won, but had these been won, it is debatable whether the attendances would have increased." [13]

Most sporting clubs cry poverty – that is the nature of the most basic communication between administrators and supporters. But the above notes also reveal a resignation. Without lottery money (plus the unspecified social club income – together with the directors' own bottomless pockets) Liverpool City was a financial non-starter. Win, lose, or draw, members of the social club were not attending fixtures. Furthermore, the most worrying aspect of this communiqué was the question of how a winning team might be funded. Win bonuses were *de rigueur* in rugby league football and although somewhat academic given City's propensity for defeat, a fundamental question was being posed: bearing in mind the match-payment system that all professional rugby league clubs were contracted to make to their players, how on earth could Liverpool City pay a winning rugby league side? It had been recorded in the *Rugby League Review* on 24 February 1950 that the Liverpool Stanley board did occasionally pay their losing players a win bonus as a loyalty payment, but these days were long gone.

By 1959 the social club was contracted to donate £25 every month to the football club and on Boxing Day 1960 it was recorded that the City board of directors was "indebted to the Rugby Social Club for their generous gift of £125. It is indeed our good fortune and an encouragement to have their support." [14] One suspects that these donations were bestowed with increasing reluctance.

A former member recalled how disgruntled colleagues expressed a lack of enthusiasm to part with subscriptions for lottery and doubles tickets knowing the profits were destined for the rugby team: "As I remember it, the supporters' club people would pester you, and you bought tickets because you thought you might win something, but a lot of members wouldn't have willingly put their hands in their pockets to support a rugby team playing two miles away. They also used to leave a bundle of programmes in the social club bar on Fridays and try to get you to buy them but not many people were interested. In fact I remember an argument one night when one chap was saying something like 'I spend enough on beer to buy this rugby team, so don't go asking me for more money'. To be honest, for most people it was somewhere to go for a cheap pint and most of them wouldn't have known one end of a rugby pitch from another - I think you had to be born to it. They probably spent their Saturdays at Anfield or Goodison or - after it was legalised - in the betting shop on Derby Lane!" [15]

Pools

Liverpool City's pools-cum-lottery was controlled by the Supporters Club and began to gather steam in the late 1950s after the passing of the Lotteries and Gaming Act in 1956. This act permitted clubs to open up for fund-raising purposes their own gaming schemes to the general public - hitherto barred by law. Those clubs that recognised this opportunity (and, initially, there were not many) found a key income stream had been unlocked. For example, Wakefield Trinity strengthened their squad with pools money and Widnes built covered accommodation at their Naughton Park ground largely on the strength of pools income. At Knotty Ash the "man in the green cap" – Arthur Pye, Ronnie Muller or another such supporter giving their services free of charge - was always present at home games to sign up willing supporters to become ticket agents. It worked well: on 10 December 1960 the Pools Committee announced there were more than 4,300 members and weekly results were published in the 'Sports Club Notices' section of the *Liverpool Echo*. Had City been able to command regular gates of even half that number, the need for a pool would have been greatly reduced. But, as it was, lottery, pontoon, doubles tickets and bingo were all-important features in the life of both supporters' and social clubs and, for the rugby team, proved to be the key to relative financial security. Several Liverpool City balance sheets indicate that year after year pools income far exceeded gate receipts. It is ironic that Liverpool City had actually developed a plan that for a more successful club would have ensured riches, but for such a club as City, it would only ever keep the wolf from the door – especially when the City Board was reliant on donations from the supporters club, not money taken at the gate on match days.

Everybody was expected to buy and sell these doubles tickets – not the least, the players. George Walker remembers: "We were all expected to sell tickets and to buy them. You couldn't walk around the ground or go to the club without someone trying to sell you something. But it was all for the good of the club and you knew that it meant that you had, say, a good meal on an away trip, or a half-decent coach to travel in, so you weighed it up like that." [16] Former City player Tom Galligan much later remarked that previously as a Widnes player he often saw the City players on away trips and was surprised at just how well they were treated, often eating at far better hostelries than the Widnes squad. This was a testimony not only to directors' generosity but also to pools income.

By the final game of the 1960–61 season the board were openly declaring: "Almost the mainstay of the club is the 1/- per week pool with its regular and growing income. The board sincerely express to Bob McCullough in particular, and his helpers, their grateful thanks for his wonderful efforts... To the Social Club at Derby Lane... thanks for its season's help and regular donations, with special thanks to its Hon. Secretary, Jack Wallis (round-ball fan) and Hon. Treasurer, Norman Lloyd, who is also a Director of the parent club." [17]

Rugby matters

As far as matters on the pitch in the early 1950s were concerned a steady influx of former St Helens, Warrington, Widnes, and occasional Wigan players did not at first improve results. Liverpool City finished bottom of the Rugby League Championship once again for the 1952–53 season. Pat Murtagh had accepted the offer to become Liverpool City's coach for the time being, but there was a desperate shortage of quality players in the squad.

On 30 August 1952 Liverpool lost at home to Workington Town 58–14 and this was the only time in the 1952–53 season that City fielded the same team in two successive games. In fact, despite a serious injury the previous season having brought his career to a close, even Murtagh had to turn out in a late-season fixture at Rochdale. One historical detail for future reference was that this season also witnessed the humble beginnings of the illustrious Wilf Hunt's career at Liverpool. He played three games as a threequarter in October and November 1952 during a 12-match losing spell.

Liverpool won only four games once again. City were victorious away to a poor Widnes team 10–2, at home to under strength Whitehaven 7–3, at home to a meagre Featherstone Rovers 16–9 and in the final game of the season at home to a second-from-bottom Bramley side 33–7.

In their league fixtures, City scored only 225 points and - disregarding the 33 scored at Bramley - a gross of less than 200 in the other matches tells a sorry tale. Donegan was the leading try scorer with a rather feeble 10 touchdowns, followed by the ever-reliable full back Dave Cox with seven to his name.

Apart from two severe hammerings at St Helens, 42–2, and Oldham, 59–3, not as many points per match were conceded as in the previous season, but this was hardly a case for celebration. Liverpool's rugby league side was feeble and the local press wasted no time in declaring it as such.

1952-53 Northern Rugby League (bottom six teams)

25 York	36	10	0	26	370	496	20
26 Doncaster	36	10	0	26	377	665	20
27 Belle Vue Rangers	36	10	0	26	301	705	20
28 Hull Kingston Rovers	36	9	1	26	337	646	19
29 Bramley	36	6	0	30	293	898	12
30 Liverpool City	**36**	**4**	**0**	**32**	**225**	**837**	**8**

City lost their opening League fixture of the 1953–54 season 46–0 at home to local rivals St Helens and this precipitated a truly woeful start to the new campaign. A run of 12 heavy defeats brought the club to the brink of closure. Liverpool only reached the try line twice in the first eight games that season. On 22 August 1953 City lost 14–8 at York, with Dave Cox running in two tries. Apart from this no touchdowns were scored at all until the last week of September when Cockram scored twice in another defeat: at home to Castleford 26–12. This ineffectiveness resulted in a general call being made by Liverpool City for assistance from their fellow Lancashire clubs. City needed a more competitive pack to survive but, with a distinct lack of financial resources brought about by only moderate gates coupled with a total absence of local talent on which to draw, this 'call to arms' was a genuine cry to save Liverpool City from extinction in this immediately pre-social club era.

The call was met with a purposeful reply from those Lancashire clubs finding themselves with surplus players. Jack Wood arrived from Leigh that October and his entrance immediately placed more points on the scoreboard, for City had thus far been without a decent goalkicker. He was joined a few weeks later by club-mate and fellow threequarter Oliver Teggin. Stand-off Hesketh was loaned from Salford, while ageing forward Bill Whittaker arrived from – but was later recalled by – St Helens. Warrington supplied hooker Holland, and it was his arrival in December, alongside that of the Wigan pair Collier and Griffin that shored-up the pack. By January 1954 an under-strength City had lost all but one of their matches. Their sole victory was against Bramley, 28–7, during October. When the mighty Wigan came to their assistance in December 1953 by loaning these two classy forwards, City were literally struggling to fulfil their fixtures.

While these loan players did not fully arrest the run of defeats, it was 6 March 1954 before City recorded a 10–0 victory against Salford, the side did become more competitive by their inclusion, conceding far less points for the rest of that grim season. Indeed a famous home victory was recorded when, the following Saturday, in front of 2,748 spectators, City defeated Warrington 5–2. Jack Wood scored both try and goal to seal the game, with a solitary goal from Bath in reply for the league leaders. S.H. Yates was moved to write in the 20 March 1954 edition of the *Football Echo*: "Now it can be told – the inside story of the circumstances by which Liverpool City were able to stagger the rugby world last week by their sensational overthrow of Warrington, the league leaders." Yates went on to disclose how a City director had informed him "my intention is to approach each chairman and ask him for the loan of two players, not just any two players, but the very best they have available, outside their own first team."

Yates continued: "St Helens promised them forwards, Leigh weighed-in with backs, and the generosity of Wigan, who drew up a list of four well-known names – Roughley, Jack Hilton, Frank Collier and Griffin – sent the life blood racing back through City's veins. Roughley went to Salford before anything could materialise and Jack Hilton preferred Central Park and said so. Off went Collier and Griffin, to join Moss and Holland, Wood and Teggin.

Along came Warrington-born Welsby from Castleford and though Warrington submitted several names, nothing came of it. Later City sought Fishwick and received Hudson. There was the pack that helped to beat Warrington."

Yates was to temper any possible enthusiasm by stating: "The struggle is not yet over. In fact the real fight is now beginning. The clubs answered the call and loaned worthwhile players. Now these lads are happy and contented at Knotty Ash. They have found a team spirit and City want to keep them. There comes the snag." He concluded negatively: "The clubs have been generous, but how much further can they extend their generosity as City seek to keep the side that has been built? Meetings next week may show how benevolent is the wind blowing over South West Lancashire's fields." [18] The Barrow RLFC programme editor remarked in his notes for the 8 April 1954 fixture against Liverpool that City's "effort to field a more attractive side result[ed] in a much improved team" [giving] "the pack renewed power and virility".[19]

Upon the arrival of the Wigan side to Knotty Ash Stadium the following season the Liverpool City board openly acknowledged Wigan's help by stating "We would take this opportunity of thanking the Wigan Board for their help to our club last season in loaning Collier and Griffin at a time when the outlook was pretty grim for us. This gesture helped to keep us going and we are grateful." [20]

In retrospect perhaps the most important event of that dreadful 1953–54 season was the arrival at Knotty Ash of Ken Grundy. Grundy began his career at St Helens but had not really made the grade at Knowsley Road. He arrived at Liverpool in the middle of City's crisis period on the pitch and played his first game for the club on 31 October at Wakefield. He was unable to prevent a sizeable defeat, 50–21, but scored two tries as a replacement for the unavailable left-winger Bill Adair. News of his arrival at Liverpool was somewhat swamped by the influx of more illustrious Lancashire players and he was considered a useful but not outstanding utility half-back: yet another squad player released by Saints.

But his decision to play for Liverpool City was, however, of great significance. Ken played for four seasons at City, was somewhat injury-prone, and notched up only 56 appearances, scoring 21 tries. But his long-term association with the club was of far greater importance than his all-too-brief playing career.

In the 1960s he became secretary of Liverpool City, and then Huyton for many years, finally retiring from the position in 1980. Indeed his association with the club lasted as long as his health. But in 1954 his time had not yet arrived, and his 11 appearances and four tries that disappointing season gave supporters few indicators to his life-long allegiance.

But for many in the world of rugby league football in the years after 1954 Ken Grundy was Liverpool City and his place in the history of sport on Merseyside deserves more than the usual footnotes awarded to the stalwarts of rugby league.

1953-54 Northern Rugby League (bottom six teams)

25 Bramley	36	11	3	22	437	746	25
26 Castleford	36	11	1	24	437	728	23
27 Belle Vue Rangers	36	7	2	27	307	714	16
28 Doncaster	36	5	2	29	340	840	12
29 Hull Kingston Rovers	36	5	2	29	298	737	12
30 Liverpool City	**36**	**4**	**0**	**32**	**304**	**777**	**8**

Loans: part of the solution or part of the problem?

In 2004 in *Our Game* Gordon Brown interviewed Harry Ody, a City scrum-half of 1956-57. Brown reported Harry remembering "City would raise teams to beat the likes of Warrington and Wigan – usually with players on loan from the same clubs who they would soon take back." [21] Ody's comments have a genuine honesty and humour to them (although Liverpool City never actually "beat the likes of Wigan") and there is considerable evidence to suggest that this quick-fix loan approach became common policy at Knotty Ash, at least for the remainder of the decade. But it was a fine line between fielding cheap-rate chopping-block teams and those capable of holding their own against sides of comparable and superior skills.

A reprieve in 1954–55, 24th out of 31 teams, was all-too-brief as Liverpool became entrenched as one, but not necessarily the last, of the perennial clubs at the bottom of the table; perm any four from: Batley, Blackpool Borough, Bradford Northern, Castleford, Dewsbury, Doncaster, Liverpool City and Rochdale Hornets, for the remainder of the 1950s. The loan policy was, in the long run, evidently unsuccessful.

Yet that 1954–55 season also held a little promise. Smith arrived on loan from Leigh in September and, together with the previous band of journeymen, Teggin, Holland, and above all Wood, made a real difference. In all, 13 fixtures were won with Barton, Adair and Wood scoring the bulk of the points. Jack Wood scored 95 goals that season – an all-time club record. Harry Ody recalled: "Jack was a really smashing player and I thought it was a bit of a surprise that he stayed with City. He was a good leader on the pitch but he was a bit injury-prone and also ran a pub in Leigh so he did go missing from time-to-time and we suffered a bit when he wasn't in the team. He had knee trouble – that might have been why Leigh let him go, but he also did his collar bone at one stage and then at another time he moved pubs. So, without him it got a bit more difficult. But I played with Jack quite a bit and thought he was a really good, strong player who understood the game." [22]

```
1st ROUND LANCASHIRE CUP
LIVERPOOL CITY v. SALFORD
          Kick off 3 p.m.
Saturday, 11th September, 1954

  LIVERPOOL CITY (Green & White)
              1. COX
            (Full-back)
2. BARTON   3. WOODS   4. RIGBY   5. ADAIR
            (Three-quarters)
   6. HAZELHURST          7. PARKES
            (Half-backs)
              13. STOTT
   12. DONEGAN       11. HOLLAND
 10. COFFEY    9. HUDSON.    8. MOSS
            (Forwards)

            (Forwards)
 8. MARSDON   9. McKINNEY   10. GRAINGER
   11. MOSES        12. GREENWOOD
              13. ROGERS
            (Half-backs)
   7. HARRISON          6. DAVIES
            (Three-quarters)
 5. BAINS  4. ROUGHLEY  3. FAIRHURST  2. HARTLEY
            (Full-back)
              1. SMITH.
             SALFORD
Referee — H. SQUIRES (Ossett).
Touch—Judges — J. WOODWARD and W. E. HIGGMAN.
```

The *Liverpool Echo* was amazed in August 1954 when City won their first three games, hammering Keighley at home 31–8, Dewsbury at Crown Flatt 16–6, and thumping the recently elected Blackpool Borough 32–7 at Knotty Ash. The City programme editor was almost gasping in disbelief when, for the visit of the mighty Wigan on 28 August 1954 he wrote: "The winning of three games in a row (four, if you include the final game last season) has given us a new lease of life, and we ask that you will not be slow to indicate your appreciation of the team. The third highest crowd in the history of the ground last Monday was most helpful financially after all our past worries and struggles: please do all you can to keep it up." [23]

That home fixture against Blackpool Borough had attracted more than 4,600 spectators to Knotty Ash Stadium. This probably had something to do with the novelty value of the visitors among local rugby league enthusiasts. They were a new outfit, in their first season, and this was one of their first visits to the rugby league heartlands on the perimeters of Liverpool. Nevertheless with attendances such as this, the City directors could be forgiven for thinking that the bad times were well and truly over. The Wigan game for which the above notes were penned also attracted a sizeable crowd and City put up a brave show against the visitors, who included a young Jack Broome, who would later coach Liverpool City, before going down to their first defeat of the season 26–16. In September, City recorded a double over Dewsbury, 20–13, and also posted a rare first round Lancashire Cup victory over a weak Salford side.

This Liverpool line-up was narrowly defeated in the midweek, second round home tie by a strong Workington 11–8, but then lost at Bramley on the Saturday, 22–9. According to the City programme editor, however "it was only an injury which robbed us in the final stages. With the bogey of injuries we had a rearranged team last week at Bramley, which resulted in a set-back." [24]

Loans might have been good in the short-term, but the squad was perilously thin and injuries immediately affected the selection process and thus results. Towards the end of September 1954, forward Holland won Lancashire county honours and on 2 October the largest recorded gate at Knotty Ash of 7,938 witnessed the league clash against St Helens. Such was the enthusiasm that Picton Hall on William Brown Street in the centre of Liverpool was booked to host the official travelling rugby league show *Focus on Rugby* for early December. Supporters were informed: "Last time this show was given in Liverpool the demand for tickets far exceeded the capacity of the hall and no doubt a similar situation will arise again. So keep watching this programme for further announcements and as soon as the tickets are placed on sale secure yours without delay." [25]

Of course, this was Liverpool City and defeats certainly followed; for example October was a difficult month with two league matches against Warrington, one against Oldham and a return match with Keighley, the last of whom extracted revenge for their earlier defeat. But progress was being made on the field of play. With the exception of a dismal March when no games were won and a home defeat against fellow strugglers Belle Vue Rangers harked back to previous seasons, City won at least one game each month.

In April, four games were won including a 10–5 victory in City's penultimate fixture of the season over a poor Widnes side. Ken Grundy starred in each of the last seven games after injury had previously blighted his season, with tries against Widnes, Workington and Whitehaven. A drawn game at Salford together with that peculiar home loss to Belle Vue probably prevented City from finishing almost halfway up the league table. In fact, it is a pity that the eccentricities of the rugby league fixture list did not (with the exception of Dewsbury) pit Liverpool against the Yorkshire teams beneath them. Further victories would have undoubtedly ensued against Batley and Doncaster and possibly against Hull Kingston Rovers.

1954-55 Northern Rugby League (bottom eight teams)

24 **Liverpool City**	36	11	1	24	402	582	23
25 Hull Kingston Rovers	36	10	0	26	347	756	20
26 Salford	36	7	3	26	279	527	17
27 Doncaster	36	8	1	27	346	664	17
28 Batley	36	7	0	29	278	677	14
29 Blackpool Borough	36	7	0	29	303	759	14
30 Belle Vue Rangers	36	7	0	29	248	666	14
31 Dewsbury	36	5	0	31	255	717	10

On the pitch the 1955–56 season came and went in a most unremarkable fashion. Bill Whittaker was brought in from St Helens as coach, but his players fired only intermittently and he was not, reportedly, an overly popular figure with the players. He later became a director of City and chairman of Huyton; former players Ray Ashby and George Walker both described him as "a bit aloof" whereas Tom Galligan joined City at Whittaker's intervention – he was evidently an enigmatic character. Jack Wood was injured in October 1955 and did not resume his duties at full-back until the New Year. The fact that he played in only 20 of that season's fixtures probably reflected City's overall record.

Nevertheless, Wood still managed 53 goals and two tries while the ever-reliable Oliver Teggin, who also scored 34 goals, took over Wood's kicking duties mid-season. There were no hammerings to speak of and despite losing 26 league games, Liverpool ran their opponents close on several occasions, but could not kill them off. Possibly the best performance was a Challenge Cup first round 13–5 victory at home to Hull Kingston Rovers with Bill Adair scoring the only try and Jack Wood hitting five goals. A 14–5 home victory against Widnes and a closely fought 12–10 win at Salford were also spirited, but while nine games resulted in victories the season was judged to have been disappointing after the previous campaign's promise.

In the final home game of the season, a 23–11 victory against Rochdale Hornets, Jack Wood created a club record by scoring seven goals. It was only many years later during the Runcorn Highfield period that his namesake Peter equalled this feat.

1955-56 Northern Rugby League (bottom six teams)

25 Doncaster	34	7	5	22	349	592	19	27.94
26 Blackpool Borough	34	9	0	25	449	745	18	26.47
27 Castleford	36	9	0	27	462	751	18	25.00
28 Liverpool City	**34**	**8**	**0**	**26**	**375**	**685**	**16**	**23.52**
29 Dewsbury	34	8	0	26	315	700	16	23.52
30 Batley	34	7	1	26	367	645	15	22.05

Belle Vue Rangers dropped out of the competition shortly before the start of the season. There was no time to reschedule matches, so percentages were used to determine the final table.

Australians

On Wednesday 10 October 1956 Liverpool City staged perhaps their most high profile match when the visiting Australian tourists graced the Knotty Ash pitch. It was initially hoped that the game would be staged at either Anfield or Goodison Park, with a possible 20,000 gate resulting, but neither ground was available and Knotty Ash Stadium became the third, albeit more authentic, choice for the fixture.

S.H. Yates was by this time also a regular columnist for the *Liverpool Daily Post*. The *Daily Post* was, and remains, the *Liverpool Echo*'s sister-paper and in its Monday edition regularly covered Merseyside's sporting minnows. It was here where

one could find Marine, South Liverpool and Runcorn football match reports, together with regular analysis of Liverpool City's rugby league games. Aside from reporting on his beloved St Helens, Yates composed a regular rugby league column for the *Post* which, if discussing goings-on at City, as usual veered towards the portentous. For example, on 5 September 1956, after rather gloomily considering City's forfeiture of ground rights to St Helens for a larger Lancashire Cup gate yield, he remarked: "When the Australians open their tour at Knotty Ash on October 10, it will be against a Liverpool City team. Consideration was given to the question of reinforcing the side with players from neighbouring clubs but it was decided that it would be more satisfactory all-round if they relied on a purely club selection." [26]

This is a somewhat belittling comment, to be sure, and one is left wondering whether this item was more than a little mischievous. Certainly by 8 October, two days before the fixture against the tourists, in his *Echo* column Yates was effectively suggesting a mismatch: "The City forwards are likely to be dwarfed by comparison with their visitors. I should say the pack averaged something like 15 stone a man, a set of giants running with the speed of threequarters.

A record crowd for Knotty Ash is expected but there are still a limited number of stand tickets on sale at the ground tonight and tomorrow night. Any remaining unsold will be offered on the day of the match." [27]

This was not exactly helping ticket sales, then. The following day he described Liverpool City's task as "a tall order indeed, and yet these lads are fired with the sort of enthusiasm that should at least guarantee a brave show." A 3pm kick-off had been scheduled and Tom Fleet remembers the day well: "Over 50 years ago, but I was there. I had only been demobbed from National Service six or seven weeks previously after two years in Iraq and alongside everything else the rugby was getting back to normality for me. The savings I had accrued overseas were spent in roughly equal parts between an engagement ring and a motorbike (I always tell my wife Pat she was the better long-term investment).

The thing that sticks most in my mind about the City versus Australians game is that it was played on a Wednesday afternoon and I took a half-day holiday and travelled to Knotty Ash by motorbike, which must have been the furthest I had ventured on what seemed like a massive Triumph twin. City lost 40–12 and former Wade Deacon classmate Wilf Hunt played. There was a decent crowd and the records show it as 4,712 with receipts of £595.

It was the first match of the tour. It was the highest score by the Australians but surprisingly the crowd bettered those at Bradford [2,743], Hunslet [4,451], Halifax [2,254] and Wakefield [3,381]. All of them were also midweek matches. The match programme states that a director who wished to remain anonymous was to donate inscribed tankards to the tour party. BICC were to lay on a dinner and the Lord Mayor had provided lunch." [28]

The Liverpool side selected that day was:
Wood, Curran, Hunt, Ashby, Walsh, Brown, Parkes, Pearson, Fishwick, Crosby, Greenhough, Hockenhull Teggin.

The *Liverpool Daily Post* provided the match report on 11 October. There on page eight were three action photos from the game, together with a report from S.H. Yates and added comments from *Daily Post* sports writer Leslie Edwards. Yates described Liverpool's performance as "a curious mixture", but confessed that the side "made a good fight of it" and while mentioning Ashby and Parkes in dispatches, he singled out Greenhough as City's star player.

Mysteriously, the Widnesian Greenhough did not play again for City. A regular in the 'A' team he had been promoted for the three previous league games, but immediately after the Australian match he retired and was never seen again - it could only happen at Liverpool City. Scrum-half Harry Ody, incidentally, was disappointed not to have played; he thought he might have been in with a shout but had been injured in the previous Saturday's 'A' team fixture versus St Helens. "Still," he was to later recall, "I've since earned myself a few bob with bets over the years about whether the Australians ever played against Liverpool City – people don't believe it. It was a great day, the lads played well and there was a smashing crowd that day." Predictably, the programme notes were to state: "There will be many paying their first visit to Knotty Ash today of whom a goodly proportion we trust will be local. We wish them a good afternoon's sport, and hope they leave convinced as to the qualities of the game, and become regular patrons. A lot of people in this sporting city don't yet know what they are missing." [29]

In the following Saturday's *Football Echo* 'Winger' observed: "The visit of the Australians will be a topic for a long time at Knotty Ash and the fact that the club will not be out of pocket over the visit is heartening. Joining the chorus of cheers (and sometimes jeers) at Knotty Ash, were a crowd of schoolboys some from Huyton and others from the Collegiate School." [30]

The "jeers" comment referred to the sending-off of Australian tourist Brian Davies who had apparently been throwing his weight about all afternoon. After a third warning from referee Mr Appleton, he was given his marching orders and left the field with a bloody nose; it had been that type of game. S.H. Yates was less than impressed by the tourists, and on Monday 15 October complained of "the combined damage of losing [at Leeds] and getting into hot water with the crowd [the tourists were] lucky not to have a man sent off for the second match in succession." Nevertheless, it was indeed a great day at Knotty Ash and the City side put up a spirited display thus helping to strengthen Liverpool City RLFC as an enduring symbol in the minds of Liverpool's sporting public.

Ian Heads in *The Kangaroos*, his history of Australian touring sides to Great Britain, says that "The serious business began at the quaintly-named Knotty Ash ground at Liverpool on 10 October 1956. Organisers eased the Roos into their tour with a "loosen up" game against the moderate Liverpool City side."[31]

Aside from the visit of the Australian touring side, the 1956–57 season was something of a 'hit-and-miss' affair. The Saturday following the defeat by the tourists, City completed the 'double' over Hull Kingston Rovers: winning 14–11. S.H. Yates remarked via his usual bitter-sweet style: "Although they completed the double over Hull Kingston Rovers, City's receipts of just over £100 were not enough to meet expenditure.

Now that the wins are mounting and it seems obvious that City have their best side since going to Knotty Ash, the attendances must surely rise, although it will be a gradual process. In the meantime City players must go on winning and City officials go on losing." [32]

But the team did not "go on winning", at least not until a remarkable late run began on 30 March 1957 with a home 21–14 victory against Workington Town. Only five victories were recorded before the New Year, and one of these was by 24–7 in the first round of the Lancashire Cup against a Lancashire Amateur representative side. Jack Wood's kicking that day resulted in six goals, but when he once again disappeared between December and March Liverpool played 15 games and won only once, 10–6 at

Batley on 22 December. His influence on the pitch was not only from his kicking, he was an expert full-back, organising his sometimes inadequate troops to compete even in the most one-sided of games.

Coach Bill Whittaker experimented with Prescott, Hockenhull, Birch, and Dickson during Wood's enforced absence but all to no avail. Before his temporary departure Wood played 14 matches and 35 tries were scored. While he was away for 14 games there were 13 defeats and only 13 tries resulted. Once Wood resumed on 9 March at Rochdale, it was quite clear that his influence would improve the team: of the seven remaining league matches, five were won. Following the aforementioned Workington victory, Barrow, Widnes, Dewsbury and Doncaster were all defeated and despite a calamitous 45–0 hammering at Widnes on the last day of the season, the 10 championship points gleaned were enough to lift City from the bottom of the league.

During this mostly victorious run-in Wood scored another 24 goals. Despite missing three months of the season he still kicked 72 goals and scored two tries in 25 appearances – a truly outstanding achievement and perhaps even more impressive than his record of 95 goals in 1955–56 when he played 33 times.

1956–57 Northern Rugby League (bottom six teams)

25 Castleford	38	11	2	25	488	739	24
26 Hull Kingston Rovers	38	11	2	25	395	672	24
27 Liverpool City	**38**	**9**	**1**	**28**	**356**	**854**	**19**
28 Batley	38	8	0	30	399	700	16
29 Dewsbury	38	5	1	32	391	818	11
30 Doncaster	38	3	0	35	321	835	6

For the remainder of the decade the team in green tended to be regarded by opponents as St Helens and Widnes 'loan' or 'reject' XIIIs. If City were not using loan players, they were signing inexperienced youngsters or trialists from the amateur leagues in St Helens, Widnes or Warrington. The club also fielded players and player-coaches somewhat past their prime. Former St Helens player Ike Fishwick might be cited as one such example, although he played admirably for the Liverpool club and contributed well on the coaching side.

The club also introduced supposed crowd pleasing novelties. For example, Olympic sprinter, and policeman, Ken Anderson, who had occasionally helped to train the City players, signed-on in 1953, but played without distinction in a few 'A' team matches.[33] Professional boxer Matt Cusack who arrived at the beginning of the 1959–60 campaign, played one game against Whitehaven that December and was never seen again. Even Alistair Liddell - the younger brother of Liverpool FC legend Billy Liddell - tried his hand at rugby league during the 1953–54 season. He played several times for City 'A', but was unable to step up to the first team.

But among this detritus of rugby league, a few arrivals began to develop both their rugby skills and a sense of belonging, and by the closing months of the decade a hard core of players began to emerge at Knotty Ash. Inaugurated by the aforementioned Ken Grundy and old hand Ike Fishwick, the list included Ray Ashby, Ron Barton, Jim Cartledge, Frank Cookson, Ken Cork, Ken Donaldson, Ken Dibble, Peter Dutton, Ernie Halton, Ray Hockenhull, Wilf Hunt, George Walker and Peter Twiss. City's playing staff was gradually consolidating.

While many players still came and went with regularity, some kinds of roots were beginning to show though – nothing to do with the Liverpool of their adopted city, of course, but developed via an identity-giving culture surrounding the club itself. Shared experiences bound together players, staff and supporters in a common identity that was 'Liverpool City'. Indeed some of the City players developed a real sense of ownership about their club and their ground, sometimes irrespective of the rather transient coaching staff.

Peter Twiss recalls: "I think the problems at City had a lot to do with poor coaching. We gelled well as a group of players but the coaching wasn't always up to much. If we'd have had better coaching, the results would have improved, I'm sure of that." [34] Harry Ody thought Pat Murtagh a good coach ("he helped me with getting the right money") but that Bill Whittaker was "not really coaching material". Ody arrived from Pilkington Recs and preferred his time at City in the 'A' team. When called-up for the first team he found Whittaker's attitude rather officious.

The pair eventually fell out when, after scoring two tries at Hull Kingston Rovers in 1957, Harry found himself dropped. Whittaker's attitude, according to Ody, left a lot to be desired — he felt it was cold, remote and rather hurtful. Harry left the club at this juncture and returned to his first love, the amateur game where he was to collect Lancashire amateur honours with the Pilkington Recs and Clock Face clubs. Although later asked to go back to the club by his good friend Ray Hockenhull, the presence of Whittaker, who by the 1960s had joined the board, and Harry's job at Pilkington's dissuaded Harry from "giving City another go".

So, despite the problems brought about by loans and coaching deficiencies, by 1960 a nucleus of reliable and willing players had arrived at City. Many took an interest in the everyday affairs at Knotty Ash Stadium and conceivably unlike their pre-war predecessors, were prepared to get their hands dirty both on and off the park. Gordon Brown (2004) reports Harry Ody recalling to him: "How, after the club had taken out a lease on the land, designated as and eventually taken back for building land by Liverpool City Council, players used to clean it up and make improvements before each game.

It was like a tip before each match and we cleared the rubbish away and took buckets of water to fill six old baths Liverpool Council gave us. We lit fires under the baths to heat the water and one bad weather day a Hull KR player dived into one of the baths, but it was far too hot for him and he dived out again." [35]

Statistically, Liverpool City's remaining four seasons of the 1950s were remarkable only by their incredible similarity. The side finished 27th out of 30 on three occasions and 28th once. City won nine games on three occasions, and eight on another, 1958–59. The club registered 19 points twice, 21 points once, and 16 points once and the points-for and against columns in each of these seasons were extraordinarily alike.

At first glance this record might appear to reflect a total lack of progress and ambition, and if becoming a force in rugby league was the major criterion, this conclusion would appear to be correct. But this results-based concept of success masks an outstanding backs-to-the-wall effort in consolidation both on and off the park. In all 26 league games were won and four were drawn. Out of a total of 114 this does not appear to be many but in comparison with the exploits of the last few years at the Stanley Track and the first few seasons at Knotty Ash, this was indeed a considerable improvement. Furthermore, by 1960 some degree of fiscal security had been reached at Liverpool while other more illustrious rugby league clubs were lurching into financial chaos. Both ground and pitch — at times severe burdens in the early to mid-1950s — were well established by the end of the decade.

Liverpool City RLFC in the late 1950s. Back: Hockenhull, ?, Payne, Teggin, Cartledge, ?, Fishwick.
Front: George Walker third from right, Hunt, Ashby.

Left: Dr Harry Roebuck, Liverpool City chairman and stalwart
Right: Wilf Hunt (Courtesy Robert Gate)

The small body of directors, supporters, and members were fully committed, and there was equally a small cohort of players devoted to playing professional rugby league football for what they viewed as their club.

Such progress, therefore, cannot be measured in results alone. In truth, Liverpool City was far from being the almost comic-failure-stereotype presented by the local media. Of course, the club that had moved to Knotty Ash Stadium in 1950 was indeed fragile; unclear about its objectives and uncertain about its future. Yet by 1960, the diminutive Knotty Ash Stadium had a look of permanence about it – something of which the Liverpool Stanley of the late 1940s could only dream. By the early years of the new decade, successive coaches Doug Greenall, Don Gullick, Dave Cox, and Jack Broome were able to assemble reasonably settled sides from this hard core of Liverpool City players, together with a selection of more transient journeymen from the south Lancashire rugby league grapevine. These sides could often play professional rugby league football to a very high standard, despite the enduring problems brought about by lack of strength-in-depth. In fact, as the 1960s seasons passed by, so the Liverpool City sides slowly but discernibly improved. Loose-forward John McGrath was an important member of this core playing staff; he later stated: "We all felt that we belonged to a club that deserved to carry on. We also helped around the ground when we could, did a bit of painting here and there, helped with the dressing rooms, anything really to help keep a team on the pitch. This wasn't because [the club] was 'amateurish'. In fact Dr Roebuck, Dr Gore and Mr Greenhill ran the club very well indeed. Alf Vickers and Jack Valance did all sorts to keep the money coming in – it was actually a very happy club." [36]

City's very existence as a competitive unit on the playing field is even more impressive when one considers that throughout the 1950s Liverpool-born players were practically nonexistent. Bill Payne was the one rarity, being an excellent Liverpool-born rugby league player – but was without doubt the exception that proved the rule. Payne was a giant of a man, very popular among his peers. He had played a little football for Tranmere Rovers and had also boxed and played rugby union before arriving at Knotty Ash. George Walker recalls: "Billy was a great bloke and a good player, actually. His physique was amazing and I remember him taking off his shirt to reveal this 'six-pack' that he had - he was like the perfect specimen. He had been a boxer in the RAF, I think. Of course over the years this changed – a couple of cauliflower ears and some bumps and bruises... but he was a real athlete. He worked at the BI in Prescot but lived in Liverpool. He was just about the only Liverpudlian I ever remember playing for us. He was well thought of as a player and went to Oldham and then Warrington before coming back to Liverpool City. Even though he was so fit he died in his mid-50s on his way to a holiday, I believe – very sad." [37]

Harry Ody suggests that Payne was perhaps not the sole Liverpudlian at Liverpool City – stating that he thought Oliver Teggin was from "over that way", but could not be certain. Teggin was, in fact, from Birkenhead. Ody remembers Teggin as a bearded Hoover salesman, trying to sell the rest of the squad vacuum cleaners on hire purchase before training. Harry recollects Payne's home address to have been in Stoneycroft, Liverpool 13 and stated that Payne had the opportunity to continue playing football at Tranmere, but preferred the conviviality of Liverpool City – and rugby league, in general. In fact, it is to the memory of Bill Payne that this book is dedicated: a Liverpudlian who actually made a name for himself as a fine professional rugby league player - he gained Lancashire honours while with Oldham.

Various attempts were made to alleviate this dearth of local interest with numerous youth initiatives emanating from both boardroom and supporters' club; sadly, as shall be seen in the next chapter, none fully succeeded. Establishing rugby league's credentials in a city where football was the dominant force proved to be as difficult as ever.

1957–58 Northern Rugby League (bottom six teams)

25 Blackpool Borough	38	12	0	26	488	726	24
26 Batley	38	10	0	28	434	722	20
27 Liverpool City	**38**	**9**	**1**	**28**	**442**	**728**	**19**
28 Dewsbury	38	6	4	28	375	946	16
29 Castleford	38	7	1	30	445	893	15
30 Doncaster	38	4	0	34	246	971	8

1958–59 Northern Rugby League (bottom six teams)

25 Castleford	38	13	0	25	527	732	26
26 Rochdale Hornets	38	11	1	26	398	649	23
27 Batley	38	10	1	27	433	679	21
28 Liverpool City	**38**	**8**	**0**	**30**	**476**	**954**	**16**
29 Dewsbury	38	7	0	31	378	859	14
30 Doncaster	38	5	0	33	329	924	10

1959–60 Northern Rugby League (bottom six teams)

25 Bramley	38	10	2	26	393	673	22
26 Bradford Northern	38	9	3	26	450	645	21
27 Liverpool City	**38**	**9**	**3**	**26**	**383**	**720**	**21**
28 Blackpool Borough	38	9	1	28	400	819	19
29 Dewsbury	38	4	1	33	337	982	9
30 Doncaster	38	2	1	35	284	1084	5

Endnotes

[1] F. Woolley, 'Editorial', *Liverpool Stanley Official Programme* [versus Workington] 23 December 1950, p.3

[2] From Liverpool Stanley RLFC minutes housed at University of Huddersfield

[3] Collins, Tony (2006), *Rugby League In Twentieth Century Britain*, London: Routledge, p.31

[4] From Liverpool Stanley RLFC minutes housed at University of Huddersfield

[5] 'Stork's Notes', *Liverpool Echo*, 15 May 1951, p.3

[6] 'Rangers' Notes', *Liverpool Echo* Monday 9 July 1951, p.3

[7] Yates, S.H. [as 'Ranger'], 'Ranger's Notes', *Liverpool Echo*, 21 August 1951, p.8

[8] Interview with Tom Fleet, August 2007

[9] Interview with Steve Higginson, April 2007

[10] Interview with Tom Fleet, August 2007

[11] Unaccredited correspondent, 'First Class Supporters Club At Liverpool', *The Rugby League Gazette no.2*, Halifax: Fawcett, Greenwood & Co, October 1952, p.21

[12] Thanks to Philip Babbs for the above *Liverpool City Official Programme* editorials concerning Liverpool City's social club development

[13] Unaccredited programme editor, 'Club Notes', *Liverpool City Official Programme* [versus Warrington] 20 December 1958, p.5

[14] Unaccredited programme editor, 'Citizen Chatter', *Liverpool City Official Programme* [versus Widnes], 26 December 1960, p.2

[15] Interview with Frank O'Connor 10 November 2007

[16] Discussion with George Walker 2 November 2007

[17] Unaccredited 'Editorial', *Liverpool City Official Programme* [versus Wigan], Thursday 27 April 1961, p.2

[18] Yates, S.H., *Liverpool Football Echo*, Saturday 20 March 1954

[19] Unaccredited programme editor, 'Our Visitors', *Barrow Official Programme* [versus Liverpool City], 8 April 1954, p.8

[20] Unaccredited programme editor, 'Editorial', *Liverpool City Official Programme* [versus Wigan] 28 August 1954, p.2

[21] Brown, Gordon (2004), 'Memories Of Liverpool City', *Our Game 9*, spring 2004, London: London League Publications, p.4

[22] Interview with Harry Ody, 22 November 2007

[23] Unaccredited 'Editorial', *Liverpool City Official Programme* [versus Wigan] 28 August 1954, p.2

[24] *ibid*

[25] *ibid*, 'Supporters' Club Notes', p.4

[26] Yates, S.H., *Liverpool Daily Post*, 5 September 1956, p.9

[27] *ibid*, 8 October 1956, p.9

[28] Email correspondence with Tom Fleet, November 2007

[29] Unaccredited editor, 'Editorial', *Liverpool City Official Programme* [versus Australia], Wednesday 10 October 1956, p.3

[30] 'Winger' *Liverpool Football Echo*, 13 October 1956, p.9

[31] Heads, Ian (1990) *The Kangaroos – the saga of Rugby League's great tours* by, Sydney: Lester Townsend Publishing, p.150

[32] Yates, S.H., 'Rugby League', *Liverpool Echo*, Monday 15 October 1956, p.9

[33] Several well-known personalities from the athletics world turned their attention to rugby league football in the immediate post-war era. The list includes Emmanuel McDonald Bailey (Leigh), Alf Meakin (Leeds, Blackpool Borough), Berwyn Jones (Wakefield, Bradford), Arthur Rowe (Oldham), and from New Zealand Peter Henderson (Huddersfield)

[34] Discussion with Peter Twiss, 2 November 2007

[35] Brown, Gordon (2004) interview with Harry Ody for 'Memories Of Liverpool City', *Our Game 9* Spring 2004, London: London League Publications, p.4

[36] Interview with John McGrath 21 September 2007

[37] Interview with George Walker 2 November 2007

6. Recruitment and support

Back in the 1930s Jimmy Green undoubtedly had a master plan, and his untimely death in 1937 probably ended one of rugby league's most ambitious development initiatives. Green must have realised that Liverpool was never going to embrace rugby league with open arms and that any enfranchisement required careful fostering before adoption took place. Consequently, and in retrospect a kind of tripartite scheme for bringing success for Liverpool on the rugby field can clearly be seen. The initial short-term solution was to bring a team of winners to the Dirt Track. This Green did with some aplomb by using seasoned professionals, some of whom like Jack Maloney had been Highfield men through-and-through, others, such as Eddie Richards, were former rugby union players; still more arrived via cagey transfer transactions between Green and his rugby league contacts and associates.

Jimmy Green's medium-term plan was to use the Tunstall Lane ground for player development. He would have appreciated that there was little to no opportunity at such an early stage to develop the game at grassroots level in Liverpool and wisely understood that good young players needed to come from the heartlands. He ran three sides in Pemberton to bring players through the ranks. If they were not to make it with Stanley they might be sold on at profit. As we have seen, Green was renowned in rugby league circles for such deals with Wigan Highfield – in fact it was the only profitable element of the original club. In addition to running the headquarters at Tunstall Lane, he was an expert rugby scout and kept a close eye on the other local clubs in the south Lancashire area in case cast-offs or players who had simply slipped through the net came his way. This was another integral part of his medium term plan and appeared to work well during his lifetime.

Green's long-term plan required far more convolution and considerable PR work: for Liverpool to acknowledge rugby league football as something of its own, schools needed to be approached and persuaded to play the code. *Rugby League Journal*'s Harry Edgar credits Jimmy Green with a towering degree of success in bringing rugby league to the schools of Liverpool in the mid-1930s, and mentions "at least 25 schools in Liverpool were playing the game during the years Liverpool Stanley were in their pomp".[1]

However, although some progress was made, the hard evidence for such a high level of active participation by Liverpool schoolboys in rugby league remains slim. First, it is not beyond the realms of possibility to suggest that such a large scale of schools activity would have produced at least one or two young players of promise and may have even led to the formation of a schools representative side – but it did not. Therefore, and secondly, as far as this evidence is concerned the boundaries of what did or did not constitute 'Liverpool' probably remain questionable. Perhaps schools in Prescot, Rainford, and Whiston might have given the game a try – but Anfield, Walton or Everton?

Jimmy Green, in fact, was probably rather less successful in this effort to convert the sporting youth of Liverpool. In any case, this initiative was not Green's alone, for he was ably assisted by a local schoolmaster Mr N.T. Railton; when Railton left Merseyside to teach elsewhere, so the game left with him. The *Rugby League Review* records: "One of the ringleaders in this movement was a young master named N.T. Railton. He is no longer in Liverpool, more's the pity from Stanley's point of view, but he is now one of the Grade 1 referees. In those days there were about 34 schools sides playing the game, producing both spectators and players of the future. Contrast that with the half-dozen or so of the present day." [2]

Nevertheless, following Green's untimely death in April 1937, plans for a junior rugby league were announced on Tuesday 4 May at the Liverpool Stanley Supporters' Club annual general meeting. The thinking behind the proposal was sound: if some schools were playing rugby league football, a local league should be established for boys to continue the game towards adulthood. Four amateur teams (Fairfield, Knotty Ash, Walmoor, and Wavertree) had already been formed in the Liverpool area. There had even been a knockout competition – the Wagstaffe Cup – which was won by Wavertree, but according to the *Liverpool Echo* on 5 May the teams "had a rather precarious existence during the past season". Indeed the victorious Wavertree team did not compete in 1937–38 and were replaced by a line-up bearing the name of 'Anfield.'

So, potential managers were selected from the Stanley Supporters' Club with the purpose of developing a league of 16 clubs. Teams were expected to consist of boys between the ages of 14 and 16 years, some of whom were to be made up from Territorial Army cadets. It all sounded very promising, but in fact little changed over the remaining pre-war years and the 16 proposed clubs failed to materialise. A combination of Jimmy Green's death, internal strife at Stanley, apathy among Liverpudlians and a shortage of playing fields all contributed to what can be seen as a false start. In the 1938–39 season a J.H. Green Memorial Shield was contested between Walmoor, Knotty Ash, Old Swan and a returning Wavertree, but by the outbreak of the Second World War few schools were playing the sport and any presence of amateur rugby league football was restricted to either Liverpool's borders or these artificial representative sides. A Liverpool Stanley programme from January 1939 predicted optimistically: "We do feel that if we can weather the present times, our problems will become much easier, for gates of the future are assured by the ever-increasing enthusiasm in our schoolboy and junior circles. The young on Merseyside are certainly very much rugby-minded and they do set an example to their elders."

Note the use of the word 'Merseyside' rather than 'Liverpool' and note, too the same editorial as it mentions the club's efforts to "establish our team firmly in a district that has so far more or less scorned our game" [3] – mixed messages and revealing language, indeed.

There was, in truth, only one code of rugby football acceptable in Liverpool schools, and that was union. The existence of a whole raft of local rugby union-playing grammar schools such as St Edward's, De La Salle, Liverpool Institute and Liverpool College, plus a handful of first-class union clubs to boot meant that there were seldom any converts from one code to another within Liverpool itself. Few rugby union players would have been able to keep pace with the fitness levels required by professional rugby league football, but there were also important issues of culture and class at work here.

The rugby union code's authenticity on Merseyside sprang from a somewhat elevated cultural font. The city of Liverpool had developed, not as an industrial or manufacturing conurbation such as Halifax or Huddersfield, but as a marketplace, a financial centre, a treasury even. The grammar schools erected in the late 19th century supported this reading of the city and viewed the amateurism of union as the code of the gentleman. For the more socially elevated Victorians and Edwardians, rugby union football was considered to display all of the characteristics necessary for military service. Furthermore, the question of playing a game for its own sake was a high priority. These middle and upper classes associated sport with morality and character-building and this was a central ethos at both public and grammar schools. The mere suggestion of professionalism tainted this concept, apart from cricket where the professional player was viewed as subservient to the amateur master, although they played together.

Rugby was, of course, part of the backbone of imperialism and inextricably linked with patriotism. Cecil Rhodes had financed the first England rugby tour to South Africa in 1891 and any hint of professionalism in rugby was considered contagious – similar to a disease – and even tantamount to treason. When in 1903 the Welsh national selectors picked men from working-class backgrounds, the Scottish referee Crawford Finlay suggested that the whole tone of the game was being lowered. He was also to advocate contemptuously that they should clear off and join the Northern Union. It is not coincidental that during the formative years of Northern Union, players were required to work in respectable jobs, and strict limits were placed on payment and compensation in order to prevent allegations of indolence being levelled at professional rugby players.

The aim of this visible respectability was to demonstrate that the moral fibre of the Northern Union professional was just as strong as that of the amateur, where ironically the trait of under-the-table payments to players, also known as 'boot money' had become endemic before the September 1895 schism.

Merseyside rugby union clubs were long among England's elite. Liverpool RFC claims to be the oldest open rugby club in the world and Waterloo, New Brighton, Liverpool University, and Birkenhead Park were also on the old senior clubs' fixture lists until the 1980s. But the post-war economic decline of Merseyside, with so many people leaving the area, contributed to a weakening of these clubs and today this higher-ranking history is not always evident. Indeed the Liverpool and St Helens rugby union clubs merged in 1986 and Liverpool-St Helens now fields its first XV in a lower regional league. Roman Catholic grammar schools in Liverpool were especially drawn to the ethos of rugby union and, in some cases literally, forced their pupils to play the XV-a-side code of rugby, despite many boys coming from areas of the city steeped in soccer traditions. Perhaps the Christian Brothers agreed with the sports reporter of 1894 who declared: "[in the north the] labourer diverted his attention from quoits and rabbit coursing and pigeon flying, and turned it to [association] football." [4]

Presumably, if association football held the attention of these impressionable Liverpool De La Salle schoolboys, they were not able to devote constructive thoughts to a healthy body, a healthy mind, Empire and the Catholic Church. Mick O'Toole was a pupil at De La Salle Grammar School in the mid-1950s: "I never even found out until I got there that the school played rugby. I had no knowledge of the game. I had to play but did so under protest – I had no choice – we were made to play. Ironically in 1959 they converted to football, but I'd left the previous year in 1958. None of the Christian Brothers actually taught rugby themselves, but they must have had some kind of tradition of playing the game when they were younger men. In fact we had a current England international - James Patrick Quinn - as our rugby master. He was the games master who taught maths on the side. I did play once, away at St Anselm's College on the Wirral: that was a Christian Brothers college, too. I hated it but I remember having sticky buns so that was OK." [5]

A similar story emerged in Wigan, but with a twist: secondary modern Catholicism was linked to the XIII-a-side code: "You were kept, without knowing it, well away from the [rugby league] amateur game because that's where the secondary moderns ended up. The physical locations made the point. Those who made it went up to Douglas Valley, a rural parkland sat on the edge of Wigan Plantations. Those who played amateur rugby league were Irish Catholics. They went to St Patrick's and played in Scholes on an ex-corporation rubbish dump next to the canal." [6]

While often secretly paying their players boot money, the various union clubs dotted around Merseyside, some founded by old boys of the aforementioned schools, frowned upon rugby league's overt professionalism as distasteful, of a lower social echelon and somewhat parochial, in the latter case despite Liverpool existing within the county of Lancashire until the mid-1970s, Scouse vernacular still portrays Lancastrians as 'woolly-backs'. It all appeared self-explanatory: the game of rugby union simply attracted a better class of people.

Rugby League Council doctrine suggested it was a duty of all professional clubs to attempt to establish open-age amateur rugby in their allotted areas. Wigan RLFC attempted to establish various youth competitions and leagues in the borough, yet even here success was limited and several grammar schools steadfastly refused to play rugby league football. What Liverpool City directors expected from equivalent schools on Merseyside is anybody's guess. Phil Melling further states: "Even in Wigan rugby union operated a vertical monopoly of control throughout the educational system making sure that from primary school to public school, via grammar school, no one was able to play rugby league. A policy of sporting apartheid was rigidly enforced in Wigan Grammar School in which rugby league was the enemy number one... even in a rugby league heartland rugby union was able to equate its game with a certain level of academic intelligence... and to limit rugby league to the secondary modern system, where the game was played by so-called academic failures from the wrong side of the tracks. Bill Fallowfield to my knowledge never challenged this system. He allowed rugby league players to be associated in the popular mind with hewers of wood and drawers of water; those who would spend their lives in manual jobs." [7]

In 1945 Liverpool Rangers, Liverpool Stanley Juniors, and Huyton Juniors all competed in a St Helens league, but when in the immediate post-war era various attempts were made by Stanley or City to launch a Liverpool-based junior rugby league competition, the results were patchy to say the least. For example, on 27 August 1949 an advertisement in the Liverpool Stanley programme stated: "MARLA are endeavouring to form new amateur teams in Liverpool from ex-schoolboy players. Any gentlemen interested in forming and managing a new club should attend a meeting between MARLA and the ex-schoolboys to be held at 29, Derby Lane, Old Swan, on September 2nd, at 8.00pm. Provision is being made for training facilities until such time as the new teams are functioning. We have the players – now we want the managers." [8]

It was an interesting stab at social engineering, one might suggest. However, another advertisement appeared almost exactly one year later in an August 1950 *Liverpool Echo* – once again for interested parties to meet at Derby Lane to investigate the possibilities of a Merseyside Amateur Rugby League. Evidently the first endeavour was met with general disinterest. There already existed a St Helens Open Age League and a team picture of the Liverpool Hornets side – who played in that league - was published in the 21 July 1950 edition of the *Liverpool Echo*. The caption states that former Liverpool Stanley forward Ronnie Preston coached the Hornets; he also acted as the club secretary. The side had won nine out of 21 league fixtures the previous season. What's more J.C. Gregson reported to the Stanley committee on 12 June 1950 that Allmark, a former Stanley player who had been playing for Liverpool Rangers, had recently died. The committee agreed to send five guineas (£5/5/0) to his widow. But none of this rugby league activity appears to have taken place west of Queens Drive. Evidence exists therefore from the immediate post-war era that several attempts were made to involve young Merseysiders in the code of rugby league football. But Liverpool Hornets and Liverpool Rangers both played their football on the outskirts of Liverpool and drew their players from these areas, not the inner city.

A junior rugby league competition, which included a Stanley youth team, but not the open-age Liverpool Hornets, did exist in 1949, but this was not the aforementioned Merseyside Amateur Rugby League, but rather another based in the St Helens area. Liverpool Stanley's official programme for 23 April 1949 reported that the Stanley Juniors beat Liverpool Rangers 11–5 the preceding week. This league consisted of 12 sides, none of which, with the possible exception of Stanley and Rangers, appear to be Liverpool-based, as such: Rainhill were top and were followed in descending order by Ring o' Bells, Vine Tavern, UGB, Uno's Dabs, New Church, Clock Face, British Sidac, Forsters' Recs, Liverpool Stanley Juniors, Brook St. Legion and Liverpool Rangers.

As suggested previously, to all intents and purposes it appears a St Helens-based league and it is probably not without significance that the two Liverpool sides were entrenched at the wrong end of the table. The official RFL publication, the *Rugby League Gazette* of March 1950 also records on page 13 that a Liverpool junior side visited the Mitcham Stadium, London, the then headquarters of

PROGRAMME 3d.

AMATEUR RUGBY LEAGUE FOOTBALL

"S·A·R·L"

LONDON
v
LIVERPOOL RANGERS

AT

MITCHAM STADIUM

ON

Saturday, 28th May, 1949

KICK-OFF 3-15 p.m.

SPECIALLY ARRANGED BY

THE SOUTHERN AMATEUR RUGBY LEAGUE

IN CONJUNCTION WITH

THE RUGBY FOOTBALL LEAGUE

REFRESHMENTS OBTAINABLE

(Courtesy Phil Babbs)

the short-lived Southern Amateur Rugby League, during 1949. This visit actually took place on 28 May when Liverpool Rangers played London – a team consisting of players from the Southern Amateur Rugby League, established with help from Sydney Parkes, who in April 1948 offered to provide four of his grounds for a new amateur league.

This would have been a nice weekend break in London, but these earlier efforts at creating interest among the youth of Liverpool for the sport of rugby league were clearly unsuccessful, and only added to the ever-growing concept that an active, participatory interest in the code came to an abrupt end at the Liverpool city limits.

By August 1954 the Liverpool City programme editorial stated that the MARL concept was still alive but in need of development. Headlined "Amateur Rugby", it went on to say "It is obvious in many ways that one of the backbones of our game is the amateur Teams. We want to see our Merseyside Amateur Rugby League develop. They are now appealing for players, especially 15 to 18 years, to play in this new league. Coaching facilities are available and no previous experience is necessary. Applicants can contact Mr Hall at the Tea Bar after the game or at 32, Everton Road, Liverpool, 6 ('phone: Anfield 3702); he would also be glad of help from adults with organisation." [9]

A collection was taken at the Liverpool City versus Warrington match on 20 December 1958 specifically for something called the Liverpool and District Amateur Rugby League. The editorial asked supporters to "dig deep", indicating that the organisers were finding funding something of a problem. The few sides competing in this league were not clubs at all, but sporting constructions brought about by the Liverpool

City Supporters' Club membership. Members would manage a handful of teams made up of aspiring players usually from St Helens or Widnes, and pitch them against each other under names such as West Derby or Longview. Other Liverpool sides also existed sporadically under the names of Black Boro' Colts, Childwall, Crosby Lions, Hunts Cross, Old Swan and Police Cadets, but none were permanent.

It was all to no avail as far as tempting any budding Scouse rugby league players was concerned but one or two players from the League strongholds did go on to play for City, one notable being Peter Twiss. More customary were George Walker's experiences: "I was playing for St Helens YMCA but one of the teams disbanded and I went off to play football. But being a rugby league person at heart I decided to present myself at City for a trial. There were a lot of good half-backs in St Helens at the time – not just Murphy – so I thought I would be better off at City. But there was also a history of the Walkers playing for the club. My dad and uncle were both Highfield players in 1933." [10]

The Merseyside & District Amateur Rugby League was, however, back in existence by 1962. In all likelihood the title reversion was based on the lack of any Liverpool players competing. The 'Supporters Club Notes' from the City programme on 21 April also discuss a trip to the Isle of Man: "It is a pleasure to draw your attention to this splendid day's outing organised by the Merseyside and District Amateur Rugby League. The excursion leaves by M.V. King Orry from the landing stage at 10am and the price of the tickets is £1 inclusive. This includes admittance to the Rugby League Isle of Man Trophy, North Lancs versus South Lancs at the Bowl King George V Park. Kick-off 7pm." [11]

So, the Liverpool City-based development programme lurched from crisis to crisis. At the outset it foundered, then staggered onward for a few seasons with a Liverpool City 'B' team briefly in existence. The City programmes of 2 December 1961 and 6 January 1962 record a 'B' team losing to Bootle Borough 29–5 on 8 November, 21–8 to Hillhouse Recs on 25 November, and 24–0 to Liverpool Hornets on 9 December, only to come to grief once again in the mid-1960s. That 2 December 1961 programme editorial enthused that young Liverpudlians were joining the 'B' team and the writer was optimistic about the future; but within two seasons the St Helens Junior League had absorbed this Liverpool League - by which time the latter consisted of only four clubs: Liverpool Hornets, Bootle Borough and two sides from Blackpool.

The forging of links with junior rugby league sides on the outskirts of Liverpool, such as in the new town of Kirkby in the late-1950s where it was reported four schools played rugby league football and a junior team – Kirkby Rangers – played at the municipal stadium, also looked promising for a short time. But it soon became clear that such teams were only one or two-man enterprises, as a Liverpool City programme editorial duly acknowledged in November 1963: "This season the Liverpool Junior League has merged with the St Helens League. It is a pity Liverpool Hornets, founded in 1946–47, could not carry on owing to lack of officials to run the club. Bootle Boro', together with Kirkby Rangers, Blackpool Amateurs and Hillhouse Recs (Blackpool) have all entered the St Helens and District League." [12]

Despite a little success in the Lancashire Junior Cup, the Bootle Borough team was to last only one further season, as J.C. Gregson was to record in March 1965: "Speaking of junior teams, it is a pity Liverpool Hornets and Bootle Boro' were unable to carry on this season, but there is every hope the Hornets will be back next season with a new ground. Our other Merseyside juniors, Kirkby Rangers and Liverpool Fire Brigade, are both going strong." [13]

However, the development of rugby league in Kirkby was also illusory: a momentary mirage created by its deceptively 'Lancashire' rather than 'Liverpool' geography. Despite being populated by the youth of Liverpool, the new secondary schools in Kirkby attracted teaching staff registered with the Lancashire Education Committee and these teachers brought with them their own sporting preferences – which left with them as they departed the schools throughout the late 1960s and early 1970s. The fact remains that rugby league was unable to generate enough symbols of legitimacy among young people from Kirkby.

An article in the February 1968 edition of *The Rugby League Magazine* (vol. 3 no. 26) discusses the purported revived amateur rugby league scenario in Liverpool; the suggestion being that prospects were good. However the narrative by D.J. Addison presents the reader with a litany of failures. It recites the disbanding in 1962 of Liverpool Rangers and Liverpool Hornets after 20 years, the closure of the Bootle Borough side soon after, but then goes on to wax lyrical about Altash under-17s and the Kirkby Rangers open-age side – neither of which were Liverpool-based and neither of which outlasted the decade.

By this time the Kirkby Rangers team, a Warrington League side, was the pet project of John Farrell who played a handful of games for Liverpool City during the 1961–62 season and then went on to play for Widnes between 1962 and 1965. He taught and coached in Kirkby, but when these positions ended, so did Kirkby Rangers RLFC. Furthermore, while the reformation of the MARL is celebrated, membership stood at only four sides, with the recent addition of Whiston Hornets. The article is clearly written more in hope than expectation and concludes by suggesting that a Merseyside League might not actually be the best to enter from the point of view of travel – logical enough if all of the players were being recruited, as usual, from the outskirts but a terrible advertisement for the code in Liverpool where, in truth, rugby league had long ago ceased to exist.

It is, therefore, within these class-ridden and culture-conscious contexts that attempts to establish a rugby league playing network in Liverpool needs to be understood. It could never be an easy task, not simply because of the pre-eminence of association football, from which the Northern Union had felt the effects of competition as early as 1905, but also because of the conscious opposition to rugby league's professionalism from the institutional backbone of the City of Liverpool. It remains a historical fact that Liverpool City's attempt at establishing professional rugby league in Liverpool did indeed fail, and that this failure was related with Liverpool's working-class preferences in sports. But it was also related to the class-based, well-educated decision-making of a cultural elite who linked rugby union with morality, nationhood and worthiness.

These tenets were central to the curricula of most late-19th and 20th century grammar schools in Liverpool. The very presence of the Liverpool Stanley and City rugby league clubs, therefore, would have been viewed by some as lowering both the tone and tenor of the game of rugby football, if not of the city itself.

It comes as no revelation to learn that the majority of the different board members at Liverpool City were businessmen and professionals – they were trades people with networks and contacts leading out into Lancashire, Cheshire and beyond. Some board members such as Councillor Tommy Mann and Dr Harry Roebuck also hailed from rugby league-playing towns and cities (Mann from Wigan and Roebuck from Leeds), whereas others such as William Rainford were wealthy traders based in Liverpool but, hailing from Lancashire, looked east as much as west for both trade and leisure. None of these willing enthusiasts appeared to fully comprehend the ramifications of what they were attempting. The importance of integration was vital in such a city as Liverpool but from the onset of the move to Knotty Ash there appeared problems concerning shared aims among the Liverpool City cohorts – especially regarding the move to make Liverpool Stanley a members-only club.

Councillor Mann, for example, was aged 46 when Liverpool Stanley moved to Knotty Ash. Perhaps typical of the Stanley or City committee-cum-boardroom, he was born in Wigan and had been a follower of rugby league since a child. He had previously served as a director of Oldham RLFC prior to moving to New Brighton, where he had entertainment business interests at the Tower Promenade. A *Liverpool Echo* photograph of Mann shows him alongside an array of rugby league trophies at his Tower Amusements business in the summer of 1950, all borrowed to raise funds for Stanley. The footballer Joe Mercer is also pictured with the Stanley chairman. But Mann appears from this historical distance to have been something of a dreamer. He certainly exaggerated his entertainment industry connections by promising that radio star Wilfred Pickles would kick-off the opening fixture at Knotty Ash. He had made his presence felt during the tortuous removal from the Stanley Track but appears to have made enemies among the Stanley supporters. Mann's loss of face over the 'Pickles Affair' and ill health eventually led to his resignation, but not before his bemoaning of Stanley's cliques.

Dr Harry Roebuck, on the other hand, had more stamina. Roebuck was a native of Leeds and was initiated into rugby league by his father when at the tender age of three he was lifted over the turnstiles at Headingley. He soon developed a keen interest in the game while in Yorkshire and when arriving in Huyton after the war as a GP he continued his dedication to rugby league by pursuing an interest in Liverpool Stanley. In 1952 Roebuck became an executive of the new limited company formed in May 1951 and so became one of the first directors of the new Liverpool City. He later became a member of the Lancashire County Committee and the Rugby League Council. During his time on the council he served on every sub-committee and also on the Management Committee of the Rugby Football League, becoming chairman. His experiences as a player were with the union code but his first love was always league. But ultimately, like Tommy Mann, Roebuck was born and bred in a thriving league stronghold and found it rather difficult to re-adjust himself to the conditions of running a rugby league club in Liverpool. Indeed he was described by two City/Huyton fans when interviewed recently as rather "distant" and "unapproachable".

A lack of cultural tradition is at the heart of the Liverpool City issue: such tradition could not be introduced to Liverpool by the likes of Mann and Roebuck as if it were a 'gift'. Sporting cultural tradition is linked to a person's character and way of thinking, and this is far more difficult to change than the board of Liverpool City perceived.

So, like its Liverpool Stanley predecessor, the Liverpool City rugby league club was compelled to recruit its playing staff from either those released by the local professional clubs or from amateur rugby league in those rugby league towns. While player development remained a forlorn hope and such schemes in Liverpool floundered and failed, amateur clubs such as the St Helens-based Blackbrook, Moss Bank Juniors, and Pilkington Recs clubs; St Marie's, St Patrick's, and West Bank from Widnes, and Warrington clubs Crosfield Recs, Latchford Albion, and Rylands Recs all found Liverpool Stanley or City constantly sniffing around their players in the post-war era – as, indeed, did the mighty Saints.

Material support: St Helens, Widnes and Warrington

St Helens other team...

"When player after player from St Helens goes to Stanley, the critics are up in arms, fearful lest a budding Wagstaffe or Fairclough or Ellaby slips though our fingers unawares. The Jack Arkwrights, I suppose are expected to find the mesh too small or is it that big ones don't roll up so frequently.

However we can't adopt a "dog in the manger" attitude. We don't want to miss any exceptional players, but we have to be fair to young players and if they don't look like supplanting one of our regular players we have to give them a chance of making their way in another camp. It is good, however, to find that these travellers still have a soft spot for Knowsley Road.

There are eight St Helens players in the Saints team and eight in the Stanley team too... sort them out for yourself." [14]

As a town, St Helens did not even exist at the beginning of the 19th century but emerged from the villages of Eccleston, Windle, Parr, and Sutton – all originally part of the parish of Prescot. The town takes its name from St Helen's Parish Church in Hardshaw in Windle. This parish church was rebuilt in 1816 and rededicated to St Mary. However, after the church was restored between 1916 and 1926 following a fire, the dedication returned to the historic 'St Helen, St Helens'. St Helens was built on coal and glass: local collieries employed up to 5,000 men as late as the 1970s, while during the boom years of the British coal industry (1913 being the peak year of production with one million employed in UK mining) the St Helens division of the Lancashire and Cheshire Miners' Federation had, at 10 per cent the largest membership of that organisation.

Primarily because of the abundance of coal reserves, the quality of local sand, the near availability of Cheshire salt and the transport revolution – first the Sankey Canal and then the railways from 1830 onwards – a glass and chemical industry was established in St Helens. Pilkington's – for many years the leaders in the float glass technique – are still based in St Helens. The Sankey Canal was opened in 1757 to transport coal from the pits in Haydock and Parr to the River Mersey. An extension to the canal (the St Helens section) was made in 1775 linking the canal to St Helens. In the 1830s, the St Helens and Runcorn Gap Railway was built for the same purpose.

St Helens is, therefore, a proud, independent borough with only a smattering of cultural links to the city it lives alongside – Liverpool. The prominence of rugby league in the town is evidence of this cultural inconsistency. The town even boasted two professional rugby league clubs up until the Second World War – St Helens and St Helens Recs, but the latter, although linked to the glass industry workers struggled for support and disbanded as a professional outfit prior to the outbreak of the war, although continued as the amateur Pilkington Recs club.

When Lord Derby (rather than Wilfred Pickles!) officially opened Liverpool Stanley's new Knotty Ash Stadium on 26 August 1950, St Helens provided the opposition and a number of former Saints players, including Large, Preston, and Waring, were part of the Stanley squad that day. But they were, by and large, cast-offs. Waring, for example, wasn't greatly valued by Saints and had been released. Stanley signed him for a direct payment of £20 to the player with a promise of another £100 if county honours were achieved and £150 if selected for Great Britain. Needless to say, the Stanley bank manager was not troubled for the latter two figures and Waring faded from view.

By October 1950 problems developed with these St Helens-based players with Lea, Cox and Preston at the centre of the disruption – they were all placed on the transfer list but, predictably, there were no takers. Full-back Cox went on to play with some distinction for Stanley and City for several seasons and briefly coached the team in the early 1960s whereas Lea played on for a further two seasons, while Preston retired from the professional game. So whether these Saints squad players consistently contributed much to the playing strength of Liverpool Stanley remains open to debate. Indeed, the St Helens presence, although welcomed by some, was not without its critics. A few weeks prior to the opening fixture of the 1950–51 season the minutes of the Stanley committee on 12 June 1950 read: "It was felt by the Supporters' Club that the preponderance of St Helens players was not a good thing for the team and the club, and should be split up. Main committee in agreement on this point." [15]

The St Helens club was forever mildly amused (and occasionally miffed) by the fact that the Liverpool club repeatedly looked towards them for prospective players. Prior to the new era beginning at Knotty Ash a St Helens programme editorial on 23 September 1948 states with not a little weariness "Stanley... might as well be called St Helens Stanley, for there is hardly a man in the side who does not come from St Helens."

Indeed, some years later in a 1962 edition of the St Helens programme, the editor that day was to remark that by the time the name 'Liverpool City' had [re] appeared... in 1951 there were "at least as many St Helens born players in the team as the Saints had in theirs." He continued: "Since then they have gone further afield in their scouting but they are well blessed with Saints talent on the official side. Don Gullick is in charge of the coaching for the first team and Ike Fishwick teaches them all the wiles he has picked up during the years with special emphasis on the 'A' team. On the Committee they are fortunate in having Bill Whittaker's assistance. One of the straightest individuals that the Saints have ever had on their books he still has friends on the Saints – as well as on other club's' managements. Ken Grundy – a well-known name in St Helens Rugby League – is their secretary." [16]

It was not however merely superfluous players and officials that made the short move from Knowsley Road to Knotty Ash.

The facilities at Knotty Ash were rudimentary: to begin with there was no cover at all for spectators and large tents were used for the dressing rooms and headquarters. However to the eternal credit of the Liverpool board the facilities were to improve considerably throughout the 1950s and 1960s. The main grandstand, with dressing rooms installed underneath, was erected over a period of two seasons, and a shelter was eventually provided behind one goal line at the Prescot end of the ground. By 1962 a new cover enclosed the embankment opposite the grandstand. This covered accommodation had actually belonged to St Helens RLFC and was donated to City by the St Helens club when they erected a new covered paddock at their Knowsley Road ground in 1961. The old wooden and brick shelter was moved by road from St Helens to Knotty Ash that same year. In a review of the season about to pass, comments from the programme editor for the final game of the 1960–61 season revealed both grateful thanks and a guarded optimism: "Allied to the disappointing results has been the poor gates for most matches. During the close season it is hoped to erect the Stand, which the St Helens club has so generously given us, free, on the far side of the ground, and it is hoped that this will afford covered accommodation for several thousand spectators. Perhaps the lukewarm supporters will be tempted to come!" [17]

Knotty Ash, showing the former St Helens stand in the background

The ever-resourceful secretary of the City Supporters' Club, Alf Vickers, was to report in December 1961: "The new stand is practically completed and already we have had most favourable comments on its warmth and the big improvement to the comfort and appearance of the ground. The next job is to get it painted and advertisers are being invited to utilise the very excellent space running along the front canopy." [18]

By the time of St Helens's visit to Knotty Ash Stadium on 21 April 1962, J.C. Gregson was to open his editorial for that day's programme: "Today we welcome St Helens and hope that they like our new stand which is of course their old one. It has been much appreciated by our supporters in the bad weather of recent months and we again ask the Saints to accept our gratitude and thanks for this splendid gift." [19] St Helens rugby league historian Denis Whittle later remarked to Mike Latham that it was "in the true spirit of rugby league; I still remember the wagons taking the construction away, brick by brick, and down the road to Liverpool. It was always a struggle for the club and they seemed to be full of players who had previously played for Saints, Warrington, Widnes, Wigan or Leigh." [20]

It was clear that St Helens RLFC and the people of St Helens had long since acknowledged that a Liverpool-based rugby league club did not constitute a threat. The St Helens supporters' club Secretary R.J. Taylor affirmed in April 1953 that he would "like to see our neighbours from Liverpool making better headway, both financially and on the field" and then – to some extent perplexed – stated "there is no lack of spirit, either among the players or in the committee room, but success still seems to elude them. There must be plenty of potential supporters in the district." [21]

In fact the material and morale-boosting assistance provided by Saints proved to be of great value to the struggling Liverpool club who, beer money aside, received precious little of either from the citizens of Liverpool. For example, City's highest official attendance at Knotty Ash was recorded on 2 October 1954 when Saints were the visitors and 7,938 attended. The editorial from that day's programme addressed the relationship that existed between the two clubs: "The management wish to express, what they are sure all City supporters heartily endorse, namely, the great appreciation for all the St Helens board have done to help us during the last 12 months in our struggle to establish the game in Liverpool. We are grateful and will not forget... we can only add that we trust our lads will this year give them a much closer run in the game than has been customary in recent years." [22]

By the 1960s Liverpool City boasted director Bill Whittaker, who was a former Saints and Widnes player – he was in fact a forward in the St Helens side that crushed Stanley 36-2 in the inaugural game at Knotty Ash Stadium. And by December 1960 former St Helens threequarter Doug Greenall was coaching City. Then former St Helens star Don Gullick replaced him in 1961. Long-serving Ray Hockenhull and Jim Cartledge who both received testimonials from Liverpool City, were St Helens men. Another former St Helens and district player was Jack Broome's assistant and City 'A' team trainer Eric Birch who had played for Clock Face RLFC.

Liverpool City secretary – and former player and 'A' team coach – Ken Grundy was the son of Harry Grundy, former St Helens Recs player and the brother of Barrow's Jack Grundy. Matters continued very much in the same vein when Liverpool City became Huyton. Once former St Helens junior John Evans joined Huyton in 1968, he became a regular at Alt Park for several seasons. In Huyton's first season Evans played alongside half-back Norman Pickersgill and Keith Mills – two former Saints juniors – and so the story continued. The material support for Liverpool City from St Helens people was great indeed and equalled only by the number of Widnesians actually fielded by Liverpool City.

Widnes RLFC

St Helens might have provided Liverpool City with a part of their ground, but on many occasions Widnes provided their entire stadium. Indeed, during the disastrous 1968-69 season when Liverpool City removed to Huyton, the Huyton club used Widnes' Naughton Park enclosure on nine occasions as their new ground was not yet ready. On 14 May 1976 Widnes provided both ground and team to play against Huyton with all proceeds going to the embattled minnows. A crowd of 2,431 attended a game with nothing at stake other than the survival of Huyton RLFC. By 1978, Huyton were again playing a home game at Widnes after vandals rendered their Alt Park ground unusable. As we have seen, the town of Widnes provided countless players for the Liverpool club – from the talented to the inept – and, like St Helens, and to a lesser extent Warrington, created an artificial chronology for Liverpool City when the city of Liverpool had no interest in the club's continuance.

Widnes is an industrial town within the present borough of Halton, but was originally in Lancashire, with Cheshire on the other side of the Mersey at Runcorn. It is located on the northern bank of the River Mersey, where the estuary narrows to form the Runcorn Gap. Upstream and eight miles to the east is the town of Warrington, and downstream 16 miles to the west is the city of Liverpool. In 1847 the first chemical factory was established in the town and it rapidly became a major centre of the chemical industry. Chemicals are no longer produced in the town, however. Widnes also lies on the southern route of the Liverpool to Manchester railway line. The Sankey Canal, now disused, terminates in an area of the town known as Spike Island.

The rugby club was formed in 1873 under the name of Farnworth & Appleton with the 'Widnes' title being assumed two years later. The club played at a number of grounds before moving to the present site at Lowerhouse Lane in 1884. Apparently, it was during these years that the famous 'Chemics' nickname – now discarded in favour of the 'Viking' moniker - became common parlance.

Widnes was a founder member of the Northern Union in 1895 and the first match was at Canal Street, Runcorn, which was lost 15–4. During its formative years, Widnes often struggled financially and, like Wigan Highfield, had to sell players to balance the books. The strength of junior rugby league in the area means that to this day the club has a steady stream of local talent to offset its losses. For example, when Widnes became the first club to make two trips to Wembley, losing to Hunslet in the 1934 Cup Final, that side was composed entirely of local players. The Chemics were proud to reveal that not one penny had been paid in transfer fees to acquire these players. This overabundance of rugby players also meant that in the days of Liverpool Stanley, City and Huyton there were players surplus to the town club's needs, or even a few who had been missed by the club's scouts; thus several Widnesians played for Liverpool.

Jack Broome

However, arguably the most important of these Widnesians was to arrive at Liverpool City when his playing days were over. At 33 years of age Jack Broome was one of the youngest coaches in Rugby League when he arrived at Knotty Ash for the 1963–64 season. This former Wigan and Widnes player was able to assemble reasonably competitive cut-priced teams based around ever-presents such as the aforementioned Ray Ashby (until 1965), Jim Cartledge, John McGrath, Ray Hockenhull, Wilf Hunt, Tom Galligan, Tom Nicholls, and Bryan Upton. A native of Widnes, Broome had played professionally for both Wigan and Widnes before joining the coaching staff at Naughton Park after his career had been cut short by a shoulder injury.

After receiving a letter while away on holiday to inform him that he was no longer required by the then faction-riven Widnes club, Broome decided to give Liverpool City a go. He became the first Liverpool coach to be awarded a three-year contract when in March 1964 he agreed to look after the side throughout the transition period that was to be brought about by the enforced move away from Liverpool 14. He continued with the club following their transformation into Huyton RLFC. Wigan were impressed by the appointment of their former player and noted in their programme "he is a very capable and knowledgeable man in dealing with players and surely with his ability and the present enthusiasm then the future must look very bright for Liverpool." [23]

Jack Broome certainly made an immediate impact by signing several useful players in that short close season of 1963. Most were fellow Widnesians, including Mick McGillicuddy from Swinton, Brian Cartwright from Leigh (following a loan period) and Alan Gregson, a former Widnes ICI rugby union player. It was contacts (as much as contracts) that were all-important to Liverpool City and the grapevines surrounding Broome certainly produced a few valuable additions to the squad. He recalls: "I was invited to meet the Liverpool City committee - there were only a few of them - and I was asked to take over, so I agreed. I'd been coaching at Widnes, went away on my holidays to Newquay and came back without a job! Widnes then was run like a members' committee – no directors and a lot of backbiting. I got a bit fed up with this and you felt that you were up against a brick wall at times. Someone also came from Huddersfield to ask me to coach there but it was too far away. Liverpool City got wind of it. I knew some of the players – Widnes and St Helens lads – so I thought 'OK'." [24]

As a Liverpool City regular John McGrath welcomed the arrival of Jack Broome as coach: "Yes, Dave Cox was before Jack but I think went to Keighley and then emigrated. He got a job with the Co-op out in Australia. Jack was a good coach but don't mention York. I think Jack's first away game as coach with Liverpool City was at York and we won 11–10. I'd had a right go at Bryan Upton – a Warrington lad – for getting sent off. We were putting up a very good show and I bollocked him all the way from the centre to the touchline. The next minute I was sent off as well. Jack was not pleased!" [25]

Modestly, Jack Broome calls to mind those days when: "we had a settled team and these lads wanted to play. We all travelled down to Liverpool to train together twice a week and we were a proper team. Also Bill Whittaker would say to people just come down and have a look. He was a well-respected former player as well and so many stayed on." [26]

The facts were that the training regimes established by Broome created not simply a bond between players but often turned average fringe players into true professionals. Tom Galligan describes Broome as "an excellent coach" and John McGrath concurs: "That's basically the way it was. I thought, well, if somebody said to me 'go down and take a look' – and they were a half decent player – I would go because it would be a genuine recommendation – Jack being there, well, said something, too."[27]

Wilf Hunt

Wilf Hunt was a bona fide stalwart of the club. At the tender age of 17, he joined Liverpool City during the 1952–53 season: "I played for West Bank amateur team in Widnes when I was 16 and the Widnes professional club had a big crop of injuries. So they came to West Bank and signed nine of us for £50 each. When their regulars had recovered from injury they could not keep us all on, but we were now professionals and West Bank were only allowed one permit [former professional] player, as were other amateur clubs. News that we were free got round and an ex-City player Pongo Riley, phoned me and asked me to go down to Knotty Ash. Believe it or not, I got a £200 signing-on fee. To a lad of 17 in 1952 that was a lot of money. I stayed for 13 years." [28]

The £200 signing-on fee appears from this distance an extremely generous act from what was a rather impoverished club, however, City were known for these gestures of generosity – Frank Cookson and Ken Cork also received substantial signing-on fees. But of course these figures came to be a rather misleading flash in the pan. From that time onward Wilf and his colleagues found themselves on the receiving end of a modest losing payment of £4 on which he had to pay £1/10 income tax rather than the more extravagant win bonus of £8. Furthermore Wilf had to find five shillings per week for bus fares between his home in Widnes and the Knotty Ash ground, only 50 per cent of which was subsidised by the club; but his loyalty to Liverpool City was unquestionable. An amazing goal and drop-kicker, Hunt often placed points on the Liverpool City scoreboard they neither expected nor deserved and he was renowned for dropping goals from the halfway line, which were worth two points in those days.

City programme editorials of the early and mid-1960s appear to complain sporadically of a goalkicking problem yet, despite his obvious talent in front of goal, the various City coaches did not always turn to Hunt's boot on a regular basis. In his last full season, however, Wilf landed a startling 79 goals. John McGrath remembers Hunt as having great ability and an interesting attitude: "I remember playing against Wigan and they got a free kick on the half way line and their South African kicked a goal. Just minutes later Wilf Hunt drop-kicked it off the half way line – bang!" [29]

In recognition of his long service to the club, Hunt was awarded a testimonial season for 1965–66 and prior to the advent of the 1966–67 season, he was presented with a not inconsiderable cheque for £900, raised by supporters, members and club officials throughout the previous testimonial season. John McGrath recalls: "But it was hard work. We would raise £10 in a pub raffle and then spend it buying drinks for everyone. We also had a few shows in Widnes, where there was more interest in rugby league than in Liverpool, and raised £100 at one full house show featuring Freddie Starr and the Delmontes." [30]

Jack Broome remembers that Wilf "had the first benefit at Liverpool City. I remember him getting Freddie Starr. He had a nightclub and was well connected in that area. He was a fitter by trade and worked at ICI to begin with. Then he went on his own and did well." Hunt was a late convert to the position of full-back but despite this, according to Liverpool City records kicked 305 goals and scored 41 tries in his long career (although the author finds 304 goals and 43 tries) – all more often than not, it must be emphasised, for a side on its way to defeat. His total points tally of 733 was a club record. Wilf scored a try against the touring Australian side in 1956 at the tender age of

A presentation to Ray Hockenhull (Courtesy Alex Service)

20 and continued playing for City until the first month of the 1966–67 campaign, when injury forced him to hang up his boots – but not before he had kicked another 16 goals in the five opening fixtures.

The grapevine surrounding Hunt was also useful for City and later Huyton. For example, there was the arrival of former Widnes scrum-half Colin Parker. He was actually Hunt's business partner in Hunt & Parker Engineering. Later, Huyton player Bob Goulding was a doorman at Wilf Hunt's night club in Widnes (his son is Bobbie Goulding the former St Helens, Wigan and Widnes star). Hunt later became chairman of the Huyton club in the mid-1970s as the club teetered on the brink of extinction, but resigned his duties in the close season of 1977 alongside several other directors.

As a consequence of this successful fundraising year for Wilf Hunt, benefits were also awarded to Ray Hockenhull and Jim Cartledge over the next few seasons. Hockenhull joined Liverpool City from UGB in St Helens, in 1954; but without initially troubling the first team selectors he joined the newly created Blackpool Borough club for a season before returning to Knotty Ash in October 1955 for a small fee. He then stayed with City for 12 years with his testimonial year in 1967 realising £1,000.

Harry Ody remembers that Hockenhull's lorry-driving skills were also put to good use: "Ray was a good example of the way we all mucked in. He would pick you up in his lorry from wherever he was coming back from and drive straight to the ground for training. He'd then give you a lift home. Sometimes it was the only way you could get to Knotty Ash from where you lived – being in another town like St Helens, it wasn't always convenient. Ray was a good player and a real club man." [31]

Although small budgets prohibited City from being involved in regular incoming transfer deals, Jack Broome was able to introduce some useful, if not exceptional, players – not all from Widnes, of course. These included Eddie McDonnell formerly of Widnes and Warrington who arrived at Knotty Ash in 1963, St Helens squad-men Jeff Heaton (scrum-half), and Arthur Johnson (stand-off) who were recruited in 1964, and experienced forward Jim Mustard who also joined City from St Helens in 1965. Heaton was to later confess to St Helens historian Alex Service in 1989: "As for City coming in to sign me – at first I said 'No way!' But the [City] secretary Ken Grundy was a major influence in my eventual decision. One of my best mates, Arthur Johnson, the former Saints winger, was there. Together with several St Helens lads like Ernie Forber, George Walker and Jim Mustard! Despite my early impressions I really enjoyed it at City. We put up some good performances. There was only one division then and so we played good quality opposition every other week, which kept your game up to scratch. The two divisions system of today has made it so different. The First Division is played on a much higher level from the Second – at one time you would get a good lad who would come through because he was up against top quality opposition every fortnight. It just isn't the same now." [32]

Jeff Heaton made something of a name for himself while at City and, after five years of service, was transferred back to a then rather injury-ridden St Helens from the renamed Huyton RLFC in August 1969 for the bargain fee of £750. Heaton recalled in the above interview: "I actually played one game for Liverpool City when they changed their name to Huyton, but I returned to Knowsley Road at the beginning of the 1969–70 season. The secretary Basil Lowe rang me at work and said they wanted me to come back. I was on offer for £1,500 originally, but I said to City that if they did not release me I would pack it in. The actual fee was £750."

It was rather disconsolately reported by the Huyton programme editor on 30 August 1969 that this deal was not considered by fans to be in the best interests of the club – there was never a truer word spoken as Heaton went on to be involved in one of the greatest St Helens sides of the modern era before finishing his career at Rochdale Hornets in the late 1970s. As confirmed by the player himself, the Jeff Heaton deal was an example of a previously inexperienced St Helens reserve moving back to his club of provenance a much-improved player. But if Liverpool City were indeed a nursery club of sorts, then (as one might suggest) this was a pretty good deal all-round. Certainly when that aforementioned Saints programme of 13 March 1962 noted – perhaps with a degree of friendly sarcasm - that Liverpool City were "trying to get the best of both worlds", they were not very far from the mark. Former rugby union hooker Bob Burdell was also transferred by Liverpool City to St Helens at the very end of 1963. He made his debut for St Helens against Keighley in January 1964 and went on to play 27 times for the Saints before moving to Salford the following year.

From Jeff Heaton's comments it also remains a moot point whether the introduction of two divisions during the 1970s was advantageous to the Huyton club. Huyton were certainly denied the chance of regular money-spinners against their local rivals and although rugby league action between City and Saints was usually a predictable David and Goliath encounter, with St Helens always having the edge, matches between the two sides were keenly contested affairs. Many of the St Helens-based City players wore their green and white jerseys with great pride and the likes of Ernie Forber, Arthur Johnson, Ray Ashby, George Walker, Bill Adair, and the aforementioned Jeff Heaton were keen to do well against their home-town team.

As has been seen, City also raided nearby Widnes for their juniors, reserves and squad members. It was noted by the Widnes RLFC programme editor on 29 February

1964 that there "will be quite a number of former Chemics in the Liverpool team today, because there are 10 Widnesians on the Knotty Ash club's books." A large number of former Widnes players turned out for City including Ronnie Bate, Jimmy Bright, Tom Galligan, Harold Lamb, Arnie Mort, Bob Sherman, Johnny Smith, Tom Smith, and John Thompson, to mention but a few. It must be stated in Liverpool's defence however, that this poaching of players from the rugby league triangle of St Helens, Warrington and Widnes was not restricted to City scouts and officials.

Salford RLFC, for example, played their rugby in Weaste, a district of their city – Salford – immediately next door to Manchester. Unlike Liverpool, Salford was a renowned rugby league city, but could not consistently produce players of the required standard without close rivals Swinton muscling-in – up until the mid-to-late 1960s Swinton were a more successful club than the Reds of Salford. A Salford programme editorial of September 1966, therefore, notes that: "almost like ourselves, the City line-up is composed of players who hail from either Widnes, Warrington or St Helens." [33]

One illustration of the importance of the St Helens, Widnes, Wigan or Warrington rugby journeyman is that of fellow Liverpool City poor relations Blackpool Borough who, like the green and whites, existed in a town with a dearth of rugby league grassroots. Time and again Borough signed junior or reject players from these three towns, only to watch them disappear – lured away by clubs closer to home territory. An example of the former would be Brian Winstanley. Second-row forward Winstanley was voted Blackpool Borough player of the year at the end of the 1966–67 season but despite this honour he signed for Liverpool City the following season simply to be nearer his home in Widnes. One must also bear in mind of course that the majority of rugby league professionals held down full-time jobs throughout the working week.

Warrington

Warrington has always been a major crossing point on the Mersey river – there was an important Roman settlement at Wilderspool. The town also played a significant role in the English Civil War with the armies of both Oliver Cromwell and the Earl of Derby encamped near the old town centre. Throughout the 20th century Warrington was renown for the production of steel – particularly wire – textiles, brewing, tanning and chemicals. When these heavy industries declined in the 1970s and 1980s, the growth of new industrial estates on the outskirts of Warrington adjacent to the M6 and M62 motorways ensured increased employment in light industry, distribution, and technology and for some people Warrington became a boom town in the mid-to-late 1980s.

Many people know the name of Warrington for two reasons. First, as the location of the Second World War Burtonwood RAF base, one of largest such bases in England and certainly the largest US Air Force base outside the United States. The base was closed in 1993. Secondly, for the Warrington rugby league team: a game synonymous with the Borough of Warrington.

Warrington Zingari RFC was founded in 1879 by Timothy Grix of Chatburn. The club committee managed to get the use of a field fronting Sankey Street, while the headquarters of the club were at the White Hart Hotel in Sankey Street. The first match was an away fixture against the Liverpool-based Walton side (see chapter 1). This game was played at Rice Field in Liverpool on 18 October 1879 and Walton won by three goals to nil. The first home game for the club was at Sankey Street against Oughtrington, with Warrington gaining their first victory by three goals to one. In their first season

Warrington played 11 games, won seven, lost two and drew two. Another local club, Padgate Excelsior amalgamated with Warrington in 1881-1882 to form a representative town side. On 29 August 1895, the committee decided to join with 20 other clubs throughout Lancashire and Yorkshire to form the new Northern Union. The club gradually became a major force in the development of the rugby league code and during the Second World War the committee decided that a limited company of 10,000 £1 shares was to be created. Warrington Football Club Ltd was born.

The early post-war years produced glory for the club. Brian Bevan made his debut for Warrington in 1945. Over the next 16 seasons he scored 740 tries for them in 620 games. With other stars such as Harry Bath and Gerry Helme, the Wire won all the major honours, including the League Championship for the only times in their history in 1947–48, 1953–54 and 1954–55. These years firmly established rugby league football as the premier sport in the Borough and as a consequence a surplus of players emerged from the schools and amateur game. It was under these circumstances that other local clubs profited – none-the-least being Liverpool Stanley and Liverpool City.

The Warrington club was very prominent in the continuance of the Liverpool Stanley and City – even though the Wire also circled the club for tasty tit-bits should the opportunity arise. Signings by the Wire from Liverpool include Bill Derbyshire, Bill Belshaw, Tom Blinkhorn, and (via Oldham) Bill Payne.

Warrington amateur rugby league continues to be strong to this day and Stanley, City, Huyton and their progenitors made many a capture from the ranks of Warrington junior football. Perhaps the most illustrious of these were the Heesom brothers, Alec and Albert, who having signed from Crosfields, a prominent Warrington amateur club, played with great distinction for City and Huyton in the late 1960s and early to mid 1970s. Indeed, one might even cite a further example of the rugby league triangle journeyman in the case of Terry Ollier. Halifax signed Ollier in May 1958 from Warrington amateur rugby league – he had been the captain of the England Amateur rugby league team. Ollier played at centre three-quarter when in the Halifax first team, but he appears to have spent most of his time at Thrum Hall captaining the reserves. The Halifax programme editor said in December 1960: "Travelling was the main cause of Terry seeking a transfer. Living in Warrington it was most irksome for him to travel to Thrum Hall twice a week for training sessions. In the best interests of the player we therefore allowed him to join Liverpool and it is pleasing to note that he has become a big asset to his new club." [34]

Ollier probably wasn't quite up to the mark as far as Halifax was concerned. For Liverpool City, however, he performed well for the 1960–61 season, scoring a few important tries along the way. Throughout the first half of the 1961–62 season he was missing from the Liverpool line-up with J.C. Gregson stating on 2 December: "It will be some time... before Ollier is able to play again". Either injured or heavily committed to his daytime job, Ollier did return to the side for a handful of games that spring but then appears to have left Liverpool City altogether – an all-too familiar story. Other former Warrington players to appear on Merseyside include the former Huyton skipper John Smith, Jim Challinor, Doug Clarke, Jim Trainor, Stan McCormick, and Barney Losh, among many others.

Doug Clarke had left Warrington during the 1964–65 season after a bad ankle injury halted his progress at Wilderspool. He joined Liverpool on the recommendation of Bill Payne and because there were so many Warrington players in the squad at that time and transport could be shared. He moved into a player-coach position and led the 'A' team to the club's only stab at post-war honours when, in 1967–68, the reserves reached the final of the Lancashire Combination Shield. It was Clarke who brought the Heesom brothers to Liverpool and combining coaching with scouting continued his time with the club into their transition to Huyton. Doug was in charge for the first-ever game at Alt Park versus Widnes 'A' and for the official opening first team game versus Salford on 10 August 1969 when he temporarily took charge of the first team from Jack Broome, who was on holiday.

Even for some Warrington fans, Liverpool City meant something a bit special. Tommy McCarthy recalls: "The green and white hoops meant only one thing to a Wire fan: an assured victory but with a difference: respect! Respect, that is, for a team that did everything to keep rugby league alive on Merseyside. Surrounded as they were by not only the resurgent Liverpool and Everton football teams but also Saints and Wigan, not to mention the superb Widnes outfit of that time, all providing not a hope in hell of a decent share of the spoils from such a huge catchment area. Yet even among all that, you got 100 per cent of everything from Liverpool City. After all, that was all they could give to the great game we all loved. How ironic, then, that one of the worst teams of that era was not the men in green and white hoops, but the now-mighty Bradford Bulls (known then as Bradford Northern). Liverpool City? We Warrington fans loved 'em!" [35]

It was also a 'family affair' in southwest Lancashire. For example, besides the Heesom brothers, the Huyton club at one stage had on their books four Westhead brothers and these four were in turn related to the Chisnalls of St Helens, Leigh and Warrington. Rugby league was (and to some extent remains) an internecine affair. Further research into the ancestral origins of all rugby league professionals might indicate that the game is even more geographically narrow than its most hardened fans would probably admit. The Warrington connection continues even to this day. Former City player Eric Seed, who lives in Warrington, runs the Liverpool City Past Players Association. If truth be told, the entire history of professional rugby league would not be the same without the players provided by the towns of St Helens, Warrington, Widnes and Wigan.

It was certainly clear to all observers of rugby league in the mid-1960s that, notwithstanding a few notable exceptions, a regular stream of rugby league journeymen and 'nearly' men - both young and old - from that rugby league triangle would forever grace the Knotty Ash Stadium pitch. As a city, Liverpool was not only unable to produce rugby league players of any note, it was actually unable to produce any players for this code at all.

This paucity begs the question that must have crossed the collective minds of the Liverpool City board of directors on several occasions: what on earth was this spirited rugby league club actually doing in Liverpool? In spite of everything (and to their eternal credit – and the mystification of most observers), the club even cultivated one or two promising younger players and, contrasting the Heaton deal, the occasional more lucrative transfer to larger clubs ensued.

In the latter days of the Stanley era Bill Riley and Bill Derbyshire were transferred to Warrington and Teddy Cahill to Rochdale Hornets for not inconsiderable transfer fees. As the 1960s dawned, Bill Payne left Liverpool City for Oldham for a sizeable fee, whereas in the mid-1960s full-back Ray Ashby and hooker Bob Burdell both left for more lucrative pastures at Wigan and St Helens respectively, leaving Liverpool City once more bereft of their best talent but with money in the bank.

Ray Ashby

Pride of place must go to Liverpool City's one international: Ray Ashby. From the moment the long-serving Ashby joined Liverpool City from St Helens junior club Blackbrook in 1956 he was the subject of constant transfer enquiries from City's more wealthy neighbours and, despite occasional transfer speculation he remained loyal to the Liverpool club for more than eight years. Ray was the skipper of the Blackbrook 18-21 age group side. They had won the Lancashire Youth Cup in 1956 and Liverpool City signed most of this successful side with the intention of having them compete for 'A' team places. Almost immediately, however, Ashby was selected for the first team and he proceeded to play with great merit as a threequarter for the majority of the 1956–57 season, scoring three tries in the process. The following season he converted from a threequarter to a full-back and it was in that latter position that he really made his mark. Harry Ody recalls Ray as "a very good player and also a very hard man." Ody remembers Ashby colliding with a goalpost in training one evening. "He said he was fine but he had lost three of his teeth!"

Former City forward John McGrath also remembers playing "with Ray Ashby for a long time and he was a class act even then; he loved to run with the ball but sometimes had no pattern to it – he'd run this way and that. I found out if you ran behind Ray down the centre of the field about 10 yards behind him you were doing the right thing – the ball would often come to you!" [36] Ashby was finally tempted away by Wigan in March 1964 for an undisclosed fee. He was at first unaware that Wigan were interested and only knew about the deal when it had all been settled in the respective boardrooms. He later informed the author that he never saw any of his percentage of the fee, even though he had not requested this transfer. Ray went on to distinguish himself for Wigan RLFC in the 1964–65 Challenge Cup Final 20–16 defeat of Hunslet at Wembley Stadium. With Hunslet's Brian Gabbitas he shared the Lance Todd Trophy that day. Of that 1965 Challenge Cup Final, Harry Edgar was later to acknowledge it as "a final that will always be remembered for the joint award to Ashby and Gabbitas, the former recently recruited by Wigan from Liverpool City and the latter in his 13th season with the Parksiders." [37] Ray Ashby was also capped for Great Britain against France at Leigh on 18 March 1964, a 39–0 home win, while still captaining Liverpool City.

There were no further international caps for Liverpool players. However, a handful of post-Second World War Stanley and City players were good enough to receive Lancashire county caps – a genuine mark of distinction. They included forward Riley and winger Aspinall of Stanley, who received county honours in 1946, Ted Cahill, Ray Ashby, John Thompson and Bill Payne (who, although having two spells at Knotty Ash, gained his county honours while with Oldham). Once Harry Ody had returned to the amateur ranks he went on to receive his Lancashire Amateur cap.

We know that statistics never tell the whole story. And by massaging statistics the Rugby League Council were able to convince itself that the city of Liverpool was a potentially thriving development area. There could be no argument that the presence of Liverpool Stanley and Liverpool City altered to a degree the sporting profile of Merseyside, but for how long and to what depth of interest is more difficult to fathom.

To a large extent players and enthusiasts from St Helens, Widnes, Warrington and Wigan inevitably propped up the club. It was an inescapable syndrome: without the assistance of these local players and fans the club could not survive. Yet without the Liverpool accent in abundance, the club could not prosper. Therefore, despite various

Ray Ashby

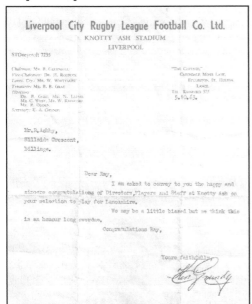

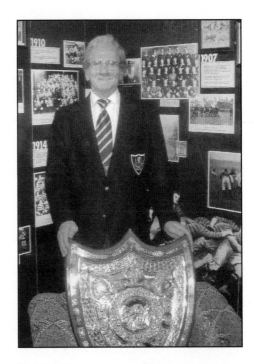

Ray Ashby – Liverpool City's only Great Britain player.
Top left: A letter from the club congratulating Ray on his selection for Lancashire
Top right: At the Gillette Rugby League Heritage Centre in 2008
Bottom: Liverpool City versus Widnes, April 1958: Saving a try. From left: Fishwick, Broome
(Widnes), Ashby tackling Bale, Tomlinson (Widnes), Galligan (Widnes), not known.
(All illustrations courtesy Ray Ashby)

attempts at development programmes throughout Liverpool City's existence the game did not flourish in Liverpool - indeed was hardly played post-war – at school level, the local clubs such as Rangers and Hornets played on the fringes of the city, and the professional club was regarded by one section of the community as an anomaly and by the other as a betrayal of the rugby union code. It was clear to all that for rugby league to prosper in Liverpool, Liverpudlians had to play the game. But for this to occur, the club and the code had to capture the imagination of the local sporting public.

Rugby league had been around long enough to be regarded as a quintessentially northern activity, this image of northern-ness was different from Liverpudlian. Rugby league could not compete with Liverpool's football heritage and myths. Local resident Mick O'Toole was later to recall the presence of Liverpool City as a local attraction: "As a schoolboy in the early 1950s and living about a mile from the ground, on several occasions (with a few mates) we would wander that way on a Saturday afternoon. The fencing around the ground consisted mainly of corrugated iron sheeting and was in a very poor state of repair with gaps everywhere. Naturally we would pop in through the holes to avoid paying at the gate. None of us had any particular interest in the game, it was just somewhere to go motivated by curiosity as to what went on in there. Usually we would get fed-up in a very short time and leave the same way we came. On a couple of occasions, we were actually chased out by the stewards or some club members." [38]

On the evidence of this comment, any attempt to develop a Liverpudlian rugby league team derived from and representing an indigenous sporting culture, was doomed from the very beginning.

Endnotes

[1] Edgar, Harry (2003), 'League and Liverpool', *Rugby League Journal* 5 winter 2003, Egremont: Edgar Publishing, pp.20-22

[2] 'Merman', 'On, Stanley, on! New Haven and Rising Hopes at Liverpool', *Rugby League Review*, 24 February 1950, p.5

[3] 'Editorial' [possibly J.A. Williams], *Liverpool Stanley Official Programme* [versus Widnes], 2 January, 1939, p.3

[4] Creston (1894), 'Football', *The Fortnightly Review* 55, p.30 cited in Boucher, David (2000), *Steel, Skill & Survival: Rugby In Ebbw Vale and the Valleys (1870-1952)*, Ebbw Vale: Ebbw Vale Rugby Football Club Ltd.

[5] Interview with Mick O'Toole, 17 September 2007

[6] Melling, Phil (2007), 'From Wigan to Wales: The 1970s and Beyond', *Rugby League Annual Review 2007* [eds. Dave Farrar & Peter Lush], London: London League Publications. p.41

[7] *ibid* pp.40-41

[8] 'Merseyside Amateur Rugby League', *Liverpool Stanley Official Programme* [versus Leigh] 27 August 1949, p.8

[9] Unaccredited programme editor, 'Editorial', *Liverpool City Official Programme* [versus Wigan], 28 August 1954, p.2

[10] Interview with George Walker 24 November 2007

[11] Unaccredited 'Supporters Club Notes', *Liverpool City Official Programme* [versus St Helens], 21 April 1962, p.7

[12] J.C. Gregson, 'Editorial', *Liverpool City Official Programme* [versus Salford], 9 November 1963, p.5

[13] J.C. Gregson, 'Editorial', *Liverpool City Official Programme* [versus Rochdale Hornets], 27 March 1965, p.2

[14] [possibly club secretary] H. Murray, untitled editorial, *Saints Programme* [official programme of St Helens RLFC – versus Liverpool Stanley], 15 November 1947, pp. 4-5

[15] Liverpool Stanley Committee Minutes 12 June 1950 housed at University of Huddersfield

[16] Unaccredited programme editor's notes, *Saints Programme* [versus Liverpool City], 13 March 1962, p.2

[17] Unaccredited 'Editorial', *Liverpool City Official Programme* [versus Wigan] 27 April 1961, p.2

[18] Vickers, A, 'Supporters' Club Notes', *Liverpool City Official Programme* [versus Doncaster], 2 December 1961, p.7

[19] J.C. Gregson, 'Editorial', *Liverpool City Official Programme* [versus St Helens], 21 April 1962, p.2

[20] Whittle, Denis, to Mike Latham (2004), 'Mike Latham's Groundhopper's Guide', *Rugby League World*, February 2004, p.42

[21] Taylor, R. J., 'Our Visitors', *Saints Programme* [the official programme of St Helens RLFC: versus Liverpool City], 4 April 1953, p.4

[22] Unaccredited programme editor, 'Editorial', *Liverpool City Official Programme* [versus St Helens], 2 October 1954, p.2

[23] [probably] Wood, J.B. [Secretary Wigan RLFC], 'Official Notes', *Wigan Official Programme* [versus Liverpool City], 28 March 1964

[24] Interview with Jack Broome, 21 September 2007

[25] Interview with John McGrath, 21 September 2007

[26] Interview with Jack Broome, 21 September 2007

[27] Interview with Tom Galligan and John McGrath, 21 September 2007

[28] Gordon Brown interview with Wilf Hunt (2004), 'Memories Of Liverpool City', *Our Game 9* Spring, London: London League Publications, p.6

[29] Interview with John McGrath, 21 September 2007

[30] *ibid*

[31] Interview with Harry Ody, 22 November 2007

[32] Service, Alex (1989?), 'Return of the Saint', *Code 13*, issue 17

[33] Unaccredited programme editor, 'Our Visitors', *Salford Football Club Official Programme* [versus Liverpool City], 28 September 1966, p.3

[34] Unaccredited programme editor, 'Sports Chat', *Halifax RLFC Official Programme* [versus Liverpool City], 3 December 1960, pp.3-4

[35] Tommy McCarthy, e-mail correspondence with author, 11 April, 2007

[36] Interview with John McGrath, 21 September 2007

[37] Edgar, Harry (2005), 'Magical Matches: The 1965 Challenge Cup Final At Wembley: Wigan 20 – Hunslet 16', *Rugby League Journal 11*, Egremont: Edgar Publishing, pp.20-21

[38] Interview with Mick O'Toole, 18 October 2006

7. Better times ahead? The 1960s

Notwithstanding the apathy from the people and press of Liverpool, the Knotty Ash pitch continued to improve as a playing surface, the Supporters' Club bar under the grandstand flourished and, most significantly, so too did the pools and the Liverpool City Social Club at Derby Lane. By the early 1960s the social club was raising about £600 per annum for the rugby club. The 'Club Notes' in the 12 September Liverpool City programme for the match against Warrington read: "This week the Supporter's Club have presented the parent club with a donation of £100, which the Directors fully appreciate; this, combined with the £25 per month from the Social Club is indeed gratifying". The aforementioned pools were also helping to balance the books; in January 1959 the Wigan programme editor noted "Their lottery has made good progress and is now bringing them in a weekly income of over £100, which must be a Godsend to their harassed directors." [1] These ambitious projects initially thrived and provided important funding for a more high-profile coaching, if not necessarily playing staff.

For instance, in February 1961 Liverpool City replaced coach Doug Greenall with Don Gullick. The Liverpool City pen picture of Gullick, printed in their programme for 15 December 1962 against York, read: "Don, who is a native of Abersychan, near Pontypool joined us midway through season 1960–61 from St Helens, where he had played as centre for several seasons. He played rugby union with Pontypool and gained county honours with Monmouth and was captain of the county team. He played for St Helens at Wembley in the 1955–56 Final but unfortunately did not get a winner's medal as St Helens lost 15–10 to Huddersfield. A schoolmaster, Don is at Ashton Grammar School, near Wigan. The good work he has put in at Liverpool City is now beginning to show results and we wish him good luck and success in the future."

Greenall's tenure in this somewhat thankless position had only lasted a few months, but first team coaches did not last very long at Knotty Ash. This might appear at first glance to be as a consequence of poor results; however, the Liverpool board only appointed coaching and playing staff one season at a time, at the discretion of the incoming coach who was free to leave at any moment he wished. This arrangement existed in full appreciation that coaches and players, alike, were usually involved with City as either a stepping-stone to bigger and better things, or as a way of playing their way into retirement.

In the case of Greenall, the Halifax RLFC programme editor in his jottings for December 1960 recognised both his credentials and the task ahead and was to rather condescendingly remark: "It is a pleasure to note that a man of Greenall's talent is preparing to devote his energies to imparting knowledge and skill to those who have been less blessed than himself. We wish him every success in his efforts to develop the talent at his disposal".[2] There were more poisoned-chalice remarks from a Halifax programme editor who appears to have known something that the Liverpool City Board did not – that perhaps Doug Greenall was not long for Knotty Ash Stadium. Sadly for Greenall he was a publican and could not keep up the pace of coaching a professional rugby league side and running a pub.

To their eternal credit the board realistically refused to stand in anybody's way and transfer requests were practically always granted. A few lines from a 1959 Liverpool City programme illustrate this well: "Billy Adams has been given permission to try his luck elsewhere, he wishes to get a club nearer his home. It was stated in the press last

Saturday, we had put a price of £2,000 on Ray Ashby, we do not know how this figure came about, but we do know we have no desire to transfer Ray. Although enquiries were made, we are more anxious to strengthen the team, not weaken it." [3]

From time to time some transfer-listed players spent long stretches on the register – they wanted away, but being considered not good enough by other professional clubs. John Thompson is an example: transfer-listed, then a trialist at Wigan during September and October 1966, but returning to Liverpool's register when he was not required at Central Park. A few, like class act Ray Ashby, were dogged by press reports of transfers (probably arising from a mixture of player's ability, and club instability) but remained loyal to City – until, in Ashby's case, one day in 1965 when an undisclosed offer from Wigan was too good to refuse.

For example, by announcing in September 1959 that Ashby was not for sale those Liverpool City 'Club Notes' above were responding to the pressure evidently forced upon them by constant speculation among a local rugby press that did not always have City's best interests at heart. The speculation did not so much report on, but feed the transfer market. City were lucky indeed that Ashby remained as loyal as he did. In fact Ray Ashby told *Our Game* writer Gordon Brown that the one thing that stood out for him as a City player was "the team spirit. It was one for all and all for one. We were all in it together." [4] This is a remarkable comment from a man who was probably far more talented than many of his colleagues. The eventual transfer deal was undisclosed at the time but was, according to Ray, probably in the region of £5,000.

Like Doug Greenall, the recognised hard man in the mid-1950s St Helens threequarter line, coach Don Gullick was a highly rated former professional player, having previously represented Wales at international level and served St Helens, Leeds and Leigh with some distinction. But even when the Warrington club came calling for his services shortly after he had agreed to coach Liverpool City, the City board still allowed him an opt-out, should he have wanted it. The Liverpool programme editorial from 4 March 1961 reported: "All at City… are delighted that our coach, Don Gullick, has informed Warrington of his desire to remain with us. This is a real tonic for us and augurs well for the future." [5]

With Ike Fishwick, another former St Helens and Warrington team member playing out his career with City, who took care of the 'A' team and youngsters, these professionals, together with the income from the social club and the remains of a £3,000 windfall from the sale of Liverpudlian Bill Payne to Oldham in the spring of 1960, held the promise of better times ahead.

That Bill Payne transfer was another indication of the equity established between players and officials at Knotty Ash Stadium. The Liverpool City programme 'Club Notes' illustrates this well: "In the sporting world, this is certainly a week of records – the Grand National televised; a multi-millionaire joining the board of a well-known local Football Club; and Liverpool City collecting a record fee for the transfer of Billy Payne.

The last event is what concerns our supporters, and the Board feels that they should know something of the background to this transfer.

Often, in the past, it has been said that City want to buy and build, not have to sell. Paradoxically, that is still true, because on many occasions the City board have discouraged potential buyers of some of our best players. Some months ago, a leading Lancashire club offered a large sum of money for a City player, but the player was not willing to move house, and so a possible deal did not materialise. The board left it entirely to the player, and with his decision, the matter ended.

138

Left: South African Duncan Pikoli, who played for Liverpool City in the early 1960s.
Right: John Thompson.

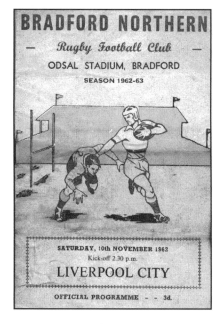

DONCASTER		LIVERPOOL
BLUE & GOLD		GREEN & WHITE
1 PRICE	- Full Back -	1 ASHBY
2 SMITH	- Right Wing -	2 PRICE
3 DAVIES	- Right Centre -	3 HUNT
4 ASKIN	- Left Centre -	4 RAINFORD
5 Mortimer/Precious	- Left Wing -	5 FARRELL
6 REED	- Out Half -	6 WALKER, G.
7 Downs/Doyle	- Scrum Half -	7 WALKER, J.
8 Yemm/Robinson	Prop Forward	8 UPTON
9 WAKEFIELD	- Hooker -	9 BURDELL
10 HEPWORTH	Prop Forward	10 CARTLEDGE
11 SWALES	2nd Row Fwd.	11 LAMB
12 ROSE	2nd Row Fwd.	12 HIGHAM
13 BOWERS	Loose Forward	13 MULLEE

Referee: N. T. Railton.   Touch Judges: H. Squires, W. Todman.

Rare away wins:

Doncaster Rovers 3 Liverpool City 5, 28 October 1961

Bradford Northern 2 Liverpool City 7, 10 November 1962

Turning to our latest transfer, it was a really 'Payne-ful' operation because everyone had the highest regard for Billy. A model clubman, an enthusiastic trainer, and a great-hearted player, big things could be in store for him, and all connected with Liverpool City – directors, training staff, players etc., wish him lots of luck in the future... The directors must now decide how to deal with this windfall – remember Payne was not on the transfer list and Oldham made the approach to City – but supporters can rest assured that every effort will be made to strengthen the team." [6]

Former City forward John McGrath recalls: "When I first went there Ike Fishwick was still there – and Billy Payne. I played with both. 'Pep' Donegan took over training for a while. Some of the people they picked to be coaches shouldn't have really been there. But you ask any player that played at Liverpool City – and a lot of them had played at other clubs as well – they'd tell you that the atmosphere was absolutely brilliant. Jeff Heaton and Arthur Johnson from St Helens enjoyed it too. Heaton went back to St Helens a better player." [7]

While Payne's transfer to Oldham in 1960 pleased board and bank manager alike, it was spoiled somewhat by the knowledge that both Barrow and St Helens had offered in excess of Oldham's £3,000. However, for the Craven Park club, "the old work and residence bogey would have again reared up its head". [8] In other words Barrow would have felt obliged to find part-time employment and a home for yet another player who came from the 'Rugby League Triangle' – which they appeared loathe so to do – early signs perhaps of the game of rugby league struggling at its fringes to find new blood.

The City directors, feeling obliged to strengthen the team, used some of the Payne windfall to dabble – mostly unsuccessfully – in the transfer market. Two unrelated examples of incoming players – probably way past their best – illustrate the frustrations of attempting to get recruits of the required standard to turn out for Liverpool City. For the 1962–63 season City brought in the displaced Oldham player George Warburton to play alongside long-serving prop Jim Cartledge. However, Warburton's move from Oldham to Liverpool City turned out to be an utter waste of money; he announced that he was to emigrate to South Africa by the end of the season. Towards the end of the same season they signed Huddersfield scrum-half Terry Gorman for a substantial fee but, sadly, Gorman never showed anything like his Huddersfield form and by November of the following season he had also left the club.

Both deals burned the collective fingers of the board and from that point local contacts rather than transfer-based contracts were of most use to the Liverpool City directors. Second-row forward Tom Galligan recalls his arrival at Knotty Ash being a consequence of the direct intervention of Bill Whittaker: "I'd left Widnes in 1962 and was going to give the game up professionally and play for St Marie's... you know, put a bit back into the game. But Bill Whittaker and Ken Grundy came to see me and said 'It's the new Second Division and we're playing Bradford Northern'. I wasn't very enthusiastic and they said 'how much are you on for Maries against Crosfields, Tom?' I said 'I don't know', and they said 'Well we play Bradford and you're on £10,' which was a lot of money – so we shook hands. Blow me Harry Owen also turned up and we beat Bradford 17–9. This was the first season of the new Second Division – and we did well. Dave Cox was there for a while as a player but also as a coach. He went to Oldham and Dewsbury and then went out to Australia with the Co-op. He only took over briefly; but with Jack [Broome] coming in 1963 things did change.

Jack was such a good coach it made you stay. Former players from Widnes were coming through and St Helens and Warrington fringe players were arriving because of

Bill Whittaker and Ken Grundy. It was a good place to be especially in the two seasons of Second Division football – we were up there with the best. It was really good company. What I found was that you were playing for and with the same people every week and you respected that... but it didn't feel like a Liverpool club. We had a bunch of university lads who would follow us around - home or away. But there was nothing noticeably 'Scouse', with one or two exceptions, one by the name of Frank, as I remember." [9]

Two divisions and another big freeze

Despite the previously discussed practical progress made by the club, out of 77 first-class fixtures played over the 1960–61 and 1961–62 seasons, Liverpool claimed victory on only 11 occasions. Moreover, by the final run-in for 1961–62, it was clear that City had all but lost interest in a season that had, as usual, become somewhat meaningless for them after the turn of the year – perhaps proving the desperate need for some kind of promotion and relegation dogfight to take place in the Rugby League Championship which was soon to be introduced. Only three matches were won between 6 January and 23 April 1962 all against fellow strugglers – 19–8 at Odsal against the dramatically declining Bradford Northern, 13–10 at the Athletic Grounds versus Rochdale Hornets, and 22–10 at home to Blackpool Borough. But sights were being set on the new Second Division the following season.

1960–61 Northern Rugby League (bottom six teams)

25 Keighley	36	10	1	25	349	553	21
26 Barrow	36	9	2	25	305	578	20
27 Dewsbury	36	8	3	25	296	573	19
28 Rochdale Hornets	36	9	0	27	296	733	18
29 Liverpool City	**36**	**5**	**1**	**30**	**296**	**768**	**11**
30 Doncaster	36	3	0	33	287	768	6

1961–62 Northern Rugby League (bottom six teams)

25 Hunslet	36	10	1	25	350	582	21
26 Batley	36	9	2	25	255	538	20
27 Dewsbury	36	8	2	26	260	543	18
28 Doncaster	36	8	1	27	294	668	17
29 Liverpool City	**36**	**6**	**0**	**30**	**224**	**753**	**12**
30 Bradford Northern	36	5	1	30	288	766	11

In an attempt to reduce polarisation and increase competition the Rugby Football League experimented with a two-division system between 1962 and 1964. The dwindling interest in fixtures following the turn of the year repeatedly worried the Liverpool City board. They felt that the Rugby League Championship was too unwieldy and overly favoured those clubs with a chance of a play-off place. In fact if a club had also been knocked out of the Challenge Cup by February, there was effectively nothing left to play for. Season after season the City board had experienced a severe decline in interest during the second half of the season which was only relieved by home fixtures against the local giants. At the very least it was thought the move to two divisions would create a competitive edge, thus perhaps attracting more support. The Liverpool City board expressed support for the two-division idea as early as 1961, as the following programme notes suggest: "Something must be done to keep interest alive in the lower reaches of the League table. At the start of each season every club is full of hope for their best ever season, but come the turn of the year, and defeat in the cup, plus a low position in the league, means merely a fulfilling of fixtures. But interest would be sustained were two divisions in existence, with relegation and promotion factors playing their part." [10]

Notwithstanding this unilateral support for the Second Division concept, come the final home game of 1961–62, programme editor J.C. Gregson was expressing some misgivings about the two division split. Discussing the fixture against St Helens he stated: "We shall miss our games with them [St Helens] but may yet meet them in the Cup or the Western R.L.F. Championship." Economics were playing their part in this expression of unease – City might defeat the likes of Batley and Blackpool Borough and in the process proceed to the higher reaches of the Second Division, but where were the lucrative takings associated with visits from the Saints?

While early season coffers-boosting derby matches against their larger local rivals remained on the Liverpool City fixture list, the more successful St Helens, Warrington, Widnes and Wigan clubs had become automatic members of the new First Division, and such fixtures against City were only relevant in terms of a newly introduced Western Regional League placing – a some what artificial competition staged to provide more fixtures. The appeal of these fixtures was therefore reduced in the minds of the travelling fans and perhaps, as forewarned by Gregson, attendances and results reflected a widely felt lack of interest.

This was further diluted for that opening Second Division 1962–63 season when the Rugby Football League decreed all eight Western Regional League fixtures were to be played at the beginning of the season. The league campaign proper therefore did not get under way until October, a ridiculous state of affairs for all clubs concerned, but particularly for minnows such as Liverpool City. For two solid months long-suffering City supporters watched their more illustrious neighbours putting City to the sword. Thankfully, for the following 1963–64 season these Western League games were dotted around the fixture list, but Liverpool City had seen their previously lucrative fixtures against the local giants reduced to little more than friendly fixtures and by the end were fielding reserves, squad players and trialists. Needless to say City's variable selections were defeated in all 16 of these Western League fixtures during this two-division era.

The 1962–63 Second Division season proper began well for City; in fact they held on to second place in the league table for several weeks at the start of the season. But, overall, playing consistency did not improve sufficiently to prevail over an entire term and, despite winning nine and drawing one of their 26 Second Division fixtures, Liverpool still finished in the bottom four and Don Gullick's contract was not extended.

The dreadful winter weather from the end of 1962 into March 1963 might have contributed to this decline. City stalwart Ray Hockenhull recalled: "We did not play for weeks and had to train in a shed. We were drawn in the first round of the Challenge Cup against Roose from Barrow-in–Furness. We could not play on our own ground, but Warrington referee Charlie Appleton, who worked at Widnes ICI, put some stuff called GL5 on the [Widnes RLFC] Naughton Park pitch and it was deemed playable. So we played there. A lot of Widnes people came along to the game, but when we knocked down a Roose player they booed us, and when Roose knocked one of us down, they cheered. It was because they were amateurs. Roose had a good team, but in the end we won." [11]

Action from Liverpool City versus St Helens 30 April 1962: Northey on the end of a high tackle.
(Courtesy Alex Service)

St Helens versus Liverpool City 8 September 1962: Parker attempts to tackle Tom van Vollenhoven
(Courtesy Alex Service)

Oldham versus Liverpool City in the early 1960s
(Courtesy Alex Service)

Liverpool City versus St Helens 10 September 1966 (Courtesy Alex Service)

Benefit collection at a Liverpool City versus St Helens match (Courtesy Alex Service)

Another new coach for Liverpool City (Courtesy Alex Service)

City's best period on the pitch came before the big freeze of that winter started. Between October and December they played 11 consecutive league matches: winning six and drawing one. But then Liverpool did not play another game of rugby until 9 February, when Roose were beaten 11–0 in the Challenge Cup as outlined above. Another gap of a month followed before they beat Blackpool Borough 5–3 on 9 March. On the heels of this, however, City's season went into freefall. Between 16 March and 1 June Liverpool played 15 matches and won only two: at home to Doncaster 9–7 and at Salford 16–11.

It came as little surprise to rugby league supporters when the two-division experiment was written-off in February 1964 only halfway through its three-year trial period. In some respects this was a pity, for the two-division system at least gave all clubs something to play for right up until the end of the season, whereas the unwieldy size of the Rugby League Championship effectively penalised clubs outside the top 16. But although the Liverpool City board had initially welcomed the two-division approach, they did not vote to continue it.

1962–63 Second Division

1 Hunslet	26	22	0	4	508	214	44
2 Keighley	26	21	0	5	450	187	42
-----							
3 York	26	16	1	9	418	243	33
4 Blackpool Borough	26	15	0	11	281	247	30
5 Rochdale Hornets	26	14	1	11	282	243	29
6 Barrow	26	14	0	12	413	280	28
7 Leigh	26	14	0	12	361	264	28
8 Batley	26	13	1	12	275	322	27
9 Whitehaven	26	12	2	12	318	306	26
10 Doncaster	26	10	0	16	283	329	20
11 Liverpool City	**26**	**9**	**1**	**16**	**159**	**328**	**19**
12 Salford	26	8	1	17	271	442	17
13 Dewsbury	26	8	0	18	200	345	16
14 Bradford Northern	26	2	1	23	163	632	5

The Liverpool City programme editorial on 8 February 1964 announced that City now "favoured one division" and it was clear that they were to vote accordingly at the extraordinary meeting called by the Rugby League Council for the following week. It was a case of pragmatics for Liverpool City; with gate receipts reliant to a vast degree on visiting supporters as much as, if not more than, home fans, any other verdict would have been akin to turkeys voting for Christmas. How could City survive without regular visits from the local south Lancashire giants?

The City teams sent out on the park had undoubtedly improved since the dark days of the 1950s, but whether they would ever be able to win promotion remained improbable – the best Liverpool could hope for was a conjoined Rugby League Championship. The system was duly scrapped at an extraordinary general meeting of the Rugby Football League in Leeds on 14 February 1964, the verdict being reached on a straight vote by 23–4. Visits from competitive St Helens, Wigan, Widnes and Warrington sides were thus assured for the next season. Eddie Waring – never a fan of Liverpool City, of course – signed the initiative off with a weary resignation at the beginning of the 1964–65 season: "Here we go again, back to the old system of one division for all, good, bad and indifferent. Farewell, for better or worse, to the two-division experiment which died a premature death in mid-season." [12]

1963–64 Second Division

1 Oldham	24	21	1	2	508	168	43
2 Leigh	24	16	2	6	411	224	34
3 Dewsbury	24	15	2	7	239	220	32
4 Barrow	24	14	1	9	351	280	29
5 Bramley	24	14	0	10	300	256	28
6 Blackpool Borough	24	12	1	11	299	303	25
7 York	24	12	0	12	317	250	24
8 Rochdale Hornets	24	8	1	15	209	271	17
9 Liverpool City	**24**	**8**	**1**	**15**	**200**	**261**	**17**
10 Batley	24	8	0	16	174	304	16
11 Whitehaven	24	8	0	16	173	341	16
12 Salford	24	8	0	16	218	392	16
13 Doncaster	24	7	1	16	182	311	15

*Bradford Northern withdrew from the league midway through the season.

Despite the general RLC mismanagement and indecision, and no doubt thanks to the social club and lottery funds, the City board actually announced a trading profit for the year ending May 1963. It was reported on the 7 March 1964 by programme editor J.C. Gregson that: "Last Monday, at City's annual general meeting, it was revealed that we had made a profit of £806 for the year ended May 31, 1963. Last season – the first in the Second Division – showed an increase in gate money over the previous season. This was our best season since coming to Knotty Ash in 1950." [13]

What an amazing little club this was. With everything on the pitch appearing to be working against their very existence, they were coordinating their fund-raising activities so well that they were trading at a profit. There was little in the way of financial support from the Rugby League Council by this stage, either. The City lottery and the Social Club were proving to be vital. Steve Higginson remembers: "In some respects they were ahead of their time. They seemed to be very good at contingency plans and understood all about key revenue streams. The club was very inventive and when you'd turn up for the match you would feel obliged to buy one of those unstapled 8-page programmes they used to print. When it was windy there were bits of programmes blowing around the ground. In the programme you were also invited to buy a badge or a pen, or something. If you left the ground without a programme nor having bought a cup of tea you would feel really guilty. City were quite good at parting you from your money." [14]

Sparks of undoubted quality radiated from Ashby, Burdell, Galligan, and Heaton, not to mention the redoubtable and phenomenal goalkicker Wilf Hunt and when they all fired in this settled side, a few positive results could almost be guaranteed on the heavy Knotty Ash pitch. On a good day City could usually beat Blackpool Borough, Dewsbury, Doncaster, Rochdale Hornets, Whitehaven and York on their own pitch and at times away from home. Batley, Bramley and Oldham were also put to the sword from time to time. These victories served Liverpool City well for although they were known as one of the Rugby Football League's bottom four clubs, they never actually finished bottom of the Championship after the disastrous run between 1951 and 1954.

The occasional encouraging result against the above, and others - there were surprises such as in the 1964–65 season when City beat Swinton 6–4, Warrington 5–0, and Barrow 11–10 over a period of only a few weeks – meant that, barring serious financial difficulties, mostly averted by income from the Derby Lane drinking establishment, continued membership of the league was never brought into question. These good results, incidentally, were actually part of a splendid run: in November and December 1964 and January 1965 a 7–7 draw at home to Blackpool Borough; 6–4 win at Swinton; 5–0 triumph at home to Warrington; 11–3 win at Blackpool Borough; defeats at Leigh and St Helens followed by a narrow 11–10 home win over Barrow.

1964–65 Northern Rugby League (bottom eight teams)

23 Liverpool City	**34**	**10**	**2**	**22**	**248**	**519**	**22**
24 Bramley	34	10	1	23	309	456	21
25 York	34	10	0	24	347	535	20
26 Batley	34	9	1	24	263	613	19
27 Keighley	34	9	0	25	303	592	18
28 Doncaster	34	9	0	25	296	616	18
29 Rochdale Hornets	34	7	1	26	293	493	15
30 Blackpool Borough	34	6	2	26	248	554	14

The Rugby League Council had come to respect Liverpool City as a small but valuable club, battling to keep rugby league alive in a football-dominated city: frequently diminished but never utterly defeated. Scrum-half between 1956 and 1964 and captain for three seasons, George Walker, called to mind: "Although we were a lowly sort of team, the spirit was fantastic. We were a small club who gave our all. We were always outweighed, but competed." [15]

Indeed, after arrangements were made to move the club to Huyton, Bill Fallowfield even went so far as to suggest that he considered City a "pace-setting" club. Writing in 1968 he stated: "Look at Liverpool City. They had no 'diddy' people working miracles for them at Knotty Ash. What did they do?

Simply this: they built a new ground and a new social club at neighbouring Huyton – the name by which they will now be known. The same can be said of Bramley – a new ground and a new social club in the last year or two. Let's hope this pace-setting duo get the rewards they richly deserve. They, like me, have confidence in the future of the game." [16]

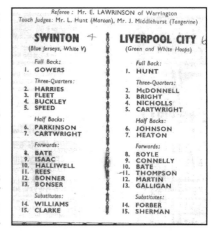

A great win at Swinton

They continued to be on the end of some hidings, however. The author's first visit to the Knotty Ash Stadium as a boy was to witness a home match versus the mighty Wigan in 1964. City eventually lost a one-sided game 34–5. I neither understood the rules nor paid to get in; perhaps typical of a diminutive Scouse 10-year-old, I took advantage of my size and was able to squeeze into the ground past a piece of rusting corrugated metal on the side opposite the main stand. That old structure from the popular side at St Helens' Knowsley Road ground, donated to City to provide some cover for the hardcore of long-suffering supporters, neither encouraged disinterested Liverpudlian football fans, such as Mick O'Toole, nor discouraged interested non-payers such as myself!

As the 1950s turned into the 1960s, declining attendances and unsteady finances became increasingly challenging for rugby league clubs. It was becoming impossible for

148

this once great spectator sport to continue to trade on gate money alone. Despite the contemporary hype about the 'Swinging Sixties' the entire country was, of course, backsliding fearlessly towards economic instability and balance of payments problems and, like many of their association football counterparts, many rugby league clubs felt uncomfortably close to insolvency. Bradford Northern were in a terrible financial state by the early 1960s and actually ceased to trade halfway through the 1963–64 season after gates had sunk to as low as 324 in their vast Odsal Stadium, less than a decade earlier the same ground held the record attendance of 102,569 for a Challenge Cup Final replay. The RFL approved of a local initiative to save the club and Northern re-emerged the following season. But the proverbial writing did appear to be on the wall – the game had to change or die. Liverpool City, already faced with a seemingly impenetrable problem of surviving in the football city of Liverpool, faced an uncertain future indeed.

Yet Oldham secretary Mr Summerscales identified in September 1964 that Liverpool City's very existence was something of a model; it was, by necessity, held together via non-rugby activities such as the social club and pools – something that had yet to be fully acknowledged by such clubs as Oldham as a survival strategy. "They cannot keep going on gate receipts alone but have a band of workers second to none in the Rugby League, who, by their social activities and pools organisation, keep the game going. It is obvious that the people who subscribe to their activities are not rugby football enthusiasts... in fact, if all subscribers to any pool organisation attended the matches of their particular club, our game would be riding on a pinnacle as regards finance, instead of the proverbial shoe-string." [17]

In an ironic twist, those clubs from the rugby league heartlands, previously able to rest on their attendance-supported laurels, were now forced to admire the entrepreneurial measures taken by Liverpool City, one of the game's anomalies. The City directors always acknowledged the value of pools proceeds in the week-to-week upkeep of the club. The Liverpool City board was made up not only of sportsmen, but also businessmen and they used their collective acumen for the benefit of their club. This was probably quite different from many a football and rugby league boardroom member of the 1960s, who repeatedly would use clubs as playthings and directorships as marks of local prestige.

For the first home fixture of the new decade, against Oldham, the City programme editor, on behalf of the board, expressed his gratitude: "For the year gone, and for the New Year, the chairman and the board are truly grateful to the many who labour so freely and sportingly to help City and if one selects the Pools Committee and agents to say an especial "thank you", that is no reflection on the efforts of the committees of the Social and Supporters Clubs. Without the combined efforts of these and others, there would just be no Liverpool City." [18]

It was, therefore, sad that these go–ahead fund-raising experiments barely kept the Liverpool City club alive. And it was ironic, too, perhaps, that just as they were being acknowledged as an entrepreneurial set up, City's woes were further exacerbated by the social disease of vandalism. As early as September of the 1963–64 season the Liverpool City Supporters' Club was reporting: "At the start of the close season, vandals again made their presence felt and our chief loss was the wrecking of the tea bar. It has cost us £50 to put this right. New steel shutters have been installed and this, together with the fact of a resident caretaker on the ground will, we hope, stop this vandalism." [19]

This was, of course, a problem that would dog all smaller sports clubs in the Merseyside region, and beyond, for the next 30 years. Indeed it is claimed by rugby league historian Harry Edgar to be a major fomenter in the downward spiral that led to the demise of the Huyton Rugby League club. The vandals of Garston and Allerton contributed in a similar fashion to the departure of Liverpool's third professional football club – South Liverpool FC – from their Holly Park ground in the 1990s. But in 1964 the game of rugby league as a whole was also in need of radical change. Summerscales also complained of "fisticuffs", "brute strength rather than skill" and a lack of "fast clean passing". Forwards slowing down the game were certainly dominating rugby league and the open rugby of which the code was justifiably proud was, by the mid-1960s, in danger of disappearing altogether.

It would be 1966 before the Rugby Football League began to address these issues. In the meantime clubs such as Oldham and Liverpool City were left to sustain interest and raise capital as best they could.

Like their Stanley forbears Liverpool City's gates, of course, had always been financially unsustainable. While the social club in Derby Lane aided the club financially, it did nothing - as the Oldham secretary suggested - to persuade Liverpudlians through the Knotty Ash stadium turnstiles. City's gross attendance figures for home games during their last three seasons at Knotty Ash certainly appeared to reflect this lack of success in promoting rugby league football. For 1965–66, the figure was 17,774; for 1966–67 the figure fell to 12,467. In their final campaign at Knotty Ash – 1967–68 – City's attendances from 17 home fixtures did actually increase, but grossed a meagre 16,488: an average of fewer than 1,000 per game. It must also be noted that these figures included home games against the likes of the distinguished St Helens, Warrington, Widnes and Wigan clubs, each of which probably brought with them up to a thousand travelling fans. Other home matches against less attractive sides such as Blackpool, Bramley, Doncaster and Whitehaven were played in front of no more than a few hundred diehards. For example, during the 1964–65 season, while enjoying a gate of more than 3,000 for a Lancashire Cup tie against St Helens, with receipts of £456, fewer than 400 were in attendance for the home games against Blackpool Borough and Barrow, and only 1,100 for the visit of mighty Wigan. With customary gate receipts of less than £100 per home game, it is a wonder that the club were able to survive at all. Such persistent inconsistencies did not go unnoticed by opponents. After all, the failure to consistently attract players of the right calibre was there for all to see in City's unenviable playing record.

During that period following the post-war boom, of falling rugby league gates – around 1951 to 1968 – Liverpool City's role as a rugby league outpost was considered by most adversaries as something of a poisoned chalice. The varying tones expressed in opponents' programme editorials, therefore, tend to make fascinating reading. For example, in his 'Welcome to Our Visitors' section of the Warrington RLFC programme for the 15 December 1951 fixture against City, the editor somewhat dryly describes Liverpool City as "one of the league's 'unfortunates' " he then continues to "offer them our best wishes for better times in 1952". [20]

The Wigan programme editor from the 31 January 1959 fixture versus City was consistent in his description of Liverpool as "certainly a team of triers, but do lack speed in crucial positions... We can expect an interesting game today, although once more our class will probably tell as the game wears on." [21] In a later edition of the Warrington official programme from the 17 September 1960 clash[22], the editor welcomes City as "the club which carries on unflinchingly its hard task of attempting to establish the RL code on Merseyside on a firm basis" and then cites six former "Warringtonians" in the probable Liverpool side as if they had been cast aside by the Wire. His final observation "perhaps our old hooker and friend Ike Fishwick will be turning out" conceivably and wryly suggests a shortage of players in the City ranks. Player-coach Fishwick was well past his best by this time and, although named in the Liverpool line-up in the programme that day, did not actually play.

In his programme notes for the March 1962 clash with City, the Oldham secretary and programme editor curtly describes Liverpool as "one of the Cinderella Clubs" [23] whereas in April 1961 Salford's editor was more generous by praising the staying power of their opponents. For example he penned the following:

Plucky Liverpool City
"They are making a Bold Fight to Cultivate the Game on Merseyside
Liverpool City, whom we entertain today, deserve the admiration of all associated with Rugby League. It requires, apart from hard cash, endless patience and fortitude to keep the flag flying in one of the strongest soccer strongholds in the Country... if good wishes are helpful, they can have ours by the ton." [24]

Similarly, the Huddersfield secretary Ken Senior was to note in his rather florid programme notes for the visit of City in a Challenge Cup fixture that same season: "Although it is many years since a Liverpool team played at Fartown we do appreciate the great efforts that have been made to foster our game in the great sea-port by the present organisation at Knotty Ash... we do look forward to the time when greater success will attend their efforts. It is sometimes forgotten that, before the last War, Liverpool Stanley were a Top Four club. May those days return." [25]

Rochdale Hornets' programme editor questioned what he saw as indifference on behalf of Liverpudlians and (to paraphrase) remarked sympathetically in December 1962[26] that despite being a difficult team to beat and showing some marked improvement City's home attendances remained woeful, with gates regularly falling below four figures, hardly statistics likely to keep a professional rugby club solvent in the 1960s, they suggested.

Rochdale ought to have known about flirting with insolvency. Like Liverpool the Rochdale playing staff was invariably conjured up from non-locals and the history of the Hornets is plagued with periodic struggles to attract rugby league players to an unfashionable and largely unsuccessful Lancashire town not altogether renowned for its interest in the game. Indeed, several transfers took place between Rochdale and Liverpool over the years. In the early 1950s Ted Cahill and Ted and Ginger Mitchell were three players who kept Liverpool afloat financially by their relocation to the Hornets' equally dilapidated Athletic Grounds.

By 1966, City's deficiencies on the field were legendary – yet so too was their resourcefulness off it. The sympathetic Workington Town programme editor was to write: "With gates that are always read in hundreds, it must be a heartbreaking business season after season to find players and finance to carry on in this hotbed of soccer... Our away game with them this season was played on February 17th under lights at Widnes and drew a two thousand and a bit gate, and we won there by 6-2. The Widnes 10 per cent [the game was played at Naughton Park] would take a little of the gate but be sure the balance was manna from heaven for the Merseysiders. On this day, to compensate their loyal supporters for the switch, they put on motor coaches from Liverpool to Widnes free, and carried one hundred and fifty people in them. If a team is worthy of a following it is the humble Liverpool, who are big enough to do this on a peppercorn takings." [27]

Many such editorial examples exist, with most opposing programme editors bringing up regularly Liverpool's unremitting problem of survival in a football city. The Rochdale Hornets editor went one further in the spring of 1965, this at a time when Liverpool itself appeared to be at the very centre of the British cultural universe: "Publicity-wise the City live very much in the shadow of Anfield, Goodison Park, the Beatles and the King of Knotty Ash himself, comedian Ken Dodd but over the years the club has done a wonderful job in keeping the rugby league flag flying against hopeless odds." [28]

No sitting on the fence there, then! But none of the above appears to grasp the essentials of rugby league's lack of realisation in Liverpool. Although actually already in some state of disintegration by the 1960s, the city of Liverpool still filed away any minorities into ones it ran, but largely ignored. The *Liverpool Echo*, for example, had its posse of rugby league correspondents in the wake of S.H. Yates, but they paid only scant lip service to the Liverpool-based club, while extolling the virtues of the more successful rugby league teams on Liverpool's outskirts, from whence, no doubt the correspondents had emerged.

From this perspective, rugby league identities could not be forged as 'Liverpudlian' because they did not relate to or exist within the frames of authenticity that gave meaning to them in a town such as, say, Warrington. Rugby league, therefore, while making some kind of imprint as a peripheral activity, could not recycle these fragments into comprehensible entities for the dominant Liverpool culture to acknowledge. In Liverpool itself, rugby league was doomed to remain peripheral – not so on the outskirts, of course. Perhaps a word on this poisoned chalice should come directly from one who knows: a dedicated local fan of rugby league.

In April 2007, Warrington supporter Tommy McCarthy said that as the Liverpool of the 1960s became a cultural icon, an image was invoked and its identity fixed via the mediation of 'Merseybeat'. For a supporter of rugby league, this image of 'place' excluded those on the periphery, discriminating the towns surrounding Liverpool to such an extent that the journey into Knotty Ash from Warrington town centre became endless and akin to a pilgrimage: "Let us not forget back then: we were all singing Beatles songs and Liverpool was the centre of the universe whether you lived in Warrington or New York; it was the place. You can imagine therefore a trip to the Knotty Ash Stadium on the Crosville H5 bus at my tender age in 1963 was like some star-spangled adventure into wonderland. The journey took hours: Great Sankey to Penketh to Widnes to Cronton and so on. My memory's not up to much these days but I think it was 1963 and I also think Warrington's ground was out of action for weeks and weeks due to the severe winter of that year. I'm sure this was technically a Warrington home fixture but played at City's ground. Whatever... Bone-chillingly cold but no worries!" [29]

Cash flow: the Supporters' Club closes

Of course, club members were able to prop up the bar under the grandstand all afternoon if they so wished. Bar takings contributed enormously to the weekly upkeep of the club. However, there was a snag, here. The bar under the stand was for members and visiting supporters only and as such was run by the Supporters' Club. Income from the bar flowed through their bank account rather than that of the rugby club. This was not good news from a cashflow point of view, especially when the membership of the supporters' club had dwindled almost to double figures. It was decided, therefore, that something should be done.

At an extraordinary general meeting held at the Knotty Ash Village Hall on 8 December 1964, the Liverpool City Supporters' Club was officially disbanded. After 30 years of service to Liverpool Stanley and City clubs – including saving the parent club from extinction in both 1938–39 and 1948–49 – there were now fewer than 100 members and only a skeletal committee.

The club directors declared their own fundraising schemes such as the weekly club lottery as the lifeblood of the club and recommended all supporters to engage in these: "Times change... In line with many other clubs the directors, through their pools committee, run their own money-raising schemes and this season have taken over the bar on the ground... the present methods of the directors are proving successful." [30]

But the demise of the Supporters Club was clearly brought about by the financial necessity of speeding-up cash flow. At a time when licensing regulations dictated a 2.30pm closure around the Liverpool pubs, the beer rather than the rugby was at least attracting a hardcore of local drinkers to the ground between the hours of 2pm and 6pm and the presence of a clique with spending power had undoubtedly been acknowledged.

It does appear, at least from this historical distance, that the Liverpool City directors had given up on any ideas of increased attendances, and were prepared to fall back on beer and weekly lottery money to supplement their meagre gate receipts, together with donations from the social club – somewhat myopic, perhaps? This might be so, but the City directors had been hit by a hammer blow from the owners of Knotty Ash Stadium six months previously – they were to be on the move yet again.

New beginnings?

As suggested above, by 1968 rugby league was finally coming to terms with itself as a declining spectator sport and gingerly setting about entering a new, more experimental but ultimately productive and popular phase of its history. The appeal of the recently introduced play the ball and four tackle rules together with Sunday kick-offs and BBC2's televised Floodlit Trophy had contributed to arresting and then upturning the long-term decline in attendances. One might even suggest that the seeds of Super League were sewn in the late-1960s. Without floodlights, however, there was never any prospect of Liverpool City entering the BBC-sponsored Floodlit Trophy; the installation of floodlights was only worthy of consideration if security of tenure on the ground could be guaranteed.

But in July 1964 the board of directors had received the news that the 20-year Knotty Ash Stadium lease would not be renewed in 1970, and that the owners wished to develop the land as soon as possible: "We have recently been informed by the owners of the ground that they will not be able to renew the lease, as owing to town planning their property in town is to be demolished and will be rebuilt here. The present lease runs to 1970 but they would like us to go by 1966. However nothing has been decided yet." [31]

The owners, according to a later Warrington programme editorial of 24 September 1968 "required the site for a new school". This was, as we have previously learnt, the Roman Catholic Church who had a school for the blind in the city centre. Huyton resident Mick O'Toole remembers his father, a devout Catholic and a member of ACTU (the Association of Catholic Trades Unionists) being heavily involved in the Blind Institute well beyond its closure and demolition in the town centre. Mr O'Toole senior, despite having visited Knotty Ash Stadium on a number of occasions, welcomed the new development. The Catholic Church in Liverpool was a cultural as well as religious institution. A two-penny rugby league club could not compete with symbolism of that magnitude.

This came as a mighty blow to the Knotty Ash board who had planned considerable ground developments, including improved training lights, for the 1964–65 season. After consultation between the Liverpool City board and the RFL it was agreed that further investment in professional rugby league in Liverpool was futile. The Leigh programme editor though the same in September 1965, saying: "Many RL clubs these days complain about their problems, but the City have a never-ending difficulty. They have to face up to terrific soccer opposition, knowing full well that every one of their home Saturday games means a counter attraction either at Liverpool or Everton. ... They will shortly be leaving their home at Knotty Ash for a site in Huyton, and we wish them well." [32]

Protracted negotiations then commenced between the Rugby League Council, Liverpool City and Huyton-with-Roby Council to relocate the club on a 21-year lease at what would be a purpose-built enclosure near the river Alt in Huyton. Once again the RFL gave substantial financial guarantees to the project, however in this case the club was to be the lessee. Unfortunately, this new pitch was so close to the Alt that it was, and remained, a nightmare to drain. This problem, together with a variety of logistic headaches ensured that delay followed delay until Alt Park was eventually ready in August 1969 – less than a year before the lease on Knotty Ash was due to end.

Towards the end of 1965, the moves to develop the site in Huyton had advanced sufficiently for locals in the area of the proposed new ground to feel threatened by its presence. An Objectors' Group was thus established in an attempt to thwart the development. The first Liverpool City official programme of 1966 reported that the board were not unduly troubled: "The Objectors' Meeting held in Huyton recently as to the proposed move of Liverpool City Rugby League to that district was, if not a roaring success, certainly not an abject failure.

It was obvious that there would be objectors but the meeting clearly showed that there was a very favourable inclination to the code in the district of Huyton. When you move a family from one house to another, the change encountered is often a little uncomfortable for a while. But as the roots take hold, so the glamour grows. This will be the case of Liverpool City when they move out of what is now comfortable surroundings to a new and challenging area. With the same courage and endeavour, which was their lot when they moved to Knotty Ash Stadium a decade or more ago, City will again show their metal. Make no mistake about that!" [33]

However, the board became far more agitated when City's slow progress to Huyton was further stalled by the 1966 General Election. Labour Prime Minister Harold Wilson needed a larger majority in parliament and called an election for 31 March. Huyton was his constituency and his local political enemies raised concerns over the funds allocated by Huyton-with-Roby Council for the new rugby league ground. While Wilson easily beat his local Conservative opponent in the election, by April Conservative allies in the national press had picked up the story in the hopes of embarrassing the Prime Minister.

Questions were tabled in the House of Commons prior to the summer recess of 1966 and Liverpool City's move to Huyton appeared at one stage jeopardised by this political speculation. The City programme editor vainly attempted to turn these setbacks into positives for his final notes of the 1965–66 season, despite the fact that a new lease at Knotty Ash was out of the question. It was clear that the club was genuinely worried by this threat to their existence: "In the face of all which has been reported in the national press of late, I am assured by those in authority that rugby will again be the focal point at Knotty Ash Stadium next season. So for the time being City fans, enjoy all the fine facilities which are available at the ground and remember it is your support, which the club urgently needs... Even though plans for the new ground have been instigated, many valuable lessons have been learned from the stay at Knotty Ash Stadium. The one really outstanding fact being that wherever you go the support has got to go with you."

A different hand, possibly that of chairman Mr Greenhill, continued on page 7 of the same edition: "As we still await Parliament decisions, and time would too short, our enforced move to the new ground will not take place this close season, and we will commence next season again here at Knotty Ash." [34]

While Liverpool as a sporting city was basking in the reflected glory of Liverpool's second First Division Championship of the decade and Everton's Mike Trebilcock-inspired FA Cup victory (and in a few weeks' time England's 1966 World Cup football triumph would create a further distinctly upbeat tone to the summer), for the officials of Liverpool City rugby league club an uncertain summer appeared to beckon. Fortunately for the board, by the autumn months of 1966 the Huyton-Wilson saga had petered out as a newsworthy item and, as promised, Liverpool City duly soldiered on for another season at Knotty Ash Stadium as one of the half dozen or so lightweights of the Rugby Football League, confident that the move to Huyton would, indeed, go ahead.

1965–66 Northern Rugby League (bottom six teams)

25 Rochdale Hornets	34	10	0	24	284	387	20
26 Liverpool City	**34**	**9**	**2**	**23**	**307**	**494**	**20**
27 Blackpool Borough	34	9	1	24	331	549	19
28 Batley	34	6	2	26	196	576	14
29 Doncaster	34	6	0	28	228	586	12
30 Whitehaven	34	4	2	28	191	585	10

On the pitch the 1966–67 season began and ended much as in previous years – heavy defeats at the hands of the game's heavyweights and occasional victories against fellow strugglers. City ended their home fixtures on an upbeat note by thrashing Whitehaven 34–5 on 1 April 1967. This was Liverpool's largest margin of victory since they beat Doncaster 32–0 in October 1959 and was their second largest points tally since the war.

The usual problem was of City being basically short-staffed. Jack Broome recalled: "The squad wasn't big enough. Once one or two got knocks it put a strain on the team. Then one or two played with knocks and the results suffered. The problem was made worse by the fact that it was difficult to watch [for the coaching staff] the amateur game because everybody kicked off on the same day so you might miss a good replacement – it was different when things [professional matches] were moved to Sundays." [35]

1966–67 Northern Rugby League (bottom six teams)

25 Hunslet	34	9	2	23	402	578	20
26 Blackpool Borough	34	9	2	23	333	509	20
27 Whitehaven	34	10	0	24	313	593	20
28 Liverpool City	**34**	**9**	**0**	**25**	**332**	**552**	**18**
29 Doncaster	34	8	1	25	361	677	17
30 Batley	34	7	0	27	280	610	14

1967–68: The final season as Liverpool City

It almost goes without saying that Liverpool City failed to win any silverware during their 17 years at the Knotty Ash Stadium. The nearest they came was via their 'A' team reaching a Lancashire Combination Shield Final in November 1967 – during their last season as Liverpool City. After defeating the reserve teams of Whitehaven, 18–7, and Rochdale Hornets, 16–11, City lost narrowly to Workington Town 11–8 in the final; but won a medal, at least. The City 'A' squad as printed in the Workington programme actually had a familiar ring about it, with several former first team players listed: Bright, Ashton, Chisnall, J. Evans, Losh, Trainor, McEwan, Sherman, R. Evans, Cartledge, Smith, Campbell, McGrath, Johnston, Poole.

The Shield Final was played at Workington's Derwent Park on Sunday 19 November – an early experiment with the soon-to-be-adopted Sunday afternoon kick-off. The Workington Town programme editor was generous in his praise for the visitors: "We hold the Shield now, having defeated Wigan in the final December last. Be sure that our players will be all out to see that it stays at Derwent Park, yet be equally sure that if it has to move from here, there is nowhere else that we would as soon see it go as to Liverpool City. I do not have to tell you how they have fought to keep the game alive on Merseyside, their courage has been the admiration of all who know them, and should we be on the losing side after today's encounter, there will be as big a cheer for Liverpool as there would have been for the Town."

Additionally, the Workington programme editor discussed the significance of this Sunday fixture experiment: "Whether we agree with it or not, it appears to be the trend to get away from Saturday afternoon now... so we have it, it will be interesting to see what our figures are today, they could go a long way towards determining what might happen on many of our tomorrows" [36] – prophetic words indeed. This important timetable move, encouraged by the Rugby League Council to avoid the relentless clashes with football's traditional Saturday 3pm kick-off, not only helped to sustain rugby league for at least the next 30 years, certainly prior to the advent of summer fixtures and Super League in 1996, but also showed the sporting world that rugby league was willing and able to change as different conditions in society developed.

There were objections, primarily from churchgoers, however this early recognition of Britain's changing socialisation patterns should never be undervalued. Certainly inspired by this reserve fixture and with due encouragement from the Rugby League Council, the Liverpool City board of directors displayed enough vision to attempt to stage rugby league's first ever Sunday afternoon league fixture. Perhaps typical of Liverpool City's luck, however, their home game against Swinton – scheduled for Sunday 10 December 1967, admission by programme only to get round the Sunday observance laws, price 4/6 – was called off owing to frost on the pitch. To further compound the loss of a trophy and the unfortunate irony concerning the Sunday fixture that never was, that final season of 1967–68 turned out to be City's most successful post-war campaign as a club.

It was not only the City 'A' team that was a force to be reckoned with. While Jack Broome remained in charge in a titular sense, the news of the arrival of former Great Britain centre Jim Challinor as player-coach and skipper for the final season at Knotty Ash had created quite a stir in the rugby league world.

Challinor, who had originally made his name with Warrington, arrived at Liverpool on the back of a Wembley appearance with Barrow. Despite his effectiveness as a player having been diminished by a knee injury that would end his playing career in that last season at Liverpool, Challinor's class told on several occasions. He played in 22 of City's 37 fixtures in all competitions and City won 11 and drew one of their 34 league fixtures, almost beating St Helens at Knowsley Road along the way,[37] and also beat Whitehaven in the first round of the Lancashire Cup.

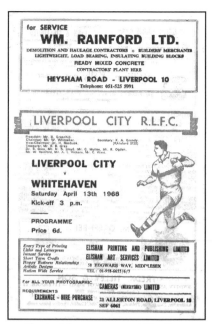

The last home game at Knotty Ash and as Liverpool City

Under Jack Broome's guidance and with Jim Challinor's enthusiasm, Liverpool City finished outside the Rugby Football League Championship bottom six for only the second time in their 23 seasons since the end of the war. But by this time few people outside the world of rugby league – in other words the majority of the population of Liverpool – could have cared less. In their very last match as Liverpool City – at Widnes on 15 April 1968 – the Widnes RLFC programme editor, notwithstanding a factual inaccuracy concerning the by-then-defunct Supporters' Club, was full of praise for the visitors and optimistic about the future of the club as Huyton RLFC: "There's no doubt that City have one of the best Supporters' Clubs in the league, and also a very enthusiastic band of officials. They have kept the club going though faced with tremendous odds. Now it would seem they have surmounted a lot of obstacles, and their playing record in recent months has given great hopes for the future." [38]

Despite one of the most wholehearted bands of officials, supporters and players in the Rugby Football League, Liverpool City had to all intents and purposes already given up their battle to keep professional rugby league alive in the city of Liverpool. In fact, despite City's fine start to their last season in Liverpool, the club programme editor was already waxing lyrical about their new home-to-be that August of 1967: "Although you all know that we will be moving 'just down the road' as it were, it is hoped that our hard core of spectators will, no doubt, support the club every bit as much as they have done since the days of Liverpool Stanley.

Great things are planned for the new headquarters of the club, which will be situated in Endmoor Road, Huyton. The new ground location will offer better spectator and training facilities and modern changing and social amenities in addition to appealing to what is in effect, an area which could produce some real rugby stars.

The ground is due to be seeded very shortly and a much larger car park than that of Knotty Ash will be instituted. There will be a proprietary club, terraces on all four sides of the new pitch with stands on three and a practice pitch at one end.

The club-house will include four changing rooms, treatment room, a large club-room, TV room, lounge, two bars, a drying room, offices, stores, kitchen and toilets.

Yes fans, the future sure looks bright for everything and everyone. The Rugby League Council has granted a substantial loan to the project and it is hoped that the ground will be in use sometime next year." [39]

At the Liverpool City AGM held in February 1968, the balance sheet revealed a profit of only £494 for the trading year – £1,000 less than the previous financial year. A fall in gate receipts of £200 was also reported. Nevertheless, the programme editorial for the following Saturday's fixture against Rochdale Hornets on 17 February remained upbeat by stating: "Despite these disappointing returns, however, club spirit is as high as ever and in these days of devaluation and inflation it is always remarkable to me that any club can finish up any season with a profit!"

These comments ring true almost 40 years later and were certainly realistic in 1968. It was indeed amazing that such a club as Liverpool City could turn a profit on a regular basis. The team may have been one of the most unremarkable in the Rugby Football League, but the club was run astutely. Predictably the programme notes for the final game at Knotty Ash Stadium on 13 April 1968 expressed mixed feelings: "This is, indeed, a sad occasion but I feel it will remind all of us connected with this great name that because our future lies elsewhere, there is still every hope for the future. You know the old saying, 'as one door closes another opens' and this must be our banner as we stride bravely towards our new home at Huyton.

We have a great future in front of us at Huyton – let no one misunderstand that and it is a very encouraging message that you all receive from directors, players and staff of the club through the medium of these notes today. It is that the heartfelt thanks of these personages go out to City fans for their wholehearted support over the past 15 years." [40]

1967–68 Northern Rugby League (bottom eight teams)

23 Rochdale Hornets	34	13	0	21	335	489	26
24 Liverpool City	**34**	**11**	**2**	**21**	**363**	**493**	**24**
25 Whitehaven	34	10	1	23	300	577	21
26 York	34	9	1	24	368	687	19
27 Keighley	34	8	0	26	295	475	16
28 Blackpool Borough	34	6	1	27	307	634	13
29 Doncaster	34	4	2	28	264	768	10
30 Batley	34	4	1	29	247	711	9

Bert Andrews of the *Prescot & Huyton Reporter* recorded with a degree of mixed emotions: "Farewell City – Hail Huyton; City Leave Knotty Ash on a high note. As if to give the old ground something to remember City set a record for the highest score of the season by beating Whitehaven 29–5." [41] It was an auspicious ending. Arthur Evans, a rare loyal Scouse Liverpool City fan who also became something of a stalwart of Huyton RLFC in the 1970s and 1980s, remembers that last home fixture against Whitehaven with some degree of satisfaction: "There were about 400 to 500 of us I suppose and City hammered them. It had actually been a pretty good season and the team was improving all of the time. It was a great day, and I remember we were all banging our fists against the pitch-surround all together. It sounded fantastic and you wouldn't have thought there were only a few hundred of us there. It was a great day. I was a bit sad at the thought of leaving Knotty Ash but like most of us I thought that we were going places with the move to Huyton." [42]

And what of the thoughts of the players and staff? John McGrath remembers that they were just hoping against hope that the move would not take place: "A lot of it went over your head and we thought it was a rumour. I wanted to stay and we thought we would be there forever; I was sad to leave. I remember playing Saints on a beautiful day with 8,000 people there all sat on the grass bank – and that's the kind of thing we had to give up – a pity." [43]

Jack Broome agrees: "I couldn't see any reason why we shouldn't have carried on at Knotty Ash and I was sad to leave. Really, the new area didn't want us at all. The first game they played on there at about ten to three there was nobody in the ground - then they didn't come through the turnstiles, they came over the walls!" [44]

End notes

[1] Unaccredited programme editor, 'Official Notes', *Wigan Football Club Official Programme*, 31 January 1959, p.3

[2] Unaccredited editor, 'Sports Chat', *Halifax RLFC Official Programme* [versus Liverpool City], 3 December 1960, p5

[3] Unaccredited programme editor, 'Club Notes', *Liverpool City Official Programme* [versus Warrington], 12 September 1959, p.5

[4] Brown, Gordon (2004), 'Memories Of Liverpool City', *Our Game 9* Spring, London: London League Publications, p.5

[5] Unaccredited programme editor, 'Editorial', *Liverpool City Official Programme* [versus St Helens], 4 March 1961, p.2

[6] Unaccredited programme editor, 'Club Notes', *Liverpool City Official Programme* [versus Batley], 26 March 1960, p.2

[7] Interview with John McGrath, October 2007

[8] Unaccredited programme editor, 'Players', *Barrow Rugby Football Club Official Programme* [versus Liverpool City], 15 April 1960, pp.4-5

[9] Interview with Tom Galligan, October 2007

[10] Unaccredited programme editor, 'Editorial', *Liverpool City Official Programme* [versus St Helens], 4 March 1961, p.2

[11] Ray Hockenhull to Gordon Brown, 'Memories Of Liverpool City', *Our Game 9* Spring 2004, London: London League Publications, p.6

[12] Waring, Eddie, Untitled editorial', *Eddie Waring Rugby League Annual No 6 1964-5,* Northwich: White Rose Publications, p.3

[13] [probably] J.C. Gregson, 'Editorial', *Liverpool City Official Programme* [versus Leigh], 7 March 1964, p.2

[14] Email correspondence with Steve Higginson, October 2007

[15] Gordon Brown (2004) interview with George Walker, 'Memories Of Liverpool City', *Our Game 9* Spring, London: London League Publications, p.5

[16] Fallowfield, W. (1968), 'All's Well: Ask Huyton and Bramley!', *Eddie Waring's Rugby League Annual 1968-69*, Castleford: MB Publications, p.47

[17] Summerscales, H, 'Watersheddings News and Views', *Oldham Football Club Official Programme* [versus Liverpool City], 12 September 1964, p.3

[18] Unaccredited programme editor, 'Editorial', *Liverpool City Official Programme* [versus Oldham], 2 January 1960, p.2

[19] Unaccredited 'Supporters' Club Notes', *Liverpool City Official Programme* [versus Oldham], 2 September 1963

[20] Unaccredited programme editor's notes, *Warrington Programme* [the official programme of Warrington RLFC: versus Liverpool City], 15 December 1951, p.2

[21] Unaccredited programme editor, 'Official Notes', *Wigan Football Club Official Programme* [versus Liverpool City], 31 January 1959, p.3

[22] Unaccredited programme editor's notes, 'Another Meeting With City', *Warrington Programme* [the official programme of Warrington RLFC: versus Liverpool City], 17 September 1960, p.3

[23] Unaccredited programme editor's notes, 'Watersheddings News and Views', *Oldham RLFC Official Programme* [versus Liverpool City], 31 March 1962

[24] Unaccredited programme editor's notes, *Salford RLFC Official Programme* [versus Liverpool City], 22 April 1961

[25] Senior, Kenneth, 'Official Notes' *Huddersfield Cricket & Athletic Club Official Programme* [versus Liverpool City] 1st round Rugby League Challenge Cup, 11 February 1961

[26] Unaccredited programme editor's notes, *Rochdale Hornets Official Programme* [versus Liverpool City], 22 December 1962 - match postponed

[27] Unaccredited programme editor's notes, *Workington Town Official Programme* [versus Liverpool City], 5 March 1966

[28] Unaccredited programme editor's notes, *Rochdale Hornets Official Programme* [versus Liverpool City], 6 March 1965

[29] Warrington RLFC supporter Tommy McCarthy: email correspondence with author 11 April 2007

[30] Unaccredited programme editor (J.C.G.?), 'The End of An Era', *Liverpool City Official Programme* [versus Oldham], 19 December 1964, p.7

[31] J.C. Gregson, 'Editorial*', Liverpool City Official Programme*, 22 August 1964, p.2

[32] Unaccredited programme editor, 'Cup Tie Night*', Leigh Football Club Official Programme* [versus Liverpool City], 8 September 1965, p.3

[33] Unaccredited programme editor, 'Editorial', *Liverpool City Official Programme* [versus Leigh], 1 January 1966, p.2

[34] Unaccredited programme editor, 'Editorial', *Liverpool City Official Programme* [versus Widnes], 11 April 1966, p.2; see also p.7

[35] Interview with Jack Broome, 21 September 2007

[36] Unaccredited programme editor, 'Notes*', Workington Town Official Programme* [versus Liverpool City 'A'], Sunday 19 November 1967

[37] Liverpool City lost 7-15 on 14 October 1967 and (according to the Liverpool City programme editor of 21 October): "but for a try that never was, we would almost certainly have beaten the Knowsley Road men before their own supporters"

[38] Unaccredited programme editor's notes, *Widnes RLFC Official Programme* [versus Liverpool City], 15 April 1968

[39] Unaccredited programme editor, 'Editorial', *Liverpool City Official Programme* [versus Blackpool Borough], 26 August 1967, pp.2-3

[40] Unaccredited programme editor, 'Editorial', *Liverpool City Official Programme* [versus Whitehaven], 13 April 1968, p.2

[41] Andrews, Bert, 'Farewell City – Hail Huyton', *Prescot & Huyton Reporter*, Friday 19 April 1968, p.4

[42] Discussion with Arthur Evans, May 2007

[43] Interview with John McGrath, 21 September 2007

[44] Interview with Jack Broome, 21 September 2007

8. Huyton RLFC – false optimism

Tom Fleet recalls that "The first year was a disaster. Any connection with any one in Liverpool was lost once the move to Huyton was made. You saw the place getting worse almost by the month"[1]

The township of Huyton is of ancient origin. In the 1086 Domesday survey the settlement was named Hitune (meaning 'high town') and a local Lord named Dot held this area along with the village of Tarboc (now Tarbock). Such hamlets were part of the land between the Ribble and the Mersey known as the 'West Derby Hundred'. The spelling 'Huyton' seems to be from 1300 onwards.

Nineteenth century railway development raised Huyton's profile considerably as transformations to the area followed the successful Rainhill Trials for steam locomotives in the 1830s. This expansion ensured that Huyton railway station became, and remains, a vital link in local and regional transport. Huyton further expanded significantly in the 1930s when large tracts of land owned by Lord Derby were sold to Liverpool Corporation. Prior to the outbreak of the Second World War housing estates gradually appeared in Huyton-with-Roby and this massive increase in population meant changes to the town's infrastructure. Further major redevelopment took place in the post–war era, including road alterations and the demolition of many old structures. Huyton's 'village' area, as it was known, was by the 1970s transformed into a modern town centre.

However, from this period, and related to the aforementioned population expansion, problems over status and profile arose as a Liverpool 'overspill' dogged the further maturity of the borough. Issues surrounding unemployment, identity and demographics created problems not fully resolved.

Vandalism intensified in the 1970s and 1980s to such an extent that the area began to depopulate. Local businesses established as a response to the earlier population growth became unstable and closures were common. Huyton is now in the borough of Knowsley, which also includes Kirkby and Halewood, but is considered by many to be a district of Liverpool. To this day local history groups in Huyton struggle to preserve the independent history of the neighbourhood.

The borough is renowned for its amateur rather than professional football clubs and St Dominic's and St Aloysius have held many County FA trophies between them. Huyton has produced several international football players such as Peter Reid and Stephen Gerrard and was also known as the constituency of former British Prime Minister Harold Wilson. Despite its close proximity to both St Helens and Widnes, the town has few historic affiliations with rugby football, although in recent seasons an amateur Huyton rugby league team has turned out at the King George V Sports Centre on Longview Road.

1968–69: The first season

On Friday 23 August 1968 on page 11 of the *Prescot & Huyton Reporter* the following article appeared: "Huyton Rugby League Football Club got into full swing last Thursday evening when its doors were opened for the first time. The club, at Endmoor Road, Longview, has taken six months to complete and was officially handed over by the contractor. Directors are Dr H. Roebuck (chairman [actually vice-chairman of the rugby club]), Mr B. Gray (treasurer), Mr K. Grundy (secretary), Mr D. Vickers (director in charge of Huyton branch), Mr N. Lloyd, Mr P. [sic] Mullee.

Good Support

On Friday, the club was opened to members of the public. Mr Grundy says they do not yet know how many members they have but are hoping for good support... The official opening of the ground is on 21 September [1968]. It will be performed by the Earl of Derby, who is president of the Rugby League." [2]

A place on page 11 of the local paper, before even a rugby ball was kicked, was rather ominous and did not bode well for the ambitions of Huyton RLFC. The message was clear: the arrival of this particular sports club in this district was by no means stop-the-presses front-page news. In fact, to say that Huyton's start was inauspicious would be one of rugby league's great understatements because that first season was an unmitigated disaster. Yet, still coached by the redoubtable Jack Broome and ably assisted by former City player Tom Smith, the former Liverpool City squad took to their opponents' fields for the 1968–69 season as Huyton RLFC in their new, distinctive colours of amber with a red and black V.

The leadership of the new club for the 1968–69 season were as follows: president, Bert Greenhill and directors: W. Whittaker, the chairman, Dr B. Gore, R. Ogden, W. Rainford, and C. West. The secretary, as always, was the unswerving Ken Grundy and a photo accompanying the above report showed Grundy behind the bar of the new club, saluting his colleagues with the aid of a pint. So, at least the new social club had opened on time, but what of the enclosure and the squad? As for the former, while a few games of rugby were played at Alt Park that season, the inauguration mentioned above did not officially occur for another 12 months; it could be argued that this interim period effectively sealed the fate of this proud little club once and for all.

On 2 September 1968 Blackpool Borough dedicated page 3 of their programme to the new visitors, stating optimistically: "Their new ground is within two miles of their old one, so they should be able to have kept their faithful supporters." The notes closed by saying "with more or less the same playing personnel we can expect another hard game today." [3]

The *Eddie Waring Rugby League Annual 1968-69* listed the Huyton playing staff as follows: "Ashton, D. Bevan, W. Bridgewater, D. Bright, J. Cartledge, J. Challinor, J.P. Chisnall, L. Cooke, T. Cork, K. Donoghue, P. Evans, J. Evans, R. Forber, E. Glynn, F. Hamilton, W. Heesom, A.B. Hardman, A. Johnson, A. Brown, D.G. Losh, B.A. Mort, A. Mustard, J. McGrath, J. McKeown, K. Newton, W. Nicholls, T. Ogburne, L. Payne, W.J. Pickersgill, N. Sherman, R. Smith, J. Smith, John. Smith, K. Sutcliffe, B. Thompson, J. Trainor, J.W.B. Winstanley."

Three players were reported as "open to transfer": B. Cartwright, J. Heaton, and A.J. Heesom.[4] Therefore, to all intents and purposes the Blackpool programme editor was correct: the squad that had performed so encouragingly the previous season was still intact, despite a few undoubtedly reaching the veteran stage. In fact the side that played in Huyton's first fixture against Keighley, a 17–12 defeat, was by and large made up from the same players that finished the previous term – but with one notable exception. Jim Challinor had decided that his knees could no longer take punishment and, although still registered as a player with the RFL, had decided to hang up his boots.

162

He had featured in fewer than two dozen games the previous season, but his influence had been immeasurable. Without him, the Huyton backs were to lack co-ordination and the forwards strength but, with scant money in the pot, there was little Jack Broome could do about it. All the money raised by the new social club was already going into the bottomless, rain-soaked pit that was Alt Park.

As the season kicked off, a postscript to the old Knotty Ash era appeared on the front page of the *Prescot & Huyton Reporter*. The 30 August edition read:

Rugby league ground is new blind centre

"The new building will replace the Catholic Blind Institute, which has been in Brunswick Road Liverpool for nearly 150 years. [the] new institute will stand on seven acres of farm land owned by the community which adjoins St Vincent's... Christopher Grange will be run by St Vincent's Committee." [5]

So, as the Huyton season began Knotty Ash Stadium was officially consigned to history. As for Alt Park, it wasn't ready and the Huyton management was compelled to organise home games at a variety of venues, and reverse other fixtures, and things were already looking more than a little messy.

Due to this unavailability, the Huyton side was forced to play 10 consecutive away games at the start of this season resulting, predictably, in 10 straight defeats. There were no out-and-out thrashings, but during August a 25–0 defeat at Hunslet and a heavy 43–7 loss at Wigan set the tone. It was clear that issues concerning the ground were to be the overriding concerns of the first season. The Warrington programme editor for Huyton's visit on 24 September confirmed: "Unfortunately, their ground, or rather the stands, are not quite ready, and therefore they have not been able to fulfil any matches for the first team at Alt Park." [6] However the *Prescot & Huyton Reporter*'s Bert Andrews had already shown that the problems at Huyton were not just incomplete building work. His description of the first competitive match played at Alt Park was discouraging. The match took place on 16 September 1968 when a Lancashire Combination Challenge Shield tie was played between Huyton 'A' and Widnes 'A'. It was, by Andrews's account, mayhem:

Youngsters spoil Huyton's first home game

"Monday saw the first match to be played on the new ground at Alt Park, and what a shambles it turned out to be. Huyton entertained Widnes in the second leg of the first round of the Combination Shield, but the whole game was spoiled by the number of youngsters who came over the walls in droves.

They invaded the pitch, climbed the goal posts, threw stones and abuse at all and sundry. Dogs by the score ran wildly about and the referee had to hold up the game more than once to clear the pitch.

Something will have to be done to stop any repetition. One official suggested barbed wire might be the answer, but others thought sterner measures would have to be taken to curb this terrible show by the children of Huyton.

Little interest could be taken in the match with children jumping on the players' backs, and my medal of the evening went to the referee who tried against great odds to bring some sort of order from the chaos.

The score, incidentally, went in favour of Widnes 15–10, and they now go into the second round." [7]

Access to the incomplete ground was evidently trouble free for the youth of Longview. Bert Andrews was to also announce in that same edition of the *Reporter* that the plans for the original Alt Park grandstand had been urgently redrafted. As suggested by the aforementioned Warrington programme editorial, problems had developed regarding the location of the grandstand. Soft sand had been discovered where the footings had been dug and the builders had been forced to fill in their excavations. A new architect had been commissioned to redesign the proposed stand, at the cost of an additional £4,000. This new structure turned out to be a rather disappointing and diminutive shelter, which in atmosphere harked back to the dark days of the Stanley Track and was nothing like that originally envisaged. In any case, it wasn't long before it too was subject to systematic vandalism.

Fortunately, with beer priced very modestly, the new social club had, perhaps unsurprisingly, become a local watering hole and at least a little cash was flowing from this source. However, any potential development of a competitive rugby team was crippled by these additional construction costs. The Derby Lane-based social club, for so long umbilical to the Liverpool City rugby team, was no longer providing anything more than a modicum of funding for the parent club and like most Liverpool-based social clubs of that era − inaugurated initially to financially support a football team − was in the process of becoming fully autonomous.

The first of Huyton's home fixtures took place at St Helens's Knowsley Road enclosure on the evening of Friday 19 October 1968 with Whitehaven as the visitors. This match resulted in Huyton's first victory of the season, 18–12, but the programme editor was compelled to confirm to the home contingent that news from Alt Park was disappointing: "In view of the public safety, the foundations for the new stand on the ground must be sunk a further 15 feet down... Officials have planned well − make no mistake." The editor continued in a typically stoic vein announcing, "This new ground is an investment for the future" [8] but even at this early stage, those 'in the know', such as stalwart forward, and later vice-chairman John McGrath, were aware that something was badly amiss: "Building a football ground next to the River Alt was crazy. We could see right away that the pitch was in a terrible mess and as for the rest of the ground, the kids were able to get over the walls and cause havoc. We couldn't train on the pitch after a while. I replaced Bill Payne as club steward. I lived at the club for a few years and, although I never experienced a break-in, the ground became a centre for vandals right away." [9]

There remained little prospect at this stage of Huyton fielding its first team at Alt Park, and as regular occupancy continued to be delayed, vandalism increased. As the builders downed tools for the day, so the hooligans swarmed over the inadequate fencing and made merry.

Huyton's second home match was played at Widnes' Naughton Park on 1 November in front of only 481 spectators. Huyton defeated Featherstone Rovers 7–5 with the talented Albert Heesom scoring the only Huyton try and Ernie Forber kicking two goals. But the programme editor noted that there was an "ever increasing number of talent now transfer listed by our club". Albert's brother Alec Heesom, Jeff Heaton, Bill Newton and the goalkicking Ernie Forber had all requested transfers, partly caused by, one suspects, sloppy and ineffective management.

Warrington were also interested in Albert Heesom and had offered full-back Keith Affleck in exchange, but the deal eventually fell through. The Huyton programme editor (perhaps Ken Grundy) further stated: "One way or another I always feel a little sad thinking in terms of players seeking or being placed on the transfer list. Whatever the problem involved it is sufficient to say – for my part – that if, and when, they are taken off, the club is, to all intents and purposes, re-strengthened." [10] The Heesoms remained whereas Newton, Forber, and Heaton were all eventually lost to the club.

A new director, James Chadwick, who had supported the Huyton venture since its infancy, was co-opted that same month in order to give the board more stability – but matters continued to deteriorate. Huyton's programme editor suggested that both the *Liverpool Daily Post & Echo* and the *Prescot & Huyton Reporter* had been unkind, feeding the public misinformation concerning the lack of matches staged at Alt Park. But for the foreseeable future the first team was playing all games away and the reserves no longer existed. At the onset of the season the Huyton 'A' team was allowed to play its Lancashire Combination fixtures at home and the first team squad was also allowed to train on the pitch. The surface appeared, according to one Huyton programme editorial of this era to be a "luscious space", but it had not settled and the sandy subsoil and defective drainage meant that within a short time the pitch had cut up badly, becoming a quagmire.

After a 23–20 win at Barrow in October 1968, the 'A' team, unable to fulfil any of its subsequent home fixtures, was temporarily disbanded. The second string had only completed six of its games (losing five) when on 11 January 1969 the Huyton versus Oldham match programme editorial (played at Widnes) announced: "The news that we are to disband the 'A' Team TEMPORARILY [editor's capitals] came as a bit of a shock to yours truly, just the same I understand that a panel of about 20 players has been chosen from which the first team will be selected.

The measure is, like I say, temporary however, and only for the season under review. The 'A' team will be reformed in time for the 1969–70 season. The main factor in the Club taking this controversial decision was to help preserve the new pitch at Alt Park.

A list of 10 home first team games are yet to be played there following the reversal and postponement of fixtures due to the ground not being ready for first team duty. Only four away League games remain and to try and fit in all their [note - he writes their not our] 'A' team games as well as the long list of first team matches would have meant very heavy wear for the new turf. Still not to worry we are still doing nicely..." [11]

"Nicely", indeed? By this time the first team squad was forced to train on an open field close to the Alt Park ground – memories of Liverpool Stanley must have flooded back for those able to recall such dismal events. The Huyton programme editor above suggested, in so many words, that 'A' team gate receipts were thin as a consequence of the poor pitch and bad press but, in reality, takings were practically non-existent after the vandals had branded Alt Park part of their territory.

In truth, apart from being a new place to either vandalise or drink on the cheap, the advent of Huyton RLFC had generated little interest among locals. Any initial curiosity had been irrevocably damaged by the failure to play even one home first team game at Alt Park in the opening months of the season. On the somewhat inauspicious date of Friday 13 December 1968 the Huyton programme editor informed the 180 souls gathered together for yet another home game at Widnes's Naughton Park that "work is progressing on the new stand at Alt Park and although hopes were high that we would at last be able to get under way at our ground by playing Doncaster there, I fear that it will be the New Year before we finally come home again." [12] That post-Christmas Doncaster match had been postponed as a consequence of the theft of roofing sheets – taken shortly after delivery.

These unforeseen problems naturally delayed the construction of the grandstand, which was then further exacerbated by the builders' annual January holidays. There was no more work on the ground until February 1969.

Furthermore, the funding for the move to Huyton had been raised via a combination of RFL, Huyton-with-Roby Council and Liverpool City capital. Each financial source was subject to its own administrative delay, which left the Huyton directors repeatedly embarrassed concerning the payment of outstanding building work invoices. The cashflow from the social club helped to alleviate this problem somewhat, but could not, on its own, clear bills that were the responsibility of each financial source. In these days when many smaller suppliers still worked from hand-to-mouth, Huyton RLFC lost the trust of their contractors, who at times would not begin work without a financial guarantee. 'Maurice Greenberg', the Old Swan-based builder's merchant and long time supporter of Liverpool City, via Bert Greenhill, found itself acting as an unpaid intermediary for supplies as the building work lurched from crisis to crisis.

As something of an overview, rugby league historian Tom Fleet records his feelings concerning Huyton's lack of impact in that first season: "It's easy to see negatives rather than positives: the ground wasn't ready at Huyton and there was absolutely zero interest in the sport in Huyton itself. For me it was such a change from the leafy lanes surrounding Knotty Ash. It was a different social area altogether – almost a deprived area. Knotty Ash seemed suburban whereas at Alt Park, well, the first problem was driving there – a bit threatening: closed shops with metal shutters. On the ground itself I would always make a point of standing where I could see my car. The car park was dangerous, too, full of glass – really hazardous. It never really looked like sustaining.

They were also nomadic in that first season so any interest that there might have been locally was lost in a short space of time and any local connection that might have been at Knotty Ash (and there was a little) was lost forever. You saw Alt Park getting worse by the month; kids throwing stones, vandalism, it was a truly horrible atmosphere. I remember an old *Bex Bissell* carpet cleaner that had been dumped in the corner of the ground, sitting there gradually rotting away.

I think Liverpool City had put down some kind of roots and the local environment was also conducive. In retrospect they were taking several steps back by moving and were also overambitious. Whatever advantages there might have been were lost in that first season – the club was just hanging on until they were eventually vandalised out of the place." [13]

For irregular enthusiast and sometimes sponsor at Alt Park (a contributor to the later "Buy Bricks For Huyton" campaign) Tom Fleet, it was a concept blinded by optimistic ignorance. In contradistinction to the earlier diatribes of Eddie Waring, Tom still believes that any genuine future for the club was lost with the dropping of that 'Liverpool City' moniker. In an era epitomised by the city of Liverpool as an apparent beacon for popular culture, to effectively give away that title does appear tantamount to self-destruction. Further, to replace it with a name that meant little or nothing to, for example, visiting Yorkshire rugby league fans was simply foolish.

Additionally, not only did rugby league mean next to nothing to Huyton residents, but Huyton RLFC did little to encourage locals along to watch the sport - rather than drink the beer - all round it was a dead loss.

Of course, unbeknown to the Huyton board of directors, the area of what was soon to be retitled 'Merseyside' was heading for a massive cultural and demographic shift. As the late 1960s witnessed dramatic movements of people across the region, changes in work patterns and shifts in cultural values occurred that still have ramifications to this day. Local sports clubs in need of a new generation of enthusiasts felt the fall-out as upwardly mobile families – such as the stalwarts at Knotty Ash – began moving away from the area. The traditional move for many Liverpudlians was 'over the water' to Wirral, but new housing estates in Bryn, Ashton-in-Makerfield, Cronton and the like began to deprive Liverpool of its sports-loving middle classes.

True, the Huyton RLFC social club was open for business but while locals might have been prepared to pop in for a pint, they showed little interest in the rugby league on offer. In the final analysis, like its Liverpool City forebears, Huyton required a regular flow of income from visiting supporters to help balance its meagre takings. But even this was not possible in this first season while most home matches were played in Widnes, St Helens or at the opposition's home ground, with only a fraction of these gates receipts reaching Huyton's bank account. In that aforementioned home programme of Friday 1 November 1968 there was a plea to any Widnesians there: "… may I remind Huyton supporters particularly and those Widnes fans who come along tonight that our 'A' team boys are running their fixtures at the new ground. Indeed, contrary to what rugby league fans read in their Sunday newspapers last week, Huyton 'A' team beat Barrow 'A' at Huyton, not Barrow. Furthermore, at Alt Park tomorrow our 'A' team play the very good St Helens 'A' side in what should prove a cracker of a match. So how about it fans – if you're doing nothing in particular tomorrow afternoon take a trip and enjoy the scenery, the excellent club facilities… and the match, of course!" [14]

Somewhat typically, the St Helens 'A' fixture was cancelled at the last minute – doubly frustrating for those who might have decided to go along. John Davies recalls: "I took the bait and hung around Alt Park for something like an hour before being told that the game had been cancelled earlier that morning. I was only 15 and was a bit scared about hanging around that area, to be honest. I nearly threw in the towel after that." [15]

But actually there were few Widnes fans at the ground on that (or any) day to watch Huyton. For example, another home match – against Barrow – took place at Widnes's Naughton Park on 17 January 1969 with only 130 in attendance. By this time Huyton were in possession of the Mackeson Golden Ball - plus the cash reward that came with it – for a successful 13–5 and 7–3 double over Oldham the previous fortnight. The nomads even managed to hang on to the trophy for another week by defeating Barrow 20–3. But it would be false to think that Widnes fans would turn out en masse for these matches.

A potentially valuable home Challenge Cup draw against Warrington, scheduled for 25 January 1969 was unfortunately postponed at the last minute by the referee. The fixture was then played at Wilderspool and a 31 January home match against Salford was also unwillingly transferred to The Willows. It was unadulterated chaos. Finally, on 30 March a home Sunday fixture took place at Alt Park against Blackpool Borough, with Ray Ashby at full-back for Blackpool, and Huyton duly recorded a 13–10 victory. But after the false starts of the previous months the game went ahead without a great amount of publicity or, indeed, interest. While a reasonable gate of 1,000 attended the fixture, how many were locals and how many were from rugby league's fraternity, remains a moot point. A match programme was not even provided for this hasty re-arrangement and, in return for 5/-, admission to the ground was obtained via a Gestetnered (duplicated) typed team sheet. The following week, 2 April 1969, the Huyton programme editor waxed lyrical in his defence of the previous Sunday's events: "Yes we finally got off the ground as it were and played that elusive first match at our new ground. The weather was kind to us and if there was some disappointment with the actual attendance (1,000) it should be looked at with some real satisfaction rather than a dubious pessimistic attitude... Make no mistake about it – this might be just what we, as a club, have been looking for. There might have been misgivings about the state of the pitch but I remind all critics that I have seen worse." [16]

This seemed like eternal optimism, yet the Widnes programme editorial for the visit of Huyton on Monday 7 April wearily declared: "It would seem that Huyton have almost made Naughton Park their second home. They have played most of their 'home' games here this season." [17]

By the end of that inaugural 1968–69 season there were many rumblings of discontent among the dwindling band of supporters. A handful of victories had been notched, mainly due to the excellence of Jeff Heaton, including that double against Oldham and an 8–5 victory at Salford in April, but spectators were so disgruntled that club officials were forced to acknowledge the problems in the final programme notes of the season. Huyton's first season would go down as one remarkable only for its lack of organisation. As outlined above, the Huyton team actually played nine of its scheduled home matches at Widnes's Naughton Park – sharing the gates with the host club. The Widnes handbook for the following season discloses information on all league gates and receipts for the previous term – including those of tenants Huyton. These latter gates were predictably and increasingly dispiriting:

Huyton versus Featherstone Rovers 1 November 1968: 481, receipts £107 (7–5)
Huyton versus Hunslet 9 November 1968: 281, receipts £58 (13–11)
Huyton versus Keighley 30 November 1968: 204, receipts £41 (3–15)
Huyton versus Rochdale Hornets 13 December 1968 180, receipts £37 (0–10)
Huyton versus Oldham 11 January 1969: 394, receipts £88 (7–3)
Huyton versus Barrow 17 January 1969: 130, receipts £28 (20–3)
Huyton versus Widnes 10 March 1969: 1,539, receipts £340 (2–16)
Huyton versus Workington Town 22 March 1969: 61, receipts £12 (7–18)
Huyton versus Doncaster 3 May 1969: 98, receipts £20 (2–12)

Receipts totalled a meagre £730, and almost half of this figure was provided by the derby with Widnes on 10 March. With matchday ancillaries added, the Widnes club received a grand total of £817 from the fixtures and paid out only £355 to Huyton – it was a financial disaster for the latter. What made things even worse for the Huyton management were the four victories in the above fixture list, making it necessary to pay four win bonuses to the players.

The final home game of the season against Doncaster on Saturday 3 May 1969 was played, and duly lost 12–2, at Widnes in front of only 98 people – the club's lowest-ever attendance up to this point. While the generosity of the Widnes club should be recorded, the local population of Widnes, it seems, was not so desperate for a game of rugby league as to venture along to Naughton Park to watch Huyton lose to Doncaster. What makes matters worse is that such an embarrassment could have been so easily avoided, for that Doncaster game had been scheduled for Alt Park the previous Sunday, 27 April, but was cancelled at the last minute – yes, it had been a wet April, but why on earth postpone the last match of the season?

The club officials acknowledged in these final programme notes: "While on the subject of thanks, the club would like to extend its appreciation also to our faithful band of supporters. Many of these have probably felt cheated about the loss of proper home matches but they can rest assured that next season will bring about a recognised fulfilment of home fixtures at Alt Park... it is hoped the drainage will have been improved considerably by next August." [18] It wasn't: the drainage problem at Alt Park was never fully resolved and even after Knowsley United FC took over the tenancy in the mid-1980s, the pitch remained a swamp in the winter and a dust bowl in the summer. The Endmoor Road ground was simply too close to the Alt and, perhaps like the Huyton team itself, this river meandered somewhat aimlessly from one end of the pitch to the other.

1968–69 Northern Rugby League (bottom six)

25 Huddersfield	34	9	1	24	296	553	19
26 Batley	34	8	1	25	294	577	17
27 Huyton	**34**	**8**	**0**	**26**	**273**	**657**	**16**
28 Bramley	34	7	0	27	313	575	14
29 Blackpool Borough	34	7	0	27	382	752	14
30 Whitehaven	34	6	1	27	360	539	13

Despite this seemingly eternal pitch problem coupled with the fact that Alt Park bore very little resemblance to the arena originally proposed and that the local Longview gangs had earmarked Alt Park for systematic destruction, it was implausibly announced by the directors at the end of this first season that notwithstanding teething problems, moving out of Liverpool had given the club a shot in the arm – this seemed naive. Coach Jack Broome was to later admit: "We were improving at Knotty Ash – a little at a time but there was improvement. But the move to Huyton was a disaster, a complete disaster – nothing went right. We couldn't train on the pitch; we had to train anywhere we could. After another season I packed it in." [19]

Harry Edgar later penned the following incisive comment on how the broader cultural transformations of the 1970s effectively ruined Huyton RLFC's chances: "With hindsight, rarely can a dumber move have been made in rugby league. Unfortunately, nobody could have bargained for the changes in society, which saw Alt Park become a persistent target for vandals and criminals during the 1970s. Eventually things got so bad in Huyton that the ground became a virtual no-go area and rugby league's favourite nomadic club had no choice but to either move again or die." [20]

Former Great Britain and Dewsbury star and now renowned Sky Television rugby league co-presenter Mike Stephenson also gloomily remembered visiting Alt Park "on a couple of occasions" in the 1970s: "Our coach would arrive at Alt Park and drop us off but wouldn't stay in the area for fear of vandalism. Both coach and driver would disappear for the length of the game and reappear at an appointed time outside the ground. It was a terrible shame, but that's the way it was." [21] Garry Clarke, son of second team coach Doug Clarke, recalls another small but decisive anti-hooligan ritual: "When the teams came out prior to the kick off the subs used to bring out of the clubhouse with them chairs or benches to place at the side of the pitch. Then at the end of the game they would take them back inside again. The reason being if they were left outside they would be vandalised or pinched. At one game while in the stand I saw several young kids climbing into the ground via a hole in the roof." [22]

Perhaps not so bad, one might suggest? But former Liverpool City player Harry Ody remembers going to Alt Park in the early 1970s and was told to follow a group of young people who had actually paid to get into the ground. They disappeared under the stand to "take drugs; I watched for only a little while in case I attracted their attention." [23]

The 1970s: A downward spiral

The Earl of Derby officially opened Alt Park on Sunday 10 August 1969 when Salford provided the opposition. The Huyton side was grossly outclassed, losing 60-5 to a team which, being one of the first British rugby league sides partly funded from variety-club and fruit-machine takings, was beginning to ascend well beyond previous under-achievements. The Huyton side still largely consisted of players who performed so inconsistently the previous season, some of whom like John Evans and Bill Payne and a returning John McGrath were at the old-hand stage, and it showed.

Jeff Heaton, the club's best player by a mile, wanted out. He was transfer listed by the Huyton Board at over £1,000 but threatened to give up the game altogether unless he was allowed to join St Helens for a smaller fee. After scoring a try in the Lancashire Cup defeat at home to Blackpool Borough on 17 August 1969, he left. The editorial in the match programme said: "The transfer of our half-back Jeff Heaton back to his native St Helens last week must surely rank as the best bargain buy of the season. On offer at a reported £750 Jeff was snapped up by a very worried Saints side, who saw the full value of Huyton's clever player. I have always admired Heaton's play but for the life of me his transfer price of £750 was a give-away price. I reckon Jeff in the Alex Murphy class and knowing his situation at St Helens I can imagine the complete satisfaction they will get from his transfer despite the fact that he left St Helens to come to Huyton (Liverpool City) a few seasons ago. Behind the heavy and mobile Saints pack, I can see Jeff hitting the headlines in the next couple of months. Yet, when many loyal fans are thinking that Heaton's move was not in the best interests of the club it should be remembered that it was he himself who decided his own future. He was of the opinion that his future lay elsewhere and so the club reluctantly allowed the deal to go through. Club officials – to a man - thought highly of Heaton but once he had made up his mind to go there was little if anything they could do." [24]

The Heaton transfer graphically illustrated the club's decline. Les Chisnall was to soon follow Heaton out of the club when Leigh paid Huyton £1,500 for his services in October 1969. It all smacked of desperation. The above quoted editorial voice speaks of the fans' disappointment and there certainly appeared to be a considerable amount of disillusionment felt by the club's long-suffering supporters after the utter disarray of 1968–69. As for the 1969–70 season the Huyton side, bereft of its two best players, fared no better, failing to record a single victory before a 6 December 1969 18–10 win at Bramley. Huyton went on to lose another five games before recording a narrow 3–2 win – again away from home – on 25 January 1970 at Workington Town. This match was followed by an unusual 0–0 draw with Swinton, together with a first round Challenge Cup triumph at Hunslet, but this Huyton side was a very low scoring one, with only 38 tries being registered for the entire season. In all, only five league matches were won, two at home, and it was that solitary point gained from the extraordinary 0–0 draw that kept Huyton off the bottom of the table.

The early departures of Jeff Heaton and Les Chisnall were undoubted factors, but so too was the overall age of the Huyton regulars who stayed behind. Quite simply, they were well past their prime – which had been limited. Bill Payne was still playing, so too John McGrath. Even Eddie McDonnell had returned to the side. These men had been playing rugby league before the Beatles had recorded their first hit record. The Huyton programme editor was to acknowledge in October 1969: "Our 'veterans' have done us proud over the years... They were the backbone of a side, which had always struggled to bring our game to the forefront of what is, after all is said and done, a soccer stronghold. But with passing seasons their strength and undoubted experience is not always the saviour." [25]

But any decision regarding the continuation of this 'veteran' policy remained unresolved because, quite simply, no other players of the required standard were available and any promising talent quickly left the club. For example, Bill Payne played in every fixture that season, apart from the opener against Salford. The side managed only 177 points from 34 league fixtures and for the *Prescot & Huyton Reporter's* Bert Andrews, it was a "pathetic" scoring return; this word fittingly featured regularly in his match reports. The aforementioned programme editor mentioned in his notes for the visit of St Helens in October 1969 that "the one thing that keeps reminding me of the seriousness of our playing position is the points for [in the league table]..." He wasn't wrong there, and as Huyton duly stuttered to the end of the season the fan base lessened proportionately and coach Jack Broome called it a day. In reality, against clubs in the bottom quarter of the championship, crowds often measured between 100 and 200, foredooming the new decade ahead. Supporter John Davies recollects "standing there rather bored and counting the crowd on one occasion towards the end of the 1970 season, I think it was against Batley. I got to 90-something and that was about it − half of them probably got in for nothing." [26]

1969–70 Northern Rugby League (bottom six)

25 Keighley	34	13	0	21	370	555	26
26 York	34	11	1	22	378	502	23
27 Doncaster	34	7	0	27	264	564	14
28 Huyton	**34**	**5**	**3**	**26**	**177**	**643**	**13**
29 Oldham	34	6	0	28	343	590	12
30 Blackpool Borough	34	6	0	28	318	762	12

For the following season, 1970–71, Wilf Hunt and Colin Parker joined the board and Joe Coan became the new coach. Hunt and Parker were former players - Hunt of considerable distinction − who had made good with their engineering company and interests in the nightclub scene in Widnes and they felt that they could offer Huyton a new lease of life. But as the new season kicked off Huyton's team was still overly reliant upon old stagers, a returning Mick McGillicuddy, for example, although Dave Leatherbarrow was showing a level of maturity that was attracting attention from other clubs.

As usual, the season began poorly and although, by the last week of October the side had won two matches on their travels, it couldn't get a result at Alt Park. This form was becoming financially punishing, for the crowds at Alt Park were becoming skeletal. The programme editorial for the 17 October 1970 home match against Oldham was to remark: "The back room boys are also playing a fine game in the organisation and running of the club and the only real regret in our full second season at Alt Park is that not enough Huyton and district folk are taking the trouble to come along and watch us play. Yet the position is far from desperate and given a little more time I feel sure we will make ourselves felt in the game of rugby league." [27]

As the season unfolded a run of important victories ensured Huyton would not dice with that final position on the table. Indeed, a respectable 24th position was achieved with six clubs beneath them in the league table. Nonetheless, Huyton almost equalled the record Liverpool defeat with a 63–0 thumping at Wakefield Trinity in September

1970, and lost the above quoted game 23–4 to an improved Oldham side in October, but throughout the course of the season the side became a little more settled and, although not high scorers, remained undefeated on 13 occasions.

The season only really came to life in the new year. Beginning with a 5–5 draw at Rochdale on 6 February 1971, Huyton played 15 league games between February and April. The club won eight of these, even recording a narrow 5–0 victory on 13 March at Alt Park against the mighty Wakefield, as outlined in the club programme: "What revenge, and how sweet it was to hear local and national critics swallowing their words... It would be true to say that the 5-nil victory will live long in the annals of our club and without fear of contradiction there wasn't one dissenting voice about who was the better side. Great stuff [coach] Mr Coan and players, and what a boost for our directors, officials and all those who have struggled to keep this club going... the future is indeed rosy." [28]

But Huyton's scoring rate remained a predicament. Swinton finished one place above them in the league table with 404 points scored. One place below were Rochdale Hornets who scored 318 points. Huyton's meagre total was 229. So, despite a respectable league position, their points-for column was the lowest in the Championship; this had been the case for the last three seasons.

Huyton's last five games of the season were all played at home. Four were won – Workington Town 13–11, Blackpool Borough 22–9, Hunslet 5–3, Dewsbury 15–13. If the attendance figures released by the club are accurate, the gate increases make for interesting reading: 250 watched the win against Workington. This grew to 280 for the victory against Blackpool. Further wins appear to account for increased attendances with 500 for the visit of Hunslet and 600 against Dewsbury. An accountant's dream attendance of 2,000 watched the final match of the season against Warrington, a 16–9 defeat. But no league games were played against Widnes, Wigan or St Helens that season and it seems a pity that the home fixture against Warrington was the final fixture of the season, because nothing was at stake for Wire.

It was indeed a season of acute contrasts: financially disappointing in that only one Lancashire Cup game against St Helens and the aforementioned Warrington league fixture attracted anything like helpful gates, but holding some promise in that the team played well enough throughout the second half of the season to merit a small growth in receipts. However, with the notable exception of the Wakefield Trinity result in March, the remaining victories were gained against weaker teams. Of course, a division between the stronger and weaker clubs had been evident for many years, but the clubs against whom Huyton were able to record victories were, like themselves, diminutive – indeed those such as Blackpool, Doncaster and Hunslet were perilously near to closure.

Huyton RLFC was on the horns of a dilemma. The monetary value of repeated home fixtures against the local giants was undeniable, but the Huyton team was only really fully competitive against the second class teams. Back in the mid-1960s Liverpool City's board of directors had publicly considered the possible nightmare scenario of being unable to pay for a winning team. With the removal of regular fixtures against the local south Lancashire giants – a perfect way of balancing the books – this nightmare was beginning to emerge as reality. Although Huyton's late run brought higher gates, the club was still unable to account for a regular stream of win bonuses. It was a confusing year, indeed, for Huyton RLFC. Off the pitch matters were made even more distressing by the announcement in January 1971 of the death of Bert Greenhill. Of all of the stalwarts to have stood by the club – particularly in the recent move to Huyton, Greenhill's name was perhaps the most loyal.

1970–71 Northern Rugby League (bottom seven)

24 Huyton	**34**	**11**	**2**	**21**	**229**	**508**	**24**
25 Rochdale Hornets	34	9	3	22	318	533	21
26 Blackpool Borough	34	10	1	23	380	647	21
27 Bradford Northern	34	8	2	24	339	662	18
28 Doncaster	34	7	3	24	306	695	17
29 Whitehaven	34	8	1	25	298	698	17
30 Hunslet	34	6	1	27	355	739	13

In any case, the locals continued to ignore the club. It wasn't that Huyton RLFC was thought of as inconsequential; the club was not considered at all. And it would be no use blaming local people for this. The experience of a rugby league club should be entertainment and information. But how could people be attracted when Huyton was built around failure and loyalty rather than success and enjoyment? In such circumstances isolation develops. The Huyton side lost many more than it won, played to waning crowds in a district that ignored this particular code of rugby for the sake of associating with the successes of football. Huyton RLFC was attempting to challenge this – an impossible task.

However, it is also worth reminding ourselves of the parlous state of the borough of Huyton-with-Roby, socially and culturally. The 1970s copies of the local newspaper, the *Prescot & Huyton Reporter*, show a lot of news of business closures, shop vandalism and youth crime. While always appreciating that local papers thrive on bad news, the extensive and varying magistrates' proceedings presented by the *Reporter* invariably suggest that a great deal of this reportage was not altogether speculative.

Throughout the 1970s the decline in the borough's infrastructure was as alarming as it was consistent. The self-image, therefore, of Huyton RLFC was forced to change dramatically: from the initial optimism portrayed by Ken Grundy and his fellow directors in 1968, seemingly at the centre of some kind of community, to the pessimism, isolation and sense of utter worthlessness associated with running a club in a depopulating area. A 1977 Huyton RLFC official programme illuminates this bewilderment as the downward spiral of vandalism and hooliganism at matches and at other times to which Huyton RLFC fell victim grew ever worse: "To revert back to our game with Workington, I don't think that there have ever been worse scenes at Alt Park since its opening and whilst I am not blaming our own junior supporters entirely, it takes two to quarrel. A lot of damage was done and it is damage we can ill afford. We have taken our own steps to stop this type of behaviour but we need the help of all supporters to stop any repetition of similar scenes." [29]

This downwards spiral was not restricted to off-the-field matters, for over the next two seasons Huyton's dream of becoming a rugby league name on the pitch was lost amid growing local hostility to the presence of the club, a lack of money-spinning fixtures against local rivals on a regular basis, and increasing vandalism. The club's existence was rightly deemed anomalous. The equally descending syndrome of unemployment in Huyton created disillusion among the borough's youth that saw no equal in the post-war era: job security on Merseyside was now an illusion.

HUYTON R.L.F.C.
ALT PARK
HUYTON

HUYTON
v
WHITEHAVEN

FRIDAY 18th OCTOBER   KICK-OFF 7-30 p.m.
(At St. Helens Ground)   OFFICIAL PROGRAMME 6d.

For ALL YOUR PHOTOGRAPHIC
REQUIREMENTS   CAMERAS (MERSEYSIDE) LIMITED
EXCHANGE - HIRE PURCHASE   21 ALLERTON ROAD, LIVERPOOL 18
733 6061

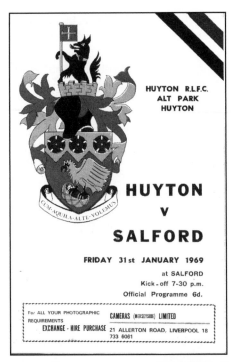

HUYTON R.L.F.C.
ALT PARK
HUYTON

HUYTON
v
SALFORD

FRIDAY 31st JANUARY 1969
at SALFORD
Kick - off 7-30 p.m.
Official Programme 6d.

For ALL YOUR PHOTOGRAPHIC
REQUIREMENTS   CAMERAS (MERSEYSIDE) LIMITED
EXCHANGE - HIRE PURCHASE   21 ALLERTON ROAD, LIVERPOOL 18
733 6061

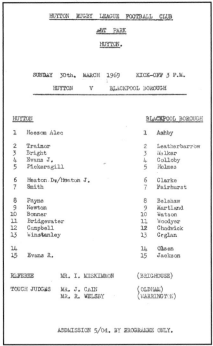

HUYTON RUGBY LEAGUE FOOTBALL CLUB

ALT PARK

HUYTON.

SUNDAY 30th. MARCH 1969   KICK-OFF 3 P.M.

HUYTON   v   BLACKPOOL BOROUGH

	HUYTON		BLACKPOOL BOROUGH
1	Heesom Alec	1	Ashby
2	Trainor	2	Leatherbarrow
3	Bright	3	Walker
4	Evans J.	4	Colloby
5	Pickersgill	5	Holmes
6	Heaton D./Heaton J.	6	Clarke
7	Smith	7	Fairhurst
8	Payne	8	Belshaw
9	Newton	9	Martland
10	Bonner	10	Watson
11	Bridgewater	11	Woodyer
12	Campbell	12	Chadwick
13	Winstanley	13	Crglan
14		14	Olsen
15	Evans R.	15	Jackson

REFEREE   MR. I. MCSKIMMON   (BRIGHOUSE)

TOUCH JUDGES   MR. J. CAIN   (OLDHAM)
MR. R. WELSBY   (WARRINGTON)

ADMISSION 5/0d. BY PROGRAMME ONLY.

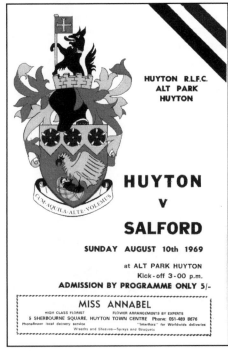

HUYTON R.L.F.C.
ALT PARK
HUYTON

HUYTON
v
SALFORD

SUNDAY AUGUST 10th 1969

at ALT PARK HUYTON
Kick-off 3-00 p.m.
ADMISSION BY PROGRAMME ONLY 5/-

MISS ANNABEL
HIGH CLASS FLORIST   FLOWER ARRANGEMENTS BY EXPERTS
5 SHERBOURNE SQUARE, HUYTON TOWN CENTRE   Phone: 051-489 8676
Phonaflower local delivery service   "Interflora" for Worldwide deliveries
Wreaths and Sheaves—Sprays and Bouquets

Moving to Alt Park: Top – two 'on the road' programmes.
Bottom left – the first match, a 13-10 win against Blackpool, who have Ray Ashby at full-back.
Bottom right, the official opening against Salford in August 1969.

Such fundamental effects on both club and team were dramatic: Huyton RLFC was unable to attract young players of the required standard and between 1971 and 1973 began to lurch from crisis to financial crisis. Matters were made worse by ill-advised speculation on players past their prime, for example in September 1971 Huyton paid out £750 – money they could ill-afford – for the services of former Wigan player Johnnie Jackson. It was a desperate act and Jackson lasted a little over a season. Decisions such as these increasingly placed the Huyton club under strain and illustrated to all involved just how tenuous the club's existence really was. According to supporter John Davies: "By 1973 it was usually down to Wilf Hunt and Colin Parker to balance to the books."

These two seasons witnessed the Huyton side victorious on only 10 occasions overall and at times it struggled to be competitive. The 1972–73 season actually kicked off on a positive note with a first-ever opening fixture win since the renaming of the club. On 10 August 1972 struggling Hunslet were beaten 14–10. The season ended with a 12–8 home win against Workington Town on 23 April 1973. In between, however, and almost equidistant to each of these results, came a solitary victory over Blackpool Borough on 19 November 1972 – all other games were lost.

Only Dave Leatherbarrow was able to make a name for himself in what would have to be described as a poor and dispirited squad. He was the top try-scorer in each of these two seasons with eight and nine tries, respectively.

1971–72 Northern Rugby League (bottom six)

25 Blackpool Borough	34	11	0	23	351	560	22
26 Keighley	34	8	0	26	330	740	16
27 Huyton	**34**	**7**	**1**	**26**	**277**	**610**	**15**
28 Batley	34	5	2	27	249	628	12
29 Doncaster	34	5	0	29	234	729	10
30 Hunslet	34	2	0	32	300	662	4

1972–73 Northern Rugby League (bottom six)

25 Hull	34	11	0	23	494	693	22
26 Barrow	34	7	0	27	351	775	14
27 Doncaster	34	6	0	28	298	911	12
28 Hunslet	34	5	0	29	371	916	10
29 Blackpool Borough	34	4	0	30	324	972	8
30 Huyton	**34**	**3**	**1**	**30**	**243**	**879**	**7**

Liverpool City old boy Dave Cox returned to the club as coach for 1973–74, but the team faired no better. This was the season when the RFL finally decided that two divisions was the answer to all of their problems: Huyton, naturally, was an automatic member of the lower tier. After a 16–6 defeat at home to Batley on the opening day of the season, Huyton provided the first visiting opposition for the revived New Hunslet club on 26 August 1973. More than 4,000 people turned up at Leeds Greyhound Stadium to welcome back the reformed Yorkshire outfit. A 23–0 loss for Huyton that day symbolised the continuance of the Merseysiders' decline, ironically in opposition to the phoenix-like rise of the New Hunslet club.

The arrival of the Second Division meant that Huyton now had a reduced fixture list to contend with, together with the certain knowledge that home league fixtures against their more successful local rivals were now in all probability consigned to history.

Under Cox's stewardship, Huyton proceeded to lose 18 games on the bounce – the club's entire fixture list up until the New Year. This only came to an end on 6 January 1974 by virtue of a narrow home 15–12 victory against fellow strugglers Blackpool Borough. Only two more wins transpired that season, both against Doncaster, one in the league, the other in the Challenge Cup, and the season petered to an inglorious end in late March with a defeat at York.

Huyton played only 30 games overall, but used almost 40 players. It was desperate stuff and the team duly finished bottom of the pile, with a retained list that would probably not have graced another club in the same division. Huyton RLFC's annual balance sheet – published on the 31 May 1974 – made for grim reading. Only £1,903 was derived from gate and programme income. The RFL provided the club with £4,061, but the bulk of Huyton's meagre turnover came from pools receipts, which amounted to £10,482. The figures speak for themselves.

1973–74 Second Division (bottom four)

11 New Hunslet	26	7	0	19	272	418	14
12 Blackpool Borough	26	7	0	19	272	585	14
13 Doncaster	26	3	0	23	158	684	6
14 Huyton	**26**	**2**	**0**	**24**	**182**	**460**	**4**

The 1974–75 season, however, witnessed a surprising recovery thanks to the arrival of new player-coach Terry Gorman. Leigh-born Gorman had been a Huddersfield player when transferred to Liverpool City in April 1963. A sound scrum-half he nevertheless proved to be rather injury prone, and appeared only 20 times for the club before moving back to Yorkshire later that year. His last game for Liverpool City was against Salford on 9 November 1963. Gorman went on to play for Dewsbury, Batley – with some merit – and Swinton. As his career began to draw to a close he became 'A' team player-coach at Oldham before moving to Huyton. Gorman initially arrived at Huyton in the summer of 1974 to assist coach Geoff Smart, but Smart stood aside to become team manager.

From the outset it was Gorman's knowledge of the game that was to prove to be relatively successful for the Huyton side – and potentially ruinous for the Huyton club. Joining Gorman at Alt Park from Wigan was fellow Leigh-born Derek Watts who had previously played such a vital part in Leigh's Challenge Cup-winning year of 1971.

Prop Doug Davies, who two seasons previously the Merseysiders had transferred to Salford for £1,500, returned to the club alongside another Leigh-born player, Norman Williams. So there was a distinct Hilton Park flavour to the side that began the new campaign. Doug Davies also took over the running of the social club from John McGrath. Gorman played 20 out of a total of 31 games at scrum-half and the side was probably the most competitive that Huyton had fielded in its short history. In fact, so improved was the defence that Huyton finished with a positive points tally of 301 for, 291 against: the first time this had occurred in the entire post-war era for the club.

The final position of seventh – exactly halfway – in the Second Division was a fair one. Gorman had managed to pull a side together by signing several experienced players such as the aforementioned Watts, Allan Nuttall and the excellent Terry Hammell. The season was one of real improvement with only a single short spell after Christmas that resulted in a losing streak – four games were lost in succession before a 16–7 win at home to Batley on 2 February 1975 restored some balance. The club reached the second round of the John Player Trophy after narrowly defeating Huddersfield 14–12 in the first round. A visit to Warrington in the second round even recalled days of old – they were hardly rivals now but a share of the gate was most welcome.

Perhaps the most impressive result of the season was a 32–10 home victory against Hull in November 1974, with seven players getting on the score sheet, including seven goals from Derek Watts. Out of the last six fixtures, three games were won, one was drawn and two were lost. Dave Leatherbarrow once more top-scored with 10 tries, while Watts kicked 51 goals and scored four tries. Huyton won 12 and lost 12 and the points-difference was marginal; at one stage the season even held the promise of promotion as Huyton actually hung onto fourth spot for a spell.

1974–75 Second Division (top seven)

1 Huddersfield	26	21	0	5	489	213	42
2 Hull KR	26	20	1	5	628	249	41
3 Oldham	26	19	0	7	406	223	38
4 Swinton	26	17	1	8	399	254	35
5 Workington Town	26	16	0	10	371	275	32
6 Whitehaven	26	14	1	11	285	234	29
7 Huyton	**26**	**12**	**2**	**12**	**301**	**291**	**26**

(Top four clubs promoted)

Matters on the pitch continued much in the same vein in 1975–76 with Terry Gorman still coach at Alt Park. He was, in fact, to carry on his heroic run as coach until 1977. Gorman, blending a mixture of old and new players, managed to get the Huyton team firing for a second consecutive season and it was not until the end of January 1976 when amid inevitable problems brought about by injuries and team changes Huyton's small squad became stretched and the season began to fall away; at one stage a top four slot had looked possible. For the first time since 1954 the club won its opening two league matches – at Batley 14–10 and at home to New Hunslet 17–9 – and the team was becoming a force to be reckoned with in the Second Division. A notable run in October and November 1975 saw them pick up 12 points from eight games. The defence continued to improve and the only hammering came at Salford, 44–17, in August in the first round of the Lancashire Cup.

But gates remained dismal and further vandalism to the ground, including sporadic fires and fence removal around Guy Fawkes Night, coupled with higher running costs – win bonuses, for example – continued to drain directors' pockets. By the end of November Gorman's successful side had emptied the Huyton coffers and chairman Wilf Hunt was forced to go cap-in-hand to the RFL and Forshaw's Brewery for money to bail the club out of its difficulties. Following this crisis, Huyton duly lost all three games in December.

The Huyton programme editor H.R.H. Andrews announced in January 1976: "We have had a lot of publicity lately covered by all the media mainly centring around our finances and indeed our future. Well, I have it on the authority of our chairman Wilf Hunt that our future is assured. We are here to stay… with help from the Rugby League and other sources." [30]

The Whitehaven programme editor of 5 March 1976 illustrated Huyton's generic problems to the home fans present that evening: "Welcome this evening to our visitors, Huyton, a team which, early in the season, suffered from the worst of all possible fates, success. Too many wins by the on-the-field side, forced the club to ask for a life line from the league. Even being early challengers for promotion did not bring the fans into

Alt Park and the club simply could not continue to pay for their league position. A local brewery and the league stepped in and here they are today." [31]

Andrews' 'Club Notes' for the 21 March 1976 visit of Workington Town stated emphatically: "Following today, there remains one more home match v. Bramley, which will bring to a close what must surely be one of the most crucial seasons in the history of the club. I am convinced that not many people realise the terrific struggle that has gone on behind the scenes in order to put on a match every week throughout the season. The devotion and utter determination of the board against all odds is to be commended." [32]

In all likelihood those few stalwarts in attendance that day were fully aware of the losing fight against both the vandals of Huyton and the inflation of the mid-1970s. But few outside Alt Park could have cared less. For example, as was the case with all members of the RFL, the club was obliged by RFL convention to attempt to cultivate local interest in rugby league (such as the aforementioned MARL – see chapter 6).

At the beginning of that 1975–76 season the club tried to encourage local teenagers to come along to Alt Park for training sessions in a vain attempt to develop a youth side – Huyton Tigers. It worked for a while but then declined though lack of interest and poor discipline from the players. Club supporter Arthur Evans recalls: "We advertised for lads to turn up at Alt Park for trials and we had an older trainer who was great with the lads. He ran a chimney sweeping business in Prescot and he loved rugby league and took a great interest. Anyway, we had what seemed like hundreds turn up on the first day, but loads of them were never seen again after they had been hit – tackled – once! All the same we assembled quite a useful team, called them Huyton Tigers and entered them into the North West Counties League. They did OK for a while but their discipline was terrible and keeping an eye on them was a major task: eventually they sort of melted away. That was pretty typical of the youth of that area in the 1970s. They came along, tried things out for a bit but then mostly disappeared." [33]

As the Huyton programme editor himself declared in September 1975: "Liverpool born rugby league players? It sounds incredible."

That 1975–76 season also witnessed the rebirth of the supporters club – for so long defunct since being decommissioned by the Liverpool City Board in the mid-1960s. Throughout 1975–76, this small band of supporters led by Andrews began to take over responsibility for the day-to-day expenses of the club. All matchday programmes were paid for by the Supporters' Club, as were the matchday refreshments. A small club shop also appeared, with the aforementioned Arthur Evans at the helm. The Huyton Tigers initiative belonged to the Supporters' Club and the duty of paying out benefits to injured players also became their responsibility. The club had, to all intents and purposes, reverted back to the organisational models once so apparent at the Stanley Track, and it was not coincidental, for the Huyton RLFC Limited Company was on the verge of collapse.

In fact, Huyton were so desperate for cash that a special friendly fixture was arranged against Widnes at Naughton Park on Friday 14 May 1976. It was in aid of the Huyton Survival Fund and this time Widnesians turned out in numbers: 2,341 spectators witnessed an entertaining and high-scoring match. Widnes had lost the Challenge Cup Final to local rivals St Helens the previous weekend and the Huyton match acted as a thank you to all supporters who had made the trip to Wembley and welcomed the team back to Widnes. So the Huyton club was able to capitalise on a wave of enthusiasm in the town for the Chemics. Widnes won the game 31-23, but the score was immaterial: Huyton had been saved from oblivion yet again by the local rugby league fraternity. The

Huyton Supporters Club chairman, H.R.H Andrews, stated on 25 May 1976: "I feel justifiably proud in presenting this, our first season's balance sheet and proud too of the amount of work that has been put in by our hard working members. They have spent many hours in running the various functions undertaken last season and this coupled with the respective duties on match days has meant a lot of hard work and no chairman could be more proud of his fellow committee men than I, not once have they flinched at extra work that has been placed upon them.

It has been a season of rumour after rumour but we have been kept fully in the picture by the directors and we realise that there is a lot of hard work to be done in order to reach the state of affairs that all of us desire." [34]

1975–76 Second Division (bottom six)

9 Huyton	**26**	**10**	**0**	**16**	**242**	**373**	**20**
10 Whitehaven	26	8	2	16	253	347	18
11 Halifax	26	7	1	18	322	460	15
12 Batley	26	6	1	19	228	432	13
13 Blackpool Borough	26	6	1	19	224	460	13
14 Doncaster	26	2	0	24	195	726	4

The supporters had once again proved to be fully capable of taking things into their own hands. However, there were insufficient numbers to run events on the scale of their post-war predecessors, who had promoted dances at some of the major Liverpool halls in support of their club, or raised money for the benefit of the entire club. The supporters' club dances of the late 1940s had now given way to the mobile discos of the late 1970s. Such affairs were less social, less communal and far more commonplace. While the bar at Alt Park benefited from the alcohol sales, other activities such as draws, raffles and the like had become the stuff of history. The Supporters' Club attempted a couple of race nights, but these backfired badly, leaving them to pick up the bill, rather than count the profits. Despite several setbacks, and as the limited company stumbled from crisis to crisis, the supporters did at least create an important income stream disconnected from the limited company and its losses.

However, unlike the club in Derby Lane, which since its autonomy had continued to thrive, the Alt Park social club was also suffering somewhat by this time. Membership had fallen and, despite continuing to provide some income to the rugby club, finances dwindled in inverse proportion to expenses.

Dave McCormick, another of that curious band of Liverpudlians who saw authenticity in both non-league association football and rugby league, spent his Saturdays following South Liverpool in the Northern Premier League and his Sundays following Huyton – but he now recognises that there were insufficient bodies at both grounds to keep things on an even keel: attendances by this time were pitiful. He looks back on it now and even questions his sanity: "Sometimes I look back on those days and wonder why I put myself through it all. Everybody else in Liverpool appeared to be celebrating the successes of Liverpool FC but not me. I seemed to dwell on the melancholy of a defeat in football at Holly Park followed by another in rugby at Alt Park. And both grounds could be very depressing experiences. There were so few active supporters by this time. Then the vandalism... I remember being at one game at Alt Park when a Mini was stolen and dumped into the river Alt in full view of everybody. 'A' team matches were even worse. You'd ring up the club to see what time the game was to kick-off and the steward would say something like 'what time can you get here?' Time without number the Huyton side could be winning at half time by a comfortable margin, only to crumble in the second half. You would say 'never again' but would be back the next week - very masochistic!"

McCormick remembered attending one game when the gate money was stolen. He blames the "daft sod" handling the cash for being naive enough to carry the takings across a small part of the ground in a bag: an indication of just how low matters had sunk at Huyton RLFC of the mid-1970s.

Typical of many council estates, the one surrounding Alt Park was divided between a retirement age population and emerging teenagers; the latter poorly educated and with few job prospects. From this doom-laden situation emerged severe social problems and the Huyton ground and social club was regarded on the one hand as something of an oasis for certain older members of the community, irrespective of the code of football played on the field, whereas for some of the younger generation it became a physical representation of pointlessness upon which one could vent one's spleen.

The problems faced by the new directorship led by Isherwood and Andrews was that money saved or raised from one sector was invariably spent on the other – either in an attempt to repair the continual and increasingly structural damage to the ground or to continue to attract the elder community into the watering hole inside the ground. During a match in November 1976 a pitch invasion had actually brought Alt Park to the brink of closure; the programme notes declared: "All those who attended must have witnessed the terrible scenes following the game. The pitch was invaded and the referee was treated to all manner of verbal abuse. Now then, whether the spectators are our own followers or whether they are supporters of the visiting team WE ARE RESPONSIBLE, and to quote the relevant passage from RL Bye Laws they shall have powers to [quote] CLOSE a ground either for a stated period or permanently..." [35]

From the Huyton versus New Hunslet February 1977 programme notes by Bill Isherwood display an all-too familiar ring, directors attempting to pull out as many financial stops as possible, but seeing expenditure outstrip income: "A steady progress has been maintained covering all aspects, the redecoration of the social club which you must admit really adds to the comfort and appearance, this was considered vital as it is our main source of income, and despite news to the contrary our gates have improved, the standard of our play is reflected in our position in the League, and our 'A' team are now a well organised body playing well... We have come to an agreement with a well known baseball club that they will play at Alt Park through the summer (all to our financial benefit) for as well as playing through the summer and paying, we feel that they will swell the coffers of the Social Club... We are not out of the woods as yet, but at least we can begin to see day-light, we can only make a call for your continued support and hope for the day when we make it and you can say 'I was there at the start'." [36]

But during the summer of 1977 the Huyton board of directors resigned en masse. Gone were Wilf Hunt and Colin Parker, sick and tired one suspects of forever dipping into their own pockets to make safe the ineffective enclosure rather than securing new players. By September 1977 a new board of directors had surfaced under the guidance of Bill Isherwood. These men, together with indefatigable secretary Ken Grundy, were able to keep the club on something resembling an even keel. They placed a considerable amount of their own money at the disposal of Huyton RLFC and via further assistance from the RFL and the negotiation of a £12,000 share investment from Forshaw's Burtonwood Brewery were able to stabilise the social club.

The problem, however, with the brewery loan was that Forshaw's gained control of the social club and over the forthcoming years, prior to Huyton's move to Runcorn, this

180

meant that the rugby club was effectively starved of working capital. Like many other football clubs in a similar position the Huyton board of directors found that their chief source of income was being condensed.

Resembling other small sports organisations of that era, the ubiquitous 'development association' lottery tickets were introduced in an attempt to alleviate the shortfall – sadly to little avail. Cities such as Liverpool were swamped by such fund raising activities and, like all similar short-term schemes the appeal of these lottery scratch cards faded in direct proportion to the irritation brought about by unwelcome canvassing.

From a playing point of view the 1976–77 season was a moderate success. Terry Gorman was once again able to provide the directors with a reasonably competitive side, but whether this was due to the standard of the players being brought into the club, or the reported dramatic drop in quality of the lower regions of the game's Second Division is open to debate. Doug Davies became Terry Gorman's assistant in September 1976. On the pitch, the form of Arthur Daley was one of the highlights of the season.

Huyton began the season well with six league wins in eight matches – good enough for a near-top placing but with a small squad, this could not be maintained and a poor second half of the season materialised. Huyton performed doubles over Swinton, Batley, Blackpool and Doncaster, but still ended up in the bottom half of the table.

As usual, lucrative cup runs did not transpire; the side lost in the first round of each of the Lancashire, John Player, and Challenge Cups. The 3 April 1977 'Club Notes' from Andrews compounded cliché upon tired cliché: "It is not sufficient that we pay our way, this is not enough if we are going to go ahead and spend money to improve our position, so whilst we have stopped the rot we now have to turn the corner and start that uphill struggle. But it will happen... we have struggled too long, we have the backing of the Rugby League, and to the many times asked question of whether RL is a viable proposition in Liverpool, the answer is a great big yes." [37]

Huyton finished the season in a respectable ninth place, with 11 wins from 26 matches, having scored 302 points, but conceding 402.

At the end of the campaign Terry Gorman, the man to whom Huyton owed so much in turning out a half-decent side, but who had also somewhat ironically brought the club to the brink of extinction by forcing it to offer its players winning pay, departed to Swinton. The club had survived the greatest threat to its existence since the days of the Stanley Track - but only just. As with many clubs of all codes of football everywhere, a board of directors in hock to the brewery and a small, but dedicated, supporters' association was now running the show. Huyton RLFC had a social club that was out of the board's full control, and an ineffectual development programme: without the required bodies, both were mere shadows of the old Liverpool City initiatives.

The team was playing a standard of rugby league in front of a faithful few that at times belied rugby league's definition as a spectator sport. These issues were not Huyton's alone, of course, but they were magnified by endless vandalism that the club was effectively crippled. As in the days of John Bilsland and the Stanley Track, while the club remained at Alt Park, development possibilities did not exist. As Harry Edgar affirms, it was the vandalism issue – one that even today scarcely brings credit to the area – that finally forced the club to move to pastures new.

With the arrival of a new coach for the start of the 1977–78 season, Geoff Fletcher, the history of the club was to enter its final, decisive phase.

181

End notes

[1] Interview with RL historian Tom Fleet, July 2007

[2] Unaccredited correspondent [possibly B. Andrews], *Prescot & Huyton Reporter*, 23 August 1968, p.11

[3] G.C.L. [probably], 'Our Visitors', *Blackpool Borough Official Programme* [versus Huyton], Monday 2 September 1968, pp. 5, 8 not inclusive

[4] Waring, Eddie [ed.], *Eddie Waring Rugby League Annual 1968-69*, Castleford: M.B. Publications, p.52

[5] 'Rugby League Ground Is New Blind Centre', *Prescot & Huyton Reporter*, 30 August 1968, p.1

[6] [probably] J.P. Worthington, 'Welcome To Huyton', *Warrington Football Club Official Programme* [versus Huyton], Tuesday 24 September 1968, p.3

[7] Andrews, Bert, 'Youngsters Spoil Huyton's First Home Game', *Prescot & Huyton Reporter*, 20 September 1968, p.1

[8] Unaccredited editor, 'Editorial', *Huyton RLFC Official Programme* [versus Whitehaven at St Helens], Friday 18 October 1968, p.2

[9] Interview with John McGrath, 21 September 2007

[10] Unaccredited editor, 'Good Evening Fans', *Huyton RLFC Official Programme* [versus Featherstone Rovers], Friday 1 November 1968, pp.2-3

[11] Unaccredited editor, 'Editorial', *Huyton RLFC Official Programme* [versus Oldham at Widnes], 11 January 1969, pp.2-3

[12] Unaccredited editor, 'Editorial', *Huyton RLFC Official Programme* [versus Rochdale Hornets], Friday 13 December 1968, p.3

[13] Interview with Tom Fleet, July 2007

[14] Unaccredited editor, 'Good Evening Fans', *Huyton RLFC Official Programme* [versus Featherstone Rovers at Widnes], 1 November 1968, p.2

[15] Rugby league supporter John Davies to author 1 February 2008

[16] Unaccredited editor, 'Editorial' *Huyton RLFC Official Programme* [versus Warrington at Wilderspool], 2 April 1969, p.2

[17] Unaccredited editorial, 'Huyton Are Here Again!', *Widnes RFC Programme* [versus Huyton], Monday 7 April, 1969, p.2

[18] Unaccredited editor, 'Editorial' *Huyton RLFC Official Programme* [versus Doncaster], Saturday 3 May 1969, p.3

[19] Discussion with Jack Broome 29 July 2007

[20] Edgar, Harry (2003), 'League and Liverpool', *Rugby League Journal* 1/5 Winter, Egremont: Edgar Publishing, pp.20-22

[21] Mike Stephenson to author July 2007

[22] Garry Clarke, correspondence with author December 2007

[23] Harry Ody to author, January 2008

[24] Unaccredited 'Editorial' (perhaps Ken Grundy?), *Huyton RLFC Official Programme* [versus Leigh], 30 August 1969, p.3

[25] *ibid* [versus St Helens], 11 October 1969, p.2

[26] John Davies to author 1 February 2008

[27] Unaccredited 'Editorial' (perhaps Ken Grundy?), *Huyton RLFC Official Programme* [versus Oldham], 17 October 1970, pp 2-3

[28] Unaccredited 'Editorial' *Huyton RLFC Official Programme* [versus Huddersfield], 29 March 1971, p.2

[29] 'H.R.H.A.', 'Club Notes', *Huyton RLFC Official Programme* [versus Hull], 6 March 1977

[30] *ibid*, [versus Batley], 4 January 1976, p. 2

[31] Unaccredited editor, 'Huyton', *Whitehaven RLFC Official Programme* [versus Huyton], Friday 5 March 1976

[32] 'H.R.H.A.', 'Club Notes', *Huyton RLFC Official Programme* [versus Workington Town], Sunday 21 March 1976, p.3

[33] Arthur Evans to author, May 2007

[34] H.R.H. Andrews, 'Chairman's Report', *Huyton Rugby League Supporters' Club AGM Notice,* 25 May 1976, p.4

[35] Unaccredited 'Club Notes', *Huyton RLFC Official Programme* [versus Blackpool Borough], 28 November 1976, p.5

[36] W. Isherwood, 'From The Chairman', *Huyton RLFC Official Programme* [versus New Hunslet], Sunday 6 February 1977, p.3

[37] H.R.H.A 'Club Notes', *Huyton RLFC Official Programme* [versus Doncaster], Sunday 3 April 1977, p.6

9. Geoff Fletcher arrives

One should never suggest that a single man can effectively make history to the exclusion of others. Historians dislike over-simplicities, 'great-man-history' that eliminates contingency, convergence, class forces and the randomness of life. Yet, on the other hand, it is undeniable that key individuals do leave their mark in a historical sense, and that the unforeseen or divergent can contribute to the events surrounding such personalities: especially when that key person happens to be a pro-active decision maker rather than passive and reactive individual.

Tom Fleet comments that "If success was not achieved on the field at Huyton, it certainly was, in ensuring survival, by an incredibly dedicated group of workers. Of the many people who gave money, time and energy in the cause of Huyton, the one man whose name became synonymous with the club was Geoff Fletcher." [1]

While it would be incorrect to suggest that the vandalism at Alt Park was directly connected with the playing career of Geoff Fletcher, one might suggest, however, that the two are historically connected: one perhaps bringing out a determination in the other. Fletcher is undoubtedly a key individual in the history of rugby league in south-west Lancashire in the 1960s, 1970s, 1980s and 1990s. Yet, his contributions to the game remain largely unsung because of his decision to dedicate the latter years of his playing career to perhaps one of the least successful clubs in the entire history of the sport – Huyton RLFC.

The legend of Jimmy Green fostered and grew, but was then lost amid the ravages of time. The legend of Geoff Fletcher similarly reached considerable stature by the mid-1990s, but in the wake of the modern Super League culture, it also receded. Following the advent of Super League such one-man-club narratives, once perhaps the very substance of which rugby league legends were made, were no longer politically correct. It now appears that such stories are consigned to another era of rugby league history – an epoch that suggests decline and parochialism: beyond, if not living memory, then certainly comprehension. However, it is interesting to note that David Hodgkinson's book *Heroes of Rugby League*, published in 1983, along with chapters on many of the game's post-war legends includes a chapter on Geoff Fletcher.

Fletcher is now back to probably what he does best – farming. However, for almost 20 years he was the single – and perhaps single-minded – driving force behind the survival of the Huyton RLFC and its later incarnations.

Bill Isherwood and Ken Grundy, the incumbent chairman and secretary respectively of this struggling club, persuaded him to join Huyton as player-coach in the summer of 1977. Fletcher had enjoyed a well-rounded career with a variety of clubs since turning professional in 1962. Born and raised in St Helens, Geoff began as an amateur with Thatto Heath, where he won an amateur international cap; this was followed by a spell with Pilkington Recs. before he signed professional terms with Leigh.

Geoff went on to win Lancashire Cup and representative honours after moving to Oldham. Indeed he made a try-scoring debut for Lancashire versus Yorkshire at Widnes on 24 January 1968. He was then transferred to Wigan before returning to Hilton Park, Leigh. Wigan once again took Fletcher from Leigh in 1974 before he returned a third time for the 1975–76 season. Following this, he spent a season at Workington Town and it was here that Isherwood and Grundy approached him about the vacant player-coach position at Alt Park. Accepting the post was to be a life-changing decision.

The *Liverpool Echo* that August of 1977 was jam-packed with news concerning Liverpool FC's latest star signing, Kenny Dalglish, but *Echo* rugby league correspondent Leslie Woodhead was able to quote Fletcher in an optimistic mood in the *Football Echo* of 13 August:

Geoff Rises to Huyton Challenge

[Woodhead quoting Fletcher]: "We are right in the centre of a well-populated area here and we want to attract as many of these people as possible to come along and watch us and see what rugby league is all about. This is a great change for the people of the district. We have a fine clubhouse at Alt Park and I want to provide a successful team."[2]

In a display of further optimism concerning Fletcher's coaching abilities, Woodhead also discussed the high fitness levels of the Huyton squad and the fact that Fletcher, during his final spell at Leigh, had steered the 'A' team to the Lancashire Combination Championship. Actually, Geoff could still play to a high level, having also received man-of-the-match awards in six of his last seven appearances for Workington. According to Woodhead, Fletcher had also made a great signing by persuading Les Chisnall to return to the professional game from amateurs Pilkington Recs. This was, indeed, quite an achievement: Geoff remembers persuading Chisnall as "quite difficult".[3] He continued: "I lost a lot of players. It's always difficult when a coach takes over and there were a lot of Leigh lads who left with Terry. But Bill [Isherwood] was a hard worker who was from Widnes and he was able to introduce Widnes-based lads. I had my contacts of course – Les Chisnall was one of these and Huyton's team became a mixture of those who stayed and newcomers."

By the summer of 1977 Huyton RLFC was, if not penniless, certainly run on a hand-to-mouth basis. Fletcher soon discovered that coaching the side was but one activity among many if the club was to survive. Fortunately he was already a successful businessman with a thriving pig-breeding farm in St Helens and a retail newsagents in Clock Face – he did not need the money that the Huyton board of directors had offered him. This was just as well because within a short space of time it was costing Geoff money to play and coach the team: "I can't remember to this day why I said 'yes'... it certainly wasn't the money... it was probably the challenge. Also I had six months at Workington, training twice a week and playing once a week. It was only a short-term arrangement with Tom Mitchell and I helped keep them up [in the First Division] but it was a long way to travel. Ken Grundy offered me the player-coach job at Huyton. Ken was a lovely man, a gentleman. He was the real administrator at the club and his heart was always in the right place. Bill also told me straight that there was a real job on at Huyton, but I said yes. I knew I would have to do other things besides coaching such as paying the wages. Eventually I was paying them out of my own pocket, near enough."

As Tom Fleet suggests, to many, Geoff became 'Mr Huyton': "His contribution to Huyton was immense. Not only was he player-coach, he was team manager, groundsman, general factotum and fundraiser. In this last activity Fletcher organised sponsorship of many club activities over and above specific matches, often with publicans from the St Helens and Widnes areas."[4]

He wasn't a bad coach either. In his first season at Huyton, his team continued to be one of the most improved, at least among the lower echelons of the Second Division. Fletcher scored a superb try on his debut in a close 19–13 Lancashire Cup defeat against Warrington at Wilderspool on 21 August 1977, but Huyton followed this result with a run of five losing matches before a 9 October 20–14 victory at Keighley began to pull the season around. Following this result, the Huyton side was able to register on average almost a win every other game as a further eight victories and two draws ensued. The double was achieved twice that season: over a rather hapless Batley (11–3 and 12–6) and a more consistent Keighley (20–14 and 17–10), but the best result of the season by far was a home 12–5 victory against high-flying Huddersfield in January 1978. The Fartowners were subsequently promoted. A little financial fortune favoured Huyton in all three knock-out competitions. Despite losing in each of the first rounds of the Lancashire Cup, John Player Trophy and Challenge Cup, Huyton had drawn the aforementioned Warrington, plus Widnes and St Helens, respectively – and all away from home. A 50 per cent share of these gates was far better, of course, than a 50 per cent dividend from home attendances would have been and, as in days of old, these fixtures against the south-west Lancashire giants ensured Huyton could meet its financial obligations.

Fletcher had effectively succeeded in maintaining Terry Gorman's resolute side, and the Merseysiders' final league position of 10th in the Second Division was well earned. In the meantime, the cup fixtures had rescued the club's finances.

Of course the Huyton team was far from being a bunch of world-beaters, but players such as Tabern, with 34 goals and three tries, Burke, Alan Bishop, Brian Grady, O'Neill, Dave Walker and Fletcher himself proved to be among the toughest of oppositions in the Second Division. John Huxley of the *Huddersfield Daily Examiner* remarked in his Fartown programme notes in September 1977: "...over the last couple of seasons they have become a tough team to beat." [5] Huxley might have used the word 'tough' in a more general sense, for Fletcher's team was becoming renown for its hard men. This reputation was infused by regular sendings-off, resulting in several inconvenient bans for such a diminutive squad. There was no 'A' team, of course.

Oddly, one player did receive something of a pardon. Forward Les Westhead, who in November 1976 had previously received a *sine die* ban from the RFL for allegedly grabbing referee Ron Moore by the collar while disputing a decision, found it revoked for the 1977–78 season after Geoff Fletcher – desperately short of players – had pleaded his case. Westhead played in the four opening games that season - he scored a try in the September 33–10 home defeat by York, but then disappeared for the rest of the season. He returned intermittently the following term but was something of a marked man and retired from the professional game in December 1978 after playing against Oldham.

1977–78 Second Division (top ten)

1 Leigh	26	21	0	5	538	231	42
2 Barrow	26	21	0	5	521	234	42
3 Rochdale Hornets	26	21	0	5	437	200	42
4 Huddersfield	26	18	0	8	502	324	36
5 York	26	16	2	8	447	286	34
6 Oldham	26	17	0	9	419	325	34
7 Keighley	26	11	3	12	357	337	25
8 Swinton	26	11	1	14	369	385	23
9 Whitehaven	26	10	2	14	277	326	22
10 Huyton	**26**	**9**	**2**	**15**	**250**	**352**	**20**

But this relative equilibrium both on and off the pitch was not to last. As any reader of the *Liverpool Echo*'s regular 'Kirkby and Huyton' feature would have noted, the social and economic infrastructure of Knowsley was rapidly deteriorating. On 9 August the

Liverpool Echo reported: "School leavers have boosted the number of jobless teenagers to a record figure of 3,600 in Knowsley. And Huyton appears to have taken over from Kirkby as the borough's unemployment black spot." [6] It was to worsen even further, for by the following month that figure had risen to 4,000 and continued an upward ascent thereafter.

During the close season of 1978 the youth of Longview caused so much destruction to Alt Park that it was declared unfit for use. One visit by local delinquents resulted in stand seats ripped out of their sockets, perimeter and partition walls demolished, parts of the playing area dug up, and the added hazard of broken glass being inserted like land mines into the surface. On another occasion the clubhouse plumbing and electrics were severely damaged. The sports editor of the *Prescot & Huyton Reporter* noted: "Huyton RL team face a tough start to the season when they face league champions Widnes in the first round of the Forshaw's Lancashire Cup. And if that task is not difficult enough Huyton have been forced to switch the game from Alt Park to Widnes because of... about £5,000 worth of damage to the ground, including stand seats being ripped out, toilets smashed and frequent break-ins to the clubhouse and social club... conditions are so bad at the ground that the tie had to be switched." [7]

Throughout that summer of 1978 vandalism was becoming the norm and the *Reporter* was constantly occupied by such events. The *Liverpool Echo*, on the other hand, did not even consider the damage at Alt Park to be newsworthy until the first edition of that season's *Football Echo* was published in late August. Leslie Woodhead merely retrospectively recorded that "as they recover from a pre-season body blow of costly vandalism on their Alt Park ground, the club are looking confidently and optimistically at the new season." This report – actually more of a press release – went on to display photos of both coach Geoff Fletcher and chairman Bill Isherwood in positive demeanours – perhaps to some extent attempting to 'play down' the vandalism.

Disorder

Prior to that opening 1978–79 fixture, RFL secretary David Oxley had paid a visit to Alt Park and declared the enclosure unsuitable for professional rugby league. Huyton RLFC appeared to be back where it had started in 1968: playing at Widnes's Naughton Park in front of a faithful few. This time only one game was staged at Widnes – the Widnes accounts show £192 was the Chemics' share of the gate – but chairman Bill Isherwood, who had placed a lot of his own money from his plumbers merchants business in Widnes at the disposal of the club, and had helped to negotiate the loan with Forshaw's brewery, had had enough and promptly resigned. The brewery was running the social club for its own ends and providing him with only a modicum of cash. Isherwood could see little future for the club and consistent with his own relocation to North Wales, decided to stand down as chairman; he later left the boardroom completely.

Supporter John Davies remembers: "Bill was incredibly upset – in fact he was incensed. He told me in an unguarded moment he saw no sense in continuing at Huyton and I think his resignation set the scene to eventually leave the borough." [8] Of course at this stage the club was in no position to up-sticks yet again – especially when a brewery loan hovered like the Sword of Damocles over the club. Before his resignation, in an attempt to show the brewery that the club was trying to cut expenses, Isherwood had cancelled first the 'A' team coach and then the 'A' team itself. But it was all to no avail as the vandalism wore him down. The Huyton programme notes for the game versus

Halifax at Widnes on 9 September 1978 simply announced in an unemotional way: "Many of you will be aware of the reason for these arrangements from press reports etc. But for the benefit of others, the position is that during the close season Alt Park has been subjected to a sustained campaign of vandalism involving damage to excess of £5,000. The result is that our ground has been rendered unfit for use. The matter has been placed in the hands of our insurers, whose due processes of course take time, but we are hopeful Alt Park will be ready for use in the near future... The main item of news from the boardroom is the resignation of our chairman, Mr Bill Isherwood, after two years in office. Bill's resignation has been reluctantly brought about by business pressure and the fact that he now lives in North Wales... Bill's contribution to the club during his period as chairman should not go unrecorded and I have no hesitation in saying that but his devoted efforts there would be no Huyton RLFC today." [9]

The new chairman, Lawrence Karalius, a member of perhaps one of rugby league football's most famous families, was soon to find the going extremely tough during his short tenure. In fact, according to Geoff Fletcher, Karalius once wanted to close down the club completely. Fletcher resisted, the closure was effectively halted, and Karalius later moved on. Fletcher recalls: "He came to me one day and said the brewery is taking over the social club and the club's closing and the team's finished. I said 'oh no it's not you've no shares in this club and you've no rights here – we'll run the rugby club'. The manager from the brewery came down and said he was shutting the social club so I just said 'OK, but you won't shut us down'. They had already put in their own steward and they were giving us nothing. I don't know what happened after that but Karalius seemed to disappear."

Vice chairman Ian Comish, a Southport resident, began to sound out the possibilities of a move to the floodlit Haig Avenue ground of Southport FC. However this bold idea was immediately put on hold, for no sooner had preliminary discussions commenced in the close season of 1978, than Southport were ejected from the Football League. Furthermore, part of Haig Avenue, the covered terrace behind one goal, was declared unsafe and closed. This was neither the first, nor the last time that the name of Southport FC became linked with that of Huyton RLFC and although a move was not to transpire, it was Comish, following-on from Isherwood's resignation, who slowly set the ball rolling concerning club relocation.

On the pitch Huyton's 1978–79 season began in a most curious fashion. In their new kit of white shirts with a red, black and amber 'V' they lost 43–6 at Widnes in the aforementioned rearranged Lancashire Cup tie in August, but after that drew the next four matches – an amazing statistic for rugby league. Owing to further destruction and the fact that the ground's infrastructure had now been weakened not only by the vandalism, but also by ineffective repairs, all of the games were played away. Following a 6–6 draw at Batley on 3 September, an 11–11 draw ensued against Halifax at Widnes on the 9th, Huyton and Swinton finished all-square 16–16 on the 17th and this was incredibly followed by 13-points-apiece draw on the 24th at Hilton Park against Leigh in the John Player Trophy. This game was replayed (again at Leigh) and only two points then separated the sides 10–8 in Leigh's favour. Normal service was resumed, however, on 1 October 1978 when the Huyton team was thrashed 32–5 at New Hunslet. It was this result that confirmed the vandal-led tone for the season: depression and slow destruction. In between the loss at New Hunslet and a win against Batley on 25 March 1979 every game was lost and Huyton managed only another two victories for the rest of the campaign – in succession in May 1979 against Dewsbury 25–21 and Whitehaven

15–12, both games back at the still partially-wrecked Alt Park. Half-back Jimmy O'Neill – according to Geoff Fletcher "one of the best I ever had – and a really funny man" – top-scored with 10 tries and 18 goals. This was an impressive feat in such a weak squad. Fletcher was unable to repeat the competitive character of previous seasons.

As a whole the club was in a sense of deep dejection following the problems with its adopted area. Indeed, Geoff Fletcher found it extremely difficult to attract and then hold onto players of the required standard while even the most basic facilities were practically non-existent. By October 1978 Huyton had only 19 players registered with the RFL and injuries and unavailability were further shrinking that already small figure: "We really struggled for players; I had to dip into the local amateur leagues all the time. Everybody I had from league teams had family problems – that's why they didn't turn out for the bigger teams... knocking at doors, lads playing under pseudonyms. 'Mick Grady' played in every position! Scrum-half and prop! Mick was the local copper who had come to control the game one day and I'd seen him and he could run, so I said 'what are you doing?' He said he was on duty and I asked him to play... so he did! When his Sergeant came around with the car after the game Mick just told him 'it's been very quiet today'. When he was running down the pitch the kids called him all sorts. Then his name became our pseudonym for trialists and amateurs.

I even dipped into the amateur leagues in Doncaster. The lad who featured in *Another Bloody Sunday* – I got him too. The problem was it was a real step up for the amateur lads. But I never had a team that didn't try, even though they could let you down because they couldn't really make that step up."

On 22 October 1978, the Dewsbury programme editor recognised the seriousness of Huyton's vandalism predicament and reported to supporters: "It is unlikely that their Alt Park ground will be fit to play on this season and that the likely costs of the vandalism are going to be well over the original estimate of £5,000. For a problem like that to hit a club like Huyton with their limited finances and prospects not that good, is a very severe blow indeed which they will do well to survive." [10]

Survival became the number one criterion, while the weather during that winter of discontent was equally miserable with heavy snowfalls, and ice lasting into late-February. When a thaw did finally arrive, most football pitches across Merseyside were waterlogged. For Huyton, an eight-week period elapsed without either a game of rugby or more than a modicum of income. Between 17 December 1978 – a 25–13 loss at home to Oldham and 21 February 1979 – a 14–2 Challenge Cup defeat at the hands of Keighley, Huyton RLFC did not play a match. The 'Wishbone' lottery ticket – a piece of card not remembered with a great deal of relish across Merseyside – came to play a major part in Huyton's survival. Between this meagre income and what little Forshaw's brewery donated after social club running expenses had been deducted, Huyton RLFC plodded on regardless.

The transfer to Whitehaven of stand-off Jimmy O'Neill in April, where he joined his brother Dennis and former Widnes player Ray Dutton, also helped the cause financially, but O'Neill was a talented player Huyton could ill-afford to lose. By 16 May 1979 chairman Karalius's programme notes for the penultimate home fixture versus Whitehaven declared the season to be: "One of our most disappointing seasons ever [yet] I feel most optimistic for the future of our club with the tremendous progress that has been made with the financial affairs of the company. The problems facing the new directors at the commencement of this season were so great that only a concerted effort averted disaster." [11] The supporters had heard that before.

1978–79 Second Division (bottom six)

9 Oldham	26	10	1	15	297	435	21
10 Whitehaven	26	8	3	15	297	408	19
11 Swinton	26	7	2	17	349	452	16
12 Doncaster	26	7	0	19	259	547	14
13 Huyton	**26**	**3**	**3**	**20**	**261**	**513**	**9**
14 Batley	26	4	1	21	194	479	9

Portents of doom?

Cutbacks were apparent everywhere at the once-more-vandalised Alt Park as the Huyton side kicked-off in 1979-80. For example, the official programme was reduced to a very basic affair with only eight pages printed on very poor quality faded blue paper. Geoff Fletcher had next-to-nothing to spend on incoming players and relied on goodwill as much as anything. Furthermore, and akin to the post-war Liverpool Stanley side, even the kit turned out to be anything on which the club could lay its hands. The team was decked-out in very basic red shirts with blue shorts for most of the season and blue shirts with red shorts as 'change' strip.

Huyton's first four games were all away from home after a designated home fixture against Bramley had been reversed, thanks again to an unfit Alt Park. Because the fixture was switched at very short notice the Bramley bar apparently remained closed and not even a programme was issued for the game. Bramley even wanted the game to count as a Huyton home fixture, but the RFL sided with the Merseyside club. Bramley won 23–18.

By the 7 October fixture against Dewsbury, Fletcher was having great difficulty raising a side, but finally managed to cobble together a line-up that went down 35-0. The amateur Reddicliffe and the ubiquitous 'Mick Grady' were drafted-in at the last minute; whereas Reddicliffe did not play again, 'Grady' was to appear on innumerable team sheets: only as a pseudonym, of course. Fellow struggling minnows Doncaster were put to the sword 24–5 at the end of October and Whitehaven defeated 23–10 at an increasingly grim-looking Alt Park, which had suffered more vandalism – this time to the perimeter walls, in November 1979.

However, following this win, 12 straight defeats ensued. It was only by virtue of two Huyton wins in April against Yorkshire strugglers Bramley, 16–10, and Keighley, 15–3, that Doncaster rather than Huyton ended up at the foot of the Second Division. It was at the end of this bleak season that Huyton was portentously given until the end of June to confirm to the RFL their intent for the following season. The Rugby League Council was actually providing Fletcher with the opportunity to resign his team from the RFL and it was noted at the RFL AGM that Huyton was the only club not represented, a matter disputed by Geoff Fletcher.

It was this season that the impeccable award-winning Yorkshire Television documentary *Another Bloody Sunday* materialised. Ostensibly concerning the day-to-day survival of the Doncaster club, it nevertheless displayed Fletcher and his players battling unsuccessfully against a Doncaster side that was in search of victory to end the longest run of defeats in the Yorkshire club's history. Predictably this run came to an end via an unconverted try against Huyton that February 1980. These two clubs were undoubtedly connected, not simply via their travails but by their indefatigability and dedication to the sport of rugby league. The activities surrounding Doncaster's survival in a seemingly uncaring town, despite the city's long affiliation with amateur rugby league its professional side has often struggled - perfectly reflected the Huyton story – with one notable exception: the squalid surroundings of Doncaster's aptly named Tattersfield were luxurious in comparison to the wreckage at Alt Park. The programme not only suggested that these enthusiasts were authentic custodians of the sport, but it also captured an important financially stricken era in Britain's sporting narrative.

It showed quite clearly that at some rugby league clubs only a 'thin red line' of supporters and players stood between appearance and disappearance. To this very day *Another Bloody Sunday* is a monumental slice of British social history and, thankfully, Doncaster survived, but one wonders how the RFL responded to this documentary at that time. Once might propose that, despite its authenticity, it did not, at least as far as the RFL was concerned, project anything like the image they wanted for the game.

For 1979–80 Huyton's squad was miniscule and somewhat aged. Alec Heesom, at 36 years of age, was still getting a game, and without the ever-reliable Dave Walker, Alan Bishop and Fletcher himself, the coach would have been unable to field a fully competitive side – indeed trialists and pseudonym AN Others, together with good old 'Mick Grady', were creeping increasingly onto the team-sheets.[12]

The club also lost forward Keith Wills to Leigh in November 1979. Wills had been injured and had only played two matches on 24 October and 4 November before Leigh came in for him. But it all seemed something of a waste of time and money, as Wills was back at Alt Park later that season for his third spell at the club, illustrating just how much disparity existed between the First and Second Divisions of the Rugby League Championship. Despite Wills' nomadic tendencies, Fletcher had no real choice but to take him back – he was short of players and Wills had been released without a fee.

In February 1980, Huyton drew First Division high-flyers Salford in the first round of the Challenge Cup. By this time Alt Park was in such a distressed condition that the RFL threatened to switch the tie to The Willows. In a concerted effort resembling a military operation, Geoff Fletcher organised his players to help repair the perimeter walls to both pitch and ground so that the tie could go ahead at Huyton. They were successful and although Salford cruised to a 25–0 victory, the share of the gate of approximately 3,000 paying customers was manna from heaven.

Fletcher was now taking more and more interest in the day-to-day affairs of his club. He played 16 games that season, which was incredibly strenuous for an ageing professional, but his off-the-field work was now becoming at least as significant as his on-the-field activities.

The directors announced prior to the Salford match: "This has been a tremendous gesture of loyalty to Huyton by Geoff Fletcher and his team." But this was, of course, a massive and rather patronising understatement. Indeed, Geoff Fletcher was beginning to regard the board of directors as a rather somnambulant group of individuals. While freely admitting that he was (and remains) a maverick Fletcher recalls being "the only one who seemed to actually get things done – I thought we had some right idiots on the board at times".

Second Division 1979–80 (bottom six)

9 Batley	26	10	2	14	232	370	22
10 Bramley	26	10	1	15	330	451	21
11 Keighley	26	10	0	16	342	396	20
12 Huddersfield	26	10	0	16	363	423	20
13 Huyton	**26**	**5**	**0**	**21**	**209**	**555**	**10**
14 Doncaster	26	1	1	24	196	733	3

Fulham

The talking point of the 1980–81 season was the arrival of the Fulham RLFC into professional rugby league. Almost 50 years had elapsed since the old Wigan Highfield club had made its pact with the Greyhound Racing Association and the experiment, of course, had not been a success. This had been followed a couple of years later by attempts to develop two more teams in London, Action & Willesden and Streatham & Mitcham. The former had only lasted a season, the latter had withdrawn from the league in February 1937. Now, Harold Genders and his cohort of enthusiasts had persuaded the hard-up Fulham FC that an extra stream of
valuable income could be sourced from a move into rugby league.

For the new season the Fulham team was placed in the Second Division of the championship, a practical but, in retrospect, perhaps unwise move. With a selection of experienced players, youngsters and a couple of recruits from rugby union, Fulham RLFC was able to breeze through that first season and gain promotion. But the yawning gap between the First and Second Divisions was fully exposed to 'the Cottagers' the following season. They were relegated and with away fixtures to come at the likes of Alt Park and Tattersfield, combined with the departure of some of the veterans who had been the fans' heroes in the first season, interest in west London waned.

Huyton's first visit to Fulham was quite an occasion: in front of nearly 6,000 at Craven Cottage, Fulham eventually ran out 25–4 winners but for a while the game was a close-run thing. Yet Geoff Fletcher remembers events following the match as rather more significant: "Yes, we ran them close, as I remember, and it was in front of over 5,000 at the ground. [Fulham chairman] Ernie Clay was really delighted with the day and came over to me and asked me how much it had cost to bring the team to Fulham. I just said 'oh about £5,000'. He took out his chequebook and wrote out a cheque for five grand. I couldn't believe it. But it was that good a day, and Fulham had brought in so many people, that he must have thought it was worth it."

Throughout 1980–81 Huyton were once more struggling against the seemingly insurmountable odds of damage and destruction. In the Warrington official programme for the 17 August 1980 Forshaw's Lancashire cup-tie against Huyton, Billy Benyon noted: "Coming back to our friends from Huyton, there has been press speculation about a possible link-up with soccer side Tranmere Rovers, at least in ground facilities and the experiment at Fulham may well produce interest in this direction. Grounds are often isolated and the mindless brigade can wreak havoc in a very short time." [13]

The Huyton directors clearly wanted out of Alt Park and the local press had got wind of this. However, the Tranmere story, while not without a level of veracity was something of a smokescreen. It was once again Southport FC, now members of the Northern Premier League, who had expressed interest in the prospect of Huyton RLFC sharing their stadium. Southport FC was by this time practically bankrupt and had rather oddly refused to join the new Alliance Premier League (now known as the Conference) on a matter of principal. The club also suffered from factionalism, mounting debts and a partially dilapidated ground so for Ian Comish, now Huyton chairman, the prospects of a ground-share with an equally weakened association football club looked burdened with difficulties. In principal, the Rugby League Council approved of these Southport-Huyton moves, but unlike on previous occasions, did not offer financial assistance, merely standing in the wings and watching as negotiations finally came to nought. It was now clear that the RLC quietly viewed Huyton RLFC as a club they could willingly do without.

As for Huyton's ground, perhaps the root of all of the club's problems since 1968, the intensity of the attacks increased exponentially; practically every week brought further bad news. By the autumn of 1980 sledgehammers had reduced the pitch surround to pieces and the playing area was therefore deemed by the RLC not to be fully enclosed; the RFL took a dim view of this for some months to come. Pressure was beginning to mount – the Liverpool newspapers largely ignored the club and the rugby league authorities questioned its validity. Even the most passive sports fan could see that results were disastrous: the Huyton team was in freefall and spent the majority of the season vying with Doncaster and Blackpool for the bottom place in the Second Division.

Only two games were won that season, predictably against the aforementioned Doncaster, 20–0, and Blackpool, 12–8. Huyton duly ended this disastrous campaign rock bottom of the league. The season ended very gloomily with Huyton conceding more than 30 points in nine of their final 13 games. The last match, at Keighley on 19 April 1981, resulted in a heavy 50–5 defeat.

Back in January 1981 the Hunslet programme editor, in congratulating Geoff Fletcher and his players for their shared aims, spoke of rugby league as "a sport that delights in self-inflicted bad publicity". The point was well made: in this era of rampant hooliganism and insensitive unemployment most of rugby league's Second Division clubs were both financially inept and socially ineffective. Rugby league had perhaps for the first time failed to generate a new cohort of supporters within its heartlands and with a palpable lack of inward investment, pitiable spectator facilities, and an often poor quality (and sometimes violent) brand of rugby, the lower echelons of the professional game had entered a dark era.

Attendances and income fell in diametric relationship with the Thatcherite economy of the 1980s – which directed much of its economic dismantling of traditional industries towards the very towns where rugby league had prospered. The borough of Huyton, never of course a rugby league heartland, was by this time also suffering from mass unemployment and economic meltdown. Over the next couple of seasons the RFL attempted to breathe new life into the Second Division by sanctioning new clubs. It was this revival of interest from the Rugby League Council itself that led to a bold, but adventurous and ultimately costly, expansion of the Second Division to an unprecedented 20 clubs by 1984. In the meantime, however, Huyton's resignation, rather than reinvention, would have pleased many council members – and perhaps even RFL secretary David Oxley.

For the visit of Fulham on Sunday 15 March 1981, Huyton attempted to pull out all the stops in welcoming the London stars and their supporters. In the absence of any cash to pay for even a plate of sandwiches and tea for the players, Geoff Fletcher had arranged the players' refreshments to come from the Cherry Tree Hotel in St Helens and the catering at the ground from The Bridge Hotel – similarly in St Helens – all free of charge. However the enclosure was once again in a terrible mess and the programme editor for that fixture, probably Ian Comish, was forced to apologise in print for: "The condition of Alt Park is not what we would like it to be - to say the least. Repeated acts of vandalism have made it difficult to carry out any improvement work but we are hoping to make improvements shortly. In the meantime we apologise to spectators for the state of the ground." [14]

Action at Alt Park

Top: Huyton versus Wigan 14 December 1980. (Photo: Mike Haddon)

Middle: Huyton versus Cardiff Blue Dragons 20 September 1981. Steve Fenwick evades a tackle. (Photo: Alex Service)

Left: The last game at Alt Park, 26 April 1984. (Bob Webster archive)

Huyton RLFC 1983-84 (Courtesy *Rugby League Journal*)

Geoff Fletcher in action for Huyton.
(Courtesy *Rugby League Journal*)

Problems at Alt Park

Left: Vandalism during a game – local youngsters trying to demolish the stand

Below: Spectators watching the action. Much of the stand roof is missing.

(Photos: Andrew Cudbertson)

195

In the same 'souvenir programme', international referee Mick Naughton stated with a genuine degree of integrity: "Most people would have called it a day long before now, but not Geoff Fletcher who refuses to let the Huyton club die, even when the youths living around the Alt Park ground go in daily and ransack the place. In Geoff Fletcher Huyton have a rugby league fanatic, he eats, sleeps, and drinks the game. While there is a ray of light Geoff will continue to work at it for the sake of Huyton, rugby league, and his love for the game.

"Everyone you speak to in the game say 'poor Huyton' and then forget it. But I can tell you Geoff doesn't want sympathy, he wants action and any help from people willing to chip in to help the Huyton club to survive the present crisis.

"I know what a state the club is in. Earlier this season I was given the job by Rugby League HQ to inspect the pitch before the game vs Doncaster and even I finished up marking the pitch with helpers like Big Chisee and Little Chisee, a father and son team who clean the dressing rooms, wash the kit, mark the pitch, and do every other little job required of them around the ground. Mrs Chisee helps with the food after the match." [15]

The game was duly lost 19-3; supporter John Davies recalls: "I went to that Fulham match and all I heard all afternoon were complaints from visiting supporters. I don't know how many were in the ground that day." [16] One is left wondering exactly what the travelling Fulham fans made of Alt Park that March afternoon – perhaps there was a mixture of feelings: admiration, maybe, for a club freely admitting to its shoestring existence, but also possible wonder that such poor facilities could (or should) exist and be endorsed by the Rugby Football League in 1981.

There might have even been a few present that day, after reading Dave Leatherbarrow's welcoming programme notes, who were both amazed and dismayed that this was the club that had set in motion the first London rugby league experiment almost 50 years previously.

By April 1981 club officials had been invited to attend an emergency meeting with RFL secretary David Oxley, who was becoming ever-worried by Huyton's thinning infrastructure. Perhaps the glaring opposites of the Huyton versus Fulham fixture had not been lost on the ambitious secretary who wished the RFL to enter a new era of prosperity. It became evident to Oxley that, alongside the small board of only a half-dozen souls, it was Geoff Fletcher and a few players, such as the aforementioned stalwart Dave Leatherbarrow, who were keeping the club alive – but what kind of existence was it - and at what cost? The Keighley programme editor for Huyton's last match of the season suggested that Fletcher and the players were now running the club and questioned this albeit steadfast continuation at Huyton: "[This is] a side whose future has been in the balance for most of the season with player-coach Geoff Fletcher and his players having virtually run the club both on and off the field. Where Huyton's future rests has been in doubt for some time and there have been suggestions that next season they could embark on a ground sharing venture with either Southport or Runcorn soccer club." [17]

Fittingly, only Geoff Fletcher actually turned up for the meeting, yet following the soul-searching, the RFL secretary David Oxley announced to all that there was no need to panic – this meeting he stated had been the first in a series of get-togethers between the Rugby League and the Huyton club. Oxley, according to Geoff Fletcher, was a "true gentleman" but was also acting on the instructions of the RFL chairman, who along with his council members was running out of patience with the pocket-sized club: "I felt that they wanted us out, but they wanted a few clubs out – Blackpool, Doncaster, Dewsbury,

Batley – they wanted them all out – I realised this but it just made me all the more determined. There was still a pool but we didn't get much, if anything. They told me we were going to be leaving but they weren't providing us with anything. But we'd stabilised the club."

Fletcher, during a discussion after lunch, produced a Huyton RLFC bank book showing £5,000 on deposit. Oxley almost certainly realised that on this evidence Huyton was probably the only club in the Second Division actually 'in the black' and withdrew from any out-and-out demands suggested by his chairman. One might suggest that the £5,000 cheque from Fulham's Ernie Clay had been the source of these funds, but in fact this was money that had been unearthed from ticket sales, dinner-dances and donations. On this showing, Geoff Fletcher's team was by now not only paying its own way but also showing a small profit for the club – but it was not to last.

1980–81 Second Division (bottom four)

12 Dewsbury	28	11	1	16	346	364	23
13 Doncaster	28	5	0	23	250	562	10
14 Blackpool Borough	28	4	1	23	212	419	9
15 Huyton	**28**	**2**	**0**	**26**	**211**	**796**	**4**

Job creation?

Geoff Fletcher recalled that "From the moment I came, there was constant vandalism – they couldn't get in the club house however – we had bars and bolts – even machine gun posts! The vandals used to lever the terracing up! It took all of the players to put it back – how they moved it, in the first place, I don't know."

For the 1981–82 season Ian Comish officially took a back seat as local JP Seth Powell was elected chairman. Powell commenced negotiations with the local council and employment services for the possibility of a government-funded Job Creation Scheme (JCS) to begin at Alt Park. Such schemes were part of the Conservative government's initiative aimed at reducing youth unemployment, especially in such deprived areas as that surrounding the Huyton rugby league ground.

Similar in some respects to the Youth Training Scheme or YTS, JCS was aimed at mostly young men and women on the long term unemployment register whose benefit would be stopped if they did not agree to join the programme. The young unemployed were then placed into a trade in an attempt to get them experienced and trained, with the hopes of being kept on in employment at the conclusion of the scheme. In fact only two major features evolved from this forlorn agenda: firstly that the youngsters mostly did not learn a trade, as such, and were only employed for menial tasks; secondly that the companies employing them did so only for the duration of the scheme as cheap labour, and released them once the prospect of paying real wages loomed large. Both of these eventualities were particularly prevalent in the building trade, where profits had been squeezed by the inflation of the early 1980s.

Nevertheless, at one stage £85,000 worth of work on Alt Park was discussed, a figure that would certainly have resulted in a refurbished enclosure. However, predictably, the plan evolved at a snail's pace and when it finally did begin it became clear to all that it would be a thoroughly disappointing exercise. Work was painfully slow and of poor quality, the work gangs brought in under the builders' supervision were ill-equipped and lacking in the most basic skills and eventually the programme petered to a close with only a little poor quality renovation work completed. Indeed it has since been argued by some that those employed were repairing their own vandalism; John Davies outlines that: "I recognised a couple who were supposed to be on the JCS or YTS. They were hanging around at a match one Sunday, and ended-up breaking the fencing on the far side of the ground that they had been repairing during the week. It didn't make much difference: their work was hopeless. It was a typical government scheme thing; they were only turning up to keep themselves on the dole." [18]

A little money came into the club that season from Liverpool businessman Ian Wallis of Cathedral Tours and the transfer of Paul Fitzpatrick to Rochdale Hornets but it was, by and large, an uneventful and disheartening period: one of constant struggles with repairs and vandalism occurring abreast of each other and, of course, the ever-failing side. Only five games were won, more than 700 points conceded, and yet again the team finished at the foot of the Second Division. There was no denying that Alt Park now gave off both the atmosphere and appearance of impermanence to all who went along.

Geoff Fletcher carried ever-increasing responsibilities, raising money here, there and everywhere from local hostelries, lottery tickets and small sponsorship deals. He remembers: "We were getting nothing from beer, so we tried everything: we sold the Wishbone lottery tickets. The lottery was run honestly and people appreciated that, and we were getting local winners, which was good. Terry Hughes inherited the scheme at Huyton and I handed the new directors like Ken Carberry that bank book with £5,000. Some of the players weren't happy because they'd helped to raise the money but it was the best thing to do. We had sportsman's dinners in St Helens and Widnes to help pay the wages. The wages were not that great but it all helped."

Despite the presence of a development officer, it was Fletcher who was now effectively in charge not only of coaching and selecting the team, but also finding the cash to pay for it. Indeed by October 1981, and much to the embarrassment of the Rugby League Council, who now clearly wanted the club removed from the competition, Fletcher was awarded an *Open Rugby* magazine Sportsmanship Award. Harry Edgar stated: "No man typifies the spirit of grassroots rugby league better than Geoff and we are proud to make him the first recipient of the... award." By November 1981 Fletcher had received another accolade, this time from the Rugby League Writer's Association for his "outstanding contribution to Rugby League". These awards symbolised a marked difference of opinion between the rugby league press and the elected officials. In a reversal of the Eddie Waring fiasco of the early 1950s, Huyton found itself at the centre of an argument over grassroots versus expansion. But this time it was the press who backed the club, not the RFL.

But, of course, unlike their coach, the Huyton side was never going to pick up any silverware. By the New Year of 1982 the club programme notes bemoaned the fact that its side had won only one game during the entire year of 1981. As time elapsed, and despite Fletcher's best efforts, the club was gradually vanishing from view. 'Groundhopper' John Bibby recalls: "For me, the whole point of watching Huyton at this time was the same as my ideas about being a non-league soccer fan. I would go to watch, say, Runcorn or Marine and enjoy the general atmosphere about the place, pick up a programme, watch a passable game of football – sometimes it could very exciting – and generally enjoy being at the ground, as much as the game. I'd also follow rugby league because it was a chance of doing the same on a Sunday and a lot of the grounds were interesting. But the point was that I wouldn't be very concerned about going to, say, Warrington or St Helens if I could find a smaller club with an interesting ground.

198

Geoff Fletcher charging forward for Huyton (Photo: Andrew Cudbertson)

That's how visits to Huyton began. But as the seasons rolled by, the place became dismal and depressing. I remember one Sunday in the early 1980s standing there at the Prescot Road end with those horrible tower blocks looming over the other side of the ground and asking myself 'what actually was the point of this place?' The ground was a complete mess, and there was a total lack of atmosphere. The club seemed to be fading before my very eyes. I answered myself that there didn't seem to be a point, and, sad to say, never returned." [19]

1981–82 Second Division (bottom four)

14 Batley	32	8	0	24	357	596	16
15 Blackpool Borough	32	7	0	25	341	608	14
16 Doncaster	32	5	1	26	319	793	11
17 Huyton	**32**	**5**	**0**	**27**	**296**	**707**	**10**

In October 1982 the boardroom was to thank "Mr Pat Kelly and his men for their work on the ground renovations." But the message was to add: "This work is progressing well but we still require financial assistance to fulfil our desire to rebuild our stadium. Details of our fund-raising schemes are elsewhere in this programme please support us if you can." [20] Reading between the lines this appears a very disappointing announcement and following the mostly unsuccessful and unsatisfactory Job Creation Scheme, the 1982-83 directors, now under a new chairman, Terry Hughes, launched their own model: Buy Bricks for Huyton. Garry Clarke remembers: "In the early 1980s Huyton, in an attempt to rebuild the vandalised Alt Park, offered supporters the opportunity to Buy bricks for Huyton. For £1 you could buy 10 bricks and get a free match ticket... so, if Warrington did not have a game, a group of us would go to watch Huyton, having first rung up to buy our 10 bricks and claim our match ticket." [21]

Tom Fleet now considers the idea as a faltering concept: "There were only a couple of dozen subscribers. You can see that from the programmes. It was just a form of sponsorship – I contributed under 'Tom Fleet & Friends' but I never saw any new bricks being purchased or used. I suspect the money went into running the team." [22]

Tom Fleet's suspicions are correct; 'Buy a Brick' was a cashflow solution as much as anything and the truth was that Alt Park was never going to recover from these incessant cancerous attacks – indeed the entire enclosure was technically unsafe. The programme notes for 2 January 1983 declared: "1983 should see a completion to the much needed ground renovation scheme. Already Alt Park is looking a lot better and we will have a stadium to be proud of" [23] but this was an actual and metaphorical whitewash: the Buy a brick campaign didn't begin to answer either the vandalism, alienation or inertia and Huyton's light began to flicker even more dimly and intermittently.

By 1 April 1983 landlords from no less than eight pubs in and around the district were sponsoring Huyton's home game against Whitehaven. This desperate act was once more the work of Geoff Fletcher who had taken to the road in an attempt to fund matchday expenses; but there was no 'thank you' from the club in the programme which, by this time was simply a pre-printed advertising medium with only one or two pages given over to match reports. In fact, the boardroom was now effectively off limits to the remaining supporters and for practically the entire season few announcements concerning Huyton's financial plight or future transpired. In the past the prime method of communication between directors and supporters had been the programme's 'Club Notes', which at times seemed to elucidate perhaps rather too much about the club's lack of progress. Ken Grundy's florid yet often unaccredited notes had previously kept supporters well informed but the redoubtable Ken had finally retired as secretary in 1980 and since that time fans were not privy to the machinations of the boardroom.

There was probably little to say after the hopes of the JCS had been all-but dashed. The team continued to struggle and the board had accordingly reduced in number. Geoff Fletcher seemed to be working alone and for some the silence spoke volumes. Perhaps the dreaded announcement was expected at any moment. John Davies recalls "You could probably learn as much from Geoff on the way out to the pitch, as from the programme or the press. For me, the club was dead on its feet and just going through the motions. At the end of the 1982–83 season I was actually waiting to be told that we'd packed-up." [24] Chairman Terry Hughes did go along to Geoff Fletcher with this thought in mind but was persuaded to give it one more season. Certainly, one look at the points-for column in the final Second Division table suggests that the team was to a large extent uncompetitive. Doncaster finished rock bottom of the pile, but scored over 50 points more than Huyton – who also won six league matches (three consecutively in October 1982) to Doncaster's two. In what turned out to be the penultimate season, the Huyton team simply could not get enough points on the scoreboard, and notched only 250 all season.

1982–83 Second Division (bottom four)

14 Dewsbury	32	8	1	23	325	507	17
15 Batley	32	6	1	25	305	719	13
16 Huyton	**32**	**6**	**0**	**26**	**250**	**687**	**12**
17 Doncaster	32	2	1	29	307	799	5

1983–84: Huyton's final season

Huyton's final season of 1983–84 did not begin with such a thought in mind, as such, although perhaps the final straw came during this season with the announcement that the ever-troublesome grandstand was decreed unsafe and closed following further attacks. It was only towards the very end of the season – which had been extended due to bad weather – that serious developments concerning the club's relocation began happen. Yet as early as the summer of 1983 a cartel involving the board of directors of football's Alliance Premier League members Runcorn FC had proposed to launch a rugby league club at their Canal Street ground for the 1984–85 season.

During 1983 there had been an enormous amount of curiosity from a variety of interested parties concerning the formation of new rugby league clubs. Fellow Alliance Premier League members Maidstone United had been granted associate membership for their Kent Invicta side in April 1983 and interest from as far away as Bristol had been shown. However, as Brian Batty of the *Daily Mail* clarified, it was all rather speculative: "Rugby league's painful experience with Carlisle this year has rightly produced a note of caution whenever there is talk of new clubs coming into the game. The Bristol connection has been severed... but the Maidstone soccer club are still keen to take up the 13-a-side code... There is the possibility of clubs going out of the game next season if the financial situation worsens. So the decision of the League bosses to tread warily at this stage is not only understandable, but highly sensible." [25]

Despite being host to a powerful non-league football club, the town of Runcorn had previously enjoyed a strong link with rugby league, indeed the Canal Street ground was originally home to a Northern Union side who played there from 1879 to 1918. Runcorn AFC's myrtle green and yellow also adorned the strip of the original rugby side. Runcorn RFC was a founder member of the Northern Union and in 1907–08 hosted the touring New Zealand All Golds. But in 1918 the Canal Street ground was sold to the owner of the Highfield and Camden Tannery who, as a football enthusiast, stipulated that the ground should play host to association football rather than Northern Union rugby. In August that year the original Runcorn rugby team was disbanded.

During the 1983–84 season it was considered that Runcorn Football Club, at this stage one of the premier non-league sides in the country, should attempt to create an income stream not dependent upon football gate revenue. While Runcorn FC had become a major force outside the Football League, gates were always rather modest. A thriving social club helped pay its way, but it was thought that further diversification of income was a wise move. It was therefore decided that an application for membership of the Rugby League's second tier for 1984–85 should be made. The *Liverpool Daily Post* reported on Tuesday 3 April 1984:

Runcorn's Bid for Rugby League Place

"Runcorn's application to join the second division next season has been received by the Rugby League. The proposal to share facilities with Alliance Premier League soccer side will be considered by clubs at a special meeting in Leeds in April 18, together with applications from Mansfield and Sheffield." [26]

But by 19 April, the day following the meeting, the news from Leeds was mixed. The Runcorn bid had been withdrawn at the last minute after discussions had taken place over the previous week with Terry Hughes, Ian Comish and Ken Carberry of Huyton

RLFC. The Huyton officials, on the look out for a move and realising that Runcorn was a far safer bet than Southport, Tranmere, or indeed any other club mooted over the previous two years, had made contact with the Runcorn FC board regarding a possible relocation to Canal Street. The *Liverpool Daily Post* of 19 April outlined:

Huyton may switch grounds

"Huyton could well be playing Second Division Rugby League at Runcorn FC's Canal Street ground at the start of next season. Officials at the Alliance Premier League club applied to enter a team in the Second Division some time ago, but at yesterday's Rugby League Council meeting, in Leeds when new clubs Mansfield and Sheffield were granted associate membership, Runcorn withdrew their application.

In a statement read out by RFL secretary-general David Oxley the club said 'we are unswerving in our determination to bring professional rugby league to Runcorn, but the more we have discussed the matter we have seen the good sense of having an established set-up.'

The statement said that the club were in an advanced stage of negotiations with Huyton."[27]

The Runcorn directors had quickly grasped that prohibitive costs were involved in establishing a new rugby league football team from scratch (Maidstone had claimed they could do it for £75,000, but this turned out to be pie in the sky) and, like the Greyhound Racing Association in the mid-1930s had decided on the lock-stock-and barrel approach.

Huyton could hardly be described as "established" and were in fact on the verge of collapse, but at least they had a franchise of sorts, a team, and name changes seemed to be allowed without too much debate, as Huddersfield, Cardiff and Kent discovered that season. For Huyton, the geographical proximity of Runcorn to both Widnes and Warrington meant that the new club would finally fall within an authentic rugby league catchment area, something on which neither the Liverpool nor Huyton clubs could capitalise. Indeed, there was already a strong Runcorn amateur side that played in Haddock's Wood in Runcorn, who would provide their new neighbours with a stream of players throughout the remainder of the 1980s.

David Oxley, who desperately wanted to see the back not so of much Huyton, but of Alt Park, agreed immediately and promptly sold the idea to the RFL members; Runcorn Highfield, a name that harked back to both Huyton's origins in Wigan and to the Highfield tannery in Runcorn, was born.

Towards the end of this very last Huyton season the team went on an amazing run of victories that saw them move steadily away from the bottom of the table. The 1983–84 season began and ended with away draws: in August at Halifax, 20–20, and in May at Doncaster, 16–16. In all competitions Huyton won 10 games that season, including a John Player victory at Huddersfield, 21–8. But it was the late run in April 1984 that, aside from the projected move to Canal Street, actually attracted a little local press attention. Beginning on 1 April with a home win against third-placed Halifax, 19–12, Huyton went on to win 15–9 at Dewsbury, beat Carlisle and Doncaster at home 17–10 and 44–22 respectively. Only a 26–16 defeat at Blackpool halted this run. If this game had been won, it would have created a club record of five consecutive victories. But Huyton then won another two home games against Batley, 30–14, and Rochdale Hornets, 14–12, before a weakened side lost to Cardiff 34–16.

The Merseysiders then played out a 16–16 draw at Tattersfield, Doncaster. In all, it was a truly wonderful ending to the final season. Out of nine games played from that first day in April, Huyton won six, drew one and lost only two – which was promotion form. Much of the credit for this run went to full-back Peter Wood, a loan signing from Widnes. Wood began playing for Huyton in October 1983, but was then out of the side until March. He returned and helped turn the team's fortunes around so dramatically that by April he was practically kicking the club to victory. Wood was assisted by an in-form Peter Middlehurst, who received constant rave reviews for his performances from April onwards. Despite infrequent appearances, Peter Wood kicked 42 goals plus 11 drop-goals during the season.

The final Huyton home victory over Rochdale Hornets 14–12 at Alt Park on 26 April 1984 was witnessed by an attendance of only 200, although the *Daily Post* recorded it as 300. The average league gate in this final season was a meagre 172. There were few who lamented the club's departure from perhaps one of the most depressing sports enclosures in the north west of England. David Ball in the Runcorn AFC newsletter *The Linnets* was to reflect on that final season at Alt Park: "Huyton had been fighting a continual battle against vandalism for years. Visiting spectators to Alt Park were discouraged by the possibility of mindless vandalism to their cars or even (admittedly on rare occasions) to their person. It was against this background that talks were first begun with Runcorn AFC who themselves were seriously considering professional rugby league at Canal Street." [28]

Most rugby league stalwarts, in fact, regarded the relocation of Huyton RLFC to Runcorn as a very positive step. Tom Fleet was to later remark: "Huyton did not fail because of Geoff Fletcher – far from it in fact. The club failed because nobody took a local interest. I never saw any signs of it either way: from the club to the locals or from the locals to the club. Runcorn was an escape from Huyton. I was very pleased with the move. I saw it as a real positive. Everything was in its favour.

But although without Geoff Fletcher the club would have folded, I also wonder what resources he had at Runcorn. For a new team to have such limited funds for players seems criminal and the team just wasn't good enough. I enjoyed watching Runcorn but it was a different level by this time. Huyton was always going to be a disappointment, but it was probably more disappointing in the long run at Runcorn (and Sutton) because it looked so promising in the first place – after all, nice ground, rugby interest in the town - what was there to go wrong?" [29]

1983–84 Second Division (bottom six)

13 Batley	34	13	0	21	477	738	26
14 Dewsbury	34	12	0	22	526	698	24
15 Carlisle	34	12	0	22	539	780	24
16 Huyton	**34**	**9**	**2**	**23**	**431**	**760**	**20**
17 Keighley	34	7	3	24	425	728	17
18 Doncaster	34	2	1	31	384	1083	5

Ironically, within a relatively short space of time, Alt Park was to undergo a thorough renovation as the Orr family – footballing proprietors of Kirkby Town FC – also decided to move lock-stock-and barrel from their equally vandalised, and then partially renovated, Simonswood Lane ground in Kirkby to Huyton, renaming their club Knowsley United, along the way. As the team began to climb the non-league football pyramid, floodlights were installed and with the assistance of Knowsley Borough Council the grandstand, the clubhouse and the social club were recommissioned and upgraded; yet even football was not to last very long at the ill-fated Alt Park. It was the old, old story: as it was for Huyton RLFC, so it was to be for Knowsley and indeed Runcorn Highfield. All places have their traditions and the linking of sport into a community can only ever be successful if the local community is able to develop clubs itself, not from imports.

---

[1] Fleet, Tom (1992), 'A History of Highfield' part 9: 'Fletcher', published as a series for the *Highfield Official Programme*

[2] Leslie Woodhead quoting Geoff Fletcher, 'Geoff Rises to Huyton Challenge', [Liverpool] *Football Echo*, 13 August 1977, p.4

[3] Geoff Fletcher to author 27 February 2008; all subsequent quotes from Geoff Fletcher from this interview

[4] Fleet, Tom (1992), 'A History of Highfield' part 9: 'Fletcher', published as a series for the *Highfield Official Programme*

[5] John Huxley, 'Hopeful Huyton – Today's Opponents', *Huddersfield C. & A.C. Official Programme* [versus Huyton], Sunday 18 September 1977, p.5

[6] Unaccredited correspondent, *Liverpool Echo*, 9 August 1977, p.8

[7] Unaccredited correspondent, *Prescot & Huyton Reporter*, Friday 18 August 1978, p.11

[8] Huyton RLFC supporter John Davies to author 4 February 2008

[9] Unaccredited programme editor, 'Club Notes', *Huyton RLFC Official Programme* [versus Halifax], Saturday 9 September 1978, p. 6

[10] Unaccredited programme editor, 'Flashback', *Dewsbury RLFC Official Programme* [versus Huyton], Sunday 22 October 1978, p.11

[11] Lawrence Karalius, 'Club Notes', *Huyton RLFC Official Programme* [versus Whitehaven], Wednesday 16 May 1979, p.4

[12] See the Rugby League Collectors' Federation: *Teams and Scorers Liverpool Stanley, Liverpool City, Huyton*. Due accreditation to Irvin Saxton and the Rugby League Record Keepers' Club

[13] Billy Benyon, 'Today The Season Starts In Earnest', *Warrington Football Club Official Programme* [versus Huyton], Sunday 17 August 1980, p.18

[14] [Probably] Ian Comish, 'Ground Conditions', *Huyton RLFC Official Programme* [versus Fulham], Sunday 15 March 1981, p. 4

[15] Mick Naughton, 'Bird's Eye View of Huyton', *ibid*, p.5

[16] John Davies to author 4 February 2008

[17] Unaccredited editor, 'Our Visitors Huyton', *Keighley RLFC Match Programme* [versus Huyton], Sunday 19 April 1981, p.3

[18] John Davies to author 4 February 2008

[19] John Bibby to author 16 February 2008; 'Groundhopper' is a term used to refer to football and rugby supporters who visit a wide variety of enclosures each season. They have their own fanzines, websites and societies and are generally non-aligned, as such. The activity began in earnest in the mid-1970s. For an example, see www.footballgroundsinfocus.com

[20] [Probably] Ian Comish, 'Message From The Board', *Huyton RLFC Official Programme* [versus Bramley], Sunday 3 October 1982, p.3

[21] Garry Clarke, correspondence with author December 2007

[22] Interview with Tom Fleet July 2007

[23] [Probably] Ian Comish, 'Message From The Board', *Huyton RLFC Official Programme* [versus Bramley], Sunday 2 January 1983, p. 3

[24] John Davies to author 4 February 2008

[25] Brian Batty of the *Daily Mail* writing in the *Bramley RLFC Official Programme* [versus Huyton], Sunday 3 April 1983, p. 21

[26] [Possibly] Trevor Peake, 'Runcorn's Bid for Rugby League Place', *Liverpool Daily Post*, Tuesday 3 April 1984, p.27

[27] [Possibly] Trevor Peake, 'Huyton May Switch Grounds', *Liverpool Daily Post*, 19 April 1984, p.34

[28] David Ball, 'Runcorn Highfield RLFC', *The Linnets*, April 1985 edition

[29] Interview with Tom Fleet, July 2007

10. The river is wide

With only a brief period left to run on the worthless lease at Alt Park, Huyton RLFC Ltd. upped-sticks and began a five-year sub-tenancy at Runcorn Football Club's Canal Street enclosure. From leaseholders to sub-tenants appears financially unwise and even dangerous, but by 1984 no alternative existed. This final move away from Merseyside was long overdue but not without a degree of poignancy. Since at least the mid-1960s it appeared obvious to most rugby league observers that Liverpool and its surrounding locality would never display a strong empathy with rugby league and, latterly, did not even participate in its social side – at least in Huyton – to any great extent. The move to Runcorn, therefore, finally showed that professional rugby league could not survive within an area so dominated by association football. Perhaps, thought the optimists, the club might be revived via a move away from Liverpool: there had once existed a relationship between the code and the Cheshire town of Runcorn. But this was a rather romantic myth. Runcorn was by the mid-1980s a town in flux, partially dependent for its survival in these tough monetarist times upon a transient population from Liverpool.

Tom Fleet recalls that "The five-year sub-tenancy with the football club at Runcorn began on 19 August 1984 with a friendly against neighbouring Widnes. The game attracted a 1,750 gate, albeit mostly Widnesians, but nonetheless some 1,500 above the average gates at Huyton and three times the size of that for Runcorn FC. It was the first time for nearly 50 years that a rugby game had been played on the football ground in a town that had its own history of defunct rugby league. Interest in the town seemed high, but was not sustained nor reflected through the turnstiles." [1]

The Linnets

Runcorn Association Football Club was founded in 1918 when a local tannery owner and benefactor acquired the Canal Street ground and the club became one of the many activities of the Highfield and Camden Tanneries Recreation Club. The football club continued to be run under the umbrella of the tanneries until the formation of a limited company – Runcorn Association Football Club Limited – in 1953. The Canal Street ground was a picturesque, albeit pocket-sized, enclosure with the old town of Runcorn alongside its main gates at one end and the Manchester Ship Canal and a little beyond the River Mersey flowing past the other.

By the end of the 1983–84 campaign Runcorn's football side had achieved fifth place in the Alliance Premier League. Fellow rugby league experimenters Maidstone United were champions and thus won the right to apply for election to the Football League. Of course, before automatic promotion and relegation, an old pals' act ensured that Maidstone failed for a second time to get elected. Notwithstanding this intransigence from the Football League, further progress up the football pyramid for Runcorn was not possible without substantial ground improvements and increased cashflow.

But the football club faced other perhaps more pressing problems; Runcorn as a town (and Halton as a newly-created borough linking the two hitherto rather estranged towns of Runcorn and Widnes) had undergone several changes in its more recent history and although Runcorn FC had established itself as a non-league force to be reckoned with, the town of Runcorn (or effectively the Runcorn New Town estates to the south of the old town) displayed only passing interest. Typically tribal, incoming Liverpool and

Everton supporters also proved to be rather less than interested in such small fry as Runcorn FC. So, as with most APL clubs based close to football giants, a hard core of supporters carried the club and most of the Linnets' cashflow came from them, plus a social club on the nearby Astmoor industrial estate. Subsequent chairmen Jim Corcoran and Dave Robinson moved heaven and earth to keep the football club financially viable – and the deal with Huyton RLFC was but one such scheme.

These underlying financial pressures were the major contributory factors in the fortunes of both Runcorn Highfield and – ultimately – the Linnets in years to come. Since the 1950s Runcorn FC had owned the Canal Street freehold but by the mid-1990s that fortunate position had been forcibly surrendered. Halton Borough Council then foolishly sealed the fate of its only football success story by expecting it to play at Widnes RLFC's Halton Stadium. This was an unmitigated disaster and typical of the artificiality of combining two towns, on opposite banks of a major river into one borough. It was financially expedient but culturally meaningless. Although the Runcorn club continues, it is a shadow of its past and, currently nomadic, plays at Witton Albion's Wincham Park.

Runcorn Highfield RLFC

As with the Liverpool Stanley of the pre-Knotty Ash era, Runcorn Highfield RLFC never fully became master of its own destiny. Furthermore, it was also, like Stanley, constantly attempting to exist within pre-existing organic sporting solidarities. The club's migration close to an area so dominated by rugby league appeared on the surface to be just what was needed, but the proximity of Widnes RLFC brought problems with establishing a new fan base, playing standards and viability. As Huyton RLFC, the club at least seemed to have some symbolic value as a struggling minnow in a football area. But the new Runcorn Highfield carried no such pre-ordained authority. To many rugby league supporters in Halton, there appeared little point in such a move. Some argued that this migration was not only rather presumptuous, but pointless. John Costello recalls: "I lived in Widnes but worked in a bakery in Runcorn in the mid-1980s and I was really pleased when it was announced that Runcorn was to have its own team. But I remember feeling far less enthusiastic when it was reported that Huyton were to be the new side. I couldn't see the point. How could you get excited about bringing in a team of losers? It wasn't even as if the Runcorn committee had assembled a new team. It was the old lock-stock-and-barrel approach, as usual. I thought, well, it's somewhere to go if Widnes are away, but for me there was no way that the Highfield idea had any permanence about it. And the way it ended... well, it was farcical." [2]

Furthermore, the notion of there being a town almost waiting for the arrival of a rugby league club for the other side of Halton was an uninformed one. By the 1980s Runcorn's estates consisted of many football-mad Merseysiders and as with Huyton, the town was hard hit by unemployment and in places had a growing drug problem.

It certainly bore little resemblance to Runcorn prior to the Runcorn-Widnes Bridge, which had opened in 1960, and Halton eras. Even then, the few Runcornians interested in rugby league usually aligned themselves not with Widnes, but with Warrington. The transport system made travel to Wilderspool relatively easy.

The new Highfield club was virtually asset less with no social club, ground, and few players of any value. The directors were the same as those who had been at Huyton: chairman Terry Hughes, vice-chairman Ken Carberry with directors Almond (secretary), Ball, Ian Comish, P. Downey (treasurer), M. Downey, Kearns and Swann.

Moving to Canal Street

The Canal Street ground before the match versus Widnes on 19 August 1984.

Action from the match.

Both photos by Mike Haddon.

Runcorn Highfield players: Top left: Arthur Daley (Courtesy *Rugby League Journal*)
Top right: Dave Crompton (Courtesy *Rugby League Journal*)
Bottom left: John Cogger (Photo: Andrew Cudbertson)
Bottom right: Peter Wood in action for Runcorn (Photo: Andrew Cudbertson)

In fact, for ease of transition, the existing limited company was not renamed and Runcorn Highfield became merely a trading arm of the old company (Huyton-with-Roby RLFC Ltd). The sub-tenancy, based around a substantial four-figure fee, existed between Runcorn Football Club and these Huyton-Runcorn directors. Yet, despite the presence of a board, it was only the old limited company that prevented Highfield from simply being a team with a committee.

Garry Clarke remembers: "The move to Canal Street revitalised the club as their fortunes took an upward turn. After many years of struggling to survive they finished their first season a respectable 14th out of 20 clubs in the Second Division and reached the second round of the Challenge Cup for the first time in over a decade." [3] However, there was very little infrastructure. The move seems to have been completed on the cheap – and it was to show.

Nevertheless, for the friendly visit of Widnes on 19 August 1984, the Runcorn Highfield programme editor was optimistic, but his notes tended to evoke a bygone era. Unquestionably, the language merely repeated what had been written in innumerable programme editorials of the past: "It is our intention to firmly establish professional rugby league in Runcorn [just as it had, of course, in London, Liverpool and Huyton] and we genuinely believe that with dedication and hard work this can be achieved. Obviously success will not come easily or overnight but it will be attained far more quickly if you, the general public, show by your support that you want Rugby League in Runcorn." [4]

These were proud words. Yet once again the onus appeared to fall on the poor willing spectator rather than the board. After 60 years of such promises it surely must have been obvious to all concerned that to succeed the club needed to pay for a winning team. An opportunity to do that was there, because the 1984–85 Second Division was weak – a half-decent side would be promotion material. However, even if a good side was provided, no evidence existed that regular support would emerge. For the board to assume that supporters would turn up to watch a Huyton side that, apart from the last six weeks of 1983–84, had performed so dismally for years, was naive.

As in days of old, local amateurs were encouraged to train with the team and it did not take long for new supporters to work out that an enthusiastic but somewhat unskilled squad was to don the myrtle and yellow of Runcorn RLFC. It was therefore considered extremely likely by those in the know that this squad would finish in the bottom half of the Second Division - unless the standard of Second Division rugby had dropped even further than fans had realised. John Costello remembered: "I must admit that I was very sceptical about their prospects. They had Peter Wood who had played in Widnes 'A' Team for a long time and was a good player – but he hadn't made the grade there; a lot of them were only average former amateur utility players – lads who had played for Widnes Tigers or St Marie's. Now, in itself, that still isn't a bad standard, but it's a long way from quality professional rugby league. I thought John Tabern and Peter Middlehurst were good footballers, and I always thought Derek Ingle could have played at a higher level. But they were getting-on a bit in rugby league terms and were probably carrying knocks. It was a piecemeal squad and with no second team, woefully short of quality and back-up players." [5] Perhaps Runcorn's only realistic target for the season was to finish above Doncaster, Keighley and the two new additions to the league: Sheffield and Mansfield.

But at least one rugby league icon was going to be around, providing the project with continuity. The programme for the first match said: "Our player-coach, Geoff Fletcher has signed a new contract with the club and this is indeed good news. Geoff is now looking forward to being able to concentrate on his coaching without having to worry about all the other problems of vandalism, ground preparation, etc. etc. that he had at Alt Park. In the close season he attended the Rugby League coaching school for five days and emerged as one of only five coaches with a Grade 1 Certificate... There seems little doubt that the players will not be lacking in fitness as the season begins." [6]

But was fitness enough? Geoff Fletcher, who was forced to drag his weary bones across a rugby pitch on 11 occasions that season, later recalled: "The Huyton lads who came to Runcorn were a good bunch but in honesty they weren't great players. I tried to bring in more players but it was very difficult. Eventually you have to rely on what you have. Peter Wood was a good lad, Arthur Daley came back to us - a real gentleman - and I picked up £19,000 from Rochdale Hornets for Brian Garrity after a couple of seasons, but a lot of the lads weren't really up to it." [7]

Predictably the friendly against Widnes was a humiliation for Highfield. The Runcorn team lost 40–8 to an under strength Widnes. Following another losing trial match at Swinton, the new season kicked off rather inauspiciously on 2 September 1984 with a home fixture against fellow newcomers Mansfield Marksman. The 'Message From the Board' in Runcorn Highfield's official programme was not only cautious, but also redolent of an increasing antipathy between club and local press, brought about perhaps by the questions surrounding this move: "Our game against Widnes two weeks ago was a disappointment to all connected with the club. We played probably our worst rugby for three years and, although we did not field our strongest side, we expected a better performance. Certain newspapers were extremely uncomplimentary in their reporting and whilst we do not make excuses, we do feel that some of the comments made were not entirely necessary. We know we played badly, we know it was not Widnes' strongest side and we know we will have to show a marked improvement. People in Runcorn are not stupid and will, hopefully, realise that we can and will play far better than in this game – we did not win seven of our last nine games last season by playing bad rugby." [8]

But the match against Mansfield was duly lost 35–6 with only Garrity and Wood getting on the Runcorn scoresheet. The crowd of 490 was a little disappointing, but as very few came from Mansfield, perhaps there were a few positive signs of local interest. But at this stage the team appeared well below the required standard.

However, largely due to the excellence of full-back Peter Wood and stand-off Brian Garrity Runcorn did improve. Wood created a new club record of scoring 98 goals and 28 drop-goals, beating the previous record of 95 goals established by his namesake Jack Wood in 1955–56. Also, he kicked six goals and five drop-goals in one game: a 33–16 victory against Batley on 21 October 1984. Successive victories in September against Sheffield Eagles, Rochdale Hornets and Fulham, followed by a doughty 16–16 draw at home to Salford on 7 October in which Wood contributed many points via his boot, set the tone for the season. Runcorn eventually won 13 fixtures and in a 46–12 victory against Keighley on 21 April 1985 Peter Wood also equalled Jack Wood's and Peter Twiss's achievement of scoring seven goals in one game. Incidentally, Peter Twiss held the Liverpool City record of most points scored in a match with 20, at Warrington on 20 August 1958.

By April 1985 Chris Reilly, manager of the Runcorn Social Club, was so pleased with the increased business brought about by rugby league, that he donated a full playing kit to the club. Overall, however, gate receipts were not overly impressive and by the end of that inaugural season the Runcorn FC board was concerned about Highfield's ability to pay the following year's rent. Like the Stanley Track's John Bilsland before them, the football club board considered Runcorn Highfield only as an income stream. The victory against Fulham in September 1984 had attracted only 400 to Canal Street and this turned out to be a little above the average for the season. Runcorn Highfield was supported less by the people of Runcorn and more by local businesses in the area. Chairman Terry Hughes was able to persuade several of Runcorn FC's existing sponsors to come on board with the rugby club; additionally, the ever-dependable Ian Comish and Geoff Fletcher canvassed new minor sponsorships. But it was acknowledged by the board that the season had not been a great success "overall commitment [on the pitch] left a lot to be desired" stated one message from the board on 21 April 1985 and this lack of discernable quality had kept attendances pitifully low level.

With average gates of only 100 more than those at Alt Park, the experiment had certainly not been a financial winner. One might be able to imagine that the season was successful but, in the cold light of day, Runcorn Highfield appeared to be something of a simulation. As in the days of old in Liverpool and its environs, for Highfield to have been a success it had to have made some kind of impact upon life in Runcorn.

However, it seemed to observers that the team existed in its own world – detached from the town. John Costello recalls: "Well, it was odd, really. The atmosphere in the ground was quite good. 400 or so at Runcorn looked like a sizeable crowd – but it always seemed to me to have an air of unreality, in a funny kind of way. There was certainly a clique and the people that stood at the top end of the ground all seemed to know each other personally. So I wasn't really greatly encouraged. It was the same in the social club down the road. I went a few times after the match but, as I remember, the licensing hours were a bit odd and there seemed to be a clique in there too." [9]

Second Division 1984–85 (bottom seven)

14 Runcorn Highfield	28	11	1	16	462	538	23
15 Keighley	28	11	0	17	495	567	22
16 Bramley	28	9	2	17	439	492	20
17 Sheffield Eagles	28	8	0	20	424	582	16
18 Doncaster	28	6	2	20	353	730	14
19 Southend Invicta	28	4	0	24	347	690	8
20 Bridgend	28	1	0	27	258	966	2

Struggle

For the 1985–86 season Runcorn Highfield struggled in a noticeably improved Second Division. Sheffield Eagles were beginning to slowly rise, two strong sides – Barrow and Leigh – had been relegated from the First Division, and a hitherto underachieving Wakefield Trinity were stronger. Bridgend and Southend Invicta had collapsed – probably denying Runcorn at least a couple of victories – and only Keighley and Mansfield appeared to equal the Cheshire side's fragility. Only nine games were won by Runcorn Highfield, mostly against fellow strugglers such as the increasingly inept Mansfield, home and away, plus the fading Fulham and Carlisle, both at home. Brian Garrity was the top try-scorer with a creditable 24, but the next in line was Paul Fitzpatrick with only eight to his name. Peter Wood kicked 51 goals and 12 drop-goals. The average gate was only 366 and, taking into account away supporters scattered across that season's home fixtures, this was dismal and an obvious discrepancy between the ambitions of the directors and the realities of existence in a New Town close to Merseyside. Yet each Highfield programme that season had an entire page given over to club sponsors and at one point over 50 sponsors were engaged in financial support. Even so, the 'Boardroom Chatter' of the official programme for Sunday 27 April 1986 confessed that it had been "a disappointing season in many respects following our encouraging beginning ... the season before". In fact, without income from these myriad funders, the season would have been a financial disaster. With only three appearances as a substitute, Geoff Fletcher finally retired from playing the game he so dearly loved.

Second Division 1985–86 (bottom four)

15 Huddersfield	34	8	4	22	542	841	20
16 Runcorn Highfield	**34**	**9**	**2**	**23**	**489**	**790**	**20**
17 Keighley	34	9	2	23	401	918	20
18 Mansfield	34	2	1	31	383	1080	5

Australians

As early as September 1986 *Widnes Weekly News* rugby league reporter Paul Cook was identifying that the 1986–87 season was going to be a tough campaign. For example, an attendance of 500 had witnessed Hunslet easily defeat Runcorn 36–0 in the opening home game and Cook correctly questioned whether this rather abject team could "hold on to their supporters for another year" – in fact at least half the crowd was from Hunslet. Moves were afoot, however, to bring about an injection of new blood. Frank Wilson had replaced Geoff Fletcher as coach and 'Fletch' was given the position of team manager – a thankless task of attempting to bring in new talent. But now that the RFL had relaxed its sanction concerning foreign players, the ever-resourceful Fletcher had set in motion a search for available talent down under and was able to persuade first Illawarra prop Seamus O'Connell, and then Western Suburbs half-back or loose-forward John Cogger to come to Runcorn. These were timely signings, for an injury to former Welsh international Paul Woods finished his career; record-scoring full-back Peter Wood also called it a day after only one competitive match and when Frank Wilson was sacked in November after only four months in charge, Paul Woods and Arthur Daley took over coaching the side leaving Fletcher time to look after the Australians.

The inclusion of both Cogger and O'Connell was eagerly awaited by many rugby league observers, and once established in the team these two predictably added strength. Highfield went on a remarkable run during September and October 1986, beating in succession Mansfield 54–8, Blackpool, Workington, Batley and Sheffield. Cogger's first game was against Blackpool and he scored two tries. But as the squad subsequently suffered from a growing injury list, form and results fell away. Following this five-game streak Runcorn then won only another four games all season.

After 20 appearances and somewhat chastened by his experiences, Seamus O'Connell returned to Australia in March. Cogger, on the other hand remained at Runcorn until the end of April, played out the season, and scored in the last game of the campaign: an 18–9 win over Fulham. For that final home game, the Runcorn Highfield official programme stated that despite the inclusion of the two Australians, and it must be noted the exceptional form of stand-off Brian Garrity, the colossal inventory of injuries had rendered the team "unable to cope and, as results went against us, our confidence went and victories became harder and harder to find." The editor added: "Having said all of this, some of our performances have been nothing short of diabolical." [10]

John Cogger top-scored with 18 tries but the remaining try-scorers were scattered across a 48-man squad. Unnamed trialists played seven times, indicating both the team's injury problems and lack of strength in depth. Nevertheless Runcorn proved to be at least a level above those weaker sides in the division and finished the campaign in a respectable 11th position, with 10 wins and a draw from 28 matches.

The Second Division expanded back to 20 clubs for the 1987–88 season, and Runcorn Highfield's bank account was also expanded as the team began the campaign £19,000 to the good after Brian Garrity was transferred to Rochdale Hornets. The official programme 'Club Topics' for the 6 September 1987 fixture versus Fulham, a 23–16 win, stated that the "money received from Brian's transfer will help keep the club in a stable position" which it did. A home Lancashire Cup fixture against the mighty Widnes in September, lost 40–6, also drew 2,679 spectators to Canal Street – a record thus far for rugby league at the ground. So any team budget worries were at least put away for a year as on the pitch a most entertaining season ensued. Bill Ashurst had become coach the previous April, ably assisted by Daley, with Fletcher increasingly taking a back seat.

An informal 'A' team began this season, too, suggesting that there were even a number of players who were keen to play for Highfield – the reserves duly fulfilled a few fixtures against Wigan and Widnes. In the boardroom, however, stalwart director Ian Comish had resigned due to pressure of work and was replaced by John Hodges.

In addition to the returning John Cogger, it was announced that two more Australians were coming over to Runcorn. Cogger, due to arrive in late November, was preceded in September by his brother Jamie and under-19 Australian international Steve Ewer. Sadly, neither of them was outstanding, certainly not of John Cogger's repute. Although Jamie Cogger stayed the course, the youthful Ewer after a disagreement with the club brought on by a bout of homesickness, returned to Australia in November 1987.

Runcorn won exactly half of the 28 league fixtures, but lost their two cup ties, and almost created parity between points for and against, scoring 420 against 469 conceded. One more victory would have placed the team in the top half of the table. They began with two wins: a rare away victory 8–0 against Rochdale Hornets and the home defeat of Fulham. They also ended the season by achieving the double over Hornets and winning in a thrilling game at Huddersfield 16–14. John Cogger, only available for half the season and injured as well, scored nine tries from 16 appearances plus three as a substitute. His brother Jamie played 14 games, scoring five tries. Terry Rose kicked 45 goals and scored nine tries. Off the pitch the joint lottery that had been established between the two codes – the Linnet's Linkline Lottery had recruited 1,500 members and was growing.

It appeared that the Garrity money, the form of Cogger and his colleagues, and the Linkline Lottery were bringing forward a new era for rugby league in Runcorn. On New Year's Day 1988 the programme for the home fixture with Keighley contained a page of supporters' club notes that make interesting reading: "Our improved performances on the field have not been matched by improved reporting of the club in either *Open Rugby* or *Rugby Leaguer*. The [Supporters' Club] committee have written to both of these publications and encourage you to do the same." [11]

This was a little unfair, especially on Harry Edgar's *Open Rugby*, always a supporter of the club; nonetheless these comments suggest a growing confidence. However, by the spring of 1988 the mood had dramatically changed. After a predictably poor second half to the season, which saw the side drop out of the top half of the table, supporters were grumbling about being chastised for their criticisms of the players and also for complaining about higher admission prices, insensitively introduced by the board during the season. On the one hand players were somewhat sensitive about touchline remarks; on the other the board appeared distant and uncaring. This growing division between board, players, and supporters was further exacerbated by the arrival of another Australian, Kerry Gibson, early in 1988. Rather than being the embodiment of hope for the supporters, the arrival of Gibson appeared for some to be little more than a gimmick.

Kerry Gibson

Gibson had been born with a left arm that ended before his elbow but was, according to reports, a good passer of the rugby ball. John Cogger suggested that Gibson join Runcorn and the latter was named as a substitute for a league game away at Springfield (formerly Blackpool) Borough on Good Friday 1988. However, there followed an extraordinary media scramble with an Australian film crew showing up at the Wigan Athletic FC's Springfield Park to report on the one-armed rugby league player. Garry Clarke recalls: "Unfortunately for them, they did not know which player was Gibson. The team had been tipped off about the filming and as the players got off the coach each player had tucked his left arm into his jumper. Each one smiled at the camera and nipped into the changing room. Needless to say the film crew were baffled." [12]

A humorous event? Possibly; however, Geoff Fletcher found the incident rather disconcerting: "That was a set up for the press. I thought it was terrible really, just a publicity stunt. Gibson's coming to Runcorn had nothing to do with me. I was out of the club by that point but I was called back after that: the RFL created hell about it. I thought that the press felt we were a bit of a laughing stock." [13]

Local rugby league fan John Lomas agrees and discounts the supposedly droll nature of this incident, suggesting perhaps some kind of parody: "From a rugby league supporter's point of view it seemed a bit like a *Carry On* [film] to me. I thought that the players were not treating the sport with due respect and I stopped going to Canal Street because I felt that the players were publicity seeking and taking the piss; out of us supporters, mostly. When that John Player Trophy game against Wigan happened the following season it struck me as having something to do with this Kerry Gibson affair – as if the players couldn't give a toss and were out for themselves." [14]

Gibson played once more for Highfield, and was never seen again. Gloom had descended on the club – there is a fine line between sporting humour and demeaning sarcasm. Somehow, thanks to the players, Runcorn Highfield had crossed that line.

The team finished 12th out of 20 clubs, with a record of 14 wins from 28 matches, scoring 420 points, an average of 15 a game, but conceding 469.

The end of the beginning?

All sport represents a microcosm of society and by the late 1980s the higher echelons of rugby league were gradually shaking off any romanticism that the sport had previously embraced. Once so pronounced in its rituals concerning kinship and sociability rugby league was, like other sports, moving towards embracing an era that abandoned such ideals – it was increasingly all about the here and now. Runcorn's position as a club was deeply affected by this de-romanticisation. No longer a sport known for its collectivism, rugby league now had an elite: competitive and exclusive. Runcorn Highfield was clearly never going to be part of this new stratum. By 1988, for better or for worse, the pre-history of Super League was beginning in earnest.

Runcorn's 1987–88 campaign had ended curiously; while enjoying its best season on the pitch since moving to Cheshire, the squad had somehow brought the club into disrepute. Now the new collective judgements of the RFL were consisting of economic projections based upon development, and these did not include the likes of Runcorn.

Geoff Fletcher recalls several discussions with Maurice Lindsay, the chief executive of the RFL, around this time that for him were very revealing. According to Geoff, Lindsay's vision for rugby league (excluding all minnows) was, he hoped, an elite division consisting only of clubs most likely to pay their way – promotion and relegation was, he hoped, a thing of the past. Naturally for Lindsay, the situation of the RFL at this important time took precedence over Runcorn Highfield's issues in determining the future of the sport. Ultimately history says that both Super League and the eventual removal of Fletcher's side were probably a wise move for the RFL. But sporting life is rarely divided into neat sides of good and bad, right and wrong. Super League reinvigorated rugby league by tapping into the traditional sporting expectations surrounding virtuosity, but in doing so left behind that British appetite for the odd and outrageous. While it may be comforting to think that Maurice Lindsay and the Rugby Football League got it right – as a check, another question also needs to be repeatedly asked: how, and at what cost?

1988–89: Wigan and all that

Following a miserable gate of 316 for the opening home game of the 1988–89 season, a close-run victory over Batley, a Lancashire Cup fixture against Warrington on 18 September 1988 drew 2,310 to Canal Street, the second 2,000-plus attendance at the ground for rugby league. The game was lost 42–4 but the coffers were, albeit briefly, filled. However, by 30 October 1988 the programme editor was forced to deny rumours concerning the future of his club: "During the last few weeks we have heard a number of stories and rumours that this is our last season at Canal Street... The simple facts are these. At the end of the season, our original five-year agreement with the soccer club finishes. At this time, we have an option to review the agreement providing, of course, that both parties wish to do so. The situation from the rugby league board of directors is very clear. As a board, we consider our home to be at Canal Street, Runcorn and, as such, have never even considered the thought that we will not be here next season. Obviously we can only comment on matters from our side of the fence but we have generally had a fine relationship with our soccer cousins and can see no reason why this should not continue." [15]

The club did appear relatively secure at this stage. The supporters' club membership had seemingly put aside its differences with the board, and several new sponsors had been located. Runcorn's ad hoc reserve squad was formalised into a functioning 'A' team by joining the Slalom Lager Alliance. This side was the co-opted Runcorn Amateurs team. However, problems were converging from a variety of different directions.

First, the financial security of the host football club was not all it should have been. Runcorn FC had continued performing well in the re-named GM Vauxhall Conference and during the 1988–89 season maintained a creditable position on the table, finishing sixth. In the first 10 years of APL and Conference football, Runcorn finished in the top eight on nine occasions, but it was a very costly operation. Furthermore, in the wake of reports concerning ground safety, some of the ageing structures around Canal Street were giving cause for concern. This was following the Bradford City disaster and subsequent Popplewell Inquiry, which led to the introduction of new legislation to improve safety at British football grounds. The football directors had already decided that, by the end of their agreement with the rugby club, they would double the rent.

Additionally, another even more calamitous event was about to happen, this time by the players. Runcorn Highfield were drawn at home to play Wigan on 13 November 1988 in the John Player Trophy. The local media suggested that the game was an ideal opportunity to promote the sport in Runcorn and even looked forward to the fixture being a sell out. The Runcorn directors, however, had other ideas and in exchange for a fee from Wigan switched the game to Wigan's Central Park. The claim from Wigan was that the Canal Street enclosure was neither large enough nor safe to hold a crowd that might exceed 5,000. While considerable justification probably existed for this claim, the switch was confrontational in various ways: the supporters' club was not consulted, the players were not involved, and the press was not advised about the switch. The authenticity of the club's existence in Runcorn was thus brought into serious doubt.

The Runcorn players, already at some degree of separation from the board following the previous season's Kerry Gibson affair, demanded an increased match fee. The Runcorn directors refused and a players' strike was called. This led to coach Bill Ashurst fielding a scratch team of local amateurs for the fixture. The first team players attended the game, along with those supporters' club members who had boycotted the club's official transport – and these groups then voiced their disapproval from the Central Park stands. The game began very badly for Runcorn. Ashurst, forced out of retirement, was sent off after 11 minutes for violent conduct – head-butting Wigan's Andy Goodway. Matters deteriorated further as Wigan's points tally grew apace. In front of nearly 8,000 spectators the Runcorn Highfield amateurs were grossly outclassed and eventually lost 92–2, the club's record defeat at this point. Ashurst was also later banned and fined for bringing the game into disrepute.

An official statement from the board said: "Once it was known that Wigan were to be our opponents in the John Player Trophy, our players demanded £150 win, lose, or draw and we honestly didn't believe this was acceptable. It was our intention to pay £250/£300 for a victory with the £50 as losing pay. This was conveyed to the players and they then threatened to withdraw their services at Wigan... On the morning of the Wigan game, at about 10.15am our chairman received a phone call from the players' spokesman. The players had decided that their actions were benefiting nobody and that they would turn out at Central Park. Whilst agreeing with the sentiment, the board was not prepared at this very late stage to accept this offer, as there would have been considerable difficulty in contacting all the amateur players who had agreed to turn out on its behalf... the club is bigger than any individual or group of individuals and will not be blackmailed by anybody be they a player, coach, director or supporter." [16]

Many contemporary commentators of the day, both amateur and professional, tended to side with the players and it can easily be seen why. Runcorn Highfield's decision to switch the tie following a blatant financial inducement appeared mercenary. However, it was perhaps the action brought about by the Highfield players that proved, in the long term, to be disastrous for all concerned.

They too were out for their own ends. Indeed, one might suggest that such actions showed the players to be little more than jobbing journeymen, and the unfolding drama revealed a growing distance at Canal Street between administrators and players. While not directly involved in these shenanigans, Geoff Fletcher now sees these players as mercenaries "putting the money in their arse pocket, trying to take advantage of the situation". The Runcorn board, on the other hand, was merely "trying to take advantage of the fixture – it couldn't be done now". Furthermore, while the directors wished to place the money from the Wigan game at the disposal of the club, what the players might have done with their increased fees is anybody's guess. It was, indeed, a disaster, but it was only one game, Runcorn Highfield was never going to win the John Player Trophy, and it was quite clear that financially, short-term stabilisation was achieved.

In the long-term however, the distress created by the players' revolt was shattering and the entire club was destabilised. Tom Fleet's sympathies were with the board, not the players. He later recalled: "It was founded on the argument that Wigan received a bigger losing payout than most other opponents. The following home programme stated that the argument had been used when they drew Warrington in the Lancashire Cup and a rise to £50 was conceded. The players wanted £150 win, lose or draw at Wigan... such confidence. Personally I feel some sympathy with the board and I guess they did well to hang out. Equally the financial sense in ceding home advantage was obvious, but what does it do as a local statement?" [17]

In December 1988 Paul Cook of the *Widnes Weekly News* wrote a damning Runcorn Highfield match report of the 25-4 defeat by Huddersfield. Reading between the lines, it seemed that the players involved were now just turning up for the money: "There have been quite a few dark days since Huyton moved to Canal Street and became Runcorn Highfield, but none as pitch black as this defeat by Huddersfield.

The worst thing was, Highfield showed no signs that things can get better, so how they set about improving their position it's impossible to say. The team lacks size, pace, and confidence and until something is done to rectify at least two of these problems Highfield will get nowhere." [18]

The Highfield squad had effectively given up on the club and, by February 1989, the board felt likewise about the players. After Bill Ashurst had been sacked, Cogger coached the side for the first six weeks of 1989. But this previously loyal star player of the squad had also been deeply involved in the revolt and was transferred in February to Oldham. Since his arrival three years before, Highfield had been under pressure to sell Cogger, however, both club and player had hitherto resisted. On this occasion, with a wide rift between board and player, it was decided to take Oldham's £12,000 offer. The board's statement read: "No doubt there will be many who will criticise the directors for agreeing to John's transfer but, realistically, with the mounting pressure from other clubs, it was inevitable that John would move on sooner or later... John cannot be blamed for wanting to better himself. We always told him that should he ever wish to move on, then we would not stand in his way. During his time at Runcorn, John has been a model professional, a very loyal member of the side and a fine ambassador for the club." [19]

John Cogger was without doubt Runcorn Highfield's most talented player, although Geoff Fletcher rates Seamus O'Connell "the best of the lot". Cogger played 61 games for Runcorn Highfield, scoring 34 tries; he was also voted Second Division Player of the Season in 1987.

Despite a hat-trick of tries on his debut, and winning the club captaincy at Oldham, Cogger never fully rediscovered his Runcorn form and his transition to a higher level was relatively unsuccessful. His record for Oldham reads remarkably similar to that of his time at Runcorn: between 1989 and 1991 he played 62 games, scoring 31 tries, but the

Oldham side was relegated from the First Division the season of his transfer, then promoted in 1990, and then immediately relegated in 1991.

Following Cogger's transfer there was little point to the rest of the Runcorn campaign. Defeat followed defeat and Highfield ended the season at the foot of the table with only two wins and a draw; almost 1,000 points were conceded. The average attendance at Canal Street for that season was fewer than 300 and the 'A' team experiment was abandoned part way through the season without a win to its name. Fifty-nine players had donned the Runcorn shirt that season. Even Peter Wood briefly returned for four games. However, the bulk of the players who turned out for Highfield only played a handful of games and then disappeared.

Only Geoff Dean, Charlie Jones and Danny Campbell played 20 games or more. It did appear to some observers that the club was on the brink of collapse. Barry Broadhead recalled: "My thoughts went back to the old days of Huyton and I thought, 'well, there we go, that's what happens when you import a bunch of no-marks'. They not only brought scorn down on themselves but also on the town of Runcorn and I didn't like that at all." [20]

Geoff Fletcher now confesses that a combination of mismanagement, hopeless coaching and disloyal playing staff brought the club to its knees: "It was grim: I'd left, really, at this point – there was a bit of animosity on the board so I packed in. Bill Ashurst had come in. But things didn't add up; I found that a 'scouting system' was taking a lot of money out of the club. I called a meeting to sack all the scouts but they never turned up, in any case. I surmised they didn't exist and I was probably right. Bill had also got very religious at this time – a born-again Christian – and I felt his mind wasn't on the job, so one thing led to another, the players were just out for themselves, and Bill was sacked. I coached the team for the rest of the season after Cogger went but it was hard putting a team out on the pitch, never mind getting a win." [21]

It may not have been the beginning of the end, but it was certainly the end of the beginning at Canal Street. The ante had been upped for clubs such as Runcorn Highfield. In the monetarist world of the 1980s, any romantic notion attached to development area rugby league was being overshadowed by financial realities. It was clear to all that another instalment in the history of the RFL had already commenced.

Second Division 1988–89 (bottom four)

17 Workington Town	28	9	1	18	365	549	19
18 Huddersfield	28	9	1	18	400	615	19
19 Mansfield Marksman	28	4	1	23	308	769	9
20 Runcorn Highfield	**28**	**2**	**1**	**25**	**224**	**998**	**5**

Runcorn's final season

A new rental agreement with the football club was signed for 1989–90 and Runcorn Highfield's immediate future was secured, but the deal did contain an annual review, and it was to be this card that would be played in 12 months' time.

Former Leigh and Great Britain star Dave Chisnall was brought in as coach in June 1989. Previously he had been the St Helens 'A' team coach but there were problems at Knowsley Road and Chisnall had been rather unceremoniously sacked; he was to later admit to Peter Oakes of the newspaper *RL Thirteen*: "No one else seemed to want me after that except Runcorn. I owe them something and I still want to prove I can become one of the top coaches in the game." [22] However, as the season commenced, Chisnall had very little to work with. From the 43-man strong squad that started the previous season only six had been retained that summer of 1989. The rest of the players had either been sacked or resigned and decided to ply their trade elsewhere.

Chisnall managed to recruit the minimum registration figure of 27 just prior to the start of the campaign, but only by signing several inexperienced rugby union amateurs such as Paul Fenney and David Hine, the latter, incidentally, a Liverpool-born player and recruitment from Blackbrook ARLFC. Chisnall was to later admit in the above article: "When I took the job I only had six players and £15,000 to spend. I built a complete team for £15,000 – that's not as much as most teams spend on one player".[23]

Predictably, the season got off to a terrible start on the pitch as every game was lost in both September and October 1989. On 5 November Rochdale Hornets defeated the inexperienced Highfield team 92–0. Following this, the emergency inclusion of a few seasoned campaigners such as Billy Platt and Frank Goodier, the latter on loan from Keighley, narrowed the points gaps, somewhat, but the team continued to lose heavily. Oldham put 60 points on the board against Highfield, Ryedale-York 52, Chorley and Batley 46 apiece; the side was being hammered every week. Speculation developed that Runcorn was up for sale and despite the board making an announcement that the club was stable with few debts, it was clear that should a buyer would be welcomed with open arms - no such purchaser emerged. On 19 November 1989 the board stated in the official programme: "Rest assured, your current board is 100% Runcorn Highfield and would only ever consider moving aside if any proposed take over or similar was for the good of Highfield. In the meantime, supporters can rest assured that we have always (and will always) carry on working as hard as we possibly can." [24]

So, perhaps rather like the infamous vote of confidence, it was quite evident by such a statement that the club was indeed open to offers. By January 1990, Terry Hughes was asking for supporters' "patience" but it was all rather fatuous. This no frills financial package was becoming an embarrassment to Chisnall, Runcorn and the RFL. Runcorn Highfield proceeded to lose every remaining game of the season. It was only by virtue of one or two closer-run results that the dreaded 1,000 points-against figure was not reached. Nevertheless, Runcorn Highfield became only the second team in the entire history of the game to go through a complete season without gaining a single point. In fact, while predecessors Liverpool City performed likewise in 1906-07 (see chapter 1), a point was removed from City's final tally after a drawn game was declared void.

By the 1990 close season the Runcorn Association Football Club, worried about its own financial future, the state of its ground, and the comic-book profile that Highfield had brought to Canal Street – by this time the rugby team had not won a fixture in over 18 months – raised the next season's rent to £15,000.

It was a move intended to bring about one of two eventualities: either the supply of more cash for the football club, or the removal an embarrassment from the ground. The former might have been the preferable option but it was the latter that took place. Matters did not come to a head until just prior to the beginning of the new season. According to Geoff Fletcher: "Terry [Hughes] wouldn't accept it and so we went to Hoghton Road." What Fletcher did not say in this interview, however, was that much of the credit for rescuing the club should go to himself. He had been a relatively inactive board member throughout the previous two seasons. However, at the last minute, with Runcorn Highfield's existence in grave doubt, he stepped in, approached certain committee members at St Helens Town FC, and made a quick agreement to take the rugby club to Town's petite Hoghton Road ground in the Sutton district of St Helens.

After all this time, the Liverpool Stanley of old was now (much to the chagrin of once close allies St Helens RLFC) St Helens-based. All of this, naturally, had to be approved by the Rugby League Council and Fletcher addressed the next council meeting.

Second Division 1989–90 (bottom four)

18 Workington Town	28	6	0	22	311	708	12
19 Keighley	28	6	0	22	436	837	12
20 Nottingham City	28	4	0	24	323	1032	8
21 Runcorn Highfield	**28**	**0**	**0**	**28**	**218**	**935**	**0**

Sutton Town

The 1 September 1990 edition of *RL Thirteen* suggested that Fletcher was in a resilient mood. Secretary Ian Swann was certainly not going to roll over: "Geoff Fletcher will take on his toughest challenge next Wednesday knowing that defeat will kill off one of the oldest clubs. Fletcher has to persuade his fellow Rugby League Council members to let Runcorn move to St Helens Town football ground – despite opposition from the Knowsley Road giants – and become Sutton Town. If he loses then the club will die although the directors are determined to take their fight into the European Court if necessary.

Director-secretary Ian Swann said: 'Geoff will argue our case. We have to leave Runcorn because we can't afford to stay there. They want us to pay £15,000 a year rent this season and £20,000 next year – we only take £600 a match through the gate. As Wigan Highfield we were a founder member of the League [not correct]. We have an awful lot of history and you can't just let that go.'" [25]

As it turned out Fletcher won perhaps one of the hardest battles of his rugby league life by persuading the Rugby League Council to agree to the move to St Helens Town, but curiously they did not agree to the change of name. Peter Oakes of *RL Thirteen* quoted Fletcher on 15 September 1990 asserting: "We survived at Huyton through the kindness of a lot of rugby league clubs. Now we have survived again. I don't think I needed to convince council members that we should be allowed to live – a lot have been in the game a great number of years and they know what it's like to survive. It's only some of the big clubs that were ready to hammer us. The small, less fashionable clubs, were behind us all the way. We are going to prove they were right. By that I mean we will be successful. We don't owe anyone, but we have got to get the team winning and get the ground up to top class condition. We have got to start developing the ground so that we get more spectators which means more money, which means we can get better players. It's going to mean a lot of hard work, getting a pick and spade and going there at night." [26]

The news was even covered in the *Daily Telegraph*. Rugby league correspondent John Whalley reported on 6 September 1990: "Runcorn have scored a rare victory by obtaining permission to share a ground with St Helens Town soccer club despite the board of directors not being in favour and an objection by St Helens Rugby Club. Runcorn were given permission at yesterday's council meeting by 26 votes to six. ... St Helens Rugby Club objected because Runcorn, now based only five miles from Knowsley Road, would be "encroaching on their development and commercial area". [27]

The result was a vindication for Fletcher; his timely return to the sharp end of Runcorn RLFC had not only helped sort out the chaos of the previous season but actually saved the club from extinction. The smaller rugby league clubs knew Fletcher of old and his indomitable spirit in the face of pressure brought out not only his bullish side, but also their admiration. One can imagine Fletcher's pitch to the RLC moving along very similar lines to his interview for *RL Thirteen*: "I don't know why I'm now a director, you seem to drift into it. But I'll tell you one thing – there's a big difference between being a director of a big club and a director of Runcorn. You won't find the big club directors going on the turnstiles at a game, you won't find them selling programmes, you won't find them making the tea, you won't find them marking out the pitch, and you won't find them washing the team jerseys. It's no good coming in and thinking that you are going to stand there watching a game – it's all about hard work at our level.

We have 15 lads on our playing register who live, were brought up and played their rugby in St Helens. We have more St Helens lads in our first team than St Helens have. What I'm hoping is that these lads' parents, uncles and aunties will come and watch us now. We will increase our crowd by playing at St Helens Town and we will go into the commercial side, which I don't think has ever been tried. We will go for the smaller businessman – the ones that Saints don't need because they are only in a small way. We have now got a permanent home, which we have never had before. We are also in a rugby league area and we've never had that before.

We are only 500 yards inside the St Helens boundary and we know we won't get Saints supporters – but we hope to get people who don't watch Saints but are still fans. We still have some of our old Huyton fans. They will keep coming and so, we hope, will the Runcorn fans. If we can get 700 or 800 we will be much happier than we were." [28]

Hoghton Road

But in the shadows of the Bold Power Station cooling towers, Hoghton Road was, of course, a very modest ground; apart from one tiny and somewhat dilapidated wooden stand on the halfway line, no cover existed at all; indeed there were very few facilities at the ground apart from an enclosed pitch – which also required considerable work to bring it up to professional rugby league standards. St Helens Town AFC had been in existence since the immediate post-Second World War era but had spent most of its time as a local also-ran in the lower echelons of the regional part-time football leagues.

Only recently had the club's finest moment arrived. Three seasons previously in 1987, as first-time entrants to the Football Association's Vase competition, St Helens Town had reached the Final at Wembley, beating Warrington Town 3-2. Despite this brush with fame, however, their ground remained unimproved, although it had a large social club. Ironically, as in the 1940s, training facilities were acquired at Clock Face – this time not the long-gone colliery club field, but the renowned Clock Face ARLFC.

If the first season was anything to go by, the move to Sutton actually held a little promise. True, the team continued its losing streak into March 1991, however, attendances did improve. This was probably a statistical anomaly and as much due to the makeup of that season's Second Division as anything else. Several larger clubs were in the bottom tier that year. By virtue of a lucrative fixture list Runcorn Highfield recorded several gates of more than 1,000 at the new ground. Only fixtures against the likes of Dewsbury, Carlisle, and Whitehaven saw attendances drop below 500. Geoff Fletcher might not have achieved 700 to 800 for home games but he wasn't far off.

One winning item that Highfield was able to bring to Sutton was the lottery. In fact, how former landlords Runcorn FC thought that this scheme would not have been missed remains beyond belief. The renamed Town Link lottery duly went into action in and around Bold, Sutton and all-points perilously close to Knowsley Road's commercial markets. This lottery added several thousands of pounds to both Hoghton Road clubs' incomes and effectively sealed what appeared to be an all-round good deal.

After a couple of early thrashings – 50–0 in the Lancashire Cup at Fulham in the first match of the season and 82–8 at Halifax on 14 October 1990, coach Dave Chisnall left the club, but not before he had signed former Saints star Chris Arkwright. Huyton stalwart Alan Bishop replaced Chisnall as coach and largely continued with Chisnall's cut-price side. However, with Bishop and Arkwright in control, it became clear to most supporters that this team would eventually win a game.

Programme columnist Frank Martin of the *St Helens Star* announced on 1 January 1991: "The club is now firmly established in a new home here at Hoghton Road... It's not been all doom and gloom on the playing front, despite what the results may suggest... There are other reasons for optimism too. Skipper Billy Platt continues to amaze all and sundry with his energy, enthusiasm and, most importantly performances... While... Simon Ashcroft is improving all the time... So let's look ahead to 1991." [29]

These notes were written in expectancy rather than blind faith, for by this time the side was performing reasonably well. By January 1991 matches against Hunslet, 11–10 and Huddersfield, 17–14, had been close and on 3 February a 12–12 home draw against Carlisle gave Highfield, now playing in red and black, their first point of the season in front of the lowest crowd of the season thus far – 250. Following two successive defeats at Keighley, 36–4 in the Challenge Cup and 33–16 in the league – the latter closer than the scoreline suggests – on Sunday 3 March 1991 the day arrived when Runcorn Highfield picked up their first victory for two years, with a 9–2 defeat of Dewsbury.

This win finally ended a truly depressing run of 75 matches without a victory. The gloom stretched as far back as 30 October 1988 when Fulham were defeated 20–12 at Canal Street. Two draws were also part of this tortuous litany of failure: 8-8 against Workington Town on 22 January 1989, and two years later the aforementioned 12–12 draw with Carlisle. Highfield programme editor Steve Burrows could barely contain his excitement: "Ecstasy, sheer ecstasy! There is no other word for it when that final hooter sounded at 4.30pm. Everyone was exuberant... If that wasn't enough – what about Monday's *Granada Reports*? [On] ITV 6.30pm when [TV] presenter John Huntley presented chairman Terry Hughes with the *Granada Reports* Perseverance Trophy, which is now pride of place in our boardroom cabinet." [30]

Highfield won another two games that season – on 31 March 54–16 at home to Keighley and on 7 April versus Nottingham City (formerly Mansfield) 42–0. Finishing 20th out of 21 teams in the Second Division might not appear auspicious, but for the first time since 1988 Runcorn had not finished bottom of the pile. The club had survived.

Second Division 1990–91 (bottom four)

18 Chorley Borough	28	7	1	20	388	721	15
19 Bramley	28	7	1	20	379	726	15
20 Runcorn Highfield	**28**	**3**	**1**	**24**	**351**	**779**	**7**
21 Nottingham City	28	2	0	26	284	945	4

In 1991 the Rugby Football League in a surprising and much-criticised move, declared that there were enough clubs in the Rugby League Championship to command three divisions, even though the Second Division would consist of only eight clubs. The three-division system lasted just two years but almost totally achieved what it set out to do – clear the bottom rungs of the championship of its apparent detritus. It was obvious to all observers of rugby league that the Rugby League board was now in the process of distancing the so-called elite clubs from the rest of the pack. This was not the only decision to have a dramatic effect on the future of Highfield but it certainly contributed to their fate. Not only was the club effectively relegated without kicking a rugby ball but also the opportunity to play book-balancing home games against well-supported sides in the lower regions of the competition had all-but vanished – probably once and for all. The eight-club Second Division had actually been introduced as a *pro tem* buffer zone in an attempt to get these clubs up to a certain standard both on and off the field. Although promotion and relegation still took place in these two seasons it was thought that the final eight would have found their true level, as it were.

The rugby league authorities – as mentioned earlier – also refused to sanction the Sutton Town title, while ordering that the Runcorn moniker be removed. There were those at the RFL who saw the title Highfield as retaining a certain level of continuity, but the name was little more than an historical footnote in the game's history. What this club now needed was a discernable geographic tag. Sutton was indeed a small community but while attendances for St Helens Town could be very low, there were hundreds of people using the social club facilities.

Disgruntled principal directors Terry Hughes and Geoff Fletcher thus began their second season at Hoghton Road as Highfield RLFC. Alan Bishop stood down as coach and was briefly replaced by Chris Arkwright, but he then left before the start of the season, being replaced by Willie Johnson. Alan Bishop also resigned from the board, which now consisted of chairman Terry Hughes and directors Fletcher, B. Morris, Swann, H. Burrows, J. Morris and secretary Dr P.R. Thomas. Programme editor Stephen Burrows became assistant secretary.

The Highfield team performed adequately in the Third Division for the 1991–92 season, winning nine matches, but gates fell to mostly fewer than 300. Simon Ashcroft and the Australian Simon Chappell were the pick of the bunch as the Highfield team pulled around a hitherto poor season by winning five out of their final 10 games. But it was evident that the St Helens locals were not interested in paying to watch third tier rugby league. The playing standards had dropped so alarmingly that the gap between the First and Third Divisions was almost immeasurable. Furthermore, newer clubs such as Scarborough, Nottingham, Chorley and Trafford barely had enough fans to produce a reasonable crowd at their home games, never mind travel away to Sutton. It was only the ever-popular and promotion-bound Huddersfield that helped swell Highfield's home attendances that season with an 803 gate for the Yorkshire side's 46–20 victory on 15 December 1991. Highfield did the double over Nottingham City, but the two games were watched by a gross attendance of only 325.

Third Division 1991–92 (bottom four)

11 Highfield	**26**	**9**	**0**	**17**	**406**	**646**	**18**
12 Chorley Borough	26	4	0	22	290	842	8
13 Trafford Borough	26	2	0	24	306	941	4
14 Nottingham City	26	0	0	26	164	1323	0

Highfield versus Nottingham (Photos: Andrew Cudbertson)

Highfield versus Hull Kingston Rovers 21 August 1994
(Photo: Mike Haddon)

For the 1992-93 season events transpired in remarkably similar mode. Highfield were, by-and-large, cannon-fodder for the heavy hitters but able to pick up enough points from the worse sides in the Third Division to keep relatively out of trouble - which was just as well because the RFL had introduced relegation to outside the game's professional structure. By spring 1993 the bottom three clubs in the Third Division dropped into the new Conference. This fate befell Chorley, Blackpool and Nottingham.

These clubs having been removed from the competition at the end of the season meant that the Third Division was scrapped and for 1993–94 the game reverted to two divisions – cynically, at a stroke three of rugby league football's four embarrassments had been eliminated. Highfield won six league matches during the season and although finishing ninth the team was effectively only a-top of the RFL base, being 16 points behind Hunslet, the eighth club in the superstructure. It was clear that the Rugby League Board considered the very lowest clubs as little more than unwanted debris.

Player-coach Willie Johnson had arrived at Highfield from Dewsbury for the 1991–92 season. He played 26 matches that year and 19 during the 1992–93 campaign, but left the club with eight matches of the season to go and the threat of Conference rugby looming large. However, in April, Mike Peers, a former Warrington professional and previously coach at Swinton came in, steadied the ship and helped steer the team to relative safety. He did so by using, in the main, willing former rugby league amateurs. Norman Barrow (who had previously played for Fulham), Mike Carr, Geoff Dean, Shaun Dolan, Paul Durnin, Paul Littler, and Eddie Tinsley were all part of that season's Highfield squad and had arrived from one local amateur club or another. Thatto Heath ARLC in St Helens was a good source of enthusiastic players, as were the Wigan St Jude's and Leigh East clubs. Significantly, out of the 50 players registered with Highfield that season over half were former amateur rugby league or union players.

Attendances and income did suffer this season, in fact Highfield were at times operating on gates well below that of their Huyton, let alone Runcorn, predecessors – but such was the case for many lower-ranking clubs. One might argue that Fletcher's economic policies at Sutton were geared around such low turnouts - not something that could be said for other clubs in the same division.

However, the club lost its most consistent patron when Terry Hughes, having inaugurated a new travel company in 1992, found that he was somewhat ahead of his time. Entitled Mersey Mouse Tours, Hughes's idea was to transport tourists to the new Euro Disney near Paris. Hughes sank a lot of his money into this activity only to find it ran into trouble. Although Geoff Fletcher was astute enough to keep Highfield on an even keel, the failure of Hughes' enterprise was a blow to Highfield. Geoff Fletcher recalls: "Terry opened something called Mersey Mouse Travel – taking out franchises to Disney in Paris and it didn't kick-off and [his company] went bust. So I took over things again, I was determined to keep it going – I don't know why... just something that's in me, I suppose." [31]

Third Division 1992–93 (bottom five)

9 Highfield	**24**	**6**	**0**	**18**	**310**	**915**	**12**
10 Barrow	24	5	0	19	476	625	10
---							
11 Chorley Borough	24	5	0	19	317	781	10
12 Blackpool Gladiators	24	4	0	20	302	958	8
13 Nottingham City	24	1	0	23	181	1132	2

With the Rugby League Conference now launched, Highfield coach Mike Peers had to be extremely careful that his inexpensive squad did not run the club into relegation territory in the new season. He therefore supplemented it with a few old hands. Two former Great Britain internationals Ian Potter and Chris Johnson, both formerly with Leigh, joined, as did an ageing, but injured Brian Garrity together with Australian Trent Jordan.

However, this squad performed woefully throughout the entire season, winning only one game and, during the final run-in suffering a humiliating 96–0 drubbing at the hands of a vastly improved Doncaster on 20 March 1994. This was now the heaviest defeat suffered by the club in its professional history. Much to Peers's embarrassment the side did indeed finish bottom of the division and a call went out for Highfield to be relegated.

Geoff Fletcher, however, once again successfully made his financial case for Highfield to persist in the Rugby League Championship. This strategy was evidently well-versed, for as early as 5 December 1993 a club programme editorial suggested that officials appreciated not only which way the wind was blowing, both on and off the pitch, but also that the RLC as a whole appreciated financial solvency, although for how long was open to conjecture: "Rugby league fans, especially those who are associated with this club which pioneered rugby league in the capital in the 1930s, and who retain one of the most financially sound regimes in the sport, don't need Mr Strudwick [coach of London Crusaders] to tell them what's wrong with rugby league in London.

Whatever Mr Strudwick, or Mr Lindsay, may suggest, the fact is that rugby league is not like American football, easily welded by rich owners to a community where it has no base. Indeed, the underlying weakness of rugby league has been the weakening of ties between clubs and the communities from which they sprang." [32]

This editorial, written by company secretary Phil Thomas, not only captures the RFL at an important phase in its projected development, but it also summarises well the geographical problems that beset Highfield. Those 'weakening ties' of which Thomas writes had been partially wrought by the RFL itself, and while the board of Highfield RLFC was under no illusion that it was also attempting to tie into a pre-existing community with no previous experience of professional rugby league, the value of such a local community was not in doubt. But while Highfield was denied its Sutton tag, a London-based import naturally possessed its London moniker almost by right. As suggested by the tone of Thomas' writing, double standards, brought about by financial gain, were clearly in evidence.

In the same edition of this programme a letter to the editor was published concerning Highfield's impending dice with relegation:

Conference Considerations
"Dear Sir,
With due respect to Hemel Hempstead can they really expect to replace Highfield if the league's only solvent club finishes the season at the bottom of division two?
Surely in view of Highfield's financial record, Rugby League Headquarters would be stupid to relegate the club to the Conference."
Highfield Regular

The programme editor replied: "I share your inference that Hemel aren't ready for Rugby League football and that financial solvency should be a condition for membership of the professional game but the only way to avoid the limbo of Conference football is not to finish bottom of the Second Division – even then it's no guarantee." [33]

However while Highfield's account books could not lie, the club was able to survive in the professional ranks for another season; not simply because of its solvency, but because no other club was prepared to take Highfield's place. It was a poisoned chalice of vast proportions and for, say, Hemel Hempstead to have been admitted to the Second Division ranks would have been utterly foolish and undoubtedly disastrous – travelling costs, alone, must have filled the southern club with dread.

Second Division 1993–94 (bottom four)

13 Carlisle	30	9	0	21	540	878	18
14 Hunslet	30	3	1	26	445	814	7
15 Bramley	30	3	0	27	376	957	6
16 Highfield	**30**	**1**	**1**	**28**	**267**	**1234**	**3**

Sky Television and Super League

Prior to the 1994–95 season, events well beyond the club's control perhaps finally instigated the beginning of the end for Highfield RLFC. Towards the end of the 1994 close season the start of what would become known as the 'Super League war' broke out in Australia when News Corporation's Rupert Murdoch tried to wrest control of the competition from the Australian Rugby League. In April 1995, Murdoch offered to inject £85 million into rugby league in Britain. The result was a speedy and at times chaotic reorganisation of British rugby league and as the Rupert Murdoch-inspired financial revolution began to take shape it was clear that Highfield was not long for this world. The Sky express train was unrelenting and extraordinary transformations were to follow, making the likes of Geoff Fletcher and his ilk appear regressive and out of touch. Mergers between local rivals were proposed – and then withdrawn – and when the dust settled, the game had moved from winter to a summer playing season, with enough funding for players in the new Super League to become full-time professionals.

With one eye cast firmly on the goings-on in Australia, the St Helens Town FC committee had already decided that the rent for the use of Hoghton Road should be raised and a figure similar to that suggested by Runcorn AFC – £15,000 a year – was mooted towards the end of the 1993–94 season. Fletcher and his board were having none of it and in March 1994 decided once again to move the club: – coincidentally to the enclosure that was so coveted by the Liverpool Stanley board of directors of 1939 to 1945 – Prescot Cables' Hope Street. This timely agreement, ostensibly between Geoff Fletcher and the owners of Hope Street (not, it must be stated, Prescot Cables FC) took place hurriedly. The owners were keen to bring in an extra revenue stream, for by the mid-1990s gate receipts had reached a wretched level and the Cables' social club was all-but closed for business. Fletcher promised to revive both club and ground and the deal was duly done. Three games were played at the end of that season at Hope Street: versus London Crusaders, Workington Town, and Keighley Cougars. On each occasion Highfield lost heavily, 58–6, 40–1 and 76–8 respectively, but attendances rose – 339, 736, 784 – and the social club reopened on match days. Was there perhaps the slenderst glint of hope for this nomadic club?

Prescot, Prescot Town and Prescot Cables FC have a long history at Hope Street. Cables were pehaps one of the first part-time professional clubs in the country to be overtly sponsored – the name Cables being added after BICC provided financial assistance. Prescot Cables joined the Lancashire Combination in 1927–28 but the years

1954 to 1960 were probably the club's most successful. By 1975, however, fortunes at the club had dipped drastically. In 1982–83 they became founder members of the North West Counties Football League. In 1986–87 they won promotion to the First Division. Hope Street housed a large brick grandstand, which exists to this day, but this had fallen into disrepair and was not used when Highfield took up tenancy at the ground. Decades of neglect and vandalism had put the Hope Street ground into a dilapidated state and it was a marvel that Fletcher persuded the RLC to go along with the move. The Cables social club was also grossly underused and so Fletcher immediately set about obtaining a brewery loan. This also meant that subsequently he was to spend long unsociable hours in the bar, building up a clientele and creating vital cash flow for his rugby team.

But on the pitch the 1994–95 season was a complete disaster for Highfield. The club won only two games all season – against amateurs Ovenden in the first round of the Regal Trophy and against Barrow 14–12 in the league. Their team of professionals lost to amateurs Beverley 27–4 in the Challenge Cup and their final game of the season (played not at Hope Street, but at Rochdale Hornets on 23 April 1995) was a humiliating 104–4 defeat at the hands of Keighley Cougars. The final home game of the season was on 17 April 1995 when Highfield lost 34–8 to Barrow in front of a paltry crowd of 195 – most of whom were away supporters. Needless to say, Highfield finished bottom of the Second Division with only two league points. The team conceded a grand total of 1,604 points in 30 league games, scoring just 224, and were 10 league points away from Barrow in 15th place, who had 12. But remarkably the club was making a profit. The brewery loan obtained by Fletcher had helped partially refurbish the social club, which was now being populated at weekends by local rugby and football enthusiasts. The team was only a little short of being hopeless, yet once again the infrastructure of the club helped pay its way. Fortunately for the Highfield board, relegation was not a consideration this season because, yet again, the RFL was reinventing itself.

At the close of the 1994–95 season, as part of moves towards the introduction of Super League in the spring of 1996, the league structure was again reorganised – this time into a top-flight Centenary Championship of 11 clubs, and First and Second Divisions of 11 teams each. The Centenary Championship consisted of the top 10 clubs from the 1994–95 First Division, plus London Broncos. The First Division (now second tier) was made up of the six clubs who had finished in places 11 to 16 in the 1994–95 First Division, plus the top five in the 1994–95 Second Division.

However, Doncaster Dragons were placed in the Second Division as a newly formed club, their predecessors having gone out of business. Doncaster and the rest of the Second Division clubs – including Highfield – formed the new Second Division (now the third tier). These changes caused a great deal of anger within the game, although some of this dissipated once the mergers were dropped. The change to summer offered a huge marketing opportunity for Super League clubs, but many of the lower echelons did not have the finance or staff to take advantage of new openings for the game.

1995–96

For Highfield, the new season began in a positive mood with coaches Frank Barrow and Tommy Frodsham replacing Mike Peers and Chris Arkwright. An Academy side coached by Les Chisnall and Dave Tickle was formed and former Wigan player Steve Chambers was signed. Dave Lever joined from Leigh and Kevin Johnson, also a former Leigh player joined the club. Perhaps one of the most historically significant signings was that of Russ

Bridge. He had started his professional career with Fulham, but then had returned to the north-west and, after having a trial with Wigan, had played regularly for Leigh. He had appeared for Highfield towards the end of the previous campaign and had agreed terms for the new season. Meanwhile, Fletcher was trying to secure a lease at Hope Street.

Fifty-five players were used in the 1995–96 season – most of them, with the exceptions of Sean Fanning and Russ Bridge, somewhat out of their depth. The team gained one point, a 24–24 draw against York in front of a crowd of 150, and the only victory came against amateurs Hemel Hempstead in the first round of the Regal Trophy, 48–18 in front of 220 supporters. In the second round of the Regal Trophy Highfield drew London Broncos and lost 82–0. Another 82–0 defeat was recorded at Hunslet Hawks. York defeated Highfield 74–14 and in three other games more than 60 points were conceded – desperate stuff and by this time truly not worthy of the professional game. Geoff Fletcher recalls: "The players by the mid-90s were asking a lot of money – £140 to lose. And they weren't worth it. It was madness, to be honest, but I was defiant; I didn't want to be the one to pull the plug!" [34]

1995–96 Second Division (bottom four)

8 Barrow Braves	20	6	0	14	342	488	12
9 Chorley Chieftans	20	5	1	14	324	608	11
10 Doncaster Dragons	20	5	0	15	348	646	10
11 Highfield	**20**	**0**	**1**	**19**	**249**	**964**	**1**

Prescot Panthers

In the spring of 1996 the RFL's professional competitions moved to a summer season and Fletcher was allowed to change his club's name once more – this time to the highly appropriate Prescot Panthers. But the playing record of this club in its death throes was scarcely worthy of this once-proud, albeit unsuccessful, club. For both 1996 and 1997 seasons the Panthers finished bottom of the Second Division and in both campaigns conceded over 800 points. In each season Prescot only won twice, in 1996 against Barrow and Chorley and in 1997 against Doncaster and Barrow. Over the two seasons more than 100 players were used by successive coaches Jim Crellin, Tommy Frodsham, Maurice Bamford and Warren Ayres; 48 in 1996 and 58 in 1997. The heaviest defeat in 1996 came from Swinton, 90–0; on another nine occasions more than 40 points were conceded. The heaviest defeat in 1997 came at Rochdale Hornets 74–6; on another eight occasions the Panthers conceded over 40 points.

Unbeknown to those at the club, the team's very last home match also came against Rochdale Hornets, ironically Liverpool Stanley's first opponents in 1934 – on Sunday 13 July - the fixture was duly lost 74–12. The following week the final fixture of the 1997 season at Carlisle's Gilford Park saw the Panthers defeated 72–10.

By the late summer of 1997 the brewery loan, previously arranged by Fletcher to open and refurbish the Hope Street social club, moved from one organisation to another. The new parent company applied pressure for the loan to be repaid with immediate effect. This simply could not be achieved and Prescot Panthers RLFC was forced into administration, then ultimately receivership. By October 1997 the ever-valiant Tom Fleet, by this stage the Widnes Vikings vice-chairman, was keen not only to save this proud club from extinction but also for Widnes to receive Prescot's share of the Sky money.

Prescot Panthers versus South Wales 5 April 1996 (Photo: Mike Haddon)

With the support of his chairman, Fleet proposed a merger between Widnes Vikings and Prescot Panthers. But the merger was not sanctioned by the RFL, who, it seems, effectively thought it mandatory that Prescot Panthers die. After discussions with a local Prescot solicitor, Fletcher was able to produce financial and legal documentation to the RLC effectively showing that the foreclosure was not due to bad management at the rugby club. Thus a one-off payment in the region of £30,000, to withdraw Prescot from all competitions, was agreed. This amount was confirmed at the Rugby League Council meeting on 3 December 1997. Neither Fletcher nor his deputy Brian Morris were present at this meeting to witness the last hurrah of this once-intrepid club. Equitable payments were subsequently made from the allotted £30,000 to the club's bankers, thence to the few remaining Huyton-with-Roby RLFC Limited Company shareholders. Geoff Fletcher recalls: "I was running the bar, and everything. I did feel let down... To be honest, I'd had enough by that time: all the hassle, I could have hung on for another 12 months and been chairman of the Council, but I'd had enough. I don't know what went on with the Prescot Council, but they had a lot to say about it – I think they wanted everybody out of Hope Street. They certainly were moaning about us being there – [someone] called us terrible people. The [Cables] football club never paid a penny towards the running of the social club. We only opened on match days or for weddings and the like - but we were paying all the rates and electricity – everything!

The worst thing was that we were actually paying the brewery loan off. We were paying off their loan regularly – the RFL were all for it. The problem was that the brewery changed and the loan was passed on and the second brewery foreclosed. But in the long run, whenever you find a football ground, there are always land-ownership problems. I think that was part the real story behind us leaving – land. I think somebody wanted to build on Hope Street. It was complicated: we had to rent the ground off the council but the buildings belong to the brewery." [35]

Longest serving player Russ Bridge was disappointed when told that the club was no more. He told *League Express*: "It's just a great shame really... other clubs are not that much better off financially... I was actually better off at Prescot than I was before I left Leigh [but] no-one from Prescot ever contacted me to update us on what was happening. I rang Warren Ayres a couple of times and he was no wiser. Chairman Geoff Fletcher had always said that the club was debt free, but when we read in the papers about a brewery making them insolvent, the alarm bells started to ring... I suppose I'd noticed his enthusiasm waning. He didn't come to many, if any, away matches last season. A club at that level ought to be able to operate on the £90,000 or so that it receives from News Corporation. There certainly wasn't a lot going to players over the last two years... It's just a big, big pity." [36]

The following week former Panthers director and secretary Brian Morris replied to Bridge: "Firstly, Prescot did not go into administration because of insolvency. That position was forced on them when the brewery called in a 10-year loan for payment immediately – an impossible task. Prescot were not behind with their monthly repayments... The club's cash flow position was more than adequate to meet its liabilities. I am certain that many Second Division chairmen would have a wry smile at Russ's statement that £90,000 per year is sufficient to run a club and perhaps hope to be given the formula. In truth, £90,000, due to be reduced this season, was barely enough to cover the costs of running three teams [Prescot ran Alliance and Academy sides]... Panthers' match terms were better than most Second Division teams and also some in the First. He implies criticism of Geoff Fletcher without realising that in addition to a very busy business life Geoff experienced a long period of serious illness to members of his family ... I doubt whether there is any other person in the Rugby League who has given more time to the game or the club... After 75 years of traversing the game's highways and byways the club is no more. But I venture to say that with Prescot's demise a little piece of the heart and soul of rugby league died too." [37]

It seems an ignominious way to end such a long, hard road: the financial cul-de-sac of a brewery loan. As Russ Bridge suggests, the demise of this club was a "big pity", but it is important not to get carried away: historically we can see both right and wrong in the closure of Prescot Panthers. Right in that self-deception is perhaps the sportsman's worst nightmare. It is certainly correct to concede that a future does not exist for a project hopelessly removed from reality. But when this is accepted there are other dangers. By not sanctioning quirkiness in sport there is the risk of only having variations on winners – all to be kept in order by a central authority, thus reducing sport to a hideous sameness. The history of this rugby league club is therefore a reminder to continually listen to local views, rather than the (often bland) sporting universalities that are ever present. From Jimmy Green to Geoff Fletcher, these increasingly seldom-heard independent voices ask to consider the positive advantages of difference... and defeat.

Second Division 1996 (bottom three)

10 Barrow Braves	22	5	0	17	354	651	10
11 Bramley	22	5	0	17	360	759	10
12 Prescot Panthers	**22**	**2**	**0**	**20**	**301**	**883**	**4**

Second Division 1997 (bottom three)

9 Bramley	20	5	1	14	353	513	11
10 Doncaster Dragons	20	3	1	16	247	668	7
11 Prescot Panthers	**20**	**2**	**0**	**18**	**247**	**817**	**4**

Endnotes

[1] Fleet, Tom (1992), 'A History of Highfield' part 10: 'To Runcorn', published as a series for the *Highfield Official Programme*

[2] John Costello to author, January 2008

[3] Clarke, Garry (2007), 'A History Of Rugby League In Runcorn', draft monograph intended for publication, p. 5

[4] [Probably] Terry Hughes, 'Message From The Board', *Runcorn Highfield Official Programme* [versus Widnes] Sunday 19 August 1984, p.3

[5] John Costello to author, January 2008

[6] [Probably] Terry Hughes, 'Message From The Board', *Runcorn Highfield Official Programme* [versus Widnes], Sunday 19 August 1984, p.3

[7] Geoff Fletcher to author 27 February 2008

[8] Unaccredited editor, 'Message From The Board', *Runcorn Highfield Official Programme* [versus Mansfield Marksman], Sunday 2 September 1984, p.3

[9] John Costello to author, January 2008

[10] Unaccredited editor, 'Club Gossip', *Runcorn Highfield Official Programme* [versus Fulham] 20 April 1987, p.5

[11] Unaccredited editor, 'Supporters' Club Notes', *Runcorn Highfield Official Programme* [versus Keighley], 1 January 1988, p.15

[12] Clarke, Garry (2007), 'A History of Rugby League In Runcorn', draft monograph intended for publication, p.5

[13] Geoff Fletcher to author 27 February 2008

[14] John Lomas to author November 2007

[15] Unaccredited editor, 'The Highfield Scene', *Runcorn Highfield Official Programme* [versus Fulham], Sunday 30 October 1988, p.5

[16] Unaccredited editor, 'The Highfield Scene', *Runcorn Highfield Official Programme* [versus Rochdale Hornets] 20 November 1988, p.5

[17] Tom Fleet: email correspondence with author, 27 March 2008

[18] Cook, Paul (1988), 'Highfield 4 Huddersfield 25', *Widnes Weekly News,* 15 December 1988, p.52

[19] Unaccredited correspondent, 'Rugby League Newsround', *Runcorn Highfield Official Programme* [versus Swinton], 19 February 1989, p.17

[20] Barry Broadhead to author November 2007

[21] Geoff Fletcher to author 27 February 2008

[22] Dave Chisnall to Oakes, Peter, 'I'm On A Winner Says Dizzy Chiz', *RL Thirteen*, reprinted in *Runcorn Highfield Official Programme* [versus Ryedale York] Sunday 16 September 1990, pp. 8-9

[23] *ibid*

[24] [Possibly] Terry Hughes, 'Comments & Opinions', *Runcorn Highfield Official Programme* [versus Bramley], Sunday 19 November 1989, p.7

[25] Unaccredited correspondent, 'Fletch Won't Flinch', *RL Thirteen no. 3,* 1 September 1990, p.2

[26] Geoff Fletcher to Oakes, Peter 'Pig Farmer Fletch Saves Runcorn's Bacon', *RL Thirteen no.5,* 15 September 1990, p.7

[27] Whalley, John (1990), 'Runcorn Win Their Point', *Daily Telegraph,* 6 September 1990, p.30

[28] Geoff Fletcher to Oakes, Peter, 'Pig Farmer Fletch Saves Runcorn's Bacon', *RL Thirteen no.5,* 15 September 1990, p.7

[29] Martin, Frank [of *the St Helens Star*] (1991), 'The Frank Martin Column', *Runcorn Highfield Official Programme* [versus Leigh], Sunday 1 January 1991, p.13

[30] Burrows, Steve (1991), 'Runcorn 9 Dewsbury 2', *Runcorn Highfield Official Programme* [versus Whitehaven], Sunday 17 March 1991, p. 26

[31] Geoff Fletcher to author 27 February 2008

[32] Phil Thomas, 'Editorial' *Highfield Official Programme* [versus Hunslet] 5 December 1993, p.3

[33] *ibid*, 'Reader's Write' *Highfield Official Programme* [versus Hunslet] 5 December 1993, p.9

[34] Geoff Fletcher to author 27 February 2008

[35] Geoff Fletcher to author 27 February 2008

[36] Unaccredited correspondent, 'Should Prescot Have Survived?': Russ Bridge to *League Express,* 8 December 1997, p.22

[37] Morris, Brian (1997), 'Panthers Put It Straight', *League Express,* 15 December 1997, p.25

11. League in Liverpool today

To claim that, following the departure of Liverpool City from the city of Liverpool in 1968, some kind of bond between the sport of rugby league and Liverpool had been broken would be highly inaccurate. To do so one would have to immediately concede to the concept that a bond had actually existed in the first place – which most certainly was not the case. However, one anomaly to emerge was that, somewhat coincidentally, the first recognised inter-university rugby league game actually took place the year of the Knotty Ash Stadium abandonment: between the universities of Liverpool and Leeds, at Widnes on 15 March 1968. This match is recognised as the start of student rugby league, although the Leeds team had been established for 18 months, playing in a local Leeds league. Andrew Cudbertson, one of the founders of the Leeds University club, recalls: "A few months after we started several of our players turned out in the chemistry department's annual rugby union fixture against their opposite numbers in Liverpool University. We discovered in the bar afterwards that that at least three of the Liverpool lads were playing amateur rugby league on Saturdays! One of those a guy called John Priestley from Huddersfield said we'll get a team together to play you in a friendly. Hence the fixture in March and later the club." [1]

Following this, the University of Liverpool has continued to maintain a long and proud history of fielding competitive rugby league teams up to today. And student rugby league has developed widely, well beyond the sport's traditional areas, with a regular World Cup competition as well.

Throughout the more recent past – and concurrent with the expansion of Liverpool's student population – attempts have been made (with varying degrees of success) to field rugby league sides from each of Liverpool's three universities. But, by and large, the students playing for these squads are ex-pats from areas of the north of England where rugby league is still regarded with great cultural esteem; this could not be regarded as an indicator *per se* of any active participation in the sport by Liverpudlians.

One noticeable exception to the lack of involvement in rugby league by Liverpudlians is James Graham, now starring in Super League with St Helens. Clearly he has had an impact on rugby league but at the present time is the exception that proves the rule, rather than the start of a trend of young Liverpudlians picking up a rugby league ball and running with it.

Liverpool Buccaneers ARLFC

However, if one looks a little more closely, one can find an independent amateur rugby league club in Liverpool. Liverpool Buccaneers ARLFC, formed during the winter of 2002 by former students and inquisitive rugby union players, runs a side in the *TotalRL.Com* RL Conference, an amateur summer competition run by the RFL to encourage non-traditional rugby league areas to play the game. The season runs from April to September with the Buccaneers' home games being played at the Sefton RUFC, Leyfield Road, West Derby, Liverpool 12 – ironically, only a 10 minute walk from the former site of Liverpool City's Knotty Ash Stadium. A little help has also made

Action from the historic first match between two British universities: Liverpool (in hoops) versus Leeds 15 March 1968 (Photo: Andrew Cudbertson)

its way to the club via St Helens RLFC and the Buccaneers have thus far been reasonably successful in illuminating the hitherto almost invisible profile in Liverpool for the sport. All very promising, one might suggest; however, the current 2008 Buccaneers player profiles listed on the club website[2] reveal that many players are either existing or former Liverpool Hope University students and are from rugby league heartlands, Ireland and even New Zealand. None, it appears, are from Liverpool – a familiar tale, to be sure.

On Monday 28 April 2008 John Farrell, Liverpool's rugby league development officer, organised an open meeting at the Liverpool Cricket Club for individuals to express their interest in the further development of the game in Liverpool. John Lawless of the *Football Echo* quoted Farrell thus: "Due to the large success of rugby league being played in many Liverpool schools, plus Liverpool Buccaneers ARLFC, the time has come to rally the communities and form some new junior teams and clubs... The new clubs and teams will need coaches, volunteers and committee members but you may be able to help out in another capacity. It would be great to see people there and if they have any questions or ideas, they shouldn't hesitate to get in touch."[3]

But does this not also sound rather familiar? Well, yes; indeed one might somewhat cynically suggest that the type of scheme proposed by John Farrell has an all-too proverbial ring. Coaches? Volunteers? Committee members? New teams? In days gone, both the MARL and Liverpool City RLFC certainly flogged this rather overworked steed almost to death. But maybe things are different now: perhaps the less ambitious nature of the suggested development programme - essentially without the attachment of a professional club - is a more realistic, long-term scheme; after all, it was eventually agreed by the RLC that the 'top down' concept, so long part of the plan to keep the Liverpool name within the Rugby Football League, was an abject failure.

However, the question still remains: will rugby league ever make a sizeable impact on the city of Liverpool? The dislocation between rugby league and the city continues to be so strong that John Farrell's call to arms will undoubtedly have to concern itself, not so much with just how the sport has thus far been ignored (this is obvious), but how it

Liverpool City past players at The George Hotel, May 2008. (Photo: Mike Brocken)

should be reconsidered, recontextualised and reconstituted in the 21st century: a truly daunting task. It is therefore probably more pragmatic as a final piece of evidence for us to briefly consider the recent experiences of the Liverpool City Past Players Association.

Liverpool City Past Players Association

Constantly in touch with each other as former colleagues, especially in and around the St Helens and Warrington areas, several City past players finally organised themselves into a recognisable group in order to attend a special Millennium 2000 event planned by the Rugby Football League. Secretary Eric Seed recalls: "Peter Dutton, who played for us, let me know that there was a call for former City players to attend a Millennium do. As the phone calls went around, people were willing to attend and it was soon realised that we should formalise it and represent the old club properly, so a tie and a blazer badge was also designed. We all got together, got up a coach and arranged to go to the Millennium dinner; there was a special menu for the players from the three counties [Yorkshire, Lancashire and Cumberland]. Peter Dutton's wife got red roses from the MC Malcolm Lord and he then announced each team in turn. When we got up with these roses, it was one of the biggest rounds of applause of the night. It took a lot to organise it but it was a good get together and we kept things going after that." [4]

As suggested by Eric Seed, it was quite apparent that the rest of the rugby league fraternity had not forgotten Liverpool City. Following this rather touching event Eric Seed assumed an organisational role and has continued to keep the former players in touch with each other from that day until this. Irrespective of any individuals' appearance record, all former City players are invited to attend LCPP social events, ranging from highly competitive bowls matches against the St Helens or Warrington past players, to a simple drink and a meal at a local hostelry – as Eric might say: "a good bit of craic". It must also be pointed out that it would unquestionably have been impossible for this book to have been written without the assistance of the Liverpool City band of brothers.

On Friday 25 April 2008, just prior to the aforementioned rallying call from rugby league development officer John Farrell, the City past players visited the Rugby League Heritage Centre at the famous George Hotel in Huddersfield. They travelled over to Yorkshire to present an original 1950s green and white Liverpool City jersey to the Heritage Centre's museum; according to George Walker they enjoyed a "wonderful time": "Yes, a very good day. Nineteen of us were there altogether. Eighteen on a coach and we met Ken Dibble at the George Hotel. Six of our party were from Warrington, 10 from St Helens and two from Widnes – plus Ken. We donated a framed photo from the Millennium do and the jersey. They made us very welcome, gave us a tour of the place and made a fuss of Ray [Ashby] of course because of the Lance Todd Trophy and Great Britain cap. After that the camaraderie kept it going. Later I spoke to a bloke who was sitting at the bar and he noticed our blazer badges. He was from Liverpool; I said 'you probably don't remember Liverpool City', he said 'oh yes I do'. Afterwards we ordered some sandwiches from the bar and that Liverpool chap said 'I'll pay for them'." [5]

Heritage

So, the Liverpool City story, of rugby league in a football city, is now officially the substance of heritage, and perhaps it is better reposing within history, certified by the Rugby League Heritage Centre, rather than re-launched without relevance, without context, without the necessary social cement. It is sometimes suggested that we record the past to learn a lesson for the present. Certainly, now that our daily lives seem to blithely move along with little recourse to the past experiences of others, we do need to remind ourselves that past, forgotten identities have great relevance.

Thinking about the partially hidden sporting heritage of Liverpool presented here provides us with examples through which we might contemplate the future. In other words, using history as something with which we can reflect – just for a moment taking ourselves out the present, making ourselves aware of how such identities were originally formulated, can show us where and how such sporting realities begin and end.

In cases such as Liverpool City Rugby League Football Club, these were contested cultural battles – in City's case, the battles were ultimately lost, but this makes the club's historical presence no less valid. By presenting genuine communal alternatives to the present day lack of substance surrounding sport the Liverpool City Past Players Association's very presence suggests those real feelings, real energies, loyalties and convictions continue to be at play. Long may these partially hidden histories continue as a reminder for any development programmes - historically biting us on the backside – or at least providing us with the occasional plate of sandwiches.

Endnotes

[1] Email to Peter Lush, 23 June 2008
[2] See: www.liverpoolbuccaneers.co.uk
[3] Lawless, John (2008), 'Rallying Call For New Clubs' (interview with Liverpool Rugby League Development Officer John Farrell), [Liverpool] Football Echo, 26 April 2008, p. 15
[4] Eric Seed to author, 3 April 2008
[5] George Walker to author, 27 April 2008

Appendix: Club Records

Honours

Lancashire League winners: 1935–36
Championship semi-finalists: 1935–36

Club records

Highest score: 59–11 versus Bramley 1933–34

Points in a match: 30 by Norman Barrow versus Keighley 1990–91
Tries in a match: 5 by John Maloney versus Bramley 1930–31
Goals in a match: 11 by Peter Wood versus Batley 1984–85

Points in a season: 240 by Peter Wood 1984–85
Tries in a season: 28 by John Maloney 1930–31
Goals in a season: 126 by Peter Wood 1984–85

Points for the club: 731 by Wilf Hunt 1955 to 1966
Tries for the club: 204 by John Maloney 1926 to 1945
Goals for the club: 304 by Wilf Hunt 1955 to 1966

Representative honours:

Great Britain: Ray Ashby, Billy Belshaw, Nat Bentham, Harry Woods.

England: Billy Belshaw, Harry Woods

Lancashire: R. Ashby, G.A. Aspinall, W. Belshaw, D. Holland, J. Maloney, W. O'Mara, W. Riley, J. Robinson, J. Thompson, K. Wills, H. Woods.

Rugby League XIII: Billy Belshaw, Harry Woods.

(NB County honours may not be complete)

References:

Discussion with Bill Adair, 2 November 2007

'Airedale' (Austin Birch?), ' 'Begun and Continued' a New Series of RL Club Histories No. 18: Liverpool C', *Rugby Leaguer*, 16 January 1959

Andrews, Bert, 'Farewell City – Hail Huyton', *Prescot & Huyton Reporter*, 19 April 1968

Ibid, 'Youngsters Spoil Huyton's First Home Game', *Prescot & Huyton Reporter*, 20 September 1968

Andrews, H.R.H (1976), 'Chairman's Report' *Huyton Rugby League Supporters' Club AGM Notice*, 25 May 1976

[Unaccredited] 'Artist's Impressions', *Wigan Examiner*, 9 September 1922

Ashby, Ray interviews 2008

The editors, ARL Australian Kangaroos Rugby League: *http://rl1908.com/Kangaroos/1937.htm* (accessed 25/07/2006)

Philip Babbs: several Liverpool City official programme editorials and memorabilia

Ball, David (1985), 'Runcorn Highfield', *The Linnets*, Runcorn AFC newsletter

'Bee's Notebook', *Liverpool Football Echo*, Saturday 28 July 1906

'Bee's Notes On Sport', *Liverpool Echo*, 8 August 1934

'Bee's Notes On Sport Of the Day', *Liverpool Echo*, 29 August 1934

ibid, Liverpool Stanley', *Liverpool Echo*, 3 March 1937

ibid, 'The Late "Jimmy" Green', *Liverpool Echo,* 1 April 1937

Discussion with John Bibby, 16 February 2008

'Blackstaff's Notes On Sport of the Day', *Liverpool Echo* 25 July 1934

Boucher, David (2000), *Steel, Skill & Survival: Rugby In Ebbw Vale and the Valleys (1870-1952)*, Ebbw Vale: Ebbw Vale Rugby Football Club Ltd

Bowes, Stephen (2003), 'My First Time: The Wonder Years', *Rugby League Journal* 1/5, Winter 2003, Egremont: Edgar Publishing

Unaccredited correspondent to Russ Bridge, 'Should Prescot Have Survived?' *League Express,* 8 December 1997

Barry Broadhead to author November 2007

Broome, Jack in discussion: 29th July 2007, interview: 21 September 2007

Brown, Gordon (2004), 'Memories of Liverpool City', *Our Game* 9, Spring 2004, London: London League Publications

Jimmy Caddick – email correspondence, May 2007

Chadwick, Stanley, *Rugby League Review*, 24 November 1950

Clarke, Garry (2007), *'History of Rugby League in Runcorn'* – draft monograph

Ibid, various correspondence with author, December 2007

Collins, Tony (2006), *Rugby League in Twentieth Century Britain*, London: Routledge

Cook, Paul (1988), 'Highfield 4 Huddersfield 25', *Widnes Weekly News*, 15 December 1988

John Costello to author, January 2008

Creston (1894), 'Football', *The Fortnightly Review* 55

Interviews with John Davies 1, 4 [February] 2008

Debord, Guy (translated 1994), *The Society of the Spectacle*, New York [USA]: Zone

Delaney, Trevor (1991), *The Grounds of Rugby League*, self published

Edgar, Harry (2003), 'League and Liverpool', *Rugby League Journal* 1/5, Winter 2003, Egremont: Edgar Publishing

Ibid (2005), 'Grounds To Remember: Knotty Ash', *Rugby League Journal* 1/11, Summer 2005, Egremont: Edgar Publishing

Ibid (2005), 'Magical Matches: The 1965 Challenge Cup Final At Wembley: Wigan 20 – Hunslet 16', *Rugby League Journal* 1/11, Egremont: Edgar Publishing

Ibid [ed.] (2006), *Rugby League Journal Annual 2006*, Egremont: Rugby League Journal Publishing

Ibid [ed.] (2007), Rugby League Journal Annual 2007, Egremont: Rugby League Journal Publishing

Ibid [ed.] (2008), Rugby League Journal Annual 2008, Egremont: Rugby League Journal Publishing

Discussion with Arthur Evans, May 2007

Fallowfield, Bill (1968), 'All's Well: Ask Huyton and Bramley!' *Eddie Waring's Rugby League Annual 1968-69*, Castleford: MB Publication

Farrar, David & Peter Lush with Michael O'Hare (1995), *Touch And Go, A History of Professional Rugby League in London*, London: London League Publications

Farrar, David & Peter Lush [eds.] (2007), *Rugby League Annual Review 2007: Rugby League Analysis, History and Vision* (incorporating *Our Game*), London: London League Publications

Firth, Vincent, 'Today In Rugby League', *Rugby League Review* 5 / 109, November 24 1950

Fleet, Tom (1991), 'A History of Highfield', series written for the *Highfield RLFC Official Programme* 1991–92 season

Various interviews and email correspondence with Tom Fleet 2007-2008

Interview with Geoff Fletcher, 27 February 2008

Flower, Peter, 'Runcorn Highfield', *Rugby League Championship Tables http://peterflower.tripod.com/table.htm* (accessed 26/07/2006)

Interview with Tom Galligan, 21 September 2007

Gaulton , A.N. 'They're Off!', *Rugby League Review* 4 / 95, 18 August 1950

Ibid, Rugby League Review, 24 November 1950

Interview, email correspondence with Steve Higginson, April 2007

Higginson, Steve & Tony Wailey (2006), *Edgy Cities*, Liverpool: Northern Lights

'Hooker', 'Liverpool Takes Up Rugby League', *Liverpool Echo*, 24 August 1934

Huxley, John (1997), 'Merseyside Mergermania', *League Express*, October 1997

Jones, John M (no date), *The History of London Highfield, Acton & Willesden, Streatham & Mitcham Rugby League Football Clubs 1933-1937*, no publishing details, privately published

Latham, Mike (1997), 'Panthers Extinct on Merseyside', *League Express* 8 December 1997

Ibid (2004), 'The Leaving of Liverpool', *Rugby League World*, February 2004

Lawless, John (2008), 'Rallying Call for New Clubs' (interview with Liverpool Rugby League Development Officer John Farrell), [*Liverpool*] *Football Echo*, 26 April 2008

www.liverpoolbuccaneers.co.uk

Liverpool City Balance Sheet May 1962 – housed at the University of Huddersfield

Liverpool Stanley Minutes – housed at University of Huddersfield

[Unaccredited correspondent], 'Liverpool Stanley's Manager, Death of Mr James Green, *Liverpool Echo*, 1 April 1937

[Unaccredited correspondent], *Liverpool Echo*, 9 August 1977

John Lomas to author, November 2007

BBC Radio Merseyside presenter Roger Lyon to author, March 2008

Mather, Tom (2007), *Snuff Out the Moon: The Development of Floodlit Rugby League*, London: London League Publications

Email correspondence with Tommy McCarthy, 11 April 2007

Interview with John McGrath, 21 September 2007

Melling, Phil (2007), 'From Wigan to Wales: The 1970s and Beyond', Rugby League Annual Review 2007 [eds. Dave Farrar & Peter Lush, London: London League Publications

'Merman', 'On, Stanley, On! New Haven and Rising Hopes at Liverpool, *Rugby League Review*, 24 February 1950

Ibid, 'Third Time Lucky?' *Rugby League Review*, 9 June 1950

Morris, Brian (1997), 'Panthers Put It Straight', *League Express*, October 1997

Interview with Frank O'Connor, 10 November 2007

Interviews with Harry Ody, 22 November 2007, January 2008

Interview with Mick O'Toole, 17 September 2007

Oakes, Peter (1990), 'I'm On a Winner Says Dizzy Chiz', *RL Thirteen – reprinted in Runcorn Highfield Official Programme,* 16 September 1990

Ibid, 'Pig Farmer Fletch Saves Runcorn's Bacon', *RL Thirteen* 5, 15 September 1990

Owe, Simon (2004), 'Following Chorley Lynx', *Our Game* 9, Spring 2004, London: London League Publications

[Possibly] Trevor Peake, 'Runcorn's Bid for Rugby League Place', *Liverpool Daily Post*, 3 April 1984

Physick, Ray (2007), *Played In Liverpool: charting the heritage of a city at play*, Manchester: English Heritage

Unaccredited correspondent [possibly B. Andrews], *Prescot & Huyton Reporter*, 23 August 1968

Unaccredited correspondent, 'Rugby League Ground Is New Blind Centre', *Prescot & Huyton Reporter*, 30 August 1968

Unaccredited correspondent, *Prescot & Huyton Reporter*, 18 August 1978

Preston, Tom (2008), 'Muddied Oafs On The Mersey: Amateur football in the Liverpool district 1879-1915', *Liverpool History Society Journal 7, 2008* [editors: McCann, Jo & Marie McQuade], Liverpool: LHS

Unaccredited correspondent, 'First Class Supporters Club at Liverpool', *The Rugby League Gazette* no. 2, October 1952

'Ranger's Notes', *Liverpool Echo*, 10 August 1950

Ibid, Liverpool Echo, 9 July 1951

Reynolds, David (1990), 'Yet Another Bloody Sunday', *RL Thirteen 8*, 6 October 1990

Unaccredited correspondent, 'Fletch Won't Finch', *RL Thirteen 3*, 1 September 1990

The editors, Rugby League Collectors' Federation (no date), *Teams and Scorers Liverpool Stanley, Liverpool City, Huyton,* due accreditation to Irving Saxton and the Rugby League Record Keepers' Club

Sadler, Martyn, *www.totalrl.com:* email correspondence with author 10 October 2006

Interview with Eric Seed, 3 April 2008

Service, Alex (1989), 'Return of The Saint', *Code 13*, issue 17

Mike Stephenson to author July 2007

'Stork's Notes', Liverpool Echo, 15 May 1951

Discussions with Peter Twiss

'Veteran', 'Northern Union', *Liverpool Football Echo*, 15 September 1906

Unaccredited correspondent 'Highfield RFC Offer From London Syndicate Accepted By Members', *Wigan Examiner* 27 May 1933

http://en.wikipedia.org/wiki/History_of_rugby_league

Walker, Gareth, 'Sharing The Wealth, *Totalrl.com*, accessed 26 July 2007

Walker, George: various discussions, interviews, telephone conversations

Waring, Eddie (1950), 'Over To Eddie Waring: Back To Nature! Distressing State Of Affairs at Liverpool', *Rugby League Review* 5/107, 10 November 1950

Ibid, untitled editorial, *Eddie Waring Rugby League Annual No 6 1964-5*, Northwich: White Rose Publications

Ibid [ed.], *Eddie Waring Rugby League Annual 1968-69*, Castleford: M.B. Publications

Wheelwright, Andy & Richard Bailey (2006-2008), *Journal of the Rugby League Collectors' Federation* 21-30, Wakefield: RLCF

Williams, Graham (1989), 'Initiating The Liverpudlians: A History of the First Liverpool City 1906/7', *Code 13*, issue 13

'Winger', *Liverpool Echo*, 11 September 1937

Ibid, Liverpool Football Echo, 13 October 1956

Ibid, 'Stanley And Apathy', *Liverpool Echo*, 2 October 1937

Ibid, Liverpool Echo, 5 August 1950

Winstanley, Ray & Derek Winstanley, *Founded On Coal* at www.sws.uiuc.edu/iswsdocs/chief/foundedon coal-winstanley.pfd (Located 16 October 2006)

Woodhead, Leslie, 'Geoff Rises to Huyton Challenge, [Liverpool] Football Echo, 13 August 1977

Yates, S.H. [as 'Ranger'], 'Ranger's Notes', *Liverpool Echo*, 21 August 1951

Ibid, Liverpool Football Echo, 20 March 1954

Ibid, Liverpool Daily Post, 5 September 1956

Ibid, 8 October 1956

Ibid, 'Rugby League', *Liverpool Echo*, 15 October 1956

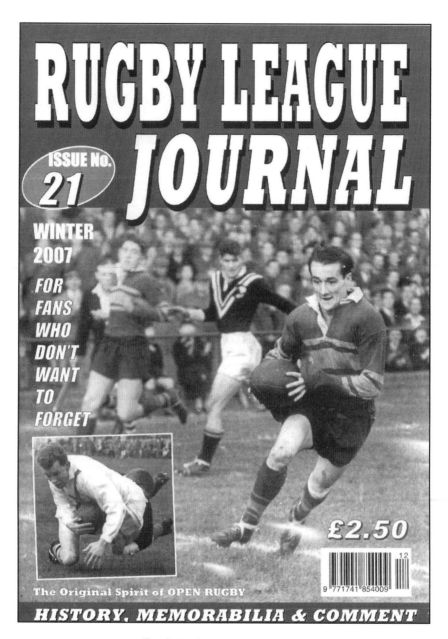

Published quarterly

History, Memorabilia and Comment with every issue packed
with wonderful old black and white photographs.

www.rugbyleaguejournal.net

For more details: e-mail: rugbyleague.journal@virgin.net
Or write to: "Rugby League Journal," PO Box 22, Egremont, Cumbria, CA23 3WA.

So close to Glory
Warrington RLFC 1919 to 1939
By Eddie Fuller and Gary Slater

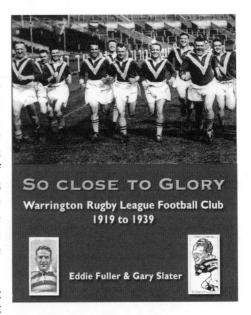

Big Jack Arkwright, Jack 'Cod' Miller, Tommy 'Tubby' Thompson, Billy Dingsdale and Bill Shankland are rugby league legends. All five made their names at Wilderspool and are now founder members of the Warrington Wolves Hall of Fame. *So close to Glory* is the story of how they and their team-mates in the club's famous primrose and blue colours helped the club to grow in size and popularity during the 1920s and 1930s. In this period the team played in three Challenge Cup Finals and three Championship Finals.

Published in April 2008 at £12.95. Available direct from London League Publications Ltd for £12.00 post free. ISBN: 9781903659373. Available at full price in the Warrington Wolves club shop.

All local lads
St Helens Recreation RLFC
By Alex Service and Denis Whittle

The full story of the only works team ever to play in professional rugby league. From their early days in rugby union, to association football, St Helens Recs and then the post-war amateur Pilkington Recs, a fascinating tale of triumph, tragedy and survival against the odds.

To be published in November 2008 at £13.95. Available direct from London League Publications Ltd for £13.00, post free. ISBN: 9781903659434

To order from London League Publications, go to www.llpshop.co.uk to pay by credit card.

Cheque payments to PO Box 10441, London E14 8WR.

All our books can be ordered from any bookshop at full price.

Peter Fox
The players' coach

Peter Fox was involved in professional rugby league for almost 50 years. After playing for Sharlston Rovers, he had a 13 year playing career with Featherstone Rovers, Batley, Hull KR and Wakefield Trinity, he became one of British rugby league's most successful coaches.

Highlights of his coaching career include:
- Coaching Great Britain and England, including beating the Australians in 1978
- Winning eight matches with Yorkshire
- Winning the Challenge Cup and promotion with **Featherstone Rovers**
- Winning the First Division title in 1980 and 1981 with **Bradford Northern**
- Winning promotion with **Bramley**
- Winning the Premiership, Yorkshire Cup and John Player Trophy

With a foreword by David Hinchliffe, this authorised biography, published in June 2008 and based on extensive interviews and research, gives the inside story of Peter's at times controversial rugby league career. It includes how he developed the teams he coached, and the players he signed. Every rugby league fan will find it of great interest.

Special offer for readers of this book: £14.00 post free (cover price £14.95). Credit card orders via www.llpshop.co.uk or from PO Box 10441, London E14 8WR (Cheques payable to London League Publications Ltd)

The book can also be ordered from any bookshop at £14.95 (ISBN: 9781903659397)

Rugby League Review No.2

RUGBY LEAGUE ANALYSIS, HISTORY & VISION

EDITED BY DAVE FARRAR AND PETER LUSH

INCORPORATING Our Game

A new edition of *Rugby League Review*, with articles on the game's history, current issues, international coverage book reviews and obituaries.

Published in September 2008 at £12.95, order for just £12.00 post free from www.llpshop.co.uk (credit card orders) or by cheque from London League Publications Ltd, PO Box 10441, London E14 8WR